THE
HERB BOOK

THE
HERB BOOK

ARABELLA BOXER
PHILIPPA BACK

HAMLYN

NOTES

* All recipes serve 4 people unless otherwise stated.
* Ovens should be preheated to the specified temperature.
* All spoon measures are level.
* Metric spoon measures in sizes 1.25 ml ($\frac{1}{4}$ teaspoon), 2.5 ml ($\frac{1}{2}$ teaspoon), 5 ml (1 teaspoon) and 15 ml (1 tablespoon) are available and should be used for accurate measurement of small quantities.
* Follow one column of measures – they are not interchangeable.

NOTES FOR AUSTRALIAN USERS

All measures in this book are given in metric, imperial and American. In Australia, the 250 ml (8 fl oz) measuring cup is used in conjunction with the imperial pint of 20 fl oz. If Australian users follow the American column they should remember that the American pint is 16 fl oz. It is also important to note that the Australian tablespoon has been converted to 20 ml, which is larger than the tablespoon used in all columns in this book, and therefore 3 level teaspoons should be used where instructed to use 1 tablespoon. Kitchen scales may be used to follow either the metric or imperial columns but only one set of measures should be followed as they are not interchangeable.

IMPORTANT

If you have experienced an allergic reaction to any products for the skin you should seek medical advice before using any of the herbal preparations described in this book.

It is recommended that all herbal infusions and decoctions for medicinal or cosmetic use be freshly prepared and used at once or within 12 hours of making up.

First published in 1980 by
Octopus Books Limited

Published in paperback in 1987 by
Hamlyn Publishing
A division of the Hamlyn Publishing Group Limited
Bridge House
London Road
Twickenham
Middlesex
England

© 1980 Octopus Books Limited

ISBN 0 600 553 671

Printed in Hong Kong

CONTENTS

THE HISTORY OF HERBS

Long before records were kept, man was using wild herbs for food and medicine. Over many years he learned that some plants were safe to eat, while others caused poisoning and death. Discovering which plants were useful must have been a matter of trial and error, sometimes no doubt with disastrous results. From remote times myths and legends grew up about the powers of herbs. Fantastic visions seen by people who had eaten a few leaves or berries from an hallucinogenic plant would deepen belief in their magical properties. These superstitions were kept alive by the wizard priests and the medicine-men, to their advantage.

In early biblical days the Hebrews used herbs as healthy flavoursome foods. The only plant put to medicinal use was the mandrake root, which was widely used as a painkiller. Although they were well aware of the healing properties of many herbs, the Hebrews held that man should not interfere with the purpose of God, the great healer, by trying to heal himself. Gradually this tradition changed. The later Prophets decreed that the power to heal diseases had been granted by God to physicians in return for their prayers. Most of the herbs used were native to the Middle East. The thymes, sages, mints and marjorams grew in the Bible lands as did rosemary and hyssop. Coriander and cumin came from Egypt.

It was in about 2000 B.C. in Babylon that the first documented account of herbs appeared. It described tried and tested medicinal uses of herbs, and included many herbs that are well-known today, such as bay tree, thyme, caraway and coriander. Instructions were given on how to prepare and administer the herbal cures.

The ancient Egyptians imported many of their herbs, spices and aromatic oils from Babylon and from distant India, learning many traditional uses for these substances through their trade. Anise, caraway, fenugreek, opium, thyme and saffron were, with others, in great demand for food, medicines, cosmetics, and perfumes. They were also used for dyes and disinfectants, and in the highly skilled art of embalming.

In their turn the ancient Greeks built upon the knowledge of herbs that had been gathered over the years and added greatly to it. Most important were the medical writings of Hippocrates, the 'Father of Medicine', who was a physician and teacher. In about 400 B.C. his students were learning the value of herbs in easing pain and curing disease. His valuable teachings and methods of practice set the pattern for modern medicine.

In the first century A.D. the Greek physician Dioscorides listed the medicinal properties of over 500 plants and herbs in *Materia Medica*. For hundreds of years this book was the standard work on the subject. It formed the basis of herbal medicine practised subsequently by Christian religious orders in medieval Europe.

A century later Galen, a physician in Imperial Rome, wrote many medical books which remained in use for 1,500 years. The old word 'galenical', describing a medicinal preparation, was derived from his name. Many of the treatments he recommended were made from herbs, whether taken as potions or applied externally.

As the Romans conquered most of Europe, they took with them a vast knowledge of herbs. Such was their faith in the strength of herbs to heal sickness and maintain good health, that wherever they went they carried herb seeds and plants to cultivate and use. Over 200 different herbs were introduced to Britain by the invading Romans, amongst them fennel, sage, borage and betony, parsley, rosemary and thyme. During the 400 years of the Roman occupation, many of the herbs they cultivated so carefully became naturalized and now grow wild.

With the establishment of the Christian church in Britain, many great monasteries were founded. The herbs left by the Romans formed the basis for the 'physick' gardens which the monks cultivated to pro-

Left: A typical herb garden of the sixteenth century, showing both men and women tending the herbs and gathering them for distilling. Such was the demand for the herb potions that two stills were required.

Opposite Above: A medieval illustration of a neat, well-planned physic garden. The gardeners are gathering herbs for the apothecary across the street. From Le Livre Rustican, a French book on healing herbs written in the fifteenth century.

Opposite Below: Portrait of John Gerard, one of the most influential herbalists in England during the sixteenth century. He collected plants from all over the world to grow in his garden in London.

vide them with the raw materials for healing medicines. The monasteries became centres of learning and medicine, and grew famous for their herbal healing methods, while throughout the Middle Ages herbal folklore flourished in the towns and villages.

During all this time little had been written about herbs and their uses, for knowledge was handed down by word of mouth. The forerunner of the English herbals, written in the eleventh century, drew heavily upon the writings of the Greeks and Romans and used the same complicated classification of plants and botanical names. In 1551, Steven Mierdman published the first part of William Turner's *New Herball*, which described some 238 British plants and was the first scientific study of plants. However, the two most famous English herbals were by John Gerard and Nicholas Culpeper.

In 1597 Gerard, an apothecary to James I, produced his well-known *Herball*. It was based on the work of the Flemish physician Dodoens, but included many of the plants growing in America, 'that new lande'. He mentioned the potato and the tomato, which he called 'Apple of Love', together with those herbs growing in his own physic garden.

In 1653 Culpeper, a physician, brought out a herbal in which he disagreed with much written by Gerard and other herbalists. Culpeper made exaggerated claims for the medicinal powers of herbs. He also

linked herbs with astrology to such an extent that, though this was popular in England at the time, it damaged the credibility of his work in the eyes of scholarly physicians.

The first herbal known in America was published in 1569 by a Spanish doctor called Nicholas Monardes. He wrote of the herbs found by the early settlers. The herb bergamot, *Monarda didyma*, commemorates him.

Amongst their few belongings those first settlers of America took with them treasured seeds and roots of their favourite herbs. Many herbs quickly flourished in their new environment and became native plants. These included soapwort, comfrey and yarrow, chamomile and coltsfoot. At the end of such a long sea journey the pioneers badly needed to eat fresh green food and soon after their arrival, set salad vegetables such as sorrel, parsley and good King Henry to grow. Friendly Indians showed the new inhabitants many plants already growing in the country that had culinary and medicinal value. The best known of these was bergamot, the leaves of which the Indians used as a tea called Oswego tea.

The cultivation of herbs in America reached its peak in the eighteenth century with the emergence of the Shakers, so-called because of their religious dances. The Shakers were a small religious group of people dedicated to the celibate life. Simplicity was the key to their way of living and they strongly believed that 'beauty rests on utility; the highest use possesses the greatest beauty'.

Shaker economy was based on agriculture: they became America's professional herbalists, the first to

Above: Red bergamot (Monarda didyma).

Left: The apothecary's workroom where herbs were dried or used fresh to make medicines. Here the herbs were weighed, mixed, chopped and ground in the huge pestle and mortar ready to sell. Healing salves and ointments, syrups and lotions were made on the stove.

Opposite: An illustration showing members of the Shaker group filling bottles with an extract of roots.

grow and sell medicinal herbs on a large scale. The Shakers cultivated a wide variety, about 150 in all, and were soon well-known for the high quality of their plants. Among the herbs sold by the Shakers were basil, borage, marjoram, tansy, sage, horehound, hyssop and thyme. They made the herbs into ointments, salves, medicines of all kinds, pills and powders.

The influence of the Shakers lasted for over 100 years, and as a result the interest in herbs continued in America without interruption. In Britain, however, the custom of growing herbs for use in the home had largely died out by the mid-nineteenth century. The Industrial Revolution brought people flocking into towns in search of work. Small terraced houses in the quickly growing towns offered no space for gardens. Much of the knowledge of the uses of herbs in cooking and for simple remedies declined as patent medicines and table condiments rose in popularity. In less intensively industrialized countries like France and Italy the use of herbs, particularly in cooking, has never ceased.

In Europe, where herbs grew vigorously in the wild, the commercial collection and cultivation of them was organized on a wide scale. Medicinal plants were imported at low cost by Britain. Some dried culinary herbs were also available, but the quality was poor and as time went by people ceased to use more than the four familiar ones: thyme, parsley, sage and rosemary.

The advance in scientific knowledge made during the twentieth century enabled scientists to isolate the chemical substance of a plant and to synthesize its properties. This meant that accurate doses of a drug could be administered, and instant medicine from the drugstore became available to all. Synthetic flavourings sold in little bottles were simple to use in the kitchen. Modern manufacturing techniques meant that there was no longer any commercial viability for an ailing and expensive herb industry to continue in Britain. In the countryside, however, and particularly in Mediterranean countries, knowledge of the uses of herbs has survived.

During the last 20 years there has been a dramatic revival of interest in herbs on both sides of the Atlantic. Bulk processing and the addition of preservatives to food has resulted in loss of natural flavour, colour and aroma. The palate is dulled by these artificial agents. Many people, anxious to use herbs again in order to taste the delicious natural flavourings, and to benefit from their nutritional value, are seeking out recipes for meals which include herbs. Others, sensitive to the possibility of dangerous side effects from certain synthetic products, are looking for ways of using herbs in cosmetics and in the treatment of minor ailments. The value and pleasure that herbs have to offer are, happily, once more being recognized.

THE HERB GARDEN

Herbs are undemanding plants, easy to grow and to look after on a small scale. Since they are not fussy as to soil, neither deep digging nor special treatment is essential, although as with all living things, the more care and attention they receive the better they flourish.

In the past it was customary for the woman of the household to look after the herb garden, and it was she who decided which herbs were to be grown and where to plant them. She weeded the beds and harvested the herbs; she added herbs to her cooking, and made wines, cordials and simple medicines. She dried the herbs for pot-pourris and perfume sachets to keep the house smelling sweet. Since most of her work was done in the kitchen, the herb bed was invariably sited as near to it as possible.

There are several important factors to be considered when deciding where it is best to grow herbs. Most herbs need the maximum amount of sunshine during the growing season. Many of them have their origins in the warmer climates of the world. In order to produce the full flavour and fragrance, you need to reproduce as nearly as you can the conditions of the natural habitat.

Where instructions state that a herb should be planted in a sunny position, they imply that ideally the plant should get about 7 hours of sunshine a day. A plant requiring partial shade needs up to 4 hours of sunshine a day. There are few plants which need to grow in total shade. Even the woodland herbs such as woodruff, wood betony and wood violet need filtered sunshine in the middle of the day and will grow in the herb garden under the shadow of the larger plants.

Herbs need protection from cold winds, which often do more damage to a plant than low temperatures. A wall, hedge or natural slope can provide good shelter, but if these are not available then a fence of some kind should be erected when the herb garden is first planted. Once the garden is established the larger herbs will provide partial protection, but a background or screen will ensure good sturdy growth.

When planning to grow your own herbs it is essential to work out how much space you can allocate to the plants. No herb garden need be very large, for a surprising number of plants can be grown in a relatively small plot. You may wish to create a small separate herb garden or to combine herbs with other plants in the herbaceous border or rock garden. Whatever you decide upon, remember that accessibility is important. You do not want to go far to collect a few herb leaves, neither do you want to walk through wet grass or cross a bed of earth to get to the herbs. Stepping stones or a narrow path could solve that problem.

Once you have decided which plants you wish to grow, a small herb bed on its own is easy to plan and to prepare.

THE HERBACEOUS BORDER

Herbs can be used as edging plants, using parsley, lady's mantle, marigold, marjoram, lemon thyme and salad burnet. Try growing a few herbs grouped together in a flower bed and plant lemon balm, bergamot, tarragon and sweet Cicely. At the back of the border plant angelica, lovage and fennel, for these are the tall herbs, and will shelter other plants and provide a handsome background.

Woody stemmed herbs make useful hedging plants in the garden but need to be kept neatly trimmed. Use rue, sage, hyssop, lavender and rosemary – or even winter savory, though it is rather slow-growing.

THE ROCK GARDEN

Add low-growing herbs such as lemon thyme, caraway-scented thyme (*T. herba-barona*), chives and golden marjoram to a collection of alpine plants. Each of these herbs can be tucked in amongst the other plants.

THE SMALL CITY GARDEN

Limited space makes growing any plant a problem. Herbs are among the easiest and most useful plants in this situation.

Where the garden is no more than a backyard, you may prefer to turn it into a patio or, to give its English name, a courtyard. The soil in city gardens is often poor and sour with little goodness left in it and you should therefore take some trouble to refresh the soil before planting herbs.

Having planned on paper the way in which you wish to plant the available space, use paving slabs, bricks or cobbles to make paths for easy access and to provide a setting in which you can create a colourful and useful herb garden. A low terrace could be another solution and would give an illusion of space.

A flat roof, a balcony or a window box may be all the space available, but however small the area and however you choose to use it, the following ideas may help you to plan where to grow herbs.

In the courtyard Grow the herbs most often needed for cutting in an old fireclay sink, standing it on bricks near the door. A mixture of annuals and perennials could include parsley, chives, dill, summer savory and garden thyme.

Make maximum use of any surrounding walls by painting them white to increase reflection of light for your plants. Attach wooden trellis work to a wall or use training wires to support a trailing plant grown in a tub at the base of the wall.

Put up a plain wooden pergola and plant hops or honeysuckle to climb over it or make use of a fragrant sweetbriar rose to provide some shade.

Remove one or two paving slabs in an existing courtyard, refresh the soil beneath and plant some low-growing evergreen herbs.

It may be more practical to have raised beds. Set two or three beds in tiers with the largest at the bottom, in a sunny corner.

Use can be made of a large strawberry jar. Fill it with parsley and useful perennials such as chives, sage, lavender and thyme and have a rosemary or lemon verbena in the top. Stand a bay tree on its own in a decorative pot. Give the shade-loving mints a container on their own and renew the plants every year or so. The container can be a shallow pottery bowl which will be easy to carry round to keep it in the shade. A wooden trough makes a striking container for the larger plants. Have one on wheels so it can be moved

to keep the herbs in the sun. Choose angelica, sweet Cicely and fennel or fill it with annuals such as chervil, dill and basil. Try caraway, cumin and anise if the courtyard gets plenty of sun.

On a terrace Use a narrow raised bed as a surround and fill it with sweet-smelling herbs. Set pillars at the corners of a terrace to give support to climbing plants grown in containers at their base. The brightly coloured nasturtium is a quick grower and a good climber.

At intervals up the pillar attach flat-sided wire baskets. Line them with polythene sheeting and fill them with herbs which spill over the sides: pennyroyal, basil, sage, lemon thyme and golden marjoram.

On a flat roof or balcony Where weight can be a problem, use light plastic pots or the attractive foamed polystyrene urns now available.

Small plastic troughs 60cm/2ft long and 15cm/6in wide, standing on a drip tray, will hold 5 plants. Plants in plastic containers do not lose moisture quite so rapidly as those in a clay pot; they will, however, need regular watering.

To control the shape of a trailing herb, construct a sturdy wire netting frame which will stand tall out of the pot. Plant the herb in the container and position the wire netting firmly over the top of it. A hop plant or a nasturtium will soon cover the wire. Rosemary can be grown and trained in the same way.

A hanging basket A basket full of herbs can be attractive and useful. Hang it by wires from a hook or iron bracket firmly attached to the wall. Baskets made from plastic-covered wire are most suitable and will hold 3 or 4 herbs. Marjoram, thyme and sage, once established, will trail downwards.

Left: Comfrey, bronze fennel and chives.
Below: A charming herb garden design making use of window boxes, hanging baskets, pots and containers.

In a window box Herbs will grow well in this situation, provided they can get 4 or 5 hours of sunshine a day. Fill the box with essential cooking herbs. For added interest grow some herbs with colourful leaves, such as the purple sage, 'Tricolor', which has pink and white streaked leaves, silver thyme, golden thyme with its gold-splashed leaves and golden balm. All these herbs can be used in cooking just as well as their green-leaved forms. Alternatively, fill the window box with fragrant herbs to scent the room when the window is open. Grow pineapple sage, lemon thyme, lemon verbena and sweet (knotted) marjoram for a good selection.

INSIDE THE HOUSE

Most herbs will grow well indoors with some care and attention. They need light, sun, watering and some ventilation. Have cooking herbs in a box on the kitchen window sill. The more fragrant herbs such as rosemary and lemon verbena would give a lovely scent if placed in the living room.

WHICH HERBS TO GROW

Having settled where to grow your herbs and how much space is available you must decide which ones you want to have and how you are going to use them. If you simply wish to add flavour to your cooking, a few herbs will be sufficient. Your interest may, however, centre around the use of herbs for natural cosmetics or the making of refreshing herbal teas, or you may prefer to make your own simple remedies for minor ailments.

It is possible to choose one herb which will cover all these requirements. Sprigs of rosemary will add a delicious flavour to lamb; a strong infusion of rosemary used as a rinse will give strength and colour to dark hair; as a herbal tea it relieves a headache and is relaxing, and dried rosemary adds fragrance to a pot-pourri.

To help you with ideas, read about the plants. Study their growing habits and discover what they look and smell like by going to garden centres and specialist herb nurseries. Visit gardens open to the public where you will find a wide variety of herbs growing. Note the height and diameter of the fully grown herbs. This is important in an overall plan.

Before you prepare the site and buy the plants or seeds, make a rough plan of the herb layout based on one of the following suggestions.

BOUQUET GARNI HERBS

One of the simplest herb collections, a *bouquet garni* pot is useful and need take up little space.

The traditional *bouquet garni* is a 'broth posy' of three common aromatic herbs tied together in a little bundle. The bundle is added to stews, sauces and casseroles and then removed before serving. The three herbs are parsley, thyme and bay and the proportions of each varies according to the dish. Recipes may call for a small, medium or large *bouquet garni* but it is as well to have the greater proportion of parsley: thyme and bay can overpower other flavours if used in too great a quantity. For special dishes a *bouquet garni* may contain rosemary, chervil, salad burnet and tarragon. Two *bouquet garni* pots are a good idea, one in which to grow parsley, thyme (or lemon thyme) and bay, the other for growing rosemary, chervil, salad burnet or tarragon. Choose your containers carefully so they will meet the growing requirements of the herbs and show them off to advantage.

One idea is to grow the three herbs in individual pots standing close together. The bay tree can then grow undisturbed, while it is easy to replace the parsley and thyme if necessary. Alternatively, put all three herbs into a deep tub at least 30 cm/12 in square. Position it so that the parsley and thyme will be in the sunshine and not overshadowed by the bay.

The second *bouquet garni* collection could be grown in an old fish kettle or container of similar shape, big enough to hold three or four herbs. Have the herbs in pots standing on the removable liner of the kettle, or plant the herbs directly into it.

Left: The bouquet garni herbs growing in pots and tubs. From left to right: thyme, bay and parsley in pots; parsley, bay and thyme in the tub; chervil, rosemary and salad burnet in the fish kettle.

Opposite: An attractive collection of herbs growing in a window box. From left to right: chives, dill, marigold, mint, summer savory and basil.

Herbs growing outside the garden door. On the left: tarragon, thyme, spearmint and rosemary. On the right: bay, fennel, sage and marjoram.

KITCHEN GARDEN HERBS

The ideal place for growing cooking herbs is immediately outside the back door. Where this is a good sunny position the herbs will grow well and provide plenty of greenery for the pot. If you grow parsley in one of the big pots and rosemary or bay in the other you need hardly put a foot outside, which is convenient in wet weather. Grow other herbs nearby, such as sage, thyme, tarragon, marjoram, spearmint and fennel.

Another kitchen herb bed could be set alongside a path. Do not make the bed wider than you can reach across unless you set slabs of stepping stones among the herbs. Put the mint in the shadiest spot in the garden and grow it surrounded by roof slates sunk into the soil or in a buried bucket (pail) so that its underground runners will not encroach upon other herbs.

Window boxes There is a wide choice of ready-made window boxes on the market from the handsome but expensive fibreglass boxes to those of simpler and cheaper construction. The plastic window boxes are light and will last for years, but those made of wood look more natural. The only material to avoid is metal; it absorbs heat so readily that the herb roots shrivel.

The box you decide upon should have efficient drainage holes and be at least 23 cm/9 in deep. Wooden boxes should be of timber 2 cm/$\frac{3}{4}$ in thick. If possible, get a size to fit your window sill exactly. Sit the box on a drip tray to avoid water running down the walls or being a nuisance to anyone below. Make sure that your window box is secure in its position before you start putting in the herbs.

For a summer window box to add flavour and interest to salads, grow basil, dill, chervil, chives, summer savory and marigold.

Herbs for the winter window box to enliven stews, casseroles and pot roasts, could be salad burnet, thyme, sage, parsley, rosemary and Welsh onion.

If a second window box is available in a shady position, you could fill it with six different mints, each in its own container to control its root growth. Peppermint, apple mint, eau-de-cologne mint, spearmint, pennyroyal and curly mint all provide delicious flavours and lovely scents.

A colourful bed of medicinal herbs. Back row: marshmallow, rosemary, comfrey and fennel. Middle row: sage, vervain, lemon balm and garlic. Front row: thyme, marigold and parsley.

A MEDICINAL HERB GARDEN

In a specialist bed of this kind it is the aim of the planner to grow herbs which will provide the basic ingredients for as many remedies as possible. Most medicinal herbs can be used for more than one ailment. It is difficult to choose herbs which, as remedies, will not overlap one another since they all contain substances to a greater or lesser degree which are good for the health. A large number, for example, are very good for indigestion or flatulence, while others are tonic herbs.

A herb bed of 12 different plants will give a wide variety from which to make remedies. To start your garden, the following herbs are suggested:

COMFREY, *Symphytum officinale* Height 60–90 cm/2–3 ft. Plant at the back of the border and give it plenty of space to grow. Use roots and leaves.

FENNEL, *Foeniculum vulgare* Height 1.5 m/5 ft. Plant at the back of the border. It will take several seasons before it reaches its full height. Use entire plant.

GARLIC, *Allium sativum* Height 60 cm/2 ft. Use bulbous root.

LEMON BALM, *Melissa officinalis* Height 45–60 cm/1½–2 ft. Use leaves.

MARIGOLD, *Calendula officinalis* Height 45 cm/18 in. Use whole plant growing above ground.

MARSHMALLOW, *Althaea officinalis* Height 90 cm/3 ft. Another plant for the back of the herb bed. Use entire plant.

PARSLEY, *Petroselinum crispum* Height 15–20 cm/6–8 in. A plant for the edge of the border.

PEPPERMINT, *Mentha piperita* Height 60 cm/2 ft. Needs to grow in the shadiest spot. Use leaves.

ROSEMARY, *Rosmarinus officinalis* Slow growing but eventual height 2 m/6 ft. Use leaves.

SAGE, *Salvia officinalis* Height 45 cm/18 in. Use leaves and flowers.

THYME, *Thymus vulgaris* Height 15–45 cm/6–18 in. Use as an edging plant. Use leaves.

VERVAIN, *Verbena officinalis* Height 45 cm/18 in. Use leaves and flowers.

A COSMETIC HERB GARDEN

In a collection of cosmetic herbs 12 different plants are suggested from which to make your choice. The herbs include those for the skin, hands, hair, nails, eyes, teeth, and feet. Grow one or two herbs for each purpose so you can try out the various cosmetic recipes and discover which ones are best suited to your particular needs.

A mixture of annuals and perennials can provide the basic ingredients for cosmetics throughout the year. Those which disappear in winter can be harvested and dried during the growing season and stored for winter use.

Elder is one of the best cosmetic herbs for the skin. It cleanses, softens and whitens the skin, is helpful for freckles and wrinkles, and it makes a soothing eyebath. Elder is not included in this design because of its large

A good selection of low-growing herbs for the rock garden. Top row: Corsican mint, dwarf lavender, prostrate rosemary and pennyroyal. Second row: golden marjoram, saffron crocus, lady's mantle, parsley and chives. Bottom row: purslane, wintergreen, winter savory and golden thyme.

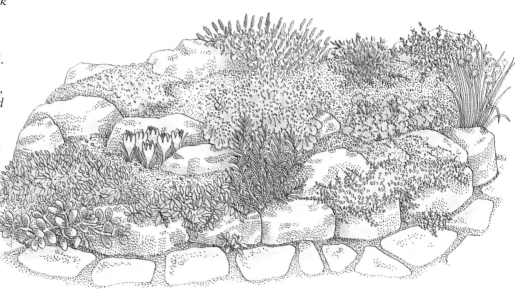

size, but where space permits it is worthwhile growing this lovely hedgerow shrub.

CHAMOMILE, *Matricaria chamomilla* Height 15–23 cm/6–9 in. For skin, hair and eyes. Use flowers and leaves.

DILL, *Anethum graveolens* Height 45–60 cm/1½–2 ft. For eyes and nails.

EYEBRIGHT, *Euphrasia officinalis* Height 15–20 cm/6–8 in. For eyes. Use the whole plant above the ground.

LADY'S MANTLE, *Alchemilla vulgaris* Height 10–50 cm/4–20 in. For skin. Use whole plant above the ground.

LAVENDER, *Lavandula spica* Height 30–90 cm/1–3 ft. For skin and feet. Use flowers and leaves.

MARIGOLD, *Calendula officinalis* Height 45 cm/18 in. For skin, feet and eyes. Use whole plant above the ground.

ROSEMARY, *Rosmarinus officinalis* Fully grown height 2 m/6 ft. For hair and skin. Use leaves.

SAGE, *Salvia officinalis* Height 45 cm/18 in. For teeth, hair and skin. Use leaves and flowers.

A cosmetic herb garden growing in a neat bed. At the back: southernwood. Second row: dill, fenugreek, lavender and rosemary. Third row: sage, marigold, yarrow, chamomile and lady's mantle. At the front: eyebright and violets.

SALAD BURNET, *Poterium sanguisorba* Height 30 cm/12 in. For skin. Use leaves.

SOUTHERNWOOD, *Artemisia abrotanum* Height 1 m/3 ft. For hair. Use leaves.

YARROW, *Achillea millefolium* Height 60 cm/2 ft. For skin and hair. Use whole plant above the ground.

HERBS FOR THE ROCK GARDEN

There are many dwarf, spreading herbs which are well-suited to growing on their own or among other rock garden plants. The suggested list of herbs will provide you with a wide choice of plants.

Most of the herbs are fragrant and attractive evergreens which can be used in cooking, for cosmetics or in medicinal preparations.

Purslane is an annual and would have to be sown each year. The flowering stems of parsley should be cut off as soon as they appear and the plant may need protection to survive the winter.

Build the rock garden in a sunny spot sheltered from the wind.

DWARF ROSEMARY, *Rosmarinus lavandulaceus* Prostrate.

WINTER SAVORY, *Satureia montana* 20–25 cm/8–9 in.

GOLDEN THYME, *Thymus × citriodorus* 'Aureus' 7 cm/3 in.

CHIVES, *Allium schoenoprasum* 30–40 cm/12–15 in.

LAVENDER, *Lavandula spica* Dwarf species.

GOLDEN MARJORAM, *Origanum vulgare aureum* 15 cm/6 in.

BASIL THYME, *Calamintha acinos* 10 cm/4 in.

WINTERGREEN, *Gaultheria procumbens* 7–15 cm/3–6 in.

CORSICAN MINT, *Mentha requienii* Prostrate.

CARAWAY THYME, *Thymus herba-barona* 5–10 cm/2–4 in.

SAFFRON CROCUS, *Crocus sativus* 10 cm/4 in.

PURSLANE, *Portulaca oleracea* 10–15 cm/4–6 in.

PENNYROYAL, *Mentha pulegium* 15 cm/6 in.

CURLY PARSLEY, *Petroselinum crispum* 15 cm/6 in.

LADY'S MANTLE, *Alchemilla alpina* 20 cm/8 in.

Left: A herb bed of plants, each having more than one use. From the path, clockwise: bay, bush basil, chives, parsley, dill, tarragon, mint, summer savory, garlic and thyme; with rosemary in the centre.

THE ALL-PURPOSE HERB GARDEN

To fulfil its function, the small all-purpose herb garden should consist of a few herbs each of which has a variety of uses.

To begin with you could grow the essential herbs, the basic flavourings for good cooking which are so delicious. Once familiar with the uses of these herbs in cooking you can study alternative ways in which to use them.

The herbs listed could easily be grown in two window boxes, if necessary, where you would get maximum value from minimum space. Each of the following 12 herbs has at least 2 other functions apart from its culinary use.

BUSH BASIL, *Ocimum minimum* Height 15 cm/6 in. Half-hardy annual.

BAY, *Laurus nobilis* Keep small by clipping. Perennial.

CHIVES, *Allium schoenoprasum* Height 30 cm/12 in. Perennial.

DILL, *Anethum graveolens* Height 60 cm/2 ft. Annual.

GARLIC, *Allium sativum* Up to 60 cm/2 ft. Perennial but lifted every year for bulb.

MARJORAM, SWEET, *Origanum majorana* Height 20 cm/8 in. Annual.

MINT, *Mentha spicata* (spearmint) Height 45 cm/18 in. Perennial.

PARSLEY, *Petroselinum crispum* Height 15–20 cm/6–8 in. Biennial: treat as annual.

ROSEMARY, *Rosmarinus officinalis* Height up to 2 m/6 ft. Perennial.

SAGE, NARROW-LEAVED, *Salvia officinalis* Height 60 cm/2 ft. Perennial.

SUMMER SAVORY, *Satureia hortensis* Height up to 30 cm/12 in. Annual.

TARRAGON, *Artemisia dracunculus* Height 1 m/3 ft. Perennial.

THYME, *Thymus vulgaris* Height 15–45 cm/6–18 in. Perennial.

A DECORATIVE HERB GARDEN

There is so much emphasis laid on the usefulness of herbs, that it is not always appreciated how decorative they can be. Herbs as ornamental plants fully deserve their place in the border, giving pleasure to the gardener with their foliage, flowers and lovely fragrances. Many herbs have variegated forms which produce very striking coloured leaves. The attractive wine-dark leaves of the purple sage, the pink, cream and green leaves of the 'Tricolor' sage and the mound of cream and pale green leaves produced by the variegated sage are all splendid plants to grow as a low hedge or ground cover in an open situation.

The grey-leaved herbs add interest and aromatic scents to hot summer days. Curry plant with its bright yellow flowers, and pink, blue or white lavender are the two grey-leaved plants suggested in the design. Santolina or catmint may equally well be included.

Other herbs which have brightly coloured leaves and make a lovely splash of colour are golden sage, golden balm, ginger mint and golden marjoram.

The vivid flowers of some herbs also stand out well and catch the eye. Hyssop flowers can be white, pink and deep blue, and borage has brilliant blue flowers which bloom for many months in the year. All the herbs suggested in this list are perennials.

BERGAMOT, *Monarda didyma* Height about 60 cm/2 ft. Bright red flowers.

BORAGE, *Borago officinalis* Height 60 cm/2 ft. Blue flowers.

CURRY PLANT, *Helichrysum angustifolium* Height up to 40 cm/15 in. Yellow flowers.

GOAT'S RUE, *Galega officinalis* Height 1 m/3 ft. White or blue flowers.

GOLDEN MARJORAM, *Origanum vulgare aureum* Height 15 cm/6 in. Gold leaves.

GOLDEN THYME, *Thymus × citriodorus* 'Aureus' Height 10 cm/4 in. Gold leaves, lemon scent.

HYSSOP, *Hyssopus officinalis* Height 60 cm/2 ft. Blue, pink or white flowers.

JACOB'S LADDER, *Polemoneum coeruleum* Height 75 cm/2½ ft. Blue or white flowers.

LADY'S MANTLE, *Alchemilla mollis* Height 30–45 cm/12–15 in. Dainty yellow flowers.

LAVENDER, *Lavandula spica* Height about 60 cm/2 ft. Blue, pink or white flowers, scented.

ORRIS, *Iris florentina* Height 60 cm/2 ft. Purple, white and yellow streaked flowers.

RUE, *Ruta graveolens* 'Jackman's Blue' Height 60 cm/2 ft. Greeny-blue leaves.

SOAPWORT, *Saponaria officinalis* Height 60 cm/2 ft. Large pink flowers.

SILVER THYME, *Thymus × citriodorus* 'Silver Queen' Height 10 cm/4 in. Silvery leaves, lilac flowers, scented.

VARIEGATED SAGES, *Salvia* spp. Height 45 cm/18 in. Varying coloured leaves, blue flowers.

Right: Herbs and other plants in an attractive garden arrangement, spilling on to the garden path.

Left: A decorative herb garden. At the back: goats rue. Second row: borage, red bergamot, hyssop and rue. Third row: orris, soapwort, Jacob's ladder and the curry plant. At the front: lady's mantle, variegated sage, golden thyme, lavender, golden marjoram and silver thyme.

PREPARING THE SITE

To get the best results from growing herbs it is worth while taking care in the preparation of your site, whether it is open ground, tubs, window boxes or indoor pots. Where you have chosen to grow herbs which require different growing conditions from one another, you can deal with specific needs after attending to the overall preparation.

Your first concern, therefore, is with the soil, and as a general rule herbs grow best in a slightly alkaline soil.

There are few soils which are so poor that they cannot be improved in some way. The ultimate aim is to have a good friable loam, not too wet and not too dry. Loam consists of a free-draining mixture of sand, clay, chalk and humus in the correct proportions.

It is not intended to go into great detail here on the substance of the various soil types or to give the special treatment required in each case. Unfortunately there is no magical method by which soil can instantly be transformed into loam. Drainage, digging and dressings can improve your soil, and the following suggestions may be of help to you.

DRAINAGE

To find out if the drainage in your garden is adequate, dig a hole double the depth of your spade at the lowest point and leave it open for a few days to see how much water collects there. If water does collect in the hole then drainage is bad and plants will not thrive because there will be insufficient air around the roots.

Improving the drainage of your soil may be just a matter of digging it over. Alternatively a simple soak-away may be required. To make one, dig a hole approximately 1 m/3 ft deep and 60 cm/2 ft square, fill it with broken bricks or stones to within 30 cm/12 in of the top, and then replace the top soil.

To put in drainage pipes is an expensive business and not worthwhile unless herbs are to be grown on a commercial scale.

DIGGING

One of the best methods by which to improve your soil is to dig it over in time for winter frosts and winds to break up the soil. This improves its texture and drainage and allows air to get to the depths of the soil. It also speeds up the decay of the humus which provides such valuable plant food.

DRESSINGS

Humus is just one of the three vital dressings needed for good soil; another is lime, which, in measured amounts, is added to the soil to build up its calcium content and is a good treatment for acid soils; the third dressing is liquid fertilizer, which is added to the soil and acts as plant food. All three dressings are necessary to get the very best results for your herbs and they will repay you by producing good sturdy plants full of flavour and aroma.

Humus is the important decomposed organic matter in soil and is usually present to a greater or lesser degree. Where the soil is highly cultivated it soon becomes exhausted and humus-producing material needs to be added. Humus can be applied in several forms, of which animal manure, hop manure and compost are the most easily obtainable.

Well-rotted animal manure is one of the best humus-makers and is added at the autumn digging, in the proportion of one barrow load to 10 m²/12 sq yds.

Hop manure is an alternative type of dressing easy to apply, but it is expensive. It is sterile so there is no smell, the quality does not vary and it is pleasant to handle. It is most suitable in the small city garden where manure would not be welcomed or where there is insufficient space to have a compost heap.

Compost is a manure consisting of a mixture of decomposed organic substances, and a garden compost heap is the least expensive way of providing a dressing for your soil. Well-made compost is a very good substitute for hop manure or well-rotted animal manure, and can be used in the same way.

Compost consists of waste plant material such as grass mowings, dead leaves and weeds, to which any waste vegetable matter from the household can be added. Natural bacterial action gradually breaks down the constituent elements into an organically rich humus.

THE COMPOST HEAP

There are several types of ready-made proprietary compost bins available on the market, or you can make you own bin tucked away in a corner of the garden. Hammer four stakes firmly into the ground to make a rectangle 90 × 120 cm/3 × 4 ft and surround these with planks of wood or wire netting to come no higher than 1 m/3 ft.

It is advisable, whatever the size of the garden, to have two small compost heaps rather than one large one. You will then have compost ready for use at an earlier date. When the first compost heap is full, build the second by moving the wire netting and four stakes to another position nearby.

To help drainage in the bin put a layer of straw or bracken, if available, on the bottom. Tip garden refuse on the top, then lawn mowings, annual weeds, leaves and non-woody plant material. From the kitchen waste use all fruit and vegetable peelings, tea leaves and eggshells. Any waste from the herbs can also be added, and comfrey is one of the best as it helps to break down the compost more quickly.

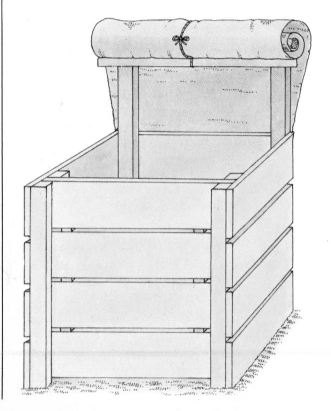

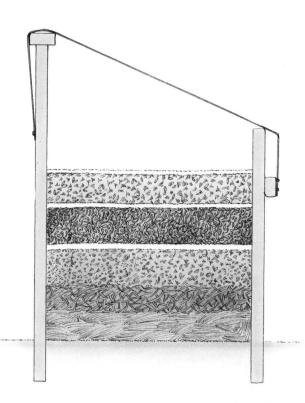

In a small city garden or courtyard it is worthwhile investing in a proper compost bin and then use an accelerator or proprietary compost-maker to break down the compost as fast as possible.

There are certain materials which should not be put on to the compost heap if it is not to become a rubbish dump. No diseased plants or lawn clippings, where the lawn has been treated with weedkiller, should be added, nor any perennial weeds of the bindweed type. Evergreen leaves, cabbage stalks, hedge clippings or woody stemmed plants take many months to decompose and should not be added to the compost heap.

If the heap is layered and, at intervals of 15 cm/6 in, the accelerator is added according to instructions, there should be no need to turn the heap once it is made. When the bin is almost full, cover the compost with soil and flatten it down. Check every now and then to see if the heap is too dry, and if it is, make holes with a stick and pour water into them. Leave the compost heap for about 4 months before using.

CHOOSING AND BUYING HERBS

The final choice of herbs to grow has to be made by the gardener, but there are one or two points that should be borne in mind when making that choice.

QUANTITY

Do not overestimate and get too many herbs for one small plot. Make a list of the herbs you wish to grow, then go carefully through it adding the ultimate height of each plant and the amount of room it is likely to need. Inadequate light or space for roots caused by overcrowding forces herbs to grow tall and spindly, and their scent and flavour suffer in consequence.

You could choose to have perennial herbs, spacing them apart correctly and, while they are young and small, sowing annual herbs in between to fill in the gaps. Such a scheme would permit you to grow several crops of chervil, caraway or dill before plants such as rosemary or southernwood had reached their full height.

HERBS FOR BEGINNERS

If you have never grown herbs before, it is wiser to start with the easy ones such as thyme, chives, dill, salad burnet or the savories. Then you will not be discouraged by the slow growth and poor showing of the difficult herbs. Basil and anise come into this category, unless you live in a very warm climate, and parsley germinates so slowly in some areas that it can be difficult to grow.

SEEDS OR PLANTS

Choosing whether to buy packets of herb seed or the herb plant itself largely depends on which herbs you have decided to grow and on the amount of time and effort you can devote to your herb garden. Expense may also be a limiting factor.

To make an instant garden by buying herb plants is obviously more expensive than growing them from seed. Nevertheless herbs such as French tarragon, purple sage and southernwood do not, except in very warm climates, produce seed, so you must begin with a plant. It is also more encouraging to start with a rosemary plant, lavender or a bay tree. Once these plants are established you will be able to increase your stock by taking cuttings.

Most herbs will grow well from seed and produce good sturdy plants with plenty of green leaves for

Opposite Left: A homemade compost bin with sacking cover.

Opposite Right: Showing the layers of waste material with the cover on top.

Right: A raised bed against a wall makes an attractive setting for the bright blue-flowered borage. Use the flowers for salads and candying; the young leaf sprigs in summer drinks.

picking. When buying seeds try to avoid choosing and buying packets that contain mixed herbs. It is far too difficult for a beginner to identify the herbs at the seedling stage.

QUALITY

It is essential to buy seeds with good, clear growing instructions on the packet. Buy from a reputable seedsman and obtain your plants from specialist herb nurseries. You can buy container-grown perennial herbs at any time of the year and annual herb plants from early summer onwards.

When choosing your plants at the nursery, look for a good fibrous root formation coming out of the base of the pot and for small stocky herbs.

GROWING HERBS IN THE GARDEN

After preparing the site, allow the ground to settle for a few weeks before planting up the herb bed. During this period you can obtain your plants. You may decide to purchase a few perennial plants, rather than grow these from seed, which can be a slow process.

PLANTING

On arriving home with your plants put them in a sheltered place until you can put them out. Do not let them get too dry.

Removing herb plant from pot.

You can plant container-grown herbs at any time of the year provided the weather is not too cold and there is no frost or snow. Thoroughly soak the plants and leave overnight before planting. Ideally, herbs should be planted on a warm damp day. Dig out a deep enough hole to accommodate the plant and remove the herb from the pot carefully, trying not to disturb its root ball, especially if the plant is a young one. Gently loosen the outside roots which tend to coil round when in the pot. Make sure you set the plant in with the top of its soil ball just beneath ground level. Fill all round with loose earth and firm it down well. Label the perennials which disappear during winter so that you will not forget where they have been planted.

When transplanting the woody-stemmed herbs southernwood, lavender and bay, you will notice the 'soil mark' on their stems. Plant these herbs deep enough for the soil to come up to this mark. Put a little leaf mould or compost in the hole, loosen the roots of the herb and place it in the hole. Fill in with earth, firming down well, and water the plant.

Gently loosening outside roots.

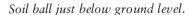

Soil ball just below ground level.

Firming the soil.

Right: When the ground has not been prepared for sowing seed, an early start can be made in a green-house. The seeds can be sown in seed trays or pots, pricked out, hardened off and then planted in their final growing position.

Left: Transplanting a woody-stemmed herb deep enough for the soil to come up to the soil mark.

GROWING FROM SEED OUTDOORS

Most herb seeds are sown either in the early autumn or the spring, but throughout the summer months successive sowings can be made of chervil, dill and parsley. Many perennial herbs can be grown from seed in the same way as annuals, but it may be a longer time before you can start using the leaves as these plants will first need to get established.

Sow herb seeds in the open ground only when the weather is warm and there is no danger of frost, and do not sow the seeds too deeply in the soil or they will not germinate. Cover the seeds lightly with soil and mark the spot where you have sown them. When the seedlings reach the 4-leaf stage, about 5 cm/2 in high, thin the plants to their appropriate distances apart. Annual herb seeds should germinate in 10 to 14 days, except for parsley which is very slow. Perennial seeds take up to 4 weeks to germinate so it is especially important to mark their position.

GROWING FROM SEED INDOORS

Sowing herb seeds indoors will give you much earlier crops and will lessen the danger of the tiny herb seedlings being mistaken for weeds and hoed out of sight!

Start with clean seed trays or flowerpots, covering the drainage holes with pieces of broken pots or a few pebbles. Fill the trays to within 1.5 cm/½ in of the top with a good seed compost such as John Innes No. 1, available from garden centres and nurseries. It is always best to use a sterile seed compost. Ordinary garden soil contains many weed seeds which will grow quickly and smother the herbs. Firm the compost down, then water the pots or trays and leave them for a day to allow the soil to warm up. Next day sow the seeds thinly and evenly and cover lightly with a thin layer of soil. The fine seed of summer savory and sweet (knotted) marjoram should be mixed with a little sharp sand for even sowing, and just lightly pressed into the soil. Cover the trays with glass, place newspaper on top to keep the seeds in the dark, and turn the glass over each day so that condensation will not form on the underside.

For best germination results keep the trays in a temperature of 13°C/58°F. After about a week, when the seeds have sprouted, remove the paper and glass and bring them into the light, but not into direct sunlight. Keep the soil damp by using a fine mist spray.

Once the seedlings have reached the 4-leaf stage prick them out 5 cm/2 in apart into a potting compost such as John Innes No 2. When the seedlings are well-established, start to harden them off by putting the trays outside for a longer period day by day when the weather is warm. After about 10 days plant the seedlings in their final growing position, spaced the correct distance apart

Covering seeds lightly with a thin layer of soil.

Seed tray covered with glass and newspaper to keep out the light.

Using a fine mist spray when seeds have sprouted, to keep soil damp.

for each herb. Until the herbs are growing strongly it is important to keep them well-watered. Tender annuals such as basil, purslane and sweet (knotted) marjoram live only a few short months and they disappear with the first frost. Protect these herbs with cloches to keep the soil warm and prolong the growing season.

Planting the seedlings in their final growing position.

MAINTENANCE

Looking after the herb garden throughout the growing season need not be an arduous task, and for the few essential jobs which have to be done you will be amply rewarded by having a healthy, colourful and fragrant herb bed.

Keep the herb garden free of weeds, doing this by hand while the herbs are small so as not to disturb their roots. Later on in the season hoe the surface of the bed to a depth of 5 cm/2 in. This action breaks up the soil, discourages weeds and allows air to circulate so that in dry weather the soil will not become hard and caked. Water the plants regularly when the weather is dry, giving special attention to moisture-loving herbs such as angelica, parsley, chervil and the mints.

To discourage weeds and prevent the soil from drying out spread a layer of peat round the herb plants. This is especially good on a heavy soil as it helps to lighten it. The use of black polythene sheeting is another way to keep the weeds down, with the added advantage of keeping the soil warm, helpful for the tender annuals and any herbs which were started late in the season.

Pick leaves and flowers for immediate use through-out the summer months. To concentrate the flavour and aroma of those herbs which are only required for their leaves, cut off the flower heads as soon as they appear.

At the end of the growing season the shrubby peren-nial herbs should be cut back to half the year's growth to maintain sturdy bushy plants. Before the first frosts arrive, cut down the fleshy-stemmed plants and dry the leaves for winter. In the autumn or early spring spread a thin dressing of a well-balanced fertilizer over the soil and lightly fork it in. A fertilizer is a concentrated plant food which, in small amounts, is good for the herb bed. Too much fertilizer will produce a lush growth but with little flavour or aroma. For the winter many of the herbs can be put into pots and brought indoors (if they are not too large). Rosemary, tarragon, thyme and salad burnet all take kindly to wintering inside the house. Pineapple sage must be brought indoors as it is a half-hardy perennial and flowers in the late autumn. If tarragon remains out of doors it should be protected from frosty weather by a covering of leaves or straw kept in place by wire netting pegged firmly into the soil.

PROPAGATION

Once your perennial herbs have become established you may wish to increase your stock without going to the expense of buying more plants, and there are a number of ways in which this can easily be done.

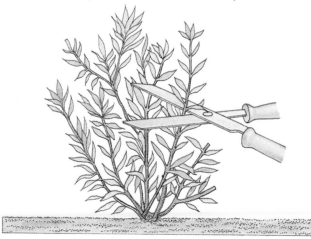

Cutting back half the year's growth from a woody-stemmed herb.

Making a slanting cut in the underside of a thick stem.

Putting hormone rooting powder on to the cut with a brush.

The stem placed firmly in the ground and secured by a peg.

Layering This is the easiest method of increasing both woody and soft-stemmed perennial herbs such as southernwood, sage, rosemary, mint, marjoram and lemon balm. Choose a strong growing flexible branch close to the ground. If the branch is thick, make a slanting cut in the underside of the stem about 20–25 cm/8–10 in from the main stem. Put some hormone rooting powder on the cut and bend the stem down so that you bury it firmly in the soil, leaving just the top-most leaves above the soil. Secure the stem in position with an old-fashioned split wooden clothes peg or piece of plastic-covered wire and leave it for 4 to 6 weeks, by which time roots will have formed. You can then sever the stem from the main plant and carefully remove the new herb plant to its final growing position.

Stem cuttings These can be taken from sturdy plants throughout the growing season. Choose strong stems with plenty of leaf growth 10 cm/4 in long and remove all the lower leaves. Fill a seed tray or shallow flower pot with sharp sand or a cutting compost, such as John Innes No 1 or 2, dip the cuttings into water and then into rooting powder, shake off the excess powder and plant the cutting firmly in the sand. Keep the sand moist and the tray out of direct sunlight. Cuttings of mint and thyme take root within 4 to 5 weeks, but rosemary, bay and lavender may take much longer.

Root division This is carried out when there is no danger of frost, in the autumn or early spring when the herb plants are dormant. Lift the plant and separate the clump carefully by pulling it apart gently or cutting. Once divided, the herbs should be replanted at once and watered well until they have become established.

CONTROL OF PESTS AND DISEASES
Fortunately there are very few pests or diseases which attack herbs, but to avoid any trouble you should follow a few basic preventive measures. Taking these measures will lessen the likelihood of trouble which may occur as a result of circumstances beyond your control. If the weather is wet there will be slugs, if it is dry there will be greenfly, and if it is cold the plants may be damaged by frost and wind.

1 Always prepare the ground thoroughly so that you will have strong-growing herbs which are more likely to resist attack than weak ones.
2 Buy the healthiest plants you can find, which will be small and stocky with plenty of fibrous root growth. Buy good fresh seed each year.
3 Try to sow or plant at the best possible time of year for the herbs to grow strong and get established before there is any danger from pests or disease. Take care when planting out container-grown plants at an unusual time of year for the reasons previously stated.

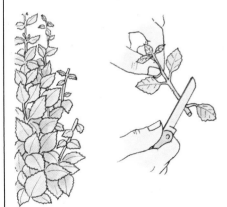

Removing the lower leaves from a strong stem 10 cm/4 in. long.

Dipping a cutting first in water and then into rooting powder.

Planting cuttings firmly into shar sand or cutting compost.

4 Remember growing plants need food; give the herbs a liquid plant feed every 2 weeks during the summer.

The disease most likely to attack in the herb garden will affect the mints. Mint rust is caused by fungi, the spores of which lie on the surface of the soil during winter. Swollen, twisted shoots of mint appear in spring covered with orange-coloured spore pustules. The leaves turn yellow and dry up, eventually dropping off. To treat this problem, remove and burn all affected shoots as soon as they come up. In the winter, when the foliage has died down, put straw over the mint bed and set fire to it. This will kill the spores in the soil. The disease does not attack the underground runners and its treatment will not damage them. Cuttings of these can be taken and planted out in a new position.

Mildew attacks herbs such as mint and tarragon and is prevalent in very damp weather where the plants or seedlings are set too close together. To treat it, spray the plants with bordeaux mixture, obtainable from garden shops.

Damping-off disease attacks seedlings and is caused by organisms in the soil. The seedlings collapse at ground level. Overcrowding in a seed tray or attempting to propagate in heavy, waterlogged soil create conditions in which this disease will flourish.

Opposite: A splendid display of white hyssop set against tall-growing pink bergamot.

Below: A well-stocked herb bed. The plants growing in pots at the front can be moved about the garden.

TUBS, WINDOW BOXES AND HANGING BASKETS

When you are choosing pots, window boxes or hanging baskets for growing herbs outside, remember you have also to fill that container with a growing medium, so buy good containers strong enough for your purpose. Do not get hanging baskets too big, for they will be heavy to handle and difficult to hang. Filling the box with soil can be a more expensive item than the box itself, so do not choose containers which are too large or cumbersome. Without overcrowding them, make the best use of the space each provides for your herbs.

The type of soil you decide to buy may be dictated by its price, but its weight should also be considered because a relatively small amount of soil, when wet, can be heavy. This could present a problem with a window box hanging on a wall, a container standing on a balcony or a hanging basket. For these special requirements you can buy a soilless compost or one of the light, peat-type composts now available.

For normal filling of containers you can use any one of a number of proprietary composts on the market which are sold for potting, such as John Innes No 2 or Levington's potting compost.

If you require soil in bulk for a large number of tubs, stone urns or window boxes, then it is better to mix your own growing medium provided you have the space to do the mixing and can obtain the necessary ingredients. It need not be as alarming as it sounds. You can measure out the ingredients with an old plastic

jug, which can be of any size so long as you keep the mixture in the right proportions.

Wash out all containers, whether old or new ones, with a weak solution of washing soda or Jeyes fluid.

To make your potting compost you need peat, sharp sand and good loam or sieved garden compost in roughly the following proportions: using a 1 pint measure, take 7 parts loam, 3 parts peat and 1 part sand. To this should be added 4 tablespoons of a base fertilizer and 1 tablespoon of lime.

Mix the parts together on a newspaper laid on a bench or even the kitchen draining board. If this is not practical, use a bucket or a plastic sack, but make sure the mixture is well-blended.

FILLING THE CONTAINERS

Large wooden or plastic tubs should stand on bricks to allow the air to circulate round them and to prevent rotting in the case of wooden tubs. Window boxes should stand on drip trays and individual pots of herbs placed on window sills should stand on trays or saucers of shingle. Put all large containers in position before filling with drainage crocks and soil. They will be too heavy to move once full.

There should be plenty of drainage holes in the base of each tub and these should be covered with pieces of broken clay pots or a few pebbles to keep the soil clear. When the tubs or boxes are very deep, more drainage material is necessary, so put in a 5 cm/2 in layer of broken crocks or gravel. To save weight, foamed polystyrene packaging can be crumbled by hand and used to replace broken crocks or gravel as a drainage medium.

Fill the containers half full of compost and firm it down well. Add remaining soil to come to within 2.5 cm/1 in of the top. Firm it down again so that the final gap between soil top and rim of container is 5 cm/2 in. This will leave room for the extra soil which comes when you plant the herbs and for the addition of fertilizers during the growing months. There is also less likelihood of the soil spilling over the sides of the container when you water the plants.

Leave the compost to settle for 7 to 10 days, especially in the larger tubs and boxes where you may find that a few weeds will have germinated in that time. Remove the weeds, water the compost well and leave for a further 24 hours before putting in the plants or sowing the seed.

Before filling a wire hanging basket with soil it should be well-lined with moist sphagnum moss so that no soil will fall through. Soak moss and soil well before planting up, by standing the basket in a shallow bowl of water until the compost is uniformly damp.

PLANTING

It is important, when putting two or more plants in one pot, to choose herbs that need similar soil conditions and the same amount of sun and watering. The most favourable time for planting up your containers is the spring, but this must depend to some extent on the type of herb chosen.

Provided the weather is not too cold, the pot-grown shrubby herbs rosemary, bay, lavender and winter savory can go into your containers at any time but preferably in the late autumn when the plants are dormant. Other perennials which die down in the winter, such as lovage, sweet Cicely, the mints and bergamot, can be planted in the early autumn to get established before the cold weather arrives. Lemon and caraway thyme, English mace and lemon verbena are half-hardy perennials and should be planted in spring.

Most annual seeds can be sown directly into the tubs and boxes in the spring, and annual herb plants can go in from late spring onwards. Sow the biannual chervil and biennial parsley in autumn as well as spring so that you have leaves through the winter or in the very early spring.

When buying your plants at the nursery look for three things. First, a good fibrous root formation coming through the base of the pot. Secondly, go for the short, vigorous stocky plants; these are well-established and will suffer less from being transplanted than tall, spindly ones. It will also be easier to cope with growing them in limited space. Thirdly, but not so important, do not purchase plants already in flower, as part of their growing energy is already expended.

Water the herbs thoroughly and leave for a few hours before transplanting. Carefully remove the plants from the pots, polythene sleeves or trays without unduly disturbing the roots. Make a hole in the soil of your container a little larger than the root ball of the plant and set it in so that the top of the root ball is just beneath the surface of the surrounding soil. Firm it down well and give it some water. Keep plants shaded from the sun and winds for the first few days while plants become established. This is especially important for hanging baskets which should be in a cool, shady position until the herbs have rooted properly.

WATERING

This is of more importance when growing plants in containers than when growing in the open ground because of the evaporation of moisture through the sides of the pot. In the hottest weather the soil needs to be kept moist, but not too wet, and this should be checked every day, especially in dry weather. Scratch the surface of the soil, and if it is dry to a depth of about 2.5 cm/1 in the plant should be watered. Where the pots can be moved, stand them in a shallow bowl of water until the surface soil is damp, otherwise water the plants thoroughly using a spray nozzle on the watering can. At the height of the growing season many herbs – annuals and other moisture-loving plants especially – will need watering every day. When the soil is thoroughly moist or water runs out at the bottom of the container the plants have had sufficient. Never allow a plant to dry out completely or the plants will be damaged when you water them.

Try to get into a habit of watering regularly or testing the soil to see if it is too dry. You cannot count on the rain providing sufficient moisture for your plants, and where the foliage is large the rain will bounce off the leaves and never reach the soil adjacent to the roots.

Hanging baskets are a special case for watering as they can very soon dry out. The soil must not be allowed to get caked. A fine spraying each evening in very hot weather will prevent this. Once a week take the basket down and give it a really good soak, then allow it to drain before rehanging.

CARE OF CONTAINER GARDENS

Keeping containers free of weeds is an important task, for no herb growing in a confined space should have to compete for soil space with unwelcome weeds. By keeping the surface free of weeds and the soil friable this will increase the amount of air in the soil which helps to release the plant foods. Where plants grow tall, like dill, Jacob's ladder or tarragon, these may need staking, especially if the container has to be in a windy position.

Herbs growing in containers need a slightly richer soil than those in the open ground, and regular feeding throughout the growing season should be maintained. A liquid feed in a weak solution is the easiest to apply, and plants should be sprayed every 10 to 12 days.

Unless you are growing herbs for their flowerheads and seeds, cut off the flowering tops as they appear to concentrate the full flavour in the leaves. Keep all plants neat and tidy, removing any dead leaves.

Herbs in containers seem to be less susceptible to pests and diseases, but unless care is taken they are subject to attacks of greenfly. If there are only a few you can remove them by hand, but where there are too many for this wash the plant in soapy water or a very weak solution of detergent washing up liquid. The greenfly should drop off. The mints are prone to mint rust disease if the plants suffer too often a rapid change in temperature. This causes brown blotches to appear on the leaves which then die and drop. The only answer is to remove the plant altogether.

Never use any insecticide sprays on the herbs, as these will only make them unfit for eating or using.

GROWING HERBS INDOORS

Herbs grown in pots, on the balcony or in the courtyard can be brought in during the winter. But if you have no facilities for growing herbs out of doors you can have them indoors all the time. Growing herbs indoors requires rather different treatment, but in fact most of the herbs which grow successfully in pots out of doors will also grow well indoors. The limiting factor is the amount of light available, and space. Stand the pots on small trays or saucers of gravel; this will allow for drainage of any excess water and keep the atmosphere humid round the plants.

Herbs growing well in pots and hanging baskets. A good thick moss is required for lining the baskets to prevent loss of moisture.

A collection of healthy plants on a sunny windowsill.

Indoor herbs need care and attention. If light, air, water and plant food can be supplied in adequate amounts, the herbs will thrive. It is also important that the containers be of a sensible size for the plants and have good drainage holes.

LIGHT

Herbs need light in which to grow and should be placed on a sunny windowsill if possible. Remove the herbs from the sill at the hottest time of the day as sunshine beating through the window pane will scorch the leaves and dry out the plant. Turn the pots round a little each day so you complete a full round every other day and all parts of the herb will get the same amount of light and air. If there is no sill, stand the pots on a table in the vicinity of the window or as near as is practical.

For the very keen herb gardener there are special fluorescent lights available emitting the photosynthetic radiation essential to plant growth, and which may be used in a dark basement kitchen or alcove. Apart from the cost, there is a great advantage in having the light exactly where it is required. The herbs should have roughly 15 hours of light per day, and the fluorescent lamp should be about 40–50 cm/16–20 in above the plants. These lamps are, however, primarily for commercial growers.

AIR

Herb plants need gentle air circulation, and when the weather permits the window can be left open. Make sure the plants will not be in a draught or where a sudden gust of wind can blow them over. In warm weather, when possible, place them outside, but if on a ledge or window be careful to secure the container. A pot falling from the ledge of a top floor window can be a danger to those below. If you only have a few herbs in pots and they are not too heavy, you can take them outside into warm, fresh air. Herbs grown in the congested atmosphere of a kitchen and subject to frequent picking will especially benefit from this change.

WATER

Watering your indoor herbs should be done carefully. The herbs will soon sicken and die if their roots have insufficient water, or conversely, are waterlogged and therefore starved of the air and nutrients present in the soil and necessary for growth. Some herbs will require more frequent watering then others, according to the species. Always keep your watering can full of water so that it will be the same temperature as the atmosphere when you water the plants. Water straight from the tap will be too cold for the herbs. Watering from above is best for the herbs, provided it can get down into the soil and does not lie on the top, and fine spraying of the leaves is important to keep the dust from clogging them.

TEMPERATURE AND HUMIDITY

It is important that the atmosphere surrounding indoor herbs does not get too dry. This can happen where there is central heating. To combat this keep a small bowl of water near the pots or trays of herbs to keep the air damp around the plants. Ideally indoor herbs should be kept in an even temperature of about 16°C/65°F. They will not grow well if subjected to extremes of temperature. If you have the central heating on one day and not the next, make sure you move the herbs to wherever it is warm.

NUTRITION

Plant foods are very necessary for indoor herbs, and regular applications of liquid plant food should be given every 10 days.

HARVESTING

Picking herb leaves for use can be done all through the growing season, but at no time should you cut more than one fifth of the total number of leaves on a herb if you want the plant to survive. Should you require leaves of a particular herb in quantity, several pots should be grown. You could have a tray holding 6 pots of chervil, parsley or dill, the herbs most often required in summer, or thyme and marjoram during the winter. Chives and Welsh onion can be cut down all at once without harm and will soon grow again, but you will need several pots of these if you are to do this often.

In the list of individual herbs you will find many that can be grown successfully indoors, even the larger-growing plants such as rosemary and bay. These plants will add fragrance and greenery to a room the whole year round, but they are very slow-growing and must be cut sparingly.

INCREASING STOCK

Once you find how comparatively simple it is to grow a few herbs indoors you may wish to increase your stock to give you more plants for cutting. Herbs such as thyme and lemon balm can be divided in the spring. Prepare the necessary number of pots as directed above and carefully take the plants out of their pots. Remove the soil and gently pull the roots apart, or cut them into as many plants as is possible, ensuring that each piece will have good roots. Put the plants into the prepared pots, firm them down well and water. Keep them out of sunshine until the herbs have recovered.

Another way to increase stock is by taking stem cuttings or 'slips' in the spring. Indoor plants suitable for this type of propagation are pineapple sage, winter savory, tarragon and rosemary. Use only the leafy vigorous growing tips of the plant. Cut off the 'slips' 10–15 cm/4–6 in long and strip off all leaves from the lower half. Dip the cuttings first in water and then in a good rooting powder. Shake off excess powder and plant the 'slips' in a tray or pots filled with cutting compost or just plain sand. Firm the cuttings down well and water them; this seals the base of the cutting into the soil so it will root and not rot and die. To speed up the rooting process cover the trays with a propagator top or the pots with plastic bags, making sure the bags do not touch the cuttings. Stand the cuttings in a good

light but not direct sunlight. When they become a bright green you will know the cuttings have rooted, but this may take some weeks. Take care when transplanting these new plants and try to leave some of the propagating medium undisturbed round the roots. When the new growth appears on the herbs you can bring the plants into the sunlight and keep them moist.

PESTS AND DISORDERS

The only pest likely to attack indoor herbs in summer is the greenfly, which clusters on the stems and the undersides of the leaves. If there are only a few, pick them off with your fingers, but if they appear in numbers up-end the plant, holding firmly on to the soil and plant, and swish the leaves in weak soapy water.

Indoor herb plants will need replacing more often than those outside because, in spite of regular feeding, the soil becomes exhausted. The herb plants can be repotted in new soil every year, and herbs such as rosemary, lemon verbena and bay will all benefit and continue from year to year. When you repot herbs, the pots should be scrubbed in a disinfectant before putting new soil into them. Remember to pot on some of the herbs as they grow bigger to allow more room for their roots to spread. You will recognize the right time for this when you see the roots growing through the drainage holes of the pots. No herb should be allowed to get pot bound. This occurs when the roots are packed very tightly in the pot. As a result there will be little growth, the plant will suffer from lack of food and need much more watering than usual. Then is the time to replant in a bigger pot in new soil.

Herbs growing in pots and containers on the patio: rose, lemon balm, tarragon, hyssop, various mints, sweet Cicely, basil, thyme, parsley and peppermint.

HARVESTING AND PRESERVING HERBS

The best time for harvesting herbs differs from plant to plant. Watch them carefully, in order not to miss the right moment. A constant factor is the weather. The day of picking must be dry: moisture is to be avoided at all costs. Gather the herbs in the morning after the dew has dried, but before the heat of the sun has fallen upon them.

Herbs should be picked just before they flower, when the flower buds have begun to form but before they actually start to open. The flavour is in the leaves, but once the plant has produced its seed, much of the flavour will disappear. Many herbs – notably fennel and dill – produce hardly any more leaves after flowering, but bear flat seed heads on long bare stems.

Pick only the tips of the branches, at the same time endeavouring to trim the plant into a neat compact shape. Cut off and discard any dead or diseased leaves. The old-fashioned way of drying herbs was certainly the most picturesque. They were tied in bunches small enough for air to flow freely through them, and hung in racks from the ceiling, often over the stove. Here they would stay for a few days, before being wrapped in paper and stored in a dark drawer.

Nowadays it is considered more efficient to dry them in racks or trays. The herbs are laid out in a single layer, and covered with a sheet of thin muslin (cheesecloth) to keep off the dust. The racks or trays are then put in a warm airy place – never in the sun – and left for about 24 hours. Suitable places are an airing cupboard, or the plate-warming drawer of an oven, with the door left open. When ready they should be totally dry and brittle, but still green; if they have turned brown this means that the heat was too high, and the flavour will have been lost. It is worth experimenting with a small amount, before consigning a year's crop to one place.

When dry, the leaves should be stored as soon as possible. They must not be allowed to come in contact with any moisture in the interim, for they will instantly re-absorb it and become musty. Take the leaves off the branches and rub or crumble them on to a sheet of paper, then pour them into small jars and seal tightly. If made of clear glass, the jars must be kept in a dark cupboard, for light causes a rapid deterioration in flavour. Ideally dried herbs should be stored in jars made of dark coloured glass.

In former times, drying was virtually the only way of preserving herbs through the winter. Nowadays the choices are infinitely wider, at least if you have a freezer, and favourite herbs may be stored in a number of different ways. In my opinion, only a few are worth the trouble of drying. Sage, rosemary, bay, mint, lovage, thyme and marjoram (or oregano) all dry well, but many others turn into dust, and many of the little jars one sees for sale in the supermarket are not worth the money. Parsley, for instance, retains none of its fresh taste, while both fennel and dill are better kept in the form of seed. Seeds always store better than leaves, since they are by their nature already dry. (Place freshly gathered seeds in a dry place, cover them with paper and leave them for 10–14 days before

Left: Drying herbs in a Swedish kitchen. This old-fashioned method of drying is not recommended today. Note how each herb is tied in its separate bundle and carefully labelled to avoid confusion when the herb is dried. Handy for the cook, these bundles were often left hanging until they were no longer any use for flavouring.

Far Left: Little bundles of dried lavender tied with ribbon.

storing in jars.) The best variety of mint for drying is spearmint, and this is excellent. In Middle Eastern countries dried mint is often used in preference to fresh, as is oregano in Greece, where during the summer when the plant is in full growth, salads are sprinkled with dried oregano. Marigold petals can also be dried quite successfully, and even retain some of their colour.

Delicate herbs like the basils, chervil, dill leaves and tarragon, are best preserved by freezing. This can be done in a number of different ways, all of which work well. With basil, for instance, the leaves should be picked off the stems and put in small plastic bags, or wrapped in small packets of cling film (plastic wrap). Tarragon, chervil, fennel and dill are best picked in little sprays, then treated in the same way. Sorrel also freezes well, but if picked in large quantities it may be more convenient first to blanch it, like spinach, in order to save space. Young black currant leaves can be frozen like basil, and used for making delicious sorbets later in the year, when the leaves on the bush are no longer young and tender. Parsley is most useful already chopped, and wrapped in tiny screws of foil, or minute

plastic bags. Treated in this way, it thaws very quickly and is ready for use almost immediately.

Another way of freezing herbs is to chop the leaves, mix them with water, and pour into ice trays. Cubes can then be melted as required. Even more useful in the freezer is a stock of various herb butters. These freeze extremely well, and can be used throughout the winter as a last-minute addition to grilled (broiled) meats, noodles, and boiled or steamed vegetables. *Pistou*, the Mediterranean sauce made from basil and pine kernels (pine nuts), also freezes well and makes a rare winter treat stirred into a vegetable soup or served on spaghetti.

If you do not have a freezer you may like to try an older method of storing herbs, that of preserving them in salt. This works particularly well with basil. Pick the leaves from the stems and lay them in a wide-necked jar or plastic box. Cover with coarse salt. Put in alternate layers of basil and coarse salt till they completely fill the container. Pour olive oil over to cover the layers, before sealing tightly. The container can be kept in the refrigerator for several weeks; the oil as well as the basil can be used in salads and in other dishes.

FENNEL
Foeniculum vulgare

LEMON BALM
Melissa officinalis

TARRAGON
Artemisia dracunculus

ROSEMARY
Rosmarinus officinalis

SPEARMINT
Mentha spicata

SWEET MARJ
Origanum mar

APPLEMINT
Mentha rotundifolia

50 POPULAR HERBS

On the following pages you will find all the well-known culinary herbs together with many that have familiar names but which are not so widely used today. The herbs have been chosen for their flavouring and seasoning properties, as well as their special therapeutic qualities. These are the herbs which have the greatest variety of uses, and while it is not intended that all the herbs should be grown in the garden, the list offers a worthwhile selection from which to make your choice. The majority of the herbs are familiar as culinary herbs but many are also good medicinal or cosmetic plants.

When you are considering which herbs to grow in your garden, you must first decide the purpose for which they are to be grown. Is it your intention to use herbs only in cooking? Would you prefer to grow a bed of medicinal herbs to make natural remedies and herbal teas? Perhaps you wish to grow the cosmetic herbs which are so fragrant and colourful.

All the plants described in this section are comparatively easy to grow, and once established in their plot, need little attention. If you cannot grow them from seed, you will find the majority are obtainable at your local garden centre or herb nursery. A few such as elder, yarrow and marshmallow, can easily be found growing in the wild – so the seed can be collected from the plants in the appropriate season.

To preserve the plants in the countryside from extinction, it is important that you only gather the seeds. It is also essential to correctly identify the plant before collecting any seeds from a herb growing in the wild. Although most herbs run true to form, some plants cross fertilize with the result that scents and flavours become mixed. If you are in doubt about the appearance of a particular herb, try to see it growing by visiting herb gardens and nursery centres. This will often give you a better idea of how to fit a particular herb into your own garden arrangement.

When planning your garden, list all the herbs you would like to grow, making a note of their heights and how you wish to use them. In this way you will find you have a good selection of herbs and a clear idea of how they can be used to their best advantage. By tradition, many herbs have a specific use, but with the emphasis today largely on the culinary herbs, most of the alternative uses remain untried. There are a great many herbs which can be used in cosmetics, and with the rising cost of these preparations in the shops, it is well worth making your own.

PARSLEY
Petroselinum crispum

BORAGE
Borago officinalis

BAY
Laurus nobilis

FAMILY: BORAGINACEAE

BORAGE

Botanical name: *Borago officinalis*

Borage is a tall hairy-leaved annual with vivid blue star-shaped flowers. It is a strong-growing plant and, whatever the weather, continues to bloom for many months of the year. Both flowers and leaves have a fresh cucumber flavour.

Borage originated in southern Europe where it was taken as a tonic herb, for it was believed to have an exhilarating effect on the mind. One of the traditional plants of the herb garden, it now grows wild throughout Europe.

CULTIVATION & PROPAGATION

Borage is best grown from seed as plants do not transplant happily. It prefers a light, rather poor soil of chalk or sand and a well-drained dry sunny position. It is not suitable for container growing because of the long tap root. Sow borage seeds 5 cm/ 2 in deep in the soil from spring to early summer where they are to flower. Thin seedlings to 60 cm/2 ft apart. Seeds germinate quickly and the plants are fully grown in 5 to 6 weeks. Borage seeds itself freely and will come up again year after year.

USES

Chop young borage leaves finely and add, with the flowers, to green salads and raw vegetable salads. Use the leaves to give a cucumber flavour to pickles and to add to pea or bean soup. Put leaves and flowers into a wine or fruit cup and allow to stand for an hour before straining. Borage makes a refreshing iced or hot drink on its own with lemon and sugar added. The flowers are an attractive edible decoration and can be candied or crystallized to decorate cakes and ice creams.

The flowers dry well and add colour to pot-pourris.

FAMILY: BORAGINACEAE

COMFREY

Botanical name:
Symphytum officinale

A tall, rather wide-spreading perennial, comfrey has big coarse rough green leaves. The flowers, which are blue or creamy-white, grow in lopsided spikes and bloom right through the summer. The whole plant grows 60–90 cm/2–3 ft tall.

For centuries comfrey has been an important medicinal healing plant taken both internally and externally. One of its synonyms is 'consound' meaning 'against swooning', probably arising from its use as a wound herb, when fresh comfrey leaves were picked and laid on cuts, bruises and open wounds to promote healing. It was also an old remedy for mending broken bones.

Comfrey is a first-class composting plant, helping the rapid breakdown of other compost materials. It is a good mulch to put round other herbs in the growing season. All parts of the plant contain valuable healing properties which are still being investigated.

CULTIVATION & PROPAGATION

Sow comfrey seed in early spring where it is to flower and thin the plants to 30–45 cm/12–18 in apart. It

grows in almost any type of soil and thrives in a damp position. Comfrey is most useful in the garden as a background plant and screen, where it seeds itself freely.

Comfrey is not really suitable for container growing because of its large roots which need a great deal of water when fully grown. Comfrey can also be propagated by dividing the roots in spring. Young leaves can be picked for use throughout the season and the roots dug up in the autumn.

USES

Fresh comfrey leaves can be cooked as a plain green vegetable like spinach. It is tastier if the cooked leaves are mixed with a good white sauce and topped with grated cheese. Add a few chopped leaves to green salads and try comfrey leaf fritters, whole leaves dipped in batter and fried in deep fat. Use only the young leaves in cooking.

A decoction of comfrey root and leaves helps to ease coughs and other bronchial ailments. Only a small quantity of this should be made at a time because of its poor keeping qualities. The roots and leaves make a poultice or ointment for treating bruises, swellings and rheumatic pains.

FAMILY: CANNABINACEAE

HOP

Botanical name: *Humulus lupulus*

The female 'cones' of the hop plant, containing flowers and embryonic fruits, when dried are used for flavouring beer and ale. They have been in use in Britain since the sixteenth century. Hop is well-known for its calming effect on the nerves: hop-filled pillows are said to cure sleeplessness.

The hop plants are vigorous perennial vines which clamber over bushes and hedgerow trees. The female cones are a greenish-yellow, while the male flowers have 5 tiny petals and hang in loose bunches.

CULTIVATION & PROPAGATION
Hop plants must have support. Grow them against a fence, wall or trellis in full sun in rich well-worked soil. Sow seeds out of doors in late spring and thin the plants to 15–30 cm/6–12 in apart. Hops can be planted to train round a pole in open ground, or over an old tree stump. They make a very attractive screen. Keep well-watered in dry weather. Top dress plants in spring. In early autumn gather female flowers for drying and cut the plant down in late autumn. Hops can also be propagated by division of the roots in spring.

USES
In summer cook young hop shoots until tender and serve with melted butter and a twist of lemon. Use hops together with other leafy vegetables to make a summer soup.

Drink hop tea last thing at night to help you sleep.

FAMILY: CAPRIFOLIACEAE

ELDER

Botanical names:
Sambucus nigra European elder
Sambucus canadensis American elder

A hardy deciduous shrub, the European elder grows up to 7 m/22 ft tall, and the American variety to 3 m/12 ft, the branches all coming out from the base. Elder is native to the British Isles where it is a common hedgerow shrub. The creamy-white blossom, elderflower, grows in clusters, and flowers for about 2 months in early summer giving out a lovely heady scent. The fruits, elderberries, are usually ready by the end of summer and will hang for many weeks, unless

the birds get to them first. Blackbirds are especially fond of the shiny black berries.

Elder is included in every herbal because of the enormous number of ways in which it can be used. It is valuable not only as a medicinal plant but also in cosmetics and for cooking.

CULTIVATION & PROPAGATION
The elder likes a sunny rather moist place in which to grow and will thrive in any good garden soil. Elder bushes should be pruned in late autumn or very early spring before growth starts.

Propagate elder by taking cuttings of leafless shoots in the autumn or by the rather more difficult method of root division. It is fairly slow-growing when started from seed.

Although elder is not suitable for container growing, those with small gardens can take comfort in the fact that its flowers and fruits may be found along the hedgerows.

USES
Elderflowers makes a heady wine, producing a flavour similar to that of muscatel grapes. The flower also makes a fragrant water ice. A light-flavoured syrup or elderflower cordial is a good basis for fruit salads and with soda water and a piece of lemon is a delicious drink. Make elderflower pancakes and serve them with stewed gooseberries, add the flowers to fruit pies, or make elderflower fritters.

The elderberries, which are best not eaten raw, make a delicious wine and other drinks. They can be used in jam- and jelly-making, combining well with crab apples. Use the berries in apple tarts and in place of currants in other puddings. An elderberry syrup effectively relieves coughs and colds. Hot elderflower tea makes a soothing nightcap.

Cosmetically, elderflowers are wonderfully beneficial to the skin. An infusion softens the complexion and is helpful as a skin cleanser. Use a compress or face pack for wrinkles, sunburn or freckles.

Elderflower lotion is pleasant and refreshing when added to the bath.

FAMILY: COMPOSITAE

CHAMOMILE

Botanical name:
Matricaria chamomilla

Chamomile is a low-growing annual with small, white, daisy-like flowers which have a lovely scent. It is the flower which distinguishes the 'true'

chamomile from other forms. As soon as it starts to flower the petals turn back, baring the receptacle. Then is the time to pick the flowers for drying.

Chamomile is a healing and cosmetic plant of great antiquity and the healing substance, azulen, is extracted from the fresh flowers.

CULTIVATION & PROPAGATION
Very easy to grow from seed, chamomile prefers a dry sunny position. Sow seed in early spring where it is to flower, mixing sand with the tiny seeds to make sowing more even. Keep seeds watered until the leaves appear. Thin the plants to 15 cm/6 in apart. Since the flowerheads are the only useful part, a fair number of plants will be required.

Chamomile grows well in containers and, though more difficult to grow in quantity, it is worthwhile for the lovely fragrance of its pretty flowers. If some of the flowers are left to go to seed in the garden, chamomile will seed itself freely and come up year after year. The plants may also be increased by division in spring.

Another fragrant plant of the same family is Roman chamomile, *Anthemis nobilis*, a dwarf species only used for making lawns. As it seldom needs cutting it is popular with busy gardeners.

USES
An infusion of chamomile is well-known as a herbal rinse for fair hair. Use it also as a mouthwash and for a soothing eyebath. As a face wash it keeps the skin soft and supple. Chamomile relieves a heavy head cold when used in a facial steam. It makes a soothing tea for stomach upsets and indigestion, and with a spoonful of honey added, is a pleasant tonic or pick-me-up. Dried flowers add their fragrance to pot-pourris.

FAMILY: COMPOSITAE

MARIGOLD

Botanical name: *Calendula officinalis*

A very popular annual, marigold has been grown for centuries in cottage gardens. A small neatly growing plant, marigold makes a brilliant splash of colour with its bright orange and yellow flowers.

Originally marigold came from India where the Hindus used it to decorate temple altars. In cooking it may be used as an inexpensive substitute for saffron. Marigold flowers have value in medicine and cosmetics as well as in cooking.

CULTIVATION & PROPAGATION

Marigold grows easily from seed sown in the spring in light rich soil and a sunny position. Thin the plants to 45–60 cm/18–24 in apart, so they can spread and make bushy growth. Though an annual, marigold seeds itself freely and will come up year after year. With its gay colour and neat growth marigold makes a good container plant.

Pick flowers for use when they are fully open. Cut off flowerheads as they fade, to prolong the flowering season. Leaves can be gathered for use at any time.

USES

Marigold infusion made from the fresh leaves will soothe tired and swollen feet. An oil or ointment made from the petals is good for sunburn and for clearing and softening the skin. Marigold tea is a pleasant drink made from the petals and sweetened with honey. The infusion taken internally is good for the complexion and for poor circulation.

Fresh or dried marigold petals add

a delicate flavour and colour to rice, cheese and savoury egg dishes. Add them to custards or a baked sponge pudding. Fresh petals add colour and nutrition to a green salad.

FAMILY: COMPOSITAE

SOUTHERNWOOD

Botanical name:
Artemisia abrotanum

Southernwood is a small perennial woody shrub of neat habit growing up to about 1 m/3 ft high. Its slender hairlike leaves are grey-green and smell strongly of lemon when crushed. The tiny yellow flowers are insignificant but southernwood rarely flowers in temperate climates.

Medicinally, southernwood was used as a stimulant and antiseptic. An old remedy using southernwood was said to cure baldness, and it is still used in some hair lotions.

CULTIVATION & PROPAGATION

In late summer take cuttings about 15 cm/6 in long with a heel, and set them 7 cm/3 in deep in sand until rooted. Plant out in the following spring. In spring cut back established plants to 45 cm/18 in to keep them bushy and compact. Choose a sunny sheltered position in well-drained good garden soil. Southernwood can also be propagated by root division in the autumn and by layering of shoots. A handsome plant for container growing.

USES

Warm southernwood tea can be sweetened with honey and taken as a tonic, though the taste is a little bitter and strong. Dried leaves in muslin (cheesecloth) bags will keep away moths. Use southernwood in flower arrangements.

FAMILY: COMPOSITAE

TARRAGON

Botanical names:
Artemisia dracunculus French tarragon *Artemisia dracunculoides* Russian tarragon

French tarragon, with its distinctive flavour, is one of the best culinary herbs for savoury cooking and no herb collection should be without it. This tall, fragrant plant can grow to 1 m/3 ft high, and is a half-hardy perennial. It spreads by underground runners. The leaves are shiny and narrow and the tiny greenish white flowers never open properly except in a very warm climate. Russian or false tarragon has a greatly inferior flavour.

CULTIVATION & PROPAGATION

Tarragon needs a very sunny well-drained position in good garden soil. It will need feeding during the growing period to reach its full flavour. As tarragon does not set seed in temperate climates, propagate by taking cuttings of rooted shoots. Start by growing three or four plants set 30 cm/ 12 in apart in spring or autumn.

Every 4 years plants should be divided and replanted in fresh soil in the early spring. Cut down outdoor plants in late autumn and protect from frost by covering them with leaves or straw. Tarragon grows well in containers and during the winter can be brought indoors.

USES

Tarragon leaves give an excellent flavour to green and raw vegetable salads. Make tarragon vinegar by steeping the fresh herb in white wine vinegar. Use it when making French dressing. Tarragon can be added to roast meat, poultry dishes and fish. It is delicious in light buttery sauces to serve with mild-flavoured vegetables like marrow and artichokes.

FAMILY: COMPOSITAE

YARROW

Botanical name: *Achillea millefolium*

A very hardy perennial, yarrow grows in bushy clumps about 60 cm/2 ft tall. The leaves are dark and feathery and have a pleasant smell when crushed. The white flat-topped flowers grow in clusters and bloom all summer. Yarrow is a cosmetic herb and can help in healing minor ailments.

Historically, yarrow was highly valued as a medicinal plant and its antiseptic properties were widely appreciated. Used to cover cuts and sores, it was claimed to help in the quick formation of scar tissue.

CULTIVATION & PROPAGATION

Yarrow is easy to grow and needs little attention. It thrives in any soil and any position. Yarrow is a common wayside plant which can be easily transplanted into the herb garden. This will repay you by helping neighbouring plants to resist disease, but keep the roots within bounds. Yarrow also seems to deepen the fragrance and flavour of nearby herbs.

USES

The flavour of yarrow leaves is pleasantly strong though a little bitter. A few chopped leaves put inside a cream cheese sandwich give it a delicious bite.

An infusion of yarrow flowers used externally is a good lotion for cleansing the skin. Add the lotion to water for a relaxing bath. A face pack for greasy skin is made from fresh flower-buds. Yarrow tea sweetened with honey can be taken as a diuretic to help in a slimming programme and is good for cramp sufferers. Strong yarrow tea is used for reducing fever.

FAMILY: CRUCIFERAE

HORSE-RADISH

Botanical name: *Cochlearia armoracia* syn. *Armoracia rusticana*

Horse-radish is a hardy perennial with large floppy leaves growing from the base of the plant to a height of about 60–100 cm/2–3 ft. The flowers are white on a single stem but they do not appear every season. The large thick white roots are used as a condiment. They are also a valuable source of vitamin C.

In the Middle Ages horse-radish was taken to improve the digestion and the crushed roots used externally for aching joints and sciatica.

Horse-radish with its hot biting taste is most often used raw. It is rarely cooked as it loses its pungency.

CULTIVATION & PROPAGATION

Horse-radish grows well in rich light soil where the roots can grow long and straight. An open sunny place is best. Plant out young shoots in early spring 30 cm/12 in apart, or bury pieces of root 5 cm/2 in deep. If seed is available sow where they are to grow and thin out as suggested. Established roots can be dug up and grated as required but as the flavour is improved by cold weather, dig them up in the winter. For an onward crop, store some roots in damp sand through the winter. Quite small pieces of root will grow into new plants. Because of the depth of soil needed to grow good horse-radish, it is not suitable for container growing.

USES

Horse-radish is primarily used as a condiment, grated into cream, and makes a pleasant change from mustard. It is a superb accompaniment to roast or boiled beef. Add grated raw root to coleslaw and uncooked vegetable chutneys. Horse-radish sauce helps in the digestion of rich smoked fish such as eel, mackerel or herring. Horse-radish paste made with cream cheese makes a tasty sandwich filling.

Horse-radish makes a good embrocation for chilblains and stiff muscles.

FAMILY: CRUCIFERAE

WATERCRESS

Botanical name: *Nasturtium officinale*

Watercress is a hardy aquatic perennial plant. Small, shiny rounded leaves grow on fleshy branching stems which at first creep through the water and then grow upright to about 30 cm/ 12 in. The tiny white flowers bloom

throughout the summer followed by long curved seed pods. The flavour of the leaves and stems, which are the edible parts, is strong and peppery.

Historically a medicinal herb, watercress is rich in iron and vitamin C and was taken to ward off scurvy.

CULTIVATION & PROPAGATION

Watercress grows best in rich sandy soil, clean running water and an open position. The depth of soil needs to be 7.5 cm/3 in and the water, for fully grown plants, 10 cm/4 in. In early summer or autumn sow seed in boxes and plant out seedlings 15 cm/6 in apart. Watercress can also be propagated by cuttings taken in spring or early autumn. Constant cutting will produce bushy plants and prevent them from flowering.

USES

Watercress is always used fresh in salads or as a garnish. Watercress soup is full of nourishment and delicious hot or chilled. An infusion of young watercress shoots, though useful for rheumatic pains, digestive upsets or bronchial catarrh, should never be taken for long periods.

FAMILY: LABIATAE

APPLE MINT

Botanical name:
Mentha rotundifolia

Apple mint is a vigorous growing perennial with long underground runners. It looks similar to a smaller variety of 'Bowles' or woolly mint. It grows up to 45 cm/18 in high. The leaves are lighter in colour, slightly longer and not so woolly as 'Bowles' mint. Apple mint has a reddish, very hairy stem and the flowers are dense spikes of pale lilac. The flavour is a pleasant combination of ripe apples and spearmint and for this reason it is not such a popular mint as other varieties. But apple mint is very hardy and less prone to rust disease. A variegated variety is available which is very attractive for flower arrangements.

CULTIVATION & PROPAGATION
Apple mint requires a moist light but rich soil set in partial shade. Mints quickly take all the goodness from the soil, so work in some compost before planting. Apple mint can be grown by planting rooted pieces of the runner 5 cm/2 in deep and 20 cm/8 in apart in early spring. Apple mint can be grown in a container but plants should be replaced each year. In a herb bed the plant will quickly spread. Set roofing slates in the soil around the apple mint to keep it within bounds. Replant mints every two or three years.

USES
The distinctive apple and mint flavour of apple mint adds a delicious taste to fruits, fruit salads and water ices. Add leaves to wine and cider cups and other fruit drinks.

FAMILY: LABIATAE

BASIL

Botanical names:
Ocimum basilicum Sweet basil
Ocimum minimum Bush basil

There are 2 kinds of basil plants, sweet and bush. They are both treated as annuals in temperate climates. Sweet basil has largish, shiny, dark green leaves and grows 30–60 cm/1–2 ft high. The flowers are white. A very popular hybrid form, opal basil has leaves of dark purple bronze with pink flowers. Bush basil, as its name suggests, is of bushy habit – only 15 cm/6 in high – and has lots of small pale green leaves and tiny white flowers. All three are of equally good flavour.

CULTIVATION & PROPAGATION
Basil has to be grown from seed or purchased as a pot plant. Sow seed in a sunny sheltered position out of doors after the danger of frost is over. Alternatively, sow in pots indoors. Use light rich soil and do not overwater because of the danger of damping-off disease. Plant out seedlings in summer 20 cm/8 in apart. When plants are established pinch out the growing centres to encourage bushy growth. The compact habit of bush basil makes it ideal for container growing, where it will provide more leaves for use over a longer growing period. It will continue indoors through the winter months.

USES
Basil is one of the best herbs to add to tomatoes and eggs, mushrooms and pasta dishes. It has a strong flavour and until this is fully appreciated it should be used rather sparingly. The flavour of the leaves tends to increase when they are cooked. Fresh leaves are good in green salads and in oil and vinegar dressings. Add to a melted butter sauce for grilled (broiled) sole.

FAMILY: LABIATAE

BERGAMOT

Botanical name: *Monarda didyma*

One of the many varieties of bergamot, the *Monarda didyma* is also called bee balm because bees are so attracted by its scent. It is a fragrant plant with pale leaves and vivid red flowers that smell and taste rather like mint. A perennial plant, bergamot grows to 45 cm–1 m/18–36 in high. The flowers appear in late summer.

Bergamot was discovered by early settlers in North America where the Oswego Indians used leaves and flowers to make the delicious soothing and relaxing tea that bears their name. It is a good plant for flower arrangements.

CULTIVATION & PROPAGATION
Bergamot needs partial shade and a rich moist soil in which to thrive. Propagate bergamot by taking cuttings or dividing the roots in spring or autumn and space the plants 60 cm/2 ft apart. Keep bergamot within bounds by periodically cutting it back. Every 2 years bergamot should be replanted in another position and the dead centre removed. Bergamot grows well in a container but needs to be kept well-watered.

USES
Chopped leaves and flowers add flavour and colour to green salads, fruit and wine cups. Use fresh or dried flowers for a tempting looking tea, or add to hot milk to take as a sedative. Add leaves and flowers to fresh fruit salads and jellies. Use dried leaves and flowers to give colour and fragrance to pot-pourris.

FAMILY: LABIATAE

HYSSOP

Botanical name: *Hyssopus officinalis*

A hardy evergreen perennial with a long flowering season, hyssop is a good herb to grow in garden or pot. It grows to about 60 cm/2 ft. It has woody stems and small pointed leaves which are pleasantly pungent. Hyssop flowers grow in long spikes of either blue or a deep pink and have a heavy fragrant scent that makes it a popular bee plant.

Hyssop is an ancient herb and was used in the Middle East many years before Christ. Its strong flavour and aroma led to the use of hyssop in the preserving of meat and medicinally as a cleansing herb. Hyssop is one of the flavouring herbs in the liqueur Chartreuse.

CULTIVATION & PROPAGATION
Hyssop will grow in light well-drained soil and a sunny position. Sow seed in moist soil in spring and thin the plants 60 cm/2 ft apart. Hyssop, once established, quite happily seeds itself. A more reliable way of increasing stock is to take stem cuttings in spring or divide the roots in autumn or early spring. If kept clipped, hyssop makes a neat hedge plant to surround the herb garden. Hyssop can be grown in a container.

USES
The faintly minty taste of hyssop leaves gives an unusual tang to green salads and vegetable soups. Try a few leaves in rabbit pie or a lamb stew. With fruit, hyssop is traditionally added to cranberries, stewed peaches or apricots, and in drinks, tarts and pies.

An infusion of hyssop makes a good cough syrup. Hot hyssop tea is an expectorant and helpful for catarrh or a cold on the chest.

Hyssop is used in the making of perfumes and the dried flowers and leaves add colour and scent to pot-pourris.

FAMILY: LABIATAE

LAVENDER

Botanical name: *Lavandula spica*

Lavender is a small perennial shrub growing from 30–90 cm/1–3 ft high, with fragrant blue, pink or white flowers. An attractive grey-leaved plant, lavender makes a lovely ever-green hedge.

Lavender was a familiar sight in the knot gardens of Tudor times, where the flower beds were laid out in a geometric design and enclosed by low hedges. In those days lavender was widely used in cooking and medicine. Nowadays the refreshing perfume of lavender is mainly used in cosmetics.

There are many different forms of lavender. Two dwarf plants are *L. stoechas* (Spanish or French lavender) and *L. nana compacta* (syn. *L. angustifolia*) both ideal for container growing or using as a surround to the herb garden. Neither lavender is likely to reach a height of more than 45 cm/ 18 in and one or two of each colour make an attractive show.

CULTIVATION & PROPAGATION
Lavender will grow from seed, root division or by cuttings. Cuttings removed from established plants with a heel and set in a box of sand in summer will be rooted by late autumn, ready for planting in the open ground the following spring. Set plants in well-drained, well-limed soil in a sunny sheltered position. Plant out seedlings 75 cm/2½ ft apart for the large varieties and 30–40 cm/12–16 in apart for dwarf lavenders. Lavender may need protection in a severe

winter, especially from high winds. Trim right back in early spring to keep plants neat and compact.

USES
Medicinally, an embrocation made from lavender oil relieves pain and muscular stiffness. An infusion of fresh lavender used as a cold compress on forehead and temples is a remedy for headaches and giddiness. Muslin (cheesecloth) bags of lavender added to the bath water are fragrant and refreshing. Cosmetically, flowers and leaves are added to other herbs in a facial steam.

Use dried lavender in herb cushions and pot-pourris. Set lavender bags or bundles amongst linen to keep away moths.

FAMILY: LABIATAE

LEMON BALM

Botanical name: *Melissa officinalis*

Lemon balm or sweet balm, is a fragrant, lemon-scented perennial which grows to about 45–60 cm/1½–2 ft. The light green leaves carry the scent, the white flowers being rather small and insignificant. The plant is highly attractive to bees.

The herb came from the Middle East where, in the past, it was taken as a refreshing tea. Its branches were used as a 'strewing herb', laid on the floor to freshen the room.

'Melissa' tea is still well-known in France as a tonic and a remedy for headaches and tiredness.

CULTIVATION & PROPAGATION
Lemon balm will grow easily from seed but they take a long time to germinate. It is best grown from stem cuttings taken in spring or autumn and set in a sunny position 30 cm/12 in apart. It will grow in any type of

soil, but the scent will be stronger if it is grown in rich moist soil. Lemon balm spreads fairly rapidly so cut it back periodically to keep it a compact shape. Lemon balm is a useful herb to grow in a window box or in a container.

USES

Since its flavour is so delicate, lemon balm can be used generously. In cooking try lemon balm in stuffings for lamb or pork, and cover a chicken with the leaves before roasting. Add to fruit drinks, wine cups, ice creams, fruit and vegetable salads. Add lemon balm to stewed fruit of all kinds and use in place of lemon when making marrow (summer squash) or rhubarb jam.

Make 'melissa' tea for a relaxing drink. Use dried leaves in pot-pourris.

FAMILY: LABIATAE

LEMON THYME

Botanical name:
Thymus × citriodorus

The sweetly scented lemon thyme is a low-growing evergreen herb of neat habit. The small leaves smell strongly of lemon. It grows to about 20–30 cm/ 8–12 in high and produces clusters of deep pink flowers rather late in the season. Lemon thyme is a good bee plant and gives honey an excellent flavour.

There are over 50 different forms of thyme, but this is one of only three kinds to be grown for culinary use. The mild flavour of lemon thyme is often preferred to that of garden thyme.

CULTIVATION & PROPAGATION

Lemon thyme can be grown in a dry

well-drained spot in full sun and ordinary garden soil. It is less hardy than garden thyme and, out of doors, may disappear altogether in a wet winter. If lemon thyme is in a very open position protect it in the winter with a covering of straw or leaf mould. Lemon thyme is a good rock garden plant and ideal for container growing if kept clipped back and well-watered in the growing season. Propagate lemon thyme by taking cuttings in the spring. Once rooted, plants should be spaced 30–45 cm/12–18 in apart. Replace lemon thyme plants every 2 or 3 years when the centres begin to die.

USES

Lemon thyme is useful for parsley and thyme stuffing, because you can dispense with the grated lemon peel normally included. Add a sprig or two to the water when boiling (stewing) a chicken. Use lemon thyme in fruit salads, jellies and a baked custard.

Cosmetically lemon thyme, when tied in a piece of muslin (cheesecloth) and added to the bath water, gives out a lovely scent. Dried leaves and flowers can be used in herb cushions and pot-pourris.

FAMILY: LABIATAE

MARJORAM

Botanical names:
Origanum onites Pot marjoram
Origanum majorana Sweet marjoram
Origanum vulgare Wild marjoram

Of the 3 forms of marjoram the sweet, or knotted, marjoram has by far the best flavour for cooking. It is sweet and spicy but mild compared to the others. Except in hot climates, sweet marjoram is treated as a half-hardy annual. It grows about 20 cm/8 in high and is a compact bushy plant with small leaves and flowers which

look like little green knots. The whole plant is strongly aromatic. Pot marjoram, a small perennial shrub, grows to 60 cm/2 ft with dense clusters of pink flowers and small rounded leaves. Wild marjoram is sometimes called oregano, from its Italian name; a perennial, it has the strongest spiciest taste of the three and grows to 75 cm/ 2½ ft high.

Throughout history the marjorams have been used in preserving food and in remedies for colds and sore throats. Dried and ground marjoram was popular as snuff.

CULTIVATION & PROPAGATION

Sweet (knotted) marjoram Sow the fine seed mixed with sand under glass in early spring. Plant out seedlings in early summer in light rich soil and a sunny sheltered position. Take pots indoors in winter. Good for container growing.

Pot marjoram Propagate by seed sown in early spring or by rooted cuttings taken in autumn or spring. It likes a well-drained light rich soil and a sheltered position. Ideal for growing in containers and indoors.

Wild marjoram Easy to grow from seed sown in spring or by division of roots taken in spring or autumn. A bit tall for container growing unless on a patio or balcony.

USES

Sweet marjoram is an excellent herb used with meat, especially homemade meat loaf, and vegetables such as marrow (summer squash) and potatoes. Add some to the rice in stuffed green peppers. Pot marjoram can be used in the same way. Wild marjoram is so much stronger that it should only be used in small quantities. Dried, it is added to Italian pizzas and spaghetti dishes.

FAMILY: LABIATAE

PENNYROYAL

Botanical name: *Mentha pulegium*

Quite unlike all other mints, pennyroyal is a prostrate creeping half-hardy perennial. During the growing season the flowering stems grow up to 15 cm/6 in high with clusters of mauve flowers.

Nowadays it is not used much in the kitchen. Years ago pennyroyal was grown in pots and carried on long sea voyages so that sailors could use it to purify or clear their casks of stale drinking water. Pennyroyal tea was also a popular drink.

CULTIVATION & PROPAGATION

As an evergreen and with its sturdy growing habit, pennyroyal makes ideal ground cover for moist open places. Plant rooted pieces of pennyroyal 15 cm/6 in apart in spring or autumn. They soon grow together and emit a lovely peppermint smell when walked upon. Pennyroyal grows in any soil but must be kept damp and may need renewing every 3 or 4 years. This is a good plant for window boxes and container growing, as it can easily be kept in check and need not take up much space.

USES

Pennyroyal has a strong flavour and scent so should be used sparingly. Finely chopped leaves can be added to soups and stuffings.

An infusion of pennyroyal is believed to be a remedy for coughs and colds and to be good for the digestion. A pot of pennyroyal, brought indoors, should keep out mosquitoes.

FAMILY: LABIATAE

PEPPERMINT

Botanical name: *Mentha piperita*

A fairly hardy perennial, peppermint is a handsome plant with reddish stems and dark green leaves growing up to 60 cm/2 ft tall. The flowers are spikes of a pinky lilac and the whole plant has a lovely strong scent.

There was no record of peppermint being used as such until John Ray, the English naturalist, published a description of the plant in 1696. The medicinal value of the plant was soon recognized. Crops from this hybrid are now grown all over the world. The oil extracted from the plant contains menthol which is used as a local analgesic for sprains, toothache and bruises. Peppermint oil is also used as a flavouring in making sweets, candies and cakes.

CULTIVATION & PROPAGATION

Peppermint thrives in a rich moist soil in open ground. Plant pieces of rooted runners 5 cm/2 in deep in spring or when danger from frost is over. It is best grown in a bottomless container set in the ground so it does not encroach on other plants nearby. Peppermint can be grown successfully in a pot on its own. Keep well-watered and clipped.

USES

Peppermint leaves can be added to fruit juices, fruit salads, and sprinkled on to split pea soup, carrots and courgettes (zucchini). A peppermint water ice is deliciously refreshing and

iced peppermint tea is cooling. Try a chopped leaf in a cup of hot chocolate and make hot peppermint tea for indigestion and as a pick-me-up. It also improves the appetite.

FAMILY: LABIATAE

ROSEMARY

Botanical name:
Rosmarinus officinalis

Sweet-smelling rosemary is an evergreen shrub and a 'must' in every herb collection. It can grow up to 2 m/6 ft high, but it is very slow-growing. A dwarf variety, only 45 cm/18 in high is neat and highly suitable for a small garden or container growing. The leaves are short, narrow and tough, rather like pine needles, and set densely on the branches. The little flowers grow in crowded clusters of pale blue. The whole plant has a strong aromatic smell.

Rosemary has always grown wild around the Mediterranean coasts. It has historical associations with the Virgin Mary: the flowers are believed to have taken their colour from her blue cloak when she threw it over a rosemary bush to dry. 'Rosemary for remembrance' is an old saying, and long ago the Greeks and Romans would twine it in their hair in the belief that it would quicken the mind and improve their memory. Rosemary was carried at weddings and funerals and used as a strewing herb, being thought to have disinfectant qualities.

CULTIVATION & PROPAGATION

Rosemary thrives in hot sun and poor soil, provided there is lime in the soil and it is well-drained. It needs a sheltered position and very little watering. Rosemary can be grown from seed but this is a slow process. Either purchase a small plant or take cuttings from an established plant in August and transplant into the ground in spring. Roots of a fairly young plant can be divided in the autumn or early spring, but cuttings are the easiest and most reliable way of propagating rosemary. Take off small side shoots about 15 cm/6 in long in late summer and put them into sand. Rosemary can equally well be grown in a container out of doors but may need protection over the winter months. Alternatively bring the plant indoors if possible.

USES

Rosemary has many medicinal and cosmetic uses. It is good for the digestion and stimulates the circulation. As a hair rinse it strengthens and deepens the colour of dark hair.

In the kitchen rosemary with lamb is an old favourite but it can be added to other meat dishes and to fish such as halibut. Try it with eggs and cheese, in biscuits (cookies), jams and jellies. Add it to fruit salad, wine and fruit cups for an unusual flavour.

FAMILY : LABIATAE

SAGE

Botanical name: *Salvia officinalis*

Garden sage is a strongly flavoured evergreen shrub which, if used carefully, can be added to many recipes other than the ubiquitous sage and onion stuffing!

Years ago it was used mainly as a remedy for coughs, colds and fevers, constipation and liver ailments and as a general tonic.

Sage can grow to a height of 60–120 cm/2–4 ft. The leaves are narrow, pale and grey-green with a rough texture. The flowers are soft purple. Other forms of sage, but not with quite such a good flavour, are the purple sage and the broad-leaved sage. All are handsome plants and ideal for container growing out of doors or inside the house.

CULTIVATION & PROPAGATION

Sage grows in any soil provided it is well-drained and in a sunny place. Sage can be grown successfully from seed sown in the early spring under glass and transplanted in late spring into the open ground. It grows rather slowly but is a good size by the end of its first season. Alternatively take cuttings from an established plant in late spring and put straight into the open ground. Plants should be 40–45 cm/16–18 in apart. When plants become leggy, pinch out the growing tips or cut the plants right back.

USES

Sage is most often used with roast pork but is also good with duck and sprinkled on to meat stews. Chopped fresh leaves can be added sparingly to green salads, cream cheese spreads, tomato dishes and to the stuffing for stuffed onions. Try sage in fruit drinks, wine and cider cups. Make an infusion of sage for a tonic and drink it hot. Use sage lotion on the skin. It also makes a good mouthwash and hair conditioner.

FAMILY : LABIATAE

SPEARMINT

Botanical name: *Mentha spicata*

Spearmint is so well-known as a flavouring that many people forget it is a growing plant! Spearmint is probably one of the oldest culinary herbs to be used in the Mediterranean region and is mentioned in all the early writings of physicians and naturalists. It was used in medicine as well as for food because of its value as a digestive.

Spearmint grows to a height of 45 cm/18 in with bright hairless leaves and long spikes of lilac flowers.

Today mint tea is still offered to guests as a mark of hospitality in North African countries.

CULTIVATION & PROPAGATION

With its long underground runners spearmint needs to be grown very much on its own or in a bottomless container, otherwise it will over-run neighbouring plants. Plant pieces of rooted runners 5 cm/2 in deep in rich moist soil and a shady position in early spring. Keep plants 20–30 cm/8–12 in apart and water them well in dry weather. This is the best mint for window box and container growing so long as the soil is kept moist. All plants should be cut back to encourage fresh growth throughout the season.

USES

Spearmint is most often used to make mint sauce or to cook with peas and new potatoes. Try it with other young vegetables such as carrots, green beans and parsnips. Cook a good handful of chopped spearmint with minced (ground) beef. Mint is excellent with fruit juices, fruit salad and in fruit and wine cups. Make a cooling mint water ice or try hot mint tea as a digestive after meals.

FAMILY : LABIATAE

SUMMER SAVORY

Botanical name: *Satureia hortensis*

An attractive herb, summer savory is a bushy low-growing annual. It reaches a height of about 23–30 cm/9–12 in with long narrow leaves and small dainty blue and white flowers. Summer savory, with its delicate spicy flavour, is essentially a cooking herb.

Summer savory was popular with the ancient Greeks and Romans who used it in highly spiced sauces poured over meat, fish and poultry.

Another form of savory is the perennial winter savory, *S. montana*. Though it is easy to grow, its flavour is not so delicate as that of summer savory.

CULTIVATION & PROPAGATION

Summer savory should be grown in light rich soil and a sunny position. Sow seeds in their flowering position in late spring and thin the plants to 15 cm/6 in apart. Seed can be sown under glass in early spring and transplanted but it does not take kindly to being moved. Summer savory is an excellent plant to grow in a container or window box.

USES

As a seasoning herb use summer savory with meats, fish and eggs. Add

to all kinds of beans and sprinkle on to vegetable soup and meat broth. Put fresh sprigs into wine vinegar and leave to permeate. Use the vinegar to make a tasty French dressing.

FAMILY: LABIATAE

THYME
Botanical name: *Thymus vulgaris*

Garden thyme is the best known of the different varieties of thyme. Its fragrant leaves are an essential ingredient in *bouquet garni*, the seasoning posy used in all good cooking.

Thyme derives its medicinal use from the component thymol, a powerful antiseptic which has been in use for hundreds of years.

Throughout history thyme has always been associated with strength and happiness. In the Middle Ages it was a symbol of courage, and high-ranking ladies embroidered sprigs of thyme on to the clothes of knights going off to fight in the Crusades.

Garden thyme is a spreading evergreen perennial and grows up to 45 cm/18 in high. Whorls of little mauve flowers bloom in summer for about a month.

CULTIVATION & PROPAGATION
Grow thyme in a dry sunny place in light well-drained soil. Raise plants from seed sown in spring where they are to flower and thin them to 30 cm/ 12 in apart. They can be grown from division of an old plant or cuttings taken in spring. Thyme is a good plant for the rockery where it virtually looks after itself. It is equally happy in a container or window box and can be used throughout the winter months.

USES
Thyme has a fairly strong flavour so needs to be added with care to meats

and fish, soups, stews and herb sauces. Try finely chopped fresh leaves on potato purée, glazed carrots and other vegetables.

A cup of hot thyme tea sweetened with honey taken last thing at night will promote sleep. As a cosmetic, thyme ointment is good for spots and pimples.

FAMILY: LAURACEAE

BAY
Botanical name: *Laurus nobilis*

Sweet bay, or bay laurel as it is sometimes known, is the name given to this perennial evergreen tree which is the only form of laurel to be used in cooking.

Bay was the ceremonial laurel of the ancient Greeks and Romans who bestowed wreaths of bay as crowns upon accomplished athletes, warrior-heroes and poets. The tree, which is very slow-growing, can reach a height of 10–12 m/30–40 ft.

Bay leaves are shiny, smooth and dark with a strong aromatic scent. The flowers are a creamy-yellow and the fruits which follow are purple. Bay is an ideal plant for container and indoor growing and it can be clipped back without harm.

CULTIVATION & PROPAGATION
Plant bay trees in ordinary garden soil in a sunny position. Where winters are likely to be severe, bring bay trees indoors. To increase stock, take cuttings from half-ripened shoots in late summer. Bay leaves can be picked for use throughout the year.

USES
Bay is one of the 3 herbs in *bouquet garni*, the 'broth posy' used to flavour good cooking. Add a bay leaf to the water when poaching fish; use a leaf in marinades. Bay leaves add their

spicy flavour to meat and vegetables, soups and stews. Store a leaf or two in a jar of rice or add to a rice pudding for a delicious flavour.

FAMILY: LILIACEAE

CHIVES
Botanical name: *Allium schoenoprasum*

An important herb in the kitchen, chives have a mild onion flavour which makes a superb seasoning for many dishes. They are hardy perennial plants with narrow grasslike

hollow leaves growing from clumps of tiny bulbs to a height of 30–40 cm/ 12–15 in. The flowerheads are small and round and pale mauve but these should be cut off to keep the flavour in the leaves. Chives make a good edging plant to the herb garden and an excellent container and indoor plant.

Little is known of its history, though one form of chives was cultivated in ancient China and was probably used throughout Asia.

CULTIVATION & PROPAGATION
Chives will grow in most soils but do best in a light rich damp soil. They need a sunny position but must not be allowed to dry out. In pots and containers, give the plants a liquid feed every 14 days to prevent the tops of the leaves turning brown. Chives can be grown from seed sown in spring and the seedlings thinned to 30 cm/12 in apart, but germination is slow. It is quicker to divide clumps of established bulbs in spring or autumn and transplant when well-rooted. Grow several clumps of chives in order to have a succession of new growth and use the plants in rotation. Lift and divide old clumps every 3 or 4 years.

USES

Chopped chives can be sprinkled on to all salads, meat broths and vegetable soups. Blend chives with cream cheese or butter to use as a topping with baked potatoes. Use chives in omelettes and other egg dishes. They are good with most cooked vegetables. Pickle any leftover chive bulbs in white wine vinegar to serve with cold meats during the winter.

FAMILY: LILIACEAE

GARLIC

Botanical name: *Allium sativum*

The distinctive taste and smell of garlic make it one of the best-known herbs. It improves the flavour of so many dishes that it is almost indispensable to good cooking. Garlic is a perennial bulb of the onion family and grows up to 60 cm/2 ft high. It is the bulb which is used as the flavouring. When fully grown it is made up of a number of small bulblets or cloves.

One of the oldest seasonings, garlic was originally believed to be a strengthening herb. It was an everyday food for Egyptian labourers working on the pyramids and it was given to the Roman soldiers to sustain them on their long marches.

CULTIVATION & PROPAGATION

Garlic thrives in a rich moist soil and a sunny position. Plant individual cloves of garlic in pots or open ground in very early spring 5 cm/2 in deep and 15 cm/6 in apart. Keep plants well-watered if there is a dry summer. In late summer when the tops die down, lift the garlic and leave it to dry out thoroughly under cover.

USES

Garlic is so strong and pungent that it should only be used sparingly; a trace of its flavour can make all the difference to the dish as a whole. One clove is usually sufficient to bring out the flavours in a savoury dish. Use the

clove whole in meat stews, vegetable dishes and soups and remove when cooking is complete. Use a cut clove to rub round the bowl for a green salad. Make garlic butter, garlic oil, garlic vinegar and add to homemade mayonnaise. Buy dried chopped garlic and garlic salt as a standby.

FAMILY: MALVACEAE

MARSHMALLOW

Botanical name: *Althaea officinalis*

An attractive hardy perennial, marshmallow can be found growing wild in marshy ground especially near the coast. It reaches a height of 1.2 m/ 4 ft with grey green leaves that are soft and velvety to the touch. The pale pink flowers grow in the axils of the leaves and bloom in early autumn. All parts of the plant contain mucilage, the highest concentration being in the roots.

Marshmallow, with its healing and soothing properties, has been highly valued through history for treating bronchial troubles. It used also to be taken as a mild laxative. The sweet-tasting white fibrous roots were dried, powdered and made into sweets and candies. The puffy marshmallow obtainable nowadays was originally flavoured with marshmallow root.

CULTIVATION & PROPAGATION

Marshmallow grows well in ordinary garden soil deeply dug and in a moist position. Sow seeds as soon as they ripen in the autumn. Space seedlings 45 cm/18 in apart and protect them through the winter. Marshmallow can also be propagated by pulling

pieces from the crown of older plants and setting them into the ground. Keep well watered until established.

USES

Marshmallow is a medicinal herb. An infusion of marshmallow leaves can be used as a gargle; a poultice made from flowers and leaves will help to reduce inflammation. In both cases the grated root is more effective. Always scrape or peel marshmallow root and use only the white fibrous pith. Make a decoction of the root for coughs and bronchial catarrh. Make an ointment to soothe skin irritations and to heal sunburn.

Cosmetically, marshmallow face pack is good for dry skins.

FAMILY: PINACEAE (CUPRESSACEAE)

JUNIPER

Botanical name: *Juniperus communis*

A handsome grey-green evergreen shrub, juniper can grow up to nearly 4 m/12 ft high, in forms either low and spreading or tall and conical. The leaves are like narrow spines and the flowers small and yellow. Male and female flowers are usually on separate bushes. The whole plant has a lovely aromatic scent. Juniper berries take 2 years to mature, being green in the first season and turning blue-black by the end of the second. The ripe berries have a spicy rather bitter-sweet taste and a dry granular texture. They are used to give gin its characteristic flavour.

Branches of the juniper bush were traditionally used to fumigate the house as a protection against disease.

CULTIVATION & PROPAGATION

Juniper grows best in good garden soil in an open well-drained position. Sow seed in spring in a cold frame and

a year later plant out of doors. Alternatively take stem cuttings from new growth and set in sandy soil under glass in early autumn, for planting out the following spring. Male and female plants need to grow alongside each other to be certain of producing berries. Gather the ripe berries in autumn for drying.

USES
Juniper berries are usually used dried. Add crushed berries to rich meats such as pork and venison, and to game. Four berries can replace a bay leaf in sauces and marinades. Use the berries in the stuffing for goose and duck, and put a few into the water when boiling ham or cooking cabbage.

Medicinally, juniper tea is diuretic and good for indigestion and bronchial complaints. It should not be taken if the kidneys are inflamed.

FAMILY: PORTULACEAE
PURSLANE
Botanical name: *Portulaca oleracea*
Purslane is an attractive tender annual with succulent leaves and small yellow flowers. It has erect reddish stems and grows up to 15 cm/6 in high. Purslane has a sharp clean flavour which is at its best when mixed with other herbs. Purslane leaves and seeds were once used for flavouring and taken as a laxative. Purslane tea was drunk as a tonic.

CULTIVATION & PROPAGATION
Purslane must be sown when all danger of frost is over, usually late spring. Sow seed in sandy soil in a sunny position and thin the plants to 10 cm/4 in apart. Purslane germinates quite quickly and leaves can be picked after 6 weeks when the shoots are about 7 cm/3 in long. It is a very easy plant to cultivate, and can be grown successfully in a container.

USES
Purslane is essentially a salad herb: a few young chopped leaves mix in well in a green salad. Young purslane shoots can be cooked as a vegetable and served with a buttery sauce. Use some fresh young leaves in broths and add to sorrel soup. Try a few leaves in a cream cheese sandwich.

FAMILY: ROSACEAE
SALAD BURNET
Botanical name:
Poterium sanguisorba
Salad burnet forms a flat rosette of leaves on the ground from which slender flowering stems grow up to 30 cm/12 in high. It is a hardy perennial and will stay green through a mild winter. The leaves are made up of coarsely toothed leaflets which have a fresh cucumber taste. The flowers are small round red heads and bloom for three months in the summer.

Salad burnet, native to the Mediterranean region, was used to flavour wines and taken as a tonic tea. In Britain burnet was planted in the knot gardens of Tudor times. Later it was taken by the Pilgrim Fathers to America where it has become naturalized.

CULTIVATION & PROPAGATION
Salad burnet is grown from seed only but if left to flower will self-sow quite freely. Sow seed during late spring or early autumn in good garden soil. For a plentiful supply of leaves keep flower-heads cut back. This is a good plant for container growing but it is better to sow new seed every year because the young leaves are so much more tender.

USES
Mainly a salad herb as its name suggests, burnet leaves are at their best when used fresh. Add them to green and raw vegetable salads. Burnet vinegar has a delicious flavour useful for making French dressing. Chop young leaves to blend with cream cheese in dips. Use liberally as a garnish in place of parsley. Add the leaves to wine cups and cooling summer drinks.

Cosmetically, an infusion of salad burnet helps to refine the skin.

FAMILY: ROSACEAE
ROSE
Botanical names:
Rosa canina Wild dog rose
Rosa rubiginosa syn.
R. eglanteria Sweetbriar
Both species of wild rose produce lovely pink or white sweet-smelling flowers in summer. In the autumn the flowers are succeeded by shining red hips. The hips are the fruit in which lies the seed. Roses are strong-growing perennials; wild dog rose is taller than sweetbriar and bears distinctive hooked thorns. Sweetbriar is, however, the more fragrant, for the leaves as well as flowers are highly scented.

For centuries rose hips have been used for food by people in European countries while rose petals have provided perfume. Rose hips are now known to be a valuable source of vitamin C.

CULTIVATION & PROPAGATION
The wild roses are so hardy they make excellent garden plants where space permits. Grow roses as a background against a fence or trellis, or plant them 1 m/3 ft apart to form an attractive hedge. Plants or rooted cuttings should be put into rich well-drained soil in early spring or late autumn. Pick rose petals in summer when they are just coming into flower and the scent is strongest. Leave the hips until after the first frost when they should be gathered and used at once.

USES
Rose petals can be used in wine and fruit cups, in jams and, when candied or crystallized, for cake decoration. Petals, if dried carefully, will give colour and fragrance to pot-pourris.

If rose hips are not required for immediate use, they should be dried or puréed and stored in screw-top jars. Use the purée as a sauce for puddings and ice cream, with breakfast cereals or thickened and spread on bread and butter. Rose hip wine is

a country favourite and rose hip jelly goes well with cold meats. Rose hips can be eaten raw but are most pleasant when made as tea, hot or iced. It is a refreshing drink and mildly diuretic.

FAMILY: RUBIACEAE
WOODRUFF
Botanical name: *Asperula odorata* syn. *Galium odoratum*

Woodruff is a very pretty little creeping woodland plant. It is a perennial herb growing 15–20 cm/6–8 in tall. The leaves grow in whorls of 6 to 8 on square stems and the tiny white flowers bloom for only a short period. The whole plant has the fragrance of new mown hay which becomes stronger when the herb is cut and dried.

Traditionally, in European countries, woodruff has been used to add its exhilarating flavour to wines and punches. In early times woodruff was dried and placed amongst the linen to keep away moths.

CULTIVATION & PROPAGATION
Woodruff makes a good ground

cover in woods or under large shrubs. It is easy to grow from seed though it takes a long time to germinate. Sow seed in summer in a shady place in ordinary garden soil. In autumn thin plants to 20 cm/8 in apart. In spring woodruff can be propagated by the division of roots of established plants. Once established, woodruff spreads quite quickly by means of its tiny burr-like seeds which stick to the fur or feathers of passing animals and birds.

USES
For a delicious summer drink add partially dried woodruff to apple juice. Woodruff imparts its lovely fresh flavour to all fruit drinks, wine or cider cups. A strong decoction of woodruff can be used as a cordial which is said to be good for the liver.

Woodruff tea made from the whole plant and taken either hot or cold, is a stimulating drink at any time of day.

FAMILY: SCROPHULARIACEAE
EYEBRIGHT
Botanical name:
Euphrasia officinalis

Eyebright is a small dainty annual. It usually grows up to about 10–15 cm/4–6 in high, but on fertile ground may grow taller. The leaves are deeply cut and the tiny, rather insignificant, flowers are white streaked with yellow and violet. They bloom in late summer. Eyebright is a common wild plant in some areas. It is essentially a medicinal herb and, as its name implies, has been used as a remedy for eye complaints for hundreds of years.

CULTIVATION & PROPAGATION
In Europe, eyebright grows in profusion in the wild and can only be grown in a garden with success if similar growing conditions can be reproduced. Eyebright roots need to feed on the roots of nearby plants, so it will only grow in a grassy patch of ground. If allowed to go to seed eyebright will come up year after year. Sow seed in spring as sparingly as possible so that thinning of the plants will not be necessary.

USES
Eyebright tea made from the whole plant, either fresh or dried, is a tonic and said to be a remedy for hay fever. Bathe tired or inflamed eyes in an infusion of eyebright made with water or milk. Used regularly, eyebright lotion is cleansing and soothing.

FAMILY: TROPAEOLACEAE
NASTURTIUM
Botanical name: *Tropaeolum majus*

Nasturtium is a round-leaved trailing or climbing annual. The trumpet-shaped flowers are brilliantly coloured in red, yellow or orange. The dwarf variety, 'Tom Thumb', grows to 30 cm/12 in high and does not trail.

The plant, which originally came from South America, was used as a remedy against scurvy and is now known to be a valuable source of vitamin C and iron. It has a strong peppery flavour similar to watercress.

CULTIVATION & PROPAGATION
Nasturtiums grow well in light sandy soil and a sunny position. Sow seed in early summer in open ground where they are to flower. Nasturtiums help to protect neighbouring plants from pests. They grow well in window boxes and other containers and provide attractive colour throughout the growing season.

USES
Nasturtium leaves and flowers should be eaten fresh and young though the leaves can be dried successfully. Use

chopped leaves on bread and butter and in sandwich spreads. Add leaves and flowers to green salads, and to cream cheese for a dip if prepared only a short time before required. Nasturtium seeds can be pickled when they are green and young. Use them as a substitute for capers to flavour sauces, relishes and as a garnish.

FAMILY: UMBELLIFERAE

ANGELICA

Botanical name:
Angelica archangelica

Angelica is a large handsome biennial plant growing up to 2 m/6 ft high in the second year. The whole plant is sweetly scented and with its big leaves, strong stems and creamy-white flowers angelica is a striking addition to the herb garden. The stems are hollow and the large leaves are divided into many leaflets arranged in groups of three. The edges of the leaves are finely toothed. The tiny flowers are massed in one large, almost round, umbel. Nowadays the bright green candied stems are used to decorate cakes, trifles and other puddings. But all parts of the plant have a use. Dig up the roots at the end of the first year of growth when they will be at their best for eating or drying. Second year roots tend to be tough and worm-eaten.

Years ago angelica seeds and roots were burned to fill the house with fragrance.

CULTIVATION & PROPAGATION

Angelica grows well in a light rich soil and partial shade. It can be grown from seed sown in late summer in the open ground where it is to flower. Thin out the seedlings to 15 cm/6 in apart. Though a biennial, angelica will continue to grow for a number of years if the flowerheads are not allowed to form. Sometimes angelica flowers do not appear until the fourth year and as the plant comes up each season the roots and stems become bigger. If it is allowed to flower, self-sown seedlings will ensure continuity.

USES

For candied angelica use the young stems or leaf stalks, which can also be used to flavour jams and jellies. Cook leaf stalks with rhubarb, gooseberries or plums to reduce acidity and save sugar. Angelica syrup made from the stems and leaves, or a decoction of the roots, can be stored in screwtop bottles in the refrigerator. The syrup can be diluted to make a refreshing drink or used in winter fruit salads. The roots and stems can be eaten cooked as a vegetable.

Angelica tea calms the nerves and reduces tension when taken last thing at night. It is also good for colds, coughs, flatulence and rheumatism but should not be taken by those suffering from diabetes. It relieves indigestion and is a pleasant warming drink to take after a heavy meal. Fresh leaves can be crushed and used in a poultice to relieve tightness in the chest. Add a muslin (cheesecloth) bag full of leaves to the water for a relaxing bath and use dried leaves in pot-pourris.

FAMILY: UMBELLIFERAE

ANISE

Botanical name: *Pimpinella anisum*

Anise is a small annual plant which produces the seed well-known in cooking, in medicine and for its commercial use as a flavouring in drinks. The plant has finely serrated leaves and tiny white flowers and grows up to 45 cm/18 in high. The seeds are small and crescent-shaped with a little tail.

Anise, native to Egypt, was mentioned in ancient Egyptian records. Later the Romans used anise both in medicine and to make a rich ceremonial cake thought to be the origin of the wedding cake.

The flavour of anise is quite strong and is similar to liquorice. The flavour has been used extensively in medicines to disguise unpleasant tastes.

CULTIVATION & PROPAGATION

Anise is propagated by seed only. Sow seed in light, well-drained soil in early summer after danger from frost is over. Sow anise in its flowering position or transplant seedlings when very small. Thin the plants to 15 cm/ 6 in apart. The seedheads are gathered in the early autumn and the drying of the seeds completed indoors. Because anise has a long tap root it is not suitable for container or indoor growing unless sufficient depth of soil can be provided.

USES

Throughout the growing season anise leaves can be used to add flavour to green and raw vegetable salads, and to fresh fruit salads. Both leaves and seeds go well with shellfish. Use seeds (aniseed) in cakes, biscuits (cookies), bread and apple pie.

Aniseed tea sweetened with honey makes a good digestive drink and a pleasant nightcap. Try chewing the seeds to cure hiccups. Anise is extremely effective for digestive ailments, and many people dislike the taste because of its association with medicines of this kind. Ground aniseed can be used in pot-pourris.

Cosmetically, a face pack made from ground aniseed will fade freckles.

FAMILY: UMBELLIFERAE

CARAWAY

Botanical name: *Carum carvi*

Caraway is a feathery-leaved biennial plant grown for its seeds and roots only. Two small crescent-shaped seeds are enclosed in each fruit which bursts open when ripe. Caraway grows up to 60 cm/2 ft high with small white flowers which are followed by the fruit in the second year.

Caraway is well-known as a digestive drink and as a flavouring in many dishes. It has long been used to flavour Kummel liqueur and the seeds used in the baking of rye bread.

CULTIVATION & PROPAGATION

Caraway seed can be sown in its flowering position in early summer or autumn. It likes a light well-drained soil and a sunny position. Thin caraway plants to 20 cm/8 in apart. The seed germinates quickly and in a severe winter the young plants may need protecting with a mulch. In the first year the plants will reach about 20 cm/8 in high, finally reaching their full height in the second year. Remove seedheads when fruit has turned brown, before it bursts open, to complete the drying indoors. Dig up roots for eating after harvesting the seeds.

Caraway can be grown in containers and window boxes provided it can get plenty of sun to ripen the seeds.

USES

Caraway seed can be used to flavour pork and liver and vegetables such as cabbage, cauliflower and potatoes. The roots can be boiled and eaten like carrots with a parsley sauce. Use caraway seed in baking cakes, biscuits (cookies), buns and sprinkled on Irish potato cakes.

Use caraway seeds in tea, a drink to help the digestion. Crush the seeds to add to pot-pourris.

FAMILY: UMBELLIFERAE

CHERVIL

Botanical name:
Anthriscus cerefolium

Chervil is a delicate fern-like biannual with a refreshing spicy flavour. A herb that can be used generously, it is well worth while having a number of plants in the garden. Chervil grows up to 45 cm/18 in tall; its fragrant leaves resemble those of French parsley and it has clusters of small white flowers.

One of the Lenten herbs of history, chervil was thought to have blood cleansing properties. It was eaten in quantity during Lent and was also used as a skin cleanser.

Chervil is one of the traditional herbs used in the *fines herbes* mixture which figures so largely in French cooking.

CULTIVATION & PROPAGATION

Chervil seeds germinate so quickly that with successive sowings it is possible to have a supply of fresh leaves almost all the year round. From early spring to late summer sow seed in well-drained garden soil in partial shade. Thin the plants to 15 cm/6 in apart. Chervil leaves can be used when the plant is about 10 cm/4 in high. Protect chervil plants with a cloche during winter for an early spring crop. Chervil can be grown in window boxes and containers and if kept well cut back will make a useful bushy plant bearing plenty of leaves.

USES

The chopped fresh leaves are at their most delicious in chervil soup. Add to butter sauces to go with delicate

vegetables and to green salads. Use chervil in herb mixtures for egg and cheese dishes. As a garnish, use chervil generously over pork or veal chops and beef steaks. Sprinkle over glazed carrots, tomatoes and peas.

FAMILY: UMBELLIFERAE

CORIANDER

Botanical name: *Coriandrum sativum*

Coriander is an annual grown for its spicy aromatic seeds. Until the seeds ripen the whole plant has an unpleasant smell. For this reason it is not the best of plants to grow in a confined space or indoors. It does deserve a place in the garden, however, for the homegrown seeds are so superior to the bought ones. The seeds are almost completely round and have a strong sweet taste.

Coriander is an ancient spice much used as a meat preservative and for flavouring foods and unpleasant medicines.

CULTIVATION & PROPAGATION

Grow coriander in a light rich soil in full sun. In early spring sow the seed where it is to flower. The plants can be thinned to 10–15 cm/4–6 in apart. Coriander needs as long a growing season as possible to make sure the seeds will ripen. In late summer when seeds have turned a light greyish brown, cut down the plants. Leave them in a dry airy place for 2 or 3 days. When completely dried shake out the seeds and store in tight stoppered jars.

USES

Ground coriander seed is an important ingredient in curry powder and other spice mixtures. Use whole seed with vegetables such as cauliflower, celery and beetroot (beet).

Add one or two crushed seeds to

give a fragrant flavour to a hot cup of coffee. Use ground seed in cakes, biscuits (cookies) and gingerbread and when making chutneys.

FAMILY: UMBELLIFERAE
CUMIN
Botanical name: *Cuminum cyminum*

Cumin is a spice herb grown for its seed only, which is strongly aromatic and has a strong warm taste. The seed is yellowish brown and about 0.5 cm/ ¼ in long. Cumin is a slender annual, growing up to 30–60 cm/1–2 ft tall. The plant has a branching stem with long thin deep green leaves and small pink or white flowers.

In Europe the use of cumin as a condiment had largely died out, but following a revival of interest in Indian and Middle Eastern cooking, it is now being cultivated again. It is also used in the spicy dishes associated with Mexican cooking.
CULTIVATION & PROPAGATION
Sow cumin seed in rich soil in a warm sheltered position in early summer and thin the plants to 15 cm/6 in apart. Provided there is plenty of sunshine the seeds should be ready for harvesting after 3 or 4 months. When seeds are ripe cut down the whole plant and complete the drying process indoors.
USES
Cumin seed is a good seasoning to add to meat casseroles and when making lentil soup. Use whole seed in the water when cooking cabbage or kidney beans. Sprinkle freshly ground cumin seed over savoury rice just before serving. Use whole seed mixed into creamed or mashed potatoes. Add whole or ground seed for flavouring cakes, bread or biscuits (cookies) and when making pickles or chutneys.

FAMILY: UMBELLIFERAE
DILL
Botanical name: *Anethum graveolens*

Dill is a fragrant hardy annual growing up to 60 cm/2 ft high. It has very finely cut blue-green leaves and deep yellow flowers. All parts of the plant are aromatic with a slightly sharp yet sweet flavour. Both leaves and seeds are used.

Medicinally dill has a calming effect and gripe water, which is made from the seeds, is given to babies for hiccups and to induce sleep. It is so mild it is quite safe. The name dill comes from the Saxon word 'dilla' and means to lull. From early times it has been taken for indigestion and stomach upsets, and as a tranquillizer.
CULTIVATION & PROPAGATION
Sow dill seed where the plants are to flower and thin the seedlings to 30 cm/ 12 in apart. Make successive sowings of dill from early to mid-summer for a continuous supply of leaves. Sow in good garden soil and a sunny position. As soon as the flowerheads are brown the seeds are ripe. The whole plant should then be cut down and the seed drying completed indoors.

USES
Dill leaves make a particularly good sauce to go with fish. Add chopped leaves to green and raw vegetable salads, especially cucumber. Blend with cream or cottage cheese for a sandwich filling. Use whole or ground dill seed in lamb stews, herb butters, bean soups and in pickled cucumber (dill pickles).

Dill seed tea taken last thing at night will promote sleep. Chew dill seeds to sweeten the breath.

FAMILY: UMBELLIFERAE
FENNEL
Botanical name: *Foeniculum vulgare*

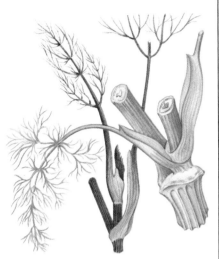

Fennel is a tall graceful perennial. It grows up to 1.5 m/5 ft tall with finely divided feathery green leaves and bright yellow flowers. In appearance, fennel closely resembles dill but has a sweet anise flavour which is altogether different. The seeds, which are dried for use, are oval in shape and have a much stronger flavour than the leaf.

Historically fennel was used as a medicine. It was believed to strengthen the eyesight and to settle an upset stomach. In ancient Greece it was considered a symbol of success.

And he who battled and subdued
A wreath of fennel wore.

CULTIVATION & PROPAGATION
Fennel can be easily grown from seed and is hardy enough to withstand most conditions. Best results are achieved if fennel is sown in moist well-drained good garden soil and a sunny position. Sow seed in early spring and thin the plants to 30 cm/ 12 in apart. Self-sown seedlings will appear freely but the main plants can be divided every 3 or 4 years. The seeds are ready to harvest when hard and a grey-green colour. Cut off the heads and complete the drying indoors. Florence fennel or finocchio (*F. v. dulce*) is a variety which has an edible swollen leaf base like celery. It needs a very long warm growing season and plenty of moisture. The leaves and seeds can be used as for garden fennel.

Another form is bronze fennel, a handsome garden plant which can be used in the same way as other fennels.

USES

Fennel is well-known as the 'fish herb'. Seeds or leaves give an excellent flavour when added to the water for poached or boiled fish. Use the chopped leaves in fish sauces or as a garnish to counteract the oiliness of rich fish. Leaves can be added to salads and raw or cooked vegetables. Try finely chopped leaves sprinkled over buttered new potatoes. Seeds can be used whole or ground to flavour bread, savoury biscuits (crackers), soups and sweet pickles.

An infusion of fennel seeds or leaves is a good treatment for inflamed eyelids and tired eyes. Warm fennel tea is diuretic and a mild laxative, helpful in a slimming programme and to those who suffer from cramp.

FAMILY : UMBELLIFERAE

LOVAGE

Botanical name:
Levisticum officinale

Lovage is a vigorous handsome perennial which can grow up to 2 m/6½ ft tall. Its large leaves are deeply divided and the greenish yellow flowers are followed by oblong deep brown seeds. All parts of the plant can be used for flavouring and have a pleasant strong yeasty taste rather like celery.

Since early times lovage was used as a 'bath herb' when it was found that, added to the bath water, it had a cleansing and deodorizing effect on the skin.

CULTIVATION & PROPAGATION

Lovage is usually propagated by dividing the roots in the spring just as the leaves start to emerge. Make sure each piece of root has a shoot. Plant them 60 cm/2 ft apart in good moist soil and a sunny position at the back of the herb garden. Lovage can be grown from seed sown as soon as the seed is ripe in summer.

USES

Use lovage leaves sparingly to enrich the flavour of vegetable soups, meat broths and casseroles. Young leaves and stalks can be cooked on their own as a vegetable. Peel or scrape the chopped stalks and put them into lightly salted boiling water; simmer until tender. Serve with a good white sauce. Add lovage to green salads and use a few chopped leaves in omelettes. The crushed seed may be used similarly, but remember it will have a much stronger flavour. The young stems can be candied like angelica and used to decorate pies and pastries.

Lovage makes an excellent cordial for a cold winter night. Lovage broth made from seeds or leaves is diuretic and stimulates the appetite.

FAMILY : UMBELLIFERAE

PARSLEY

Botanical name:
Petroselinum crispum

All varieties of parsley are hardy biennials but are usually treated as annuals. They vary in height from dwarf to 60 cm/2 ft high. No herb garden is complete without one or two plants. The most familar ones are the curly-leaved parsley and the French or plain-leaved parsley. Curly parsley is perhaps the most widely used because it makes an attractive garnish. Grow curly parsley for decoration and French parsley for flavour.

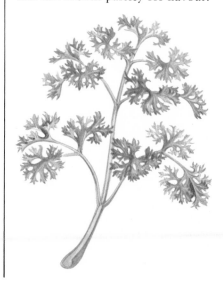

Hamburg parsley is a variety grown not only for the foliage but also for its roots which may be used as a winter vegetable rather like parsnips. Parsley is rich in vitamin C and valuable in the daily diet.

CULTIVATION & PROPAGATION

In spring, when the soil has warmed up, sow parsley seeds where the plants are to grow. The seeds can take up to 3 or 4 weeks to germinate. To hasten germination try soaking the seeds overnight or, once sown, water the seeds in with hot water. Choose a sunny position in rich, well-worked moist soil. Thin the seedlings to 20 cm/8 in apart. Keep the seedlings watered in dry weather. Cover the plants in cold weather. Parsley is a good plant for edging the herb garden, and ideal for container growing outside or indoors, when the leaves can be used throughout the year.

USES

The amount of parsley to use in savoury dishes is a matter of individual taste but as a general rule it can be added generously. Chopped leaves can go into green salads, soups, sauces and cooked vegetables. Deep fry parsley in oil until crisp and serve as an accompaniment to fish. Add parsley to dishes which contain garlic to soften the flavour.

Hot parsley tea is a tonic and a diuretic. It is believed to help those who suffer from rheumatism, and is of use to slimmers as it helps remove excess fluid from body tissue. Chew parsley leaves to sweeten the breath.

FAMILY : UMBELLIFERAE

SWEET CICELY

Botanical name: *Myrrhis odorata*

Sweet Cicely is a handsome slow-growing perennial that may reach from 60–150 cm/2–5 ft in height. It is a very fragrant plant and has a lovely sweet anise flavour. The lacy leaves are large and covered with a fine down. The tiny white flowers grow in clusters and appear very early in the season. These should be cut off to retain the full flavour in the leaves. Let one or two remain to set seed. The seeds are long and jet black.

In former times the seeds were pounded down and used to polish furniture. All parts of the plant were used in medicine, and the roots were boiled until tender and given to the elderly to eat: it was believed to strengthen the digestion.

flowers bloom briefly in high summer. The root is a short rhizome with numerous straggly roots.

CULTIVATION & PROPAGATION
Valerian seed is slow to germinate. Sow in boxes under glass in spring and plant out seedlings in summer about 60 cm/2 ft apart. Choose a sunny position in damp well-drained soil so the rhizomes can develop well. Cut off flowering tops as they appear. Harvest the rhizomes at the end of the second season. Remove fibrous roots before using or drying. Valerian is a suitable plant for container growing if kept well-watered. It is highly

CULTIVATION & PROPAGATION
Sweet Cicely germinates easily from seed sown in early spring where the plants are to grow. Choose a position in partial shade in good moist garden soil. Space the seedlings 45 cm/18 in apart. Sweet Cicely seeds itself very readily and the seedlings can be transplanted without difficulty even when a year old.

USES
Sweet Cicely is the 'sugar saver' herb and can be used generously with tart fruits to cut down acidity and reduce the amount of sugar needed. Add finely chopped leaves when cooking gooseberries, rhubarb or red currants. Use sweet Cicely in green salads, salad dressings and omelettes. Put some leaves or seeds in the water when cooking cabbage. Add leaves to fresh fruit salads and cooling summer drinks.

For indigestion, chew the ripe seeds or make sweet Cicely tea using chopped leaves and drink it hot.

FAMILY: VALERIANACEAE
VALERIAN
Botanical name: *Valeriana officinalis*

Valerian is a medicinal herb of ancient reputation and took its name from the Latin *valere*, to be healthy. The root of the plant is the main part used and this has a strong unpleasant rancid smell when first lifted. It is nevertheless an effective remedy for minor complaints.

A hardy perennial, valerian grows about 1 m/3 ft tall. The leaves are sharply divided and sometimes hairy. Clusters of small, very pale pink

attractive to cats; one of its common names in cat's valerian.

USES
Valerian has a calming effect on the whole nervous system and helps to promote sleep. Make a decoction of the roots to take for a nervous headache and as a nerve tonic. Drink valerian tea an hour before going to bed over a number of days to encourage natural sleep. While valerian is a soothing herb it should not be taken regularly for a long period of time. Doses which are too large and too strong will cause lethargy and pains in the head. An ointment of the leaves or root is used for healing sores and skin complaints.

FAMILY: VERBENACEAE
LEMON VERBENA
Botanical name: *Lippia citriodora*

Lemon verbena is a sweet-scented, tender perennial shrub which can grow up to 1.5 m/5 ft tall. The highly fragrant leaves, smelling strongly of lemon, are long and

narrow and grow in groups of 3 or 4. The tiny white or lilac flowers grow in panicles and bloom in late summer.

This lovely shrub comes from South America and is well worth nurturing in the herb garden or as a pot plant.

CULTIVATION & PROPAGATION
Lemon verbena must be grown in a warm sheltered position preferably at the base of a south-facing wall. The soil can be poor and dry. Either buy in a lemon verbena plant or take stem cuttings from an established plant at any time in the growing season. In the winter lemon verbena needs protection from the cold weather. Alternatively it can be potted up and taken indoors.

USES
The very strong lemon-flavoured leaves can be used sparingly in fruit salad, fruit jellies, punch and refreshing summer drinks. Try lemon verbena leaves in a homemade ice cream for a strong fragrant flavour. Place a leaf on the bottom of the dish in which a baked custard is to be cooked.

Hot lemon verbena tea has a mild sedative effect. An excellent herb to dry, lemon verbena leaves keep their scent for many months. Use dried leaves in pot-pourris and sachets to put amongst linen.

Use lemon verbena to scent the bath water. Pour boiling water over fresh leaves and allow to steep until quite cold. Strain and add to the bath.

An infusion of lemon verbena used nightly for cleaning the teeth is said to be good for the gums and to help prevent tooth decay.

MEDICINAL HERBS

It is of significance that pharmacologists are today beginning to assess the increasing value of herbal extracts in the treatment of disease. No longer do we depend on the trial-and-error method, which of necessity had to be used by early man, to discover the effects of a herb. Pharmacologists observe the same exacting standards followed in the evaluation of synthetic drugs to determine if the extracts have the effects attributed to them in the writings and herbals of hundreds of years ago. This method can provide precise information as to the truth or otherwise of the claims made for a particular herb. By this means it can also be discovered whether a plant has medicinal properties which up to now have had no known use.

Herbalism is the study and use of plants for medicinal purposes and is the earliest form of medicine. One of the earliest texts to be discovered was the Ebers Papyrus, written about 1550 B.C., in which the ancient Egyptians wrote down many of their prescriptions and showed their standards of medicine to be surprisingly high. Later their knowledge was to influence Greek medicine to a considerable extent.

The first physicians were all herbalists, as evidenced by the valuable description of herbs used in medicine set down by Hippocrates in the fifth century B.C. Hippocrates firmly believed that treatment of a specific complaint should be carried out only as a part of the treatment of the whole man. He stressed the importance of diet to a man's health as well as his habits and the environment in which he lived.

In the first and second centuries A.D. two eminent men figured prominently in the advancement of herbalism, Dioscorides and Galen. Dioscorides was a Greek physician and botanist who lived in Asia Minor yet travelled extensively throughout Europe studying the flora and fauna and recording the special properties of many new plants. He wrote the *Materia Medica*, a detailed list of plants and the drugs to be obtained from them, which is said to be a valuable source of information on the botany of the ancient herbalists.

With the rise of the Roman Empire the centre of medical knowledge moved to Rome, and in the second century A.D. Claudius Galenus, known as Galen, became Imperial Physician. He was a Greek physician who was the first man to diagnose by the pulse. He wrote copious works, gathering together all the medical knowledge of his time which included herbs and how they were used. His medical books were held in great respect for 1,500 years and he was considered one of the finest authorities on herbs during that time.

While pharmacology and botany were infant sciences in those days, the bases for future standard practices of the two disciplines were laid down in the experiences which were then recorded. It is perhaps unfortunate that between then and now so much mumbo jumbo was preached about herbalism that finally the old science was brought into disrepute.

With the decline of the Roman Empire came the rise of Byzantium and the Eastern Empire in the sixth century. The Byzantines, and later the Arabs, continued the medical traditions of the Greeks and Romans. In Europe, however, medicine as practised by the Romans declined until revived by the monasteries and other religious bodies, who founded hospitals and laid out herb gardens, some of which can still be seen today. The knowledge of herbal cures and methods of practice was jealously guarded by the monks. In England at the time of the Reformation, much of this knowledge was lost with the sacking of the monasteries.

In sixteenth century Europe another upheaval in the traditions of medicine was brought about by Paracelsus, a Swiss physician. A chemist and an alchemist, he tried, with no small success, to revolutionize medical practices. His methods, however, were not popular: he was an intemperate arrogant man who defined and defended the 'doctrine of signatures' (described below), emphasizing its importance. Nevertheless, Paracelsus did much to encourage research and experiment in the development of pharmacology; he distilled the essential oils from herbs to use as remedies, which was a great step forward for pharmacy.

At about the same time, illustrated herbals began to be compiled, cataloguing individual herbs with their use. These books included elegant and sometimes colourful drawings of the plants to help in their recognition.

Once printing was invented, many herbals were published and became available to all those who could read, instead of being exclusive to the religious orders and medical practitioners. People began to treat themselves when necessary, because it was so easy. Provided the correct plant was gathered from the wild all was well: it needed no skill to apply it. This practice became widespread. As country people had been using herbs in their own special way for generations, two forms of 'green' medicine were being carried on side by side. Qualified doctors were administering their herbal drugs on principles derived from their scientific training, while totally unqualified people were making and taking their own remedies based on folklore but

assisted by the newly available printed herbals.

Both forms of medical practice developed independently of one another. Orthodox medicine advanced with such rapidity that it superseded amateurish forms of herbalism, though many of the drugs used were still of plant origin.

ASTROLOGY

There were two important factors which more than any others caused herbalism to be regarded with suspicion by so many people. The first of these factors was the alleged link with astrology and the second the doctrine, or law, of signatures. This suspicion continues in large measure to the present day.

Astrology is said to have begun in ancient Babylon where the high priests were the first to study and record the positions and movements of the stars. They linked these to the happenings of their time, imbuing each of the major planets with characteristics and influence for good or evil. The zodiac was evolved, that imaginary belt in the sky in which the 12 constellations lie and along which the planets were thought to travel. The zodiac was divided into 12 parts, to each of which was attributed its own sign and characteristics; these corresponded to each separate constellation.

As the Babylonians increased their knowledge, so it spread via the trade routes to the Mediterranean lands, where the astrological systems were changed and interpreted to meet local needs. Much of the pattern of astrology as we know it today was developed by the ancient Greeks.

During the Middle Ages the rise in popularity of astrology, magic and the slavish following of signs and portents reached its height and as these came increasingly to be linked with herbs and their uses so the gap between herbalism and orthodox medicine began to widen. It was at this time that physicians produced the theory that each part of the body is ruled by a sign of the zodiac which in turn has a ruling planet. Colours, precious stones and herbs were all said to be connected to the different signs. To treat a specific ailment the herbalist needed only to know the herb which came under the sign and planet ruling over that part of the body which had been afflicted. This was the theory behind the simplified form of medicine which flourished during the fifteenth and sixteenth centuries. The astrologer herbalists of that time wrote down what they knew. One of the best known in seventeenth century England was Nicholas Culpeper. His herbal was heavily overlaid with superstition, giving each herb a dominant planet, and some of his directions appear rather farfetched in the light of present-day knowledge. Nevertheless, beneath the superstitious beliefs was a deep learning of the medicinal value of herbs, and he was certainly a successful herbalist physician of his time.

Today practical herbalists dislike the emphasis still laid on the connection between astrology and herbalism. The link with astrology and the occult gave herbalism a dubious reputation, but there was a second factor which also contributed to this.

Above: Nicholas Culpeper (1616–1654), was a well-known exponent of the Doctrine of Signatures, and also many astrological theories, by which herbs were set under the influence of the sun, moon and planets.

Opposite: The apothecary's shop where herbal medicines and potions were dispensed. Often the physic garden would be situated behind the shop.

THE DOCTRINE OF SIGNATURES

The doctrine of signatures set forth the theory that every herb has its own 'sign'. It was thought that the appearance of the plant, its colour, scent or habitat indicated the disease for which it provided a cure. To give examples, skullcap is a remedy for insomnia and the flower closely resembles the shape of the human skull. The red flowers of burdock and red clover point to their use as blood purifiers. Herbs used to cure jaundice have yellow flowers, like marigold, dandelion and toadflax. The knotted roots of figwort indicate that it is used to treat varicose veins, and the unpleasant smell of stinking motherwort links it with the treatment of suppurating sores. The bark of the willow tree, which grows in damp situations, is used for rheumatism. The theory goes so far as to suggest that not only habitat but also climate will produce plants in a particular region to cure all the diseases of the local population.

The effectiveness of the doctrine of signatures was supported most strongly by Paracelsus, but the greatest proponent of the theory was an Italian philosopher called Giambattista della Porta who lived from 1543 to 1615. He wrote books on natural magic and gardening and this last interest led him to study herbs in detail. He described the plants and through their signatures he added imaginary origins and medicinal values.

The theory does not hold up because there are so many exceptions to the rule. One of the best herbs for purifying the blood is yellow gentian; centaury, which has pink flowers, is good for jaundice and valerian, unlike skullcap, has white flat-topped clusters of flowers and is an excellent sedative.

In spite of these strange theories, some of the herbs are used with good results for the ailment to which their signatures originally pointed. The heart-shaped leaves of pansy do provide a remedy for heart troubles, and the willow bark does ease rheumatic pain.

The brief reign of the doctrine of signatures lasted about 100 years but with the advancement of experimental medicine, theories of this kind tended to lose support.

POISONOUS HERBS

It is essential when gathering herbs for either food or medicine that you correctly identify the herb with absolute certainty and know to which use the particular plant may be put. There are many poisonous herbs which grow side by side or intertwined with food plants, and which can be very similar in appearance at either the leaf, flower or fruit stage. Along damp hedgerows the bright red berries of the black bryony, which are highly poisonous, can be mistaken for the wholesome fruits of the common hawthorn. Black bryony is a vigorous climber that will twine in clockwise fashion around the stems of hawthorn and its vivid berries catch the eye.

Until you can be certain of identifying the plants it would be sensible to buy your herbs from a reliable herbalist. Most recipes call for the fresh herb, but where it is not possible to buy these you can use the dried plants with confidence. If the herb is gathered at the correct time of year, and carefully dried, the healing nature of the herb will not have been impaired. Dried herbs, however, do have a comparatively short shelf life and contain little goodness after 6 or 7 months.

Many herbs are poisonous only if eaten to excess and great care must be taken at all times when dealing with these dubious healing plants. Some herbs are used for external treatment only and the instructions must be carefully carried out when using plants which might be violent in action even though they are not listed as poisonous. When using herbs for treating minor ailments, if any of the treatments should make you feel worse, then stop them at once. The following are poisonous herbs:

Baneberry	Ivy
Black bryony	Laburnum
Buttercup	Meadow saffron
Columbine	Mistletoe
Common buckthorn	Monkshood
Deadly nightshade	Spindle tree
Fool's parsley	White bryony
Foxglove	White hellebore
Hemlock	Woody nightshade
Henbane	Yew (leaves and berries)

The danger of self diagnosis and treatment cannot be stressed too highly and where there is obviously a serious condition, a doctor should always be consulted.

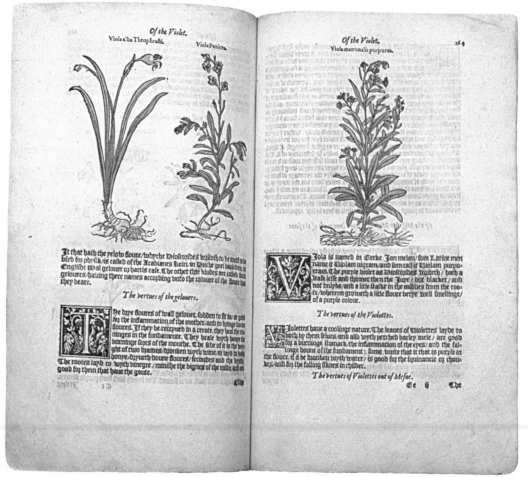

Left: The sweet-scented violet has been cultivated for centuries as a colouring agent for medications and syrups and for its delightful perfume. It is also used in medicines for throat and chest infections. This illustration is from A New Herball *written by William Turner.*

Opposite Above: A page from Phytognomonica *written by Jo Baptistae Porta, an Italian botanist of the sixteenth century. This illustration shows herbs once used to produce a healthy head of hair and to prevent baldness.*

Opposite Below: Coltsfoot (Tussilago farfara) *used to relieve coughs, sore throats and inflammation of the mouth.*

Herbal remedies are of great value to the layman where only minor ailments are concerned, for herbs provide efficient remedies that are easy to make and to apply. It must be remembered when using herbal remedies that they are unlikely to be as highly concentrated as a chemical medicine, and will have to be taken or applied over a longer period of time to achieve results.

HERBS FOR SPECIFIC AILMENTS

It is important when using herbs as remedies for minor ailments that all infusions and decoctions are used fresh and thrown away after a few hours, and that syrups are stored for no longer than a few days.

Many herbs can be used for more than one complaint and if the specific herb mentioned is not available to you, look in the individual list of herbs to find an alternative herb which you can obtain. Definitions of the terms used in the list are as follows:

An infusion is the pouring of water over a herb in order to extract its active qualities.

A decoction is an extract of a herb obtained by boiling.

A compress is a folded cloth moistened with a herbal infusion and applied to the skin.

A poultice is a soft composition applied in a cloth.

ACNE, SPOTS AND BOILS

For external treatment use compresses made from warm infusions of any of the following herbs: elderflowers, coltsfoot (leaves and flower), lady's mantle, sorrel and thyme leaves, decoction of burdock or marshmallow roots. Poultices used as hot as possible can be made from hops, marshmallow leaves or roots, or thyme leaves and flowers. Ointments of marshmallow root or marigold petals are effective.

BRUISES AND SPRAINS

Apply crushed leaves of comfrey or hyssop directly on to bruises; apply parsley leaves or St John's wort to sprains. Use cold compresses made from an infusion of witch-hazel, marigold or wintergreen; a cold poultice may be made of burdock leaves. Use St John's wort oil for both bruises and sprains.

CATARRH AND COLDS

For catarrh, drink a hot infusion made from leaves of borage, coltsfoot, comfrey or hyssop. For feverish colds, drink an infusion of equal parts of elderflower, peppermint and yarrow. For head colds, drink a hot infusion of any of the following: verbascum flowers, lime (linden) flowers, chamomile flowers, agrimony leaves, eyebright (the whole herb), fennel or sage leaves. Inhalation of chamomile flowers relieves stuffiness.

CHILBLAINS

For external treatment, paint on to unbroken chilblains the raw juice of garlic or nettle. Carefully massage with ointment made from horse-radish root, elderflower or marshmallow root. Drink nettle or elderflower tea.

CONSTIPATION

Take an infusion of basil leaves, dandelion leaves, liquorice root, parsley or feverfew leaves as a mild laxative. Chewing juniper berries helps to relieve the symptoms.

COUGHS

To ease a painful hacking cough, drink verbascum tea made from the flowers, or boil crushed comfrey root in

juniper berries, dill, parsley, fennel or caraway. For indigestion take infusions of angelica, coriander, peppermint, anise or red sage.

EARACHE

For a mild inflammation use a few drops of warm infusion of chamomile flowers or fennel leaves or seeds. To dissolve the build-up of wax which can cause pain and discomfort, make a strong infusion of marjoram leaves or a weak infusion of agrimony leaves. Use the drops warm several times a day until relief is felt.

EYE INFLAMMATIONS AND STYES

Inflamed eyelids and tired eyes are refreshed with a cold compress wrung out in an infusion of eyebright made from all parts of the herb. The same infusion may be used warm in an eyebath. Other soothing lotions for bathing the eyes can be made from chamomile flowers, vervain leaves, verbascum flowers or hyssop leaves. For styes any of the above infusions will help if used as hot as possible and applied frequently. Bathe the eye with a hot decoction of comfrey root to relieve the pain of a stye and to bring it to a head, or use a poultice made from the pounded seeds of nasturtium. An infusion of hyssop stems and leaves relieves a black eye, as does St John's wort oil.

FLATULENCE

For this troublesome complaint take an infusion of dill, sweet Cicely or peppermint leaves, or aniseed on a regular basis. Chew caraway seed for quick relief. Look to your diet and give up eating root vegetables until the complaint has subsided.

water for 10 minutes, add an equal amount of milk and simmer gently for 15 minutes. Crushed clove of garlic can be used in the same way. Sip when the cough is troublesome. Other herbs to use are marshmallow root, elecampane root, and the leaves and flowers of white horehound. Angelica syrup made from the stems is soothing; suck coltsfoot candy to ease a tight dry cough.

CRAMP

Drink infusions of chamomile flower, lime (linden) flower or fennel leaves and seeds; if taken regularly any one of these will help reduce muscular spasms. Use crushed calamint leaves to massage the affected muscles.

CUTS AND ABRASIONS

First clean the cut, then apply cotton wool pads soaked in an infusion of agrimony, yarrow or comfrey leaves or marigold petals. Apply powdered root of marshmallow directly on to the cut. Use an ointment made from lady's mantle or comfrey leaves to smooth on to abrasions. Alternatively, make a soothing oil of St John's wort using the stems, leaves and flowers. (The method for making oils is on page 66.)

DIGESTION AND INDIGESTION

Many herbs taken regularly in the form of herbal teas help in the assimilation of food, from which the body will get maximum benefit. It therefore follows that the addition of herbs to the diet greatly assists the digestion. Include in the diet at least once a day one or two of the following: sweet Cicely, garlic, dandelion, rosemary,

Weybrode. Wyld tanse.

Right: An illustration from a sixteenth century Herbal and Bestiary. On the left: Ribwort plantain (Plantago major), *which used to be known as 'weybread'; its roots made a useful flour for baking. Today the crushed leaves are used to relieve stings and bites. On the right: Wild tansy* (Tanacetum vulgare), *a tonic herb. Tansy pudding is a rather strong-tasting dish which used to be eaten during Lent.*

Opposite Above: Juniper (Juniperus Communis).

Opposite Below: Lime (linden) flowers (Tilia cordata).

HAEMORRHOIDS

This uncomfortable ailment can be eased fairly quickly. Drink parsley leaf tea regularly and dab the painful area frequently with an astringent herb infusion of agrimony leaves or witch-hazel.

HEADACHES

When these are brought on by overtiredness due to lack of sleep, nervous tension, eyestrain, stuffy rooms or other minor reasons there are many herbs which help to relieve headaches. By trying out some of them you will soon find the ones which suit you best. Drink the herb teas warm or hot to relax and soothe. Try any of the following: lemon balm, rosemary, sage, thyme, woodruff, violet, lavender flowers, chamomile flowers, or lime (linden) flowers. Rub lavender oil on to the temples or crushed peppermint leaves over the forehead.

INSECT BITES AND STINGS

For mosquito and other insect bites, rub on an ointment made of thyme and summer savory, or use a poultice of freshly grated horse-radish or freshly crushed burdock leaves. Squeeze parsley juice on to the bite for quick relief. Apply raw leaves of plantain to relieve the pain of a sting or use witch-hazel, which is good for wasp stings. Dab on an infusion of hyssop stems and leaves, or use feverfew leaves.

MUSCULAR ACHES AND PAINS

Should these persist you must visit a doctor, but for minor troubles use bay or wintergreen oil, horse-radish or elecampane ointment and massage lightly into the affected part.

NAUSEA

For travel sickness a cold infusion of basil leaves is effective. Drink it just before you start the journey. Other forms of nausea can be relieved by taking un-sweetened peppermint or lemon balm tea made from the leaves. Mint teas are pleasant antidotes to 'morning sickness' in pregnancy and, unlike chemical remedies, hold no possibility of harming the unborn child.

NERVOUS TENSION

The calming herbs are used to reduce tension when due to a nervous complaint. While it is vitally necessary that people with such a complaint should consult their doctor, the taking of a herb tea can help. Try angelica, vervain or lemon balm sweetened with honey. Use a mixture of 2 parts sage to 1 part basil leaves, or take an infusion of hops.

SLEEPLESSNESS

A sedative herb should be taken hot last thing at night. This will become more effective if taken over a period of time. The one exception to this rule is valerian, the roots of which are made into a decoction and taken cold about an hour before going to sleep. It should be used nightly for about 2 or 3 weeks, after which take a break for another week before resuming your nightly drink. It should be taken in this way and not become a habit or it will make you restless and not sleepy. Other sleep-inducing herbs are elderflower, bergamot, hops, chamomile and lime (linden) flower.

SORE THROAT AND MOUTH

Mild inflammation of the throat and mouth can be relieved by using gargles and mouthwashes. Gargle last thing at night with a warm infusion of a mixture of angelica, peppermint and lemon balm. Make honey-suckle syrup for the relief of a sore throat or suck coltsfoot candy. Make an infusion for a mouthwash using sorrel, comfrey or violet leaves. Add honey if the infusion is unpleasant to the taste.

STIFF JOINTS

When joints are temporarily stiff due to vigorous exercise or gardening, lightly rub in herbal oils made from lavender or bay. The juice of crushed mistletoe berries or juice from the dandelion stem smoothed on to the joint sometimes brings relief. Horse-radish embrocation provides an alternative remedy. Drink dandelion tea while following the treatment.

STOMACH ACHE

When stomach ache is due to eating excessively rich or acid food, or general upset, try an infusion of lime (linden) flower, peppermint, horsetail or fenugreek seeds. Chew the seeds of dill, anise or fennel.

Opposite: A pot of marigolds (Calendula officinalis). The flower-heads are used to relieve sunburn and minor burns, and for many other cosmetic and skin preparations. The petals are added to salads and used to make herbal tea.

Left: The medicinal herb garden at Acorn Bank, Cumbria, showing herbs growing well in a sheltered position by a wall. Familiar herbs are narrow-leaved sage, mullein, tansy, St. John's wort, juniper, mugwort, myrtle, lovage and southernwood.

SUNBURN AND MINOR BURNS

For relief from sunburn, smoothe on to the skin any of the following herbal ointments: marigold, honeysuckle or elderflower. Dab on witch-hazel or use a compress made from an infusion of burdock leaves, angelica, salad burnet or elderflowers. For burns, apply oil of peppermint directly on to the skin, or use fresh elder-flowers or marigold petals. St John's wort oil will soothe the pain.

TOOTHACHE

To relieve nagging toothache until a visit to the dentist is possible, drink an infusion of lemon balm and put a few drops of either oil of marjoram or oil of peppermint directly on to the tooth. Chewing yarrow leaves is another remedy.

TONIC HERBS

A tonic is something which gives tone and vigour to the system, providing a general feeling of well-being. There are many tonic herbs which are also used for other ailments, but a selection of these are dandelion, sage, parsley, rosemary, purslane, tansy, vervain, cost-mary, elderberry, rose hips and thyme.

METHODS OF MAKING MEDICINAL PREPARATIONS

It is important when making your herbal remedies that all the healing substances be fully extracted from the herbs. Most of the remedies are quite simple to make and no expensive equipment is required. It is suggested that all the herbs used be fresh but, if necessary, dried herbs can be used. When using dried herbs, you need only one-third of the quantity given for fresh herbs.

INFUSION

This is the easiest method of making a herbal medicine. You can use fresh or dried leaves, flowers or petals, soft stems and sometimes the whole herb, as with eye-bright. Seeds too can be used in this way but are more effective if slightly decocted. Fold fresh leaves and stems in a clean cloth and bruise them lightly to extract their healing juices. Place the herbs in a warm glass or china

Left: Preparing an infusion of basil and a decoction of burdock root. Honeysuckle, peppermint and dandelion are also illustrated.

Opposite: Making a poultice – a pestle and mortar are used to crush hop flowers and thyme leaves, which are then folded in muslin (cheesecloth) and moistened with hot water.

pot using 3 tablespoons of a fresh herb or 1 tablespoon if dried. Pour on 600 ml/1 pint/2½ cups boiling water, cover closely and allow to stand for 4 to 6 minutes. Strain it carefully, and it is then ready for use. Infusions will keep for a few hours but are best used hot or cold when absolutely fresh. If the infusion is for drinking you can sweeten it with a little honey.

DECOCTION

A decoction extracts the goodness from the bark or roots of a herb. It is not sufficient to add boiling water and as a general rule the herb has to be boiled. Herb bark should be crushed before being put in the pan; roots should be washed, scraped and chopped or grated. Use 25 g/1 oz of the herb to 1 litre/1¾ pints/4¼ cups cold water and bring this slowly to the boil. Simmer gently with the lid on the whole time until the liquid is reduced by half. Remove from the heat, stir and leave to get cold. Stir again, strain off the decoction and use. Roots of marshmallow or valerian are more effective if steeped in cold water beforehand. For valerian use 3 level teaspoons chopped root to 1 teacupful of cold water. Cover and leave for 12 hours in a cool place. For marshmallow use 3 teaspoons finely chopped root to 1 cup of cold water. Cover and leave for 8 hours, strain, then warm up before using. For a decoction of seeds, bruise or crush the seeds using a pestle and mortar; alternatively, put the seeds between pieces of cloth and use a rolling pin: this will release the oil. Use 1 tablespoon of seeds to 600 ml/1 pint/2½ cups of water. Add the seeds to boiling water and simmer for 6 to 8 minutes, strain and use hot.

TINCTURES

The use of alcohol instead of water as a means of extracting the properties of a herb is sometimes more effective; it will keep indefinitely. Use rubbing alcohol or vodka in which to steep the herb. Quantities will vary according to each herb but as a general guide use 40 g/1½ oz crushed or powdered herb to 600 ml/1 pint/2½ cups of alcohol. Place the tincture in an airtight jar in a warm place and shake the bottle vigorously every other day for 3 to 4 weeks, by which time it should be ready to use.

OILS

Herbs release their properties in oil. The greater the proportion of herb to oil, the more effective the mixture will become. Put 50 g/2 oz crushed herb into a glass screwtop jar. Add 300 ml/½ pint/1¼ cups of pure vegetable oil and 1 tablespoon of wine vinegar. Leave the jar in a warm place (preferably in the sun) and shake the bottle each day. Leave for 2 weeks and strain. Add some more fresh herbs and continue shaking the bottle each day. After 4 to 5 weeks the oil should be ready to use.

MEDICINAL SYRUP

Pleasant to take and soothing, herb syrups are made by pouring 300 ml/½ pint/1¼ cups of boiling water on to 75 g/3 oz of crushed herbs and leaving it to get cold. Strain the infusion, heat until it is warm then add 112 g/4 oz/½ cup sugar. When the sugar has melted, bring the mixture to the boil and simmer gently until it is of a syrupy consistency. Cool slightly, then pot and seal.

OINTMENT

The base used for an ointment can be either pure lard or white petroleum jelly. Slowly heat 225 g/8 oz of pure lard in a pan. When it has melted, add 25 g/1 oz of crushed herbs and stir until the mixture is boiling. Simmer gently for 30 minutes, then strain it into little pots and cover them when cold. The same method is used for petroleum jelly, but use 25 g/1 oz of the crushed herb to 112 g/4 oz petroleum jelly and simmer for only 20 minutes.

POULTICES

A poultice is made with crushed or chopped herbs, heated and applied directly to the affected part, soothing and drawing out the poisons. Place the herbs on a piece of muslin (cheesecloth) and fold it in so that none will escape. Immerse the muslin (cheesecloth) in boiling water until the herb is soft and mushy, being careful to leave the ends of the muslin (cheesecloth) out of the water to assist removal. Twist the ends of the piece of muslin (cheesecloth) to squeeze out the water and apply at once, bandaging lightly in position. This poultice can be heated up two or three times before all the goodness has gone. Alternatively add the herbs to slippery elm powder, moisten the mixture and spread on to pieces of lint. Heat the poultice between two plates set over a pan of boiling water. The piece of lint could equally well be spread with a paste made of slippery elm, folded in muslin (cheesecloth) and heated in an infusion of the herb.

COMPRESS

By tradition, a compress is taken to mean a cold application. The familiar bruised crushed dock leaf held on to a nettle sting is a simple herb compress. A compress consists of pieces of lint dipped into a cold herbal infusion and laid over the affected part. When it becomes warm, through contact with the skin, it is removed and replaced with another piece of cold lint until relief is felt. Hot compresses, however, can be used where they will do more good, but compresses are usually used to reduce swellings, black eyes and bruising so are more suitable when used cold.

HERBAL TEAS

Many herbs make deliciously flavoured teas, which are soothing, relaxing, refreshing or invigorating. These healthy wholesome drinks can be taken warm in winter and cooled in summer. They make a valuable addition to the daily diet if taken on a regular basis replacing ordinary tea at mealtimes. While many herb teas are taken for their therapeutic properties, most are very pleasant to drink and can continue to be taken after the treatment is finished.

Dried or fresh herbs can be used but if dried they should be kept in airtight containers. Just as ordinary tea suffers from being too long in the pot so can a herb tea: overlong steeping can ruin a delicate flavour. If stronger tea is desired, add more herb at the outset. For average strength tea use 1 teaspoon dried herb for 1 teacupful. If using fresh herbs allow 3 teaspoons and crush the leaves before adding boiling water. Cover the

cup and leave to stand for 5 minutes before straining and drinking. For iced tea follow the same method, strain the tea, cover and leave to cool in a refrigerator.

Seed tea is made by adding bruised seeds to a pan of boiling water and simmering for 5 minutes. All teas can be sweetened with a spoonful of honey or a little sugar if necessary.

There are a number of exceptions to this general rule, different methods being used to bring out the best flavour of a particular herb.

Bergamot tea is best made by using 1 teaspoon dried flowers per cupful and simmering it gently for 5 to 6 minutes. This is a clear dark red colour which looks very attractive.

Bergamot milk is made by pouring 300 ml/½ pint/1¼ cups of hot milk over 1 tablespoon of dried leaves. Leave to stand for a few minutes, then strain and drink while hot.

Chamomile tea is made from the flowers only, dried or fresh. Do not allow to steep for more than 3 to 4 minutes, then strain. It is a very delicately flavoured tea.

Elderflower cordial for hot summer days is a particularly refreshing and delicious drink. Wash a lemon and peel the rind thinly. Put 50 g/2 oz/¼ cup sugar into a jug together with the lemon rind and 4 fresh elderflower heads. Pour over this 300 ml/½ pint/1¼ cups of boiling water. Stir until the sugar has dissolved, then leave to cool. When cold, strain the tea and use diluted with cold milk or iced water.

Hop tea is made from the female hop cones and drunk warm. Use 2 teaspoons per cupful of boiling water and strain after 3 to 4 minutes.

Horsetail tea is made from the dried herb only, and to obtain the full benefit it is necessary to soak 1 to 2 teaspoons per cup for 1 hour. Bring the mixture to the boil and simmer for 10 minutes. Allow to stand another 10 minutes before straining and using. Warm it up again if necessary to drink it really hot.

Juniper berry tea is made from fresh or dried crushed berries and stimulates the appetite. Use 12 to 15 crushed berries to a cup of boiling water. Allow to stand for about 10 minutes, then strain, add honey and use. A tea can also be made using young juniper shoots which must be cleaned and then soaked in cold water for 24 hours before being used for tea.

Lime (linden) flower tea is another delicately flavoured drink and the flowers should only be allowed to steep for 3 to 4 minutes, otherwise the flavour will be lost.

Lovage broth is made in the same way as other leaf teas but as it tastes like celery, add a little sea salt to enhance the flavour.

Marigold tea is made from the petals only, either fresh or dried. It has rather an insipid taste so try adding a little lemon juice and honey to bring out the flavour.

Peppermint tea is not only attractive to look at but also has an excellent flavour and is a very good 'pick-me-up'. Make the tea using whole slightly crushed leaves for a subtle taste.

Peppermint milk is made by pouring 300 ml/$\frac{1}{2}$ pint/$1\frac{1}{4}$ cups of boiling milk over 1 tablespoon of crushed leaves. It makes a good nightcap.

Rose hip tea is made from dried rose hips, finely crushed. It is important that they are very finely crushed to extract the maximum goodness from the herb. Use 1 teaspoon per cupful, pour on boiling water, cover and leave to stand for 5 to 7 minutes. Sweeten with honey if necessary or add a slice of lemon to make a refreshing drink. The brilliant red colour makes it an attractive tea.

Thyme tea can be made from fresh or dried thyme leaves and flowers, which automatically includes the stems since it is a long job to strip the tiny leaves off the stems. Any of the species of thyme can be used for tea, lemon thyme being particularly fragrant. To make 300 ml/$\frac{1}{2}$ pint/$1\frac{1}{4}$ cups of tea use 2 to 3 sprigs of fresh thyme or 1 dessertspoonful of dried thyme. Pour the boiling water over it and leave to stand for about 8 to 10 minutes.

Valerian tea is made from the roots only and they can be fresh or dried. It can be made in the usual way – 1 teaspoon per cupful of boiling water – but is more effective if the whole process is cold. Soak $\frac{1}{2}$–1 level teaspoon of roots chopped small or grated, in a teacupful of cold water. Cover and leave in a cool place for a whole day. Strain and use.

Verbascum tea, so effective for persistent coughs, is made with the vivid yellow flowers. Use 3 to 4 flowerheads per cupful of boiling water and leave to stand for 7 to 10 minutes until the tea is a bright yellow colour: Strain the liquid carefully through fine muslin (cheese-cloth) in case any pollen remains behind, as this may further aggravate the cough.

Woodruff tea is a stimulating invigorating drink and can be made with either dried or half-dried leaves, when they have slightly wilted. Use 1 teaspoon per cup and cover with hot water – on no account should the water be boiling. Leave to stand for up to 1 hour before using. Strain and heat again or drink cold with a slice of lemon and a little honey.

THE IMPORTANCE OF HERBS IN THE DIET

Culinary herbs can play an important part in the daily diet in spite of the fact that a relatively small amount of herbs are eaten each day. Herbs contain nutritional substances which are beneficial to health, and when added to other foods they bring out the full flavour and make them more enjoyable.

The specific substances contained in herbs are the volatile oils, mineral salts and bitter principles which consist of glycerols, saponines, tannins and carbohydrates. All of these play their part in the interaction of the herb's effect.

The volatile or essential oil in a herb provides the fragrance which can have such an important effect on the body and is responsible for the healing properties of the herb. The volatile oil is easily lost if the herb is not carefully handled and dried. The mineral salts in a herb provide calcium, potassium, silicic and other acids important to the proper functioning of the body. The aperient qualities of certain herbs provide the laxative elements, being smooth and gentle. The remaining bitter principles all taste bitter, yet increase the flow of juices necessary for complete digestion. They have an effect on the circulation, the lining of the stomach, and they are antibiotic in nature, all of which contribute to full and satisfactory digestion of food.

The digestion depends to a large extent upon the palate, the sense of smell and the enjoyment of food. If food smells good and tastes good, then the saliva in the mouth begins to flow, which helps in the mastication of that food. The enjoyment in eating the food provides a relaxed frame of mind and body and is again helpful to the digestion.

Culinary herbs can also help in the diet by replacing spicy condiments such as pepper, which if used to excess can be harmful and in some cases is totally forbidden. Use summer savory, basil and nasturtium instead.

Herbs can provide flavour and interest to food for those on a salt-reduced or salt-free diet, replacing altogether the need for salt; thyme and marjoram are particularly helpful.

There are sweet herbs such as sweet Cicely, angelica, lemon balm and lemon thyme which, if used judiciously, will reduce the amount of sugar required for tart fruits and do away with the need for sugar altogether in other sweets. These herbs add subtle delicious flavours as well as sweetness, and are a boon to those on a slimming diet.

HERBS FOR BEAUTY AND PERFUMERY

Skin, hair, eyes, nails and body all look and function better if your general health is good. Cosmetics will do little to improve the appearance of women who are not getting sufficient fresh air, exercise, good sleep or relaxation and who are not eating the correct foods the body needs to maintain good health.

When beginning to use homemade herbal cosmetics for the first time, study how these same herbs can be taken internally in order to back up the action of the cosmetics and accelerate their effectiveness overall.

The benefits to be gained from using your own herbal cosmetics are many: the lovely scents and fragrance of herbs, and the other natural ingredients which you will use, have a relaxing effect that increases the beneficial action of your mixture.

Most of the ingredients required to make cosmetics are already standing on the kitchen shelf. They are safe and natural, and most of them form part of the daily diet. On the whole they are inexpensive to buy, but cost is an important point, since homemade cosmetics do not keep as well as proprietary items which contain preservative chemicals; it is these chemical constituents that can harm the skin.

Once you have become familiar with making your own herbal cosmetics, you will soon discover which herbs are best suited to your particular needs. Fresh herbs are preferable, but dried ones are fine so long as they have a good colour and aroma.

FACE PACKS

These are some of the most rewarding treatments to give yourself. A face pack cleanses, nourishes and restores a smooth fresh appearance to the skin.

A face pack must be used on a scrupulously clean face and neck. Wash the face and neck with a pure soap and a soft brush using a circular motion. Pay particular attention to the areas around chin and nose. Rinse well in clear tepid water and pat dry with a soft towel. You are now ready to apply the face pack.

When smoothing a herb pack on to the face, be careful not to cover the lips. Avoid contact with the eyes. Protect the eyes with cotton wool pads soaked in an infusion of fennel or plain water. Once you have applied the face pack, lie down and rest for the specified time; use a kitchen timer if you are worried about leaving the pack on for too long. After removing the pack, apply moisturizer to the face and neck.

BASIC HERB MOISTURIZER

To 2 tablespoons of glycerine, add 2 tablespoons of rosewater and 2 tablespoons of marigold flower water.

Whisk these ingredients together so that they are well-blended, and store in a screwtop bottle. Shake the bottle before use. Smooth the moisturizer lightly over the skin after using a face pack, then wipe the skin with a tissue. Leave only the merest film behind for protection.

To make the marigold flower water, place 25 g/1 oz of marigold petals in a pan with 400 ml/14 fl oz/1$\frac{3}{4}$ cups water to cover. Simmer gently for 30 minutes. Strain and repeat the process with 25 g/1 oz of fresh petals, trying not to add more water. This quantity should make about 300 ml/$\frac{1}{2}$ pint/1$\frac{1}{4}$ cups.

Glycerine and rosewater may both be bought from your local chemist (drugstore), but you can easily make your own. 225 g/8 oz of flower petals should produce 300 ml/$\frac{1}{2}$ pint/1$\frac{1}{4}$ cups of rosewater. Pick strong-scented rose petals from the wild dog rose or sweetbriar rose bush. Place them in a pan with sufficient water just to cover the petals. Cover the pan and bring the water to the boil; simmer over a gentle heat for 30 minutes. Pour through a strainer and discard the petals. Using the same amount of fresh petals, repeat the process, simmering for a further 30 minutes. When all the petals have been used in this way, cool and strain the rosewater into sterilized jars. Leave for 3 days before using.

NORMAL SKIN

SAGE AND APPLE PACK

Clean an apple and cut it up into small pieces. Purée the pieces in a blender, with 2 tablespoons of honey and 15 g/$\frac{1}{2}$ oz of thoroughly bruised and chopped sage leaves. Two tablespoons of rosewater may be used in place of the sage if preferred. Smooth the mixture over the skin and leave it for 15 minutes. Rinse it off with tepid water and end by splashing the skin with cold water. Pat dry with a soft towel and apply moisturizer.

LADY'S MANTLE PACK

Mix together 3 tablespoons of wheat germ, 1 tablespoon of honey and 2 tablespoons of a strong infusion of lady's mantle made from 1 tablespoon of the chopped herb to 150 ml/$\frac{1}{4}$ pint/$\frac{2}{3}$ cup of boiling water, allowed to cool. When thoroughly mixed, smooth on to the skin and leave for 20 minutes. Remove the pack with tepid water and rinse with cold water. Pat the skin dry with a soft towel and apply moisturizer. This is a stimulating and refreshing face pack.

FENNEL SEED PACK

For this tonic face pack, mix together 50 g/2 oz of yogurt, 3 tablespoons of honey, 2 tablespoons of oatmeal and 3 tablespoons of a strong infusion of fennel

seeds made from 3 teaspoons of crushed seeds to 150 ml/ $\frac{1}{4}$ pint/$\frac{2}{3}$ cup of boiling water and left to cool. Smooth on to the skin and leave for 10 to 15 minutes. Rinse it off with warm water and then dab with cold water. Pat the face dry with a soft towel and apply moisturizer.

JUNIPER STIMULATING FACE PACK

Mix together into a thick paste the white of 1 egg, 1 tablespoon of kaolin or Fuller's earth and 2 tablespoons of a strong infusion of juniper made by steeping 25 g/1 oz of juniper shoots in 150 ml/$\frac{1}{4}$ pint/$\frac{2}{3}$ cup of cold water for 24 hours. Spread the paste thickly on to the face and leave to dry for 15 minutes. Remove and rinse with tepid water then dab with cold water. Pat dry and smooth on moisturizer.

PEPPERMINT AND YEAST PACK

For a quick pick-me-up for the skin, try this stimulating pack. Mix together 1 teaspoon dried baker's yeast with 1 tablespoon of a strong infusion of peppermint leaves, made by pouring 150 ml/$\frac{1}{4}$ pint/$\frac{2}{3}$ cup of boiling water on to 2 tablespoons of chopped peppermint leaves. Leave to cool, then strain and use. Spread this mixture on to the face and neck and leave to dry completely – 10 to 15 minutes. Rinse it off with warm water, dab with cold water, pat dry and smooth on moisturizer.

DRY SKIN

An excessively dry skin can benefit from a face pack if a few simple points are observed. After cleansing the skin, smooth a light film of almond oil over the face before applying the pack. Always wash off the pack with warm water. Do not splash the face with cold water afterwards, as this contracts the skin, closes the skin pores and has a drying effect. Immediately after using a pack, cover the skin with basic herb moisturizer. Herbs helpful for dry skins include comfrey, fennel, marigold, red clover, borage, coltsfoot, lady's mantle, salad burnet, marshmallow and elderflower.

SALAD BURNET, OIL AND YEAST PACK

Blend together 1 tablespoon of powdered brewer's yeast, $\frac{1}{2}$ teaspoon of wheat germ oil and 2 tablespoons of a strong infusion of salad burnet leaves made by pouring a cupful of boiling water over 2 tablespoons of chopped burnet leaves. While it is still warm spread the mixture over the face and leave for 10 to 15 minutes. Wash it off with warm water, pat the face dry and apply moisturizer.

COMFREY PACK

One of the most soothing face packs for a dry skin is made from comfrey leaves. Put 4 tablespoons of boiled water into a blender with a handful of chopped comfrey leaves and blend until the comfrey is well-pulped. Strain the pulp through a piece of muslin (cheesecloth) expressing as much as possible of the juice. Smooth the juice on to a clean face and leave for 10 minutes; wash it off with warm water, pat dry and apply moisturizer.

MALLOW, EGG AND HONEY PACK

Beat together 1 egg yolk, 1 teaspoon of honey and 1 tablespoon of strong marshmallow decoction. The decoction is made by soaking 25 g/1 oz cleaned and chopped marshmallow root in 200 ml/$\frac{1}{2}$ pint/$\frac{7}{8}$ cup of cold water for 24 hours. Smooth the mixture on to cleaned skin and leave for 15 to 20 minutes to dry. Wash in tepid water, pat dry and apply moisturizer.

MARIGOLD, PEACH AND YOGURT PACK

Peel 1 peach and remove the stone (pit). Mash it to a pulp mixing it with 2 teaspoons of natural (unflavored) yogurt and 1 tablespoon strong marigold infusion made by pouring a cupful of boiling water on to 2 tablespoons of crushed marigold petals and leaves. Smooth over the skin and leave to dry for about 10 to 15 minutes. Wash it off with warm water, pat dry and apply moisturizer.

BORAGE, EGG, YEAST AND ALMOND OIL PACK

Beat together 1 egg yolk, 2 teaspoons of almond oil and 7 g/$\frac{1}{4}$ oz of fresh yeast, or use dried yeast mixed with a little warm water to make a paste. Add 1 tablespoon of strong borage infusion made by pouring a cupful of boiling water on to 2 tablespoons of crushed or chopped leaves. Smooth the mixture on to the skin and leave for 10 minutes. Wash it off with warm water, pat dry and apply moisturizer.

OILY SKIN

There are a number of herbs which are astringent in nature and can be used with success in face packs for an oily skin. The best of these include chamomile flowers, yarrow flowers and leaves, nettle, sage and parsley leaves.

CHAMOMILE FLOWER PACK WITH YARROW, CARROT AND EGG WHITE

Mix together 1 medium carrot, finely grated, 1 beaten egg white and 1 or 2 tablespoons of a strong infusion of chamomile flowers and yarrow leaves or flowers. Pour a cupful of boiling water over 3 teaspoons each of chamomile and yarrow and leave to cool. Spread the mixture over the face and leave for 10 to 15 minutes. Remove and rinse with warm water then dab with cold water. Pat dry and apply moisturizer.

PARSLEY PACK WITH EGG OR YOGURT

This is a very good face pack for those with an excessively oily skin. Wash a large bunch of parsley, chop it roughly and purée in a blender with enough boiled water to prevent the machine jamming. Alternatively, a juice extractor may be used. If neither of these is available, make a strong infusion by pouring a cupful of boiling water over 3 tablespoons of chopped parsley. Mix the juice with an equal quantity of egg white or natural (unflavored) yogurt and smooth on to the skin. Leave for 15 to 20 minutes. Remove the pack and rinse the skin with cold water. Pat dry and apply moisturizer.

NETTLE, MILK AND OATMEAL PACK

Mix 2 tablespoons of oatmeal with enough milk to make a thick paste. Add sufficient nettle juice to make the paste easy to spread. Express the nettle juice by means of a blender or juice extractor, or use a strong infusion made by pouring a cupful of boiling water over 2 tablespoons of chopped leaves and stems. Spread the paste over the skin and leave for 15 minutes. Remove the pack and rinse with cold water. Pat dry and apply moisturizer.

PEPPERMINT, EGG, LEMON AND CUCUMBER PACK

Purée in a blender 1 egg white, half a cucumber, peeled and roughly chopped, 1 teaspoon lemon juice and a small handful of freshly picked peppermint leaves. Spread the mixture over the skin and leave for 10 to 15 minutes, during which time a pleasant tingling sensation will be felt. Remove the pack and bathe the face with tepid water. Pat dry with a soft towel and smooth on a little moisturizer.

SAGE PACK WITH MILK AND ALUM

Make a strong infusion of sage by pouring a cupful of boiling water on to 2 tablespoons of chopped sage and leaving it for 15 minutes. Strain the infusion and leave to cool. To 1 tablespoon of sage infusion add 2 tablespoons of milk and a pinch of alum. Spread the pack over the face and leave for 10 minutes. Rinse it off with warm water, pat dry with a soft towel and apply a little moisturizer.

YARROW AND DRIED MILK PACK WITH HONEY AND EGG

Mix 2 teaspoons of dried milk with 1 teaspoon of honey. Add 2 tablespoons of strong yarrow infusion made by pouring a cupful of boiling water over 2 tablespoons of yarrow leaves and flowers. Whip up the white of 1 egg to a froth and add to the mixture, blending well. Smooth the pack over the skin and leave for 20 minutes. Rinse it off with warm water followed by a dab of cold water. Pat dry and apply a light film of moisturizer.

SKIN CLEANSERS

To function properly, the skin needs to be well cleansed every day and preferably twice a day. A good cleansing programme is important as it performs several duties. As well as removing dirt and old make-up, it takes away dead cells which would otherwise remain on the surface of the skin, spoiling its appearance and preventing it from breathing. Cleansing also softens the skin.

Start the cleansing process by using a suitable cream or lotion lightly smoothed over the skin; leave it for a few moments and then wipe it off gently with a tissue. For most skins further cleansing with a good non-alkaline soap and tepid water is recommended; this will remove all traces of the cleansing cream and make-up and leave your skin 'squeaking' clean. Immediately afterwards use a skin freshening lotion, tonic or rinse suitable for your type of skin, followed by a light application of moisturizer.

Whenever the skin feels clogged or looks dull and is a poor colour, give yourself a herb facial steam. Facial steams using herbs are a simple and effective way of deep cleansing and softening the skin. This helps in the removal of blackheads and is also very good for those suffering from acne and large pores.

A steam is not recommended for those with an exceptionally dry skin unless the skin is first covered with a thin film of oil.

Opposite: Preparing herbal cleansing creams and oils.

Below: Preparing a facial steam. The herbs illustrated are nettle, comfrey, lady's mantle, fennel, salad burnet and chamomile.

PREPARATION FOR A FACIAL STEAM

If you have long hair, tie it back from your face. Cleanse the face and neck with a light cleansing cream. Remove the cream with tissues. Wash with pure soap and water using a soft complexion brush. Rinse with clear tepid water and pat dry. Place 4 tablespoons of the herb, or mixture of herbs, in a bowl and pour on 1 litre/1¾ pints/4½ cups of boiling water. Lean over the bowl without putting your face too close to the water, and cover your head with a towel so that none of the steam will escape. Remain for 10 minutes, longer if you are able to do so. Wipe the face with a clean damp cloth and dab lightly all over the skin with a freshening lotion. Do not go outside directly after using a facial steam but allow the skin to cool down for at least an hour. Use any of the following herbs for a steam, on their own or in a mixture: marigold petals or the flowers of chamomile, lime, yarrow and elder; leaves of comfrey, fennel, lady's mantle, nettle, salad burnet, sage and peppermint.

HERBAL CLEANSING CREAMS AND OILS

The following cleansers are most suitable for normal and dry skin, but can be used for oily skins if followed by a skin freshener or astringent lotion.

CREAMY CLEANSER

Place in a bowl 25 g/1 oz lanolin, 25 g/1 oz cocoa butter and 4 tablespoons of sweet almond oil. Stand the bowl in a pan of boiling water and leave the ingredients to melt, stirring them occasionally. Remove the bowl from the pan and add 4 tablespoons of a strong infusion of violet flowers and leaves, lady's mantle leaves or chamomile flowers. Whisk the mixture by hand or with an electric mixer until it is slightly cooled and well blended. Pour into a screwtop jar. Shake before use.

Alternatively, mix together in a pan over gentle heat 4 tablespoons of vegetable margarine with 3 dessertspoons of either dried elderflower, lime (linden) flower, rosemary, sage or salad burnet leaves. When well-blended, cool slightly and pour into a screwtop jar adding a few drops of lavender or rosewater.

HERBAL CLEANSING OIL

Herbs steeped in natural oils provide particularly good cleansers for dry skins and they soften and condition the skin at the same time. Use any of the following oils as a base: safflower, almond, sunflower seed, coconut or wheat germ oil. The first 3 are probably the easiest to use as coconut oil is solid at room temperature and wheat germ oil rather thick. Add to your small jar of oil any one of the following herbs: flowers of chamomile, elder and lime; nettle, comfrey or peppermint leaves; rosemary or violet flowers and leaves. Coconut oil based cleansers need slightly different preparation. Melt 4 tablespoons of coconut oil in a pan over a gentle heat. Add 3 dessertspoons of the dried herb of your choice and simmer gently for 5 minutes. Cool, and strain into a screwtop jar. The mixture will solidify, so warm it a little in the palm of your hand before putting it on to the skin.

HERBAL CLEANSING LOTIONS

All types of skin respond to cleansing with a herb lotion and they are particularly good for oily skins. They are best kept in the refrigerator or a cool place rather than on the bathroom shelf. The lotions will keep for a few days only.

VIOLET LOTION

To 300 ml/½ pint/1¼ cups of fresh milk add 3 tablespoons of freshly picked violet flowers. Put in a pan and warm over a very gentle heat until it smells strongly of violets. Do not allow the milk to boil or a skin to form. Remove from the heat, cool and strain into a screwtop bottle. Make other cleansing milk lotions in the same way using nettle or coltsfoot leaves or chamomile flowers.

FENNEL AND YOGURT CLEANSER

It is advisable to use a fresh live yogurt. To a 150 g/5 oz carton of natural (unflavored) yogurt add 150 ml/¼ pint/⅔ cup of a strong infusion of fennel. Make the infusion by pouring 150 ml/¼ pint/⅔ cup of boiling water on to 2 tablespoons of fennel leaves. Leave to cool, strain and add to the yogurt. Mix well and pour into screwtop bottles. Store in the refrigerator.

YARROW LOTION

Make up a medium-strength infusion of yarrow leaves and flowers by pouring 150 ml/¼ pint/⅔ cup of boiling water on to 3 dessertspoons of yarrow and leaving it to get quite cold. Strain and bottle. This is a good cleanser for oily skins. For other types of skin use lady's mantle, lemon balm or lime (linden) flower.

SOAPWORT LOTION

Cover a handful of chopped soapwort leaves and stems with water in a pan. Bring slowly to the boil and simmer for 5 minutes. Cool and drain into screwtop bottles. Use as a cleanser for all types of skin.

LADY'S MANTLE AND BUTTERMILK LOTION

Buttermilk is a beneficial cleanser for oily skins and mixing it with a herbal infusion makes it still more effective. Mix together equal quantities of buttermilk and a strong infusion of lady's mantle. Make the infusion by pouring 150 ml/¼ pint/⅔ cup of boiling water over 2 tablespoons of leaves. Cool and strain before adding to the buttermilk. This is a good cleanser for those with spotty skins.

SKIN FRESHENING LOTIONS

Cleansing of the skin should be followed by the application of a herbal skin lotion which will finally remove the last traces of cleanser or soap. Soak cotton wool pads in the lotion and wipe over the skin. Lotions, fresheners, tonics and rinses can be used on all types of skin and have a soothing, healing and refreshing effect. Cosmetic vinegars and astringent lotions are for occasional use only on oily skins as they have a very strong drying action.

A simple infusion of a herb makes an effective refreshing lotion. Choose from the following herbs, all of which are helpful to the skin. Many of them have extra qualities which may be needed for your particular skin problem. Use within 12 hours.

Lime (linden) flower has a slight bleaching action. It improves the circulation and smoothes wrinkles.
Lemon balm is also used against wrinkles.
Elderflower softens and whitens the skin and is good for spots.
Lady's mantle is used for large pores and freckles.
Salad burnet helps to soften and refine the skin.
Fennel is used against wrinkles.
Violet helps to keep the skin clear of blemishes.
Yarrow infusion is for use on oily skin and it is good for facial thread veins.
Parsley helps to fade freckles.
Marigold reduces large pores, nourishes and clears the skin. It is also good for spots and pimples.
Sage is for large pores and an oily skin. It is rather more astringent than other herbs.
Coltsfoot helps to reduce facial thread veins.

A skin tonic helps to revive tired, dull skins by improving circulation of blood to the skin. Herbs are especially good for this. They can be used in an infusion using 1 teaspoon of the crushed dried herb to a cupful of boiling water. Leave to stand for 30 minutes, strain and pour into a screwtop bottle. Choose from the following herbs: chamomile and lavender flowers; dandelion, nettle, sage and horsetail leaves; rosemary, yarrow and thyme flowers and leaves.

FRESHENER FOR OILY SKIN

Whisk up the white of an egg with equal amounts of strained lemon juice and a strong infusion of rosemary. Make the infusion by pouring 150 ml/¼ pint/⅔ cup of boiling water over 2 tablespoons of the chopped herb. Leave the infusion to cool and strain it before adding it to the egg and lemon juice. Pour into a screwtop bottle.

ROSEMARY FACE RINSE

Boil a handful of rosemary leaves and flowers in 300 ml/½ pint/1¼ cups of water for 5 minutes. Leave to cool. Strain and pour into a screwtop bottle. Use as a freshener on the skin and allow it to dry completely before applying moisturizer.

ROSE LOTION

A simple astringent for oily skin, to be used once or twice a week. To 450 ml/¾ pint/2 cups of white wine vinegar add 2 tablespoons of dried rose petals, prefer-

ably those from the sweetbriar or eglantine rose. Leave to stand in a screwtop jar for 2 to 3 weeks. Strain and add 250 ml/8 fl oz/1 cup of rosewater. A similar astringent lotion can be made using marigold petals in place of the rose petals and witch-hazel in place of the rosewater.

SAGE OR HORSETAIL LOTION

Make a strong infusion of either sage leaves or horsetail by pouring 150 ml/¼ pint/⅔ cup of boiling water over 2 tablespoons of the chopped herb. Allow to stand until cold. Strain and add to an equal quantity of milk or cider vinegar. Pour into a screwtop bottle. For an extra tightening effect on the skin add a pinch of alum with the milk or cider vinegar.

MOISTURIZERS

Moisturizers help to prevent the skin from losing its moisture content. They protect the skin from harmful bacteria, harsh weather and the dry atmosphere of centrally heated houses and offices. The moisturizer need only be a thin film over the skin to provide adequate protection, rather than a heavy pore-clogging cream. Herbal moisturizers are pleasant to use and easy to make. They can be applied at any time of the day but will do most good in the mornings and evenings.

Directions for making a basic herb moisturizer have already been given. The simplest moisturizers to use are honey, lanolin and glycerine. Add these to herbal infusions to provide more protection for the skin. Use 2 tablespoons of a strong herb infusion to 1 teaspoon of honey or 1 tablespoon of lanolin or glycerine.

Opposite: Herbal cleansing lotions and skin fresheners made using yogurt, buttermilk, vinegars and infusions. The herbs illustrated are violet, rose, rosemary and lady's mantle.

Below: Preparing marigold moisturizer.

MARIGOLD MOISTURIZER CREAM

In a bowl set over a pan of hot water, melt together 1 tablespoon each of lanolin, honey, almond oil and white wax. Remove from the heat and add 2 tablespoons of a strong infusion of marigold petals made by pouring 150 ml/¼ pint/⅔ cup of boiling water over 2 tablespoons of marigold petals. Leave to cool slightly then strain. Whisk the mixture until thick and creamy and quite cold. Put into screwtop pots.

Other herbs suitable for adding to this cream in place of marigold are comfrey leaves, or the flowers of elder, lime (linden) and chamomile.

A quick way of making a moisturizer cream is to add 1 tablespoon of a very strong herb infusion to 100 g/4 oz of a good proprietary scent-free moisturizing cream. Melt the cream slightly and whip in the herb infusion. Use fennel, salad burnet, lady's mantle or elderflower.

SALAD BURNET NOURISHING CREAM

Salad burnet helps to refine the skin. Other herbs to use in its place are lady's mantle, soapwort or violet flowers. Beat 1 egg yolk with 1 teaspoon of honey, 1 teaspoon of sweet almond oil and 1 tablespoon of a very strong infusion of salad burnet leaves made by pouring 150 ml/¼ pint/⅔ cup of boiling water on to 3 tablespoons of chopped burnet leaves.

Herbs used for eye compresses and poultices: fennel, chamomile and elderflower.

EYES

There are a number of herbs which can help in soothing, toning and brightening the eyes. Some herbs can help in reducing puffiness and dark circles under the eyes, while others help to relieve tiredness and eyestrain.

Many people use eye baths, but compresses or poultices are recommended as they lessen the danger of any infection getting into the eye itself. The following preparations must be used fresh and should be stored for no longer than 12 hours.

EYE COMPRESSES

For a compress, cut 2 layers of lint for each eye so they will keep moist for longer. Soak the lint pads in a cold infusion, squeeze slightly and place over each eyelid. Rest for 10 minutes, replacing the soaked lint once it becomes warm. Finally dab the eyes with fresh cold water and pat dry with a soft clean towel.

Eyebright is one of the most helpful herbs and can be used for all eye troubles. Make an infusion using 1 tablespoon of chopped eyebright to 150 ml/¼ pint/⅔ cup of boiling water. Leave until cold, and strain into a screwtop bottle. A good time to apply a compress is while lying in your bath.

Elderflower infusion is mildly stimulant and makes a good compress to brighten the eyes.

Chamomile flowers make an infusion which is soothing and reduces inflammation.

Horsetail decoction reduces swollen eyelids and redness.

Fennel infusion is very good for strengthening the eyes and frequent bathing with cotton wool pads soaked in the solution is effective for watering eyes.

Vervain infusion is cleansing and soothes tired eyes and heavy eyelids.

Golden seal is a very effective herb for soothing and healing the eyes. Pour 450 ml/¾ pint/2 cups of boiling water on to 1 teaspoon each of golden seal and boracic acid powder. Leave to cool. Strain carefully and use warm or cold.

Wormwood infusion will reduce redness and soothe sore eyelids.

EYE POULTICES

For puffiness and for dark circles under the eyes, for aching, tired or sore eyes a poultice can be very effective. Prepare whichever herb you have decided to use by pulping leaves or flowers, or by finely chopping and bruising them and adding just a little water. Lay this mixture between two pieces of muslin (cheesecloth) for each eye. Place over and round the eyes making sure to cover the skin beneath the eyes. Discard after use.

Chamomile Use two chamomile tea bags, available from health food stores. Pour a cupful of boiling water over the bags and leave them to steep for 3 minutes. Remove the tea bags and as soon as they have cooled sufficiently place them over the eyes. Leave for 10 minutes. Sip the tea while resting.

Rose hip Use the same method as for chamomile. This poultice is particularly good for puffiness under the eyes.

Fennel Mix fresh bruised fennel leaves with a grated raw potato and spread the mixture on to muslin (cheesecloth). Lay the pad over the lids and outside of the eyes to soothe the delicate skin. Leave on for 15 minutes then dab with cold water and dry with a soft clean towel.

Coltsfoot To reduce puffy eyes, bruise or mince (grind) fresh coltsfoot leaves and add enough water to make a pulp. Place between layers of muslin (cheesecloth) to make 2 eye pads and chill them in the refrigerator for 20 minutes. Put the poultices over puffy eyes and leave for 15 minutes. Dab with fresh cold water and dry with a soft clean towel.

HANDS

Nowadays hands are subjected to fairly harsh treatment and tend to get neglected in one's general day-to-day activities. Cold weather, detergents and too much hot water ruin the skin of the hands and weaken the nails. Rubber gloves should be worn for washing up the dishes and where possible cotton gloves for working round the house. Suitable gloves should be worn when gardening, for protection against the weather as well as dirt. For those who cannot bear wearing gloves at any time use a barrier cream to smooth over the hands before doing any dirty work. Keep a bottle of hand cream near the sink in the kitchen for use after every washing-up session, and always wash your hands with a good pure soap.

Herbs can help to keep the hands in good condition, whether used on their own as a hand rinse or backing up the effectiveness of other natural substances used in the preparations. These natural substances are almond oil, glycerine, oatmeal, ground almonds, carragheen moss, white wax, cocoa butter and arrowroot.

HAND RINSE

For a single hand rinse use an infusion of one of the following skin care herbs: lady's mantle, fennel, marigold petals, marshmallow, comfrey or chamomile flowers. Make up the infusion by pouring 600 ml/1 pint/2½ cups of boiling water over 2 tablespoons of the prepared herb. For soothing rough, chapped hands make up the quantity first thing in the morning and leave in a small bowl beside the basin. After washing your hands dip them into the herb rinse for a minute or two before drying them on a soft muslin (cheesecloth) towel.

MARSHMALLOW CREAM

Make a strong decoction of marshmallow root by soaking 25 g/1 oz scraped and finely chopped root in 150 ml/¼ pint/⅔ cup of cold water for 24 hours. Strain well. Add 1 tablespoon of the decoction to 2 tablespoons of ground almonds, 1 teaspoon of milk and 1 teaspoon of cider vinegar. Beat together until well blended and add a few drops of lavender oil to scent the cream. Put into a small screwtop pot. This is a good hand cream to use whenever the hands feel dry.

FENNEL CREAM

Make a strong infusion of fennel by pouring 120 ml/4 fl oz/½ cup of boiling water on to 1 tablespoon of the prepared herb and leaving it to cool; strain. In a pan blend together 2 teaspoons of arrowroot, 2 tablespoons of glycerine, 2 tablespoons of lavender water and the fennel infusion. Stir over gentle heat until the mixture is thick and creamy. Cool slightly and pour into a screwtop pot.

CHAMOMILE CREAM

In a pan over gentle heat melt together 1 tablespoon each of cocoa butter, sweet almond oil and white wax. Add 1 teaspoon of lemon juice and 1 tablespoon of a strong infusion of chamomile flowers. Make this by pouring 120 ml/4 fl oz/½ cup of boiling water on to 1 tablespoon of the prepared herb. Leave it to cool, then strain. When the hand cream mixture is melted, remove it from the heat and stir until cold. Pour into screwtop pots. This hand cream is for softening and whitening the skin while being also slightly astringent.

LADY'S MANTLE LOTION

Melt 2 teaspoons of carragheen moss in a little hot water. Add to this 2 tablespoons of glycerine, 4 tablespoons of rubbing alcohol and 2 tablespoons of a strong

infusion of lady's mantle. For the infusion pour 120 ml/ 4 fl oz/½ cup of boiling water on to 1 tablespoon of the prepared herb. Cool and then strain. Blend all hand lotion ingredients together well and pour into a screwtop jar, adding a few drops of a herb oil to scent the lotion.

MARIGOLD OIL

Good for dry rough skin, this hand oil can also be made using St John's wort. To 250 ml/8 fl oz/1 cup of sweet almond oil add 25 g/1 oz of marigold petals and put into a clear glass screwtop jar. Stand the jar on a sunny windowsill or in any other warm place and leave for 3 or 4 weeks, shaking the bottle once a day. At the end of that time heat the oil until the petals become crisp, strain and pour into jars.

COMFREY BARRIER CREAM

Work this cream into the hands thoroughly before commencing any dirty work. Mix together 2 teaspoons of kaolin, 2 teaspoons of sweet almond oil and 1 tablespoon of a strong infusion of comfrey made by pouring 120 ml/4 fl oz/½ cup of boiling water over 1 tablespoon of the prepared herb. Leave to cool, strain and use. When work is finished, wash off the cream with pure soap and finally use a herbal hand rinse.

NAILS

Any treatment given to your hands will also help the nails and the recommendations for hand care should be followed while carrying out specific treatment for the nails.

There are one or two herbs which are particularly good for strengthening the nails, being full of silicic acid, a substance known to improve nail structure.

Mix dried dill or horsetail with other herbs, or use each on its own to make up a hand rinse infusion. The two combined will help to strengthen weak nails.

Supplement your diet by taking brewer's yeast, vitamins A and D and by drinking a glass of horsetail or dill seed tea with a teaspoon of gelatine in it every night. Chew dill seeds whenever you can. Keep a little block of beeswax by your bedside and rub or buff this on to the nails each night to improve circulation. If you wear nail enamel, always use an oily remover to take it off, for it is kinder to the nails than pure acetone. Use orange sticks rather than metal implements for cleaning the nails and a large emery board, not a metal file for shaping.

HORSETAIL NAIL BATH

Make a strong infusion of horsetail by pouring 150 ml/ ¼ pint/⅔ cup of boiling water on to 2 tablespoons of chopped horsetail. Leave to cool; strain into a bottle. Use the infusion warm and soak the nails for 10 minutes every other day. On alternate days soak the nails in warm olive oil for 5 minutes.

FEET

Feet deserve more care and attention than they usually receive, and until they start to give trouble are invariably forgotten in the day-to-day care of the body. Massage, exercise, herbs and baths can all help to make life easier for the feet.

After a long tiring day, try to spend 10 minutes lying down with your feet higher than your head. Using a massage oil, gently massage the feet to relieve stiffness. Take one foot at a time in both hands and press the fingers into the arch with thumbs on top of the foot working down from ankle to toes. Rub along the base of the toes with your thumb and then give each toe a gentle pull.

Massage the leg from the foot to the knee gently working upwards to improve the circulation.

LIME (LINDEN) FLOWER OIL

Add as many lime (linden) flower blossoms as possible to 300 ml/½ pint/1¼ cups of sweet almond oil in a screwtop jar. Leave for 2 to 3 weeks in the sun or a warm place and shake the jar every other day. Finally heat the oil in a pan until the lime (linden) flowers become crisp, then strain and bottle. This is a pleasant massage oil which helps to reduce swollen tired feet. Mugwort or marigold, comfrey or burdock can all be used in the same way.

After washing the hands, dipping them into a soothing and refreshing infusion of lady's mantle.

HERBAL TALCUM POWDER

Mix together equal quantities of Fuller's earth and a dried powdered herb such as elder leaves or mugwort. Keep it in a jar with a perforated top and sprinkle a little in the shoes each day. It helps to prevent tired, aching and perspiring feet.

MUGWORT FOOT BATH

Make up a large quantity of mugwort infusion using 2 tablespoons of mugwort leaves to 600 ml/1 pint/2½ cups of boiling water. You will probably need about 3 litres/5 or 6 pints. Pour the boiling water on to the mugwort and divide the amount into two bowls. Keep one bowlful hot and let the other get cold. Put the feet alternately into the cold and then the hot infusion ending with the cold. Leave the feet in each infusion for about 5 minutes. Dry with a soft towel and sprinkle with talcum powder. This relieves tired swollen feet and is soothing at any time.

ROSEMARY FOOT BATH

Use rosemary in the proportion of 1 tablespoon to 2.25 litres/4 or 5 pints boiling water. Allow to stand for 15 minutes, strain and use while warm. Leave your feet in the infusion for 20 minutes. Juniper berries and mint can also be used as refreshing foot baths either on their own or mixed with rosemary.

HAIR

Since the appearance of one's hair is frequently a good indicator of the general state of health, it follows that the components of the daily diet can improve or spoil the appearance of the hair. While trying to follow a sensible eating plan, include plenty of green salads and herbs especially dill and watercress, root vegetables such as carrots, and leeks, liver, fresh fish and shellfish. To supplement the diet take brewer's yeast, vitamins A and D and calcium.

As an external treatment, try a good scalp exercise to increase the flow of blood to the roots of the hair. Press the fingertips down on to the scalp using a circular motion until you feel a slight tingling sensation, then move on to another position, gradually covering the whole scalp. Dip your fingers into an infusion of rosemary mixed with a few drops of rosemary oil to give greater effect to the massage of your scalp. Use a good bristle brush on the hair at least once a day to remove dust and distribute the oils secreted by the gland at the base of each hair follicle.

Herbs can play a vital role in keeping hair looking healthy and lustrous, stimulating its growth and strengthening it. Good herbs for the hair are nettle, horsetail, burdock root, chamomile, rosemary, red sage and parsley, southernwood and yarrow.

A simple infusion made of any one of those herbs (or decoction in the case of burdock root), rubbed daily into the scalp or used as a rinse after shampooing will stimulate hair growth and keep the scalp clean. Infusions of mixed herbs can be used for specific treatment; combine chamomile and yarrow flowers and use it on blonde hair to highlight the colour; combine sage and rosemary to use on dark hair for a lustrous sheen.

HERBAL HAIR OIL

To get the full benefit from a herbal hair oil it is necessary to extract the essential oil from the herb. Take 2 tablespoons of your chosen herb and crush and bruise it well or put it through a mincer (grinder). Place in a 250 ml/8 fl oz/1 cup bottle and fill it with 175 ml/6 fl oz/1¾ cups of sunflower oil. Put a cork in the bottle and leave it in a hot sunny position for at least 3 weeks, longer if there is only intermittent sun. Shake the bottle carefully every day. Strain, expressing all the oil out of the herb and repeat the process with another 2 tablespoons of the herb. Continue until the oil smells strongly of the herb. Obviously the more often the process is repeated the stronger and more effective will be the oil. The oils can be made from any one of the herbs for hair already mentioned.

Herbal hair oils can be used to massage the scalp at night or as a hair conditioner. Use a herbal hair oil as a once-a-week conditioner, leaving it on the head for as long as possible. First massage warm oil into the scalp, saturating the hair. Cover the hair with a plastic bath cap and then with a hot damp towel. After 30 minutes remove the coverings and shampoo the hair. Continue the treatment until the hair is once more in good condition.

After shampooing the hair with a good herbal shampoo and before the hair dries, use a herbal hair oil as a quick conditioner on a clean head. Rub a little warm oil on to the scalp and massage well. Use a herbal hair rinse then set and dry the hair in the usual way.

HERBAL SHAMPOOS

Shampooing the hair is an important part of hair care and should be carried out at least once a week. For those who prefer not to wash the hair too often a pleasant way to keep it clean and lustrous is to use a dry shampoo.

DRY SHAMPOO

This consists simply of dried powdered orris root available from a herbalist. It smells faintly of violets and if you wish can be mixed with an equal quantity of Fuller's earth to make it go further. Part the hair in sections across the scalp and sprinkle the shampoo on to each parting; use a salt shaker for even distribution and do not rub the shampoo into the scalp. When the whole head has been covered leave for 5 minutes, then vigorously brush the hair with long easy strokes until all the shampoo has been removed. Place a towel over your shoulders before brushing out.

HERBAL SHAMPOO FOR DANDRUFF

Beat together 2 egg whites, 1 tablespoon of green soft soap and 1 tablespoon of a strong infusion of nettle leaves. Make the infusion by pouring 120 ml/4 fl oz/½ cup of boiling water on to 1 tablespoon of chopped nettles. Allow to cool before straining.

Make up the shampoo just before you are ready to use it and brush the hair well before shampooing.

Rinsing fair hair in an infusion of chamomile flowers.

BASIC HERBAL SHAMPOO

Make a strong infusion of soapwort leaves and stems by just covering them with soft water in a pan. Bring slowly to the boil and simmer gently for 5 minutes. Strain and use as a shampoo base to which you can add an infusion of any one, or a mixture of, the herbs for hair which have already been mentioned. Use in the proportion of 3 parts soapwort infusion to 1 part herb infusion. The herb infusion must be very strong, and made by pouring 120 ml/4 fl oz/½ cup of boiling water on to 2 tablespoons of the chosen herb and left to get cold before straining and adding to the soapwort infusion.

After shampooing the hair use a suitable herb rinse to give body to the hair.

SETTING LOTION

If your hair is inclined to lose its set quickly and become limp, try the following lotion. Mix the strained juice of a lemon with 1 teaspoon of vodka or brandy and 2 teaspoons of a strong herbal infusion. Use rosemary for dark hair and chamomile for light hair.

BATH HERBS

Most people take a bath every day with the basic intention of getting clean. But there are many herbs which, when added to the water, transform the bath into a beauty treatment and can be soothing and healing, refreshing and stimulating according to your mood or needs. A herbal bath can soften the skin, provide a tonic and correct minor skin disorders.

PREPARATION OF HERBS

The simplest and easiest way to add herbs to your bath water, without needless mess, is to make 2 or 3 little drawstring bags out of cotton cloth or closely woven muslin (cheesecloth). Make them about 10 × 7.5 cm/ 4 × 3 in with a good long drawstring so that it can hang down well into the water. Hang the bag from the hot water tap deep into the bathtub so that the flow of hot water transmits the goodness of the herb as the bath is drawn. Alternatively use a round plastic container of the kind usually used for holding small blocks of disinfectant, using a long piece of tape looped over the tap.

Fill the muslin (cheesecloth) bags with the bath herb of your choice. To benefit still further from the herbs by making the water soft, mix them with either oatmeal or bran and fill the little bags with this mixture.

Where preferred, make up a strong infusion of single or mixed herbs and add about 1 litre/1¾ pints/4¼ cups to a normal size bath.

Lovage leaves or root Use crushed leaves or grated fresh cleaned roots in a bath bag or add a strong infusion to the water for a refreshing deodorizing bath on a hot day. Do not have the water too hot.

Chamomile flowers A soothing bath additive which is a good cleansing treatment: combine the chamomile with yarrow if you have oily skin.

Elder Use leaves, bark or flowers to provide a softening, healing skin cleanser.

Rosemary bath rub Add finely crushed rosemary leaves to oatmeal in a bath bag. Wet the bag and, standing in the bath, rub it quickly over the entire body using moderate pressure. Especially good for an excessively oil skin.

Valerian root Use a strong decoction in the bath water to calm the nerves and act as a tonic to the skin.

Peppermint leaves These can be bought in tea-bag form from a herbalist. Suspend 2 or 3 bags in the water, or use a muslin (cheesecloth) bag full of leaves, or a strong infusion for a soothing cooling bath, so refreshing in the summer. For those suffering from skin complaints mix horsetail with the peppermint for a beneficial bath.

Tonic herbal bath Add strong infusions of comfrey, nettle, dandelion and daisy to warm water for a tonic bath to revitalize the skin after the long winter months.

Other bath herbs to use are thyme, lavender, lime (linden) flower and marigold.

Herbal bath oils Mix 3 parts of glycerine to 1 part of herbal oil and add a teaspoon of this mixture to the bath water. Alternatively lightly rub all over the body with a herbal oil before getting into the bath.

Herbs for the bath: herb bags, herb-scented waters and herb vinegar.

HERB-SCENTED WATERS

Keep bottles of herb-scented waters in the bathroom or on the dressing table to use as a refreshing lotion. Add to the water in the bath or use them to scent the body afterwards. Dab the face with lotion in hot weather or use it as rinsing water for hands.

Fragrant waters are so easy to make that you can afford to be lavish. You can use any herb you like. The favourites are rosemary, lemon balm, bergamot, hyssop, lovage, violet, thyme and lemon thyme, chamomile and elder. Men might prefer a scented water using coriander or cinnamon or the spiciness of cloves.

CHAMOMILE WATER

Fill a jar with fresh or dried chamomile flowers and cover them with boiling water. Leave to cool slightly and then add surgical spirit in the proportion of 2 tablespoons of spirit to 1 litre/1¾ pints/4½ cups of water. Cover with a cloth and leave to get completely cold. Strain and pour into stoppered bottles. For other herb-scented waters using leaves or flowers follow the above directions.

SPICY CORIANDER WATER

Use coarsely ground or crushed seed infused in rubbing alcohol in the proportion 1 part seed to 5 parts spirit. Leave them in a covered jar for 3 to 4 weeks, shaking it frequently. Strain and store in screwtop bottles. If you use crushed cloves or broken cinnamon sticks, do not leave the spice in the spirit for longer than a week.

To make a scented water quickly use a strong infusion of any herb leaves or flowers and add 1 tablespoon of glycerine. This will keep for several days.

HERB VINEGARS

Nowadays vinegar is associated more with salads and sauces than with cosmetics. Nevertheless, a vinegar smelling strongly of an aromatic herb can be most refreshing to the skin and the scent lingers in the same way as a herb water; it also keeps for much longer.

Years ago a herb vinegar did double duty as both scent and disinfectant. Small vinaigrettes held by a chain and worn round the neck were ready to revive those feeling faint, to ease a headache and to refresh hot perspiring hands.

BASIC HERB VINEGAR

As the base, use a white or cider vinegar, or a good wine vinegar which is soft and mellow. To 250 ml/8 fl oz/1 cup of vinegar add the same amount of water. Put in a pan and heat until it is very nearly boiling. Remove from the heat and immediately add dried crushed herbs. Try using 1 tablespoon of lemon balm and 2 tablespoons of peppermint. Leave overnight, then strain the liquid into bottles. You can make a stronger version if you wish and use any one herb or a mixture of herbs of your choice. Suggested herbs include violet, thyme, southernwood, lavender, rosemary, lovage or eau-de-cologne mint.

PERFUMING THE HOUSE

Sweet-scented and colourful pot-pourris, sachets, cushions, lavender bags and pomanders make delightful Christmas and birthday gifts.

POT-POURRI

A pot-pourri is a mixture of sweet smelling materials, chiefly dried flower petals. To these are added aromatic herbs, seeds and spices, and sometimes essential oils or spirits.

There are no hard and fast rules to follow when making pot-pourris but a few basic points should be remembered. The petals and leaves must be carefully dried to preserve their colour and scent so that they will remain fragrant for a long time. To add bulk and extra colour to your pot-pourri dry brightly coloured flowers and buds, even those without much scent of their own. Include larkspur, marigolds, anchusa, grape hyacinth and the curry plant, which does not retain its rather strong smell when dried.

Pot-pourri mixtures can be made dry or moist. The latter, generally made moist with brandy or orange peel, is best kept in china jars with perforated lids. Stored in this way the mixture will stay fragrant for many years. Dry pot-pourris are placed in open glass or china bowls around the house with a lid put on only when no one is in the room. Colour is important in dry mixtures to make them look as attractive as possible.

The bulk of most pot-pourris is made up of strong-smelling rose petals from the sweet-scented wild dog rose as well as the sweetbriar or eglantine rose. Gather these when dry and spread out on sheets of paper in a shaded but airy room. Other flowers and herbs especially good in pot-pourris are: sage, costmary, bay, lemon balm, eau-de-cologne mint, peppermint, bergamot, myrtle, rosemary and lemon verbena leaves. As well as rose petals add flowers of violets, summer flowering jasmine, lily of the valley, lavender, red bergamot, chamomile, philadelphus (mock orange) and the sweet-smelling pinks. Once the fragrant flowers and leaves have been collected and dried, mix them all up in a bowl and add a fixative.

A fixative of some kind must be added to pot-pourris to blend all the fragrances together and to retard the evaporation of essential oils which provide the scents. The fixatives most often used are: common salt for use in moist pot-pourris; orris root which comes from the rhizomes of *Iris florentina*, and gum benzoin, from a tree native to the Far East. Both the last 2 have a fragrant scent of their own which enhances the pot-pourris. Crushed or ground spices are also added to the mixtures. For these choose from coriander, nutmeg, cloves, cinnamon, allspice and mace, anise and tonka beans or vanilla pods (beans). Use 1 tablespoon of fixative to about 1.2 litres/2 pints/5 cups of petals whether you are making a moist or dry pot-pourri.

Although oils may be added to strengthen the scents they should be used with care, for too many different ones will be overpowering. Try rosemary, geranium, lavender, rose, peppermint or bergamot oil.

A SIMPLE MOIST POT-POURRI

Use a large earthenware crock and put in a 10 cm/4 in deep layer of rose petals. Immediately over this put a thin layer of common salt. Continue to add alternate layers of petals and salt until the jar is filled. Cover and leave for about 10 days, or until the mixture has settled, in a dark but airy place. Break up the rose and salt mixture with a wooden spoon and add dried orange peel, crushed clove and orris root. Blend all together and leave, covered and sealed, for 5 or 6 weeks. Shake frequently to keep it well mixed. Add a few drops of essential oil if required and reseal for another 2 weeks. The pot-pourri is then ready to put into small pottery jars.

LEMON POT-POURRI

To make a dry fragrant pot-pourri use 4 parts of dried rose petals to 1 part each of lemon verbena, lemon thyme and lavender flowers. Mix with the finely grated rind of an orange and a lemon. Leave for two days then add the fixatives – orris root and gum benzoin – and the spices – finely ground allspice and cloves. Use in the proportion of 15 g/½ oz of each spice and fixative to 9 litres/2 gallons/20 pints of petals, flowers and leaves. Stir the pot-pourri every day for a week, then put out into open glass or china bowls.

HERB CUSHIONS

Traditionally cushions of dried sweet-smelling herbs have always been used to calm the nerves, induce sleep and soothe aching heads. The little cushions, now made small enough to take from room to room or when travelling, are the direct descendant of the herb-stuffed mattress. Herbs such as lavender and lady's bedstraw were in common use before the development of modern mattress fillings.

To make the cushion use a piece of muslin (cheese-cloth) cut to size and sewn firmly round 3 sides ready to fill with herbs. Use crumbled, not powdered, herbs and stuff the cushion as full as possible. Sew up the fourth side. For a sleep cushion add to the mixture a few drops of rose or lavender oil so that the herbs will not crackle inside it. Make the outer cover as attractive as you wish in cotton, linen, silk or any other fine fabric through which the scents can pass. Choose soft colours, plain or prints, or embroider your own covers. The advantage of a slip cover is that it can easily be changed and laundered without disturbing the herb mixture.

Basic herbs for scented cushions are peppermint, sage, lemon balm and lavender, to which you can add dill, thyme, marjoram, woodruff, angelica, rosemary, bergamot and lemon verbena.

HEADACHE CUSHION

Use equal quantities of peppermint, spearmint and eau-de-cologne mint with bergamot, and 1 tablespoon of crushed orris root as the fixative. Fill the muslin (cheesecloth) and use a slip cover of a soft green printed cotton to enhance by its colour the soothing nature of the cushion.

HOP

A simple cushion of hop cones sprinkled with a few drops of vodka makes an effective little pillow for those who cannot sleep or who suffer from asthma.

LEMON-SCENTED

Mix together 1 part each of lemon balm, costmary and lemon thyme with 2 parts lemon verbena for a lovely fresh scent. Add a trace of valerian if you like it, but not so much that it overpowers the other scents.

SPICE-SCENTED

Use equal quantities of rose petals, rosemary and spearmint with a few crushed cloves. Add a little valerian, but not enough to overpower the other scents.

Attractive sweet-scented pot-pourri, herb cushions and sachets.

HERB SACHETS

A herb sachet is distinguished from herb cushions and moth bags by the fact that it includes only the strongest smelling herbs.

In years past herb sachets were used for perfuming linen and clothes, laid on bookshelves, in cupboards, carried in pockets, tied to the bedpost and slipped amongst sheets of writing paper. The favourites of old were lavender and violet, rosemary and rose, for they were heavily scented and easily available. Other herbs used were pot marjoram, costmary, basil, thyme and lemon thyme as well as the milder spices, anise, caraway and coriander. Nowadays you can add lemon verbena, sweet-leaved geranium and mint to this list. All these herbs are strong enough to use in sachets without the need for a fixative, but the addition of a little dried orange or lemon peel will retain the scents.

To make a herb sachet, use fine material such as cotton lawn which is most suitable, and make up small pads about 10 × 7.5 cm/4 × 3 in in size so they will lie flat. When filled, bind the edges of the pads with tape or ribbon to make them stronger. Fill with a single herb from the list above or make up your own mixture.

A MIXED HERB SACHET

For a lovely fresh clean-smelling sachet for general use, use 2 parts each of lavender and lemon thyme and add 1 part of lemon balm.

LAVENDER

Lavender is one of the most versatile and best-known of all herbs. Its clean, fresh, long-lasting scent makes lavender an excellent herb for using in many different ways in the home, and made into small gifts it always seems to be welcomed. There are several varieties of lavender and, with their deep scents and the lovely colours of its pink, white and blue flowers it is especially attractive.

USING LAVENDER

1 Set little bowls of the lovely dried flowerheads in the hall or cloakroom to dip your fingers into as you pass by.
2 Rub fresh lavender flowers from the heads and use them at weddings to shower the bride and groom in place of confetti.
3 Use lavender on its own to fill sachets and cushions made of organdie, through which you can see the colour; bind them prettily with ribbon or silk. Keep a sachet in your pocket or purse to refresh you in a stuffy room or when travelling. Use the cushion to relieve a nervous headache. Place sachets amongst your lingerie and handkerchiefs.
4 Make little lavender bundles using about 10 fresh long-stemmed flower heads to each bundle. Fit the heads together and bind them firmly with narrow ribbon or thread ending at the top of the stems. Carefully bend back the stems, gently pressing them to enclose the heads completely. Bind strong thread around the stems just below the bulge of the flower-

heads and cut the stems off neatly. Cover the thread and stalk ends with ribbon and leave a loop for hanging up the bundle.

5 Make lavender bags of muslin (cheesecloth) using fresh flowers and tie them up with a long piece of tape. Loop the tape over the hot water tap when running a bath for a refreshing soak after a tiring day or before an evening party.

6 Make lavender water by putting together in a glass screwtop jar 1 part of lavender flowers to 4 parts of rubbing alcohol. Leave for 3 or 4 weeks shaking it every other day. Strain and pour into small stoppered jars.

POMANDERS

Traditionally pomanders were small pieces of a strongly scented fixative called ambergris which comes from the sperm whale. The word pomander comes from the French *pomme d'ambre*, meaning 'apple of ambergris'. These little apple-shaped pieces were enclosed in beautifully made cases of gold, silver, ivory or wood. They were worn on chains round the neck or waist and acted as a protection against infection and un-pleasant smells.

Nowadays there are pomanders made of china. They are almost round and have perforations in the top through which the scents can pass, and are simply filled with a pot-pourri mixture.

The homemade pomander which has come to be

Dried lavender flowers, lavender bags and pomanders.

associated with Christmas is an orange stuck with cloves. Easy to make, it is a charming gift for a friend and the spicy scent lasts for years.

A CITRUS POMANDER

Use an orange or a lemon and push cloves into the fruit close together until it is completely covered. Make small holes using a meat skewer so that the cloves will go easily into the fruit. Put the fruit into a bowl and pour over it 3 or 4 tablespoons of powdered orris root. Keep scooping up the orris and pouring it over the fruit until it is well covered. Leave it in the orris until it has dried out or put it in a bag in a dark cupboard or drawer. Make these pomanders 3 or 4 weeks before Christmas.

MOTH BAGS

There are a number of fragrant herbs which, when dried, act effectively as moth repellents. Lay them amongst linen and blankets which are not in frequent use or put them between layers of winter clothes when in store over the summer months. If coats and suits are stored on coat hangers, attach a moth bag to each hanger by a piece of ribbon and cover the clothing with a polythene (plastic) garment bag.

The sweet-smelling herbs add a pleasant delicate scent to the clothes and linen not at all like the rather harsh strong smell of proprietary camphorated moth balls which lingers on clothes for so long.

To make moth bags cut out pieces of thin cotton cloth the required size. A bag 7.5 cm/3 in square would be sufficient to provide protection for a blanket; several of these would be needed for a drawerful of clothes. Alternatively, make a muslin (cheesecloth) bag to fit the drawer exactly and fill it with a thin even layer of herbs. Coat hanger herb bags could be triangular in shape with each side 5 cm/2 in long. The shape and design of the moth bag can be printed or plain, whichever you prefer. Dried herbs can be used on their own or in mixtures and the moth bag will be effective over a longer period if the herbs are mixed with a crushed spice such as cinnamon or cloves.

The moth-protective herbs, which should be dried and crumbled, are southernwood, thyme, santolina (cotton lavender), mint, mugwort, woodruff, rosemary, sage, sweet marjoram and lavender.

SINGLE HERB MOTH BAGS

Choose from southernwood, woodruff, mint, rosemary or mugwort and to 1 heaped tablespoon of the herb add 3 or 4 pieces of chopped orris root or 1 teaspoon of crushed cinnamon stick.

MIXED HERB MOTH BAGS

1 Take a handful each of southernwood, thyme and tansy and mix with 1 tablespoon of crushed clove.

2 Mix a handful each of mugworth, mint, santolina and rosemary with 1 tablespoon of crushed cori-ander.

3 Use 2 tablespoons of lavender flowers with 1 each of sweet marjoram and woodruff.

4 Mix sage, rosemary and southernwood in equal quantities and add a few pieces of chopped orris root.

COOKING WITH HERBS

From ancient times herbs have been cultivated for culinary and medicinal purposes; yet in recent years the use of fresh herbs in cookery has been sadly neglected. In the fourteenth, fifteenth and sixteenth centuries, herbs were considered of prime importance in England; every monastery and manor house had its own herb garden. Herbs at that time were rated higher than vegetables, although the two were so closely linked as to be almost inseparable. In fact, the word 'vegetable' has been in use for less than 200 years and many of the plants growing in our vegetable gardens today were once known as 'pot' herbs. The plants we consider to be culinary herbs, such as marjoram, tarragon, rosemary and basil, were known as 'sweet' herbs. Throughout the centuries the cooks developed the art of combining and contrasting the different flavours to bring out the very best in a favourite dish. Flowers also had their place in the herb garden, for any flower whose petal or leaf could be put to some culinary or medicinal use was automatically classified as a herb. Thus our earliest herb gardens included lilies, damask and briar roses, marigolds, mallow and gilly-flowers. The petals and flower-heads were used to add colour to salad dishes.

The familiar plan of the formal herb garden, with geometric beds bordered with lavender, hyssop or rosemary, only evolved in the sixteenth century when the kitchen and flower gardens were for the first time cultivated as separate entities; and the herb garden accordingly decreased in size.

In the last 150 years, the use of herbs in England has declined almost to the point of extinction. Apart from mint sauce, sage and onion stuffing, and the use of chopped parsley as a garnish, they have hardly rated as worthy of cultivation. Fortunately, however, other European countries have been more faithful to the old traditions, and in France particularly the belief in the health-giving powers of tisanes made from infusions of herbs has helped to perpetuate their growth and use. In Italy also, the faith in the cleansing powers of young herbs, taken in the early spring in the form of broths and infusions, has remained constant. With the innovation of the *nouvelle cuisine* and its related *cuisine minceur* in recent years, the value of herbs has once again been made evident. For herbs are at their best in light wholesome dishes of this sort; they can be used to advantage in uncooked dishes, and their addition to our diet adds only vitamins and healing properties, without weight or richness.

Soups

Soups, and vegetable soups in particular, are among my favourite foods. They also provide one of the best opportunities for using herbs, and one of the simplest ways to learn to cook with them. I like to use them for the most part individually; by adding one well-chosen herb to a soup of blended cooked vegetables it is possible to produce an almost perfect dish.

The main use of herbs in soups is as a contrast, both in flavour and in colour. Since most soups involve prolonged boiling, which induces the more delicate herbs to lose their flavour, colour and vitamin content, herbs are best added, uncooked, to the finished soup just before serving. By adding a couple of spoonfuls of finely chopped lovage to a soup of blended puréed root vegetables, for instance, one gains the contrast of a quite separate flavour – a slightly hot, peppery taste redolent of celery – against the background of a bland creamy base, and the visual appeal of bright green against the warm orangey colour of the soup itself. Used in this way, even the most delicate herbs retain their flavour, while the stronger ones, like lovage and parsley, are not allowed to dominate the dish. I like to add chopped parsley in large amounts, and for this reason often have a bowl of it on the table, in case others like it only in moderation.

Infusion is another method used for flavouring soups with herbs. In this instance, the herb is left to stand for 20 to 30 minutes in a liquid which has been brought almost to boiling point, then covered and drawn to the side of the fire. The liquid, usually stock, sometimes cream, is then strained and used as the base for a light soup. A little of the same herb, finely chopped, is added as a garnish at the last moment. Tarragon, chervil and dill are all good used in this way. Chervil has a subtle taste like a more delicate parsley and it is one of my three or four favourite herbs. It makes a most delicious soup, in combination with chicken stock, lemon juice and egg yolks.

I always use fresh herbs in soups, as dried herbs look so dull. Even so, many soups can be served throughout the winter, since parsley at least is always available. Pots of bush basil brought into the house in early autumn can be used until mid-winter; when left in a sunny spot they will continue to produce new leaves for quite some time.

Opposite: Bean soup with parsley; Carrot and turnip soup with coriander; Celery consommé with lovage

BEAN SOUP WITH PARSLEY

Metric/Imperial	American
200g/7oz dried haricot beans	1 cup navy beans
1 onion	1 onion
2 carrots	2 carrots
2 leeks	2 leeks
2 sticks celery	2 stalks celery
4 tablespoons olive oil	¼ cup olive oil
225g/8oz tomatoes	½lb tomatoes
1.5 litres/2½ pints chicken stock or game stock	6¼ cups chicken stock or game stock
sea salt and black pepper	sea salt and black pepper
6 tablespoons chopped parsley	6 tablespoons chopped parsley

Before cooking, soak the beans in water for 3 to 4 hours. Using fresh unsalted water, cook them until tender, about 45 minutes. Drain, reserving the water. Peel the onion, and clean the carrots, leeks and celery. Chop the vegetables. Heat the oil in a saucepan and cook the onion until slightly softened. Add the carrots, leeks and celery and cook for 5 to 6 minutes. Skin and chop the tomatoes and add them to the other vegetables. Cook for a further 3 to 4 minutes then heat the stock and pour it on. (If you do not have enough stock, use some of the cooking liquid from the beans.) Bring to the boil and simmer for 30 minutes, until the vegetables are soft. Add the beans and reheat. Add salt and pepper to taste, then stir in the chopped parsley. This makes a substantial soup for 6 to 8.

CARROT AND TURNIP SOUP WITH CORIANDER

Metric/Imperial	American
225g/8oz carrots	½lb carrots
225g/8oz turnips	½lb turnips
40g/1½oz butter	3 tablespoons butter
1 litre/1¾ pints chicken stock	4¼ cups chicken stock
sea salt and black pepper	sea salt and black pepper
2 tablespoons sour cream	2 tablespoons sour cream
2 teaspoons ground coriander	2 teaspoons ground coriander
1 teaspoon ground cumin	1 teaspoon ground cumin
1 tablespoon finely chopped coriander leaves	1 tablespoon finely chopped coriander leaves

Clean and slice the carrots and turnips. Heat the butter in a saucepan and stew the carrots and turnips gently for about 6 minutes, stirring now and then. Heat the stock and pour it on to the vegetables. Bring to the boil, add salt and pepper, and simmer for 30 minutes, covered. Put through a coarse food mill and return to the clean pan. Reheat, adding more salt and pepper as needed, and stir in the sour cream. Add the spices and the chopped coriander leaves, mix well, and stand for 5 minutes before serving.

CAULIFLOWER SOUP WITH CHERVIL

Metric/Imperial	American
1 medium cauliflower	1 medium cauliflower
50g/2oz butter	¼ cup butter
900ml/1½ pints chicken stock	3¾ cups chicken stock
sea salt and black pepper	sea salt and black pepper
4 tablespoons thin cream	¼ cup light cream
3 tablespoons chopped chervil	3 tablespoons chopped chervil

Cut the cauliflower into sprigs and wash them well. Chop the sprigs. Heat the butter in a heavy pan. Toss the chopped cauliflower in the butter for 4 minutes, then add the heated stock. Bring to the boil, cover the pan, and simmer for 20 minutes. Purée in a blender until smooth, then return to a clean pan and reheat. Add salt and pepper to taste and stir in the cream. Add the chopped chervil and stand for a few minutes before serving. This soup is also good cold; in this case, chill it before adding the chervil.

CELERY CONSOMMÉ WITH LOVAGE

Metric/Imperial	American
1 large head celery	1 large bunch celery
1.2 litres/2 pints game or beef stock	5 cups game or beef stock
sea salt and black pepper	sea salt and black pepper
lemon juice, to taste	lemon juice, to taste
2 tablespoons chopped lovage	2 tablespoons chopped lovage

Scrub the celery well and chop it roughly, root, leaves and all. Put it in a pan with the cold stock and bring very slowly to the boil. Cover and simmer for 30 minutes, until it is well flavoured. Strain the stock and return to a clean pan. Reheat, adding salt and pepper to taste, with a little lemon juice. Stir in the chopped lovage and stand, covered, for 3 or 4 minutes before serving.

CHERVIL SOUP

Metric/Imperial	American
3 leeks	3 leeks
350g/12oz potatoes	¾lb potatoes
50g/2oz butter	¼ cup butter
50g/2oz chopped chervil or chervil and parsley mixed	1½ cups chopped chervil or chervil and parsley mixed
900ml/1½ pints chicken stock	3¾ cups chicken stock
juice of ½ lemon	juice of ½ lemon
1 tablespoon dill vinegar or white wine vinegar	1 tablespoon dill vinegar or white wine vinegar
sea salt and black pepper	sea salt and black pepper
1 large egg yolk	1 large egg yolk
4 tablespoons whipped cream	¼ cup whipped cream

Wash and slice the leeks; peel and slice the potatoes. Melt the butter in a saucepan and stew the leeks for 4 minutes. Add the potatoes and the chervil and cook for a further 2 minutes. Heat the stock and pour it on to the vegetables. Cover and simmer for 25 minutes. Cool slightly, then purée in a blender until smooth and return to a clean pan. Reheat, adding the juice of half a lemon and the vinegar. Add salt and pepper to taste.

Beat the egg yolk in a small bowl, stir in 3 to 4 tablespoons of the hot soup and mix with the egg yolk. Stir this mixture into the soup for a moment or two without allowing it to boil. Pour into cups and garnish each one with a spoonful of whipped cream. (This soup can be made with a mixture of parsley and chervil or parsley alone when chervil is unobtainable.)

QUICK CHERVIL SOUP

Metric/Imperial	American
3 eggs	3 eggs
3 tablespoons chopped chervil	3 tablespoons chopped chervil
1 litre/1¾ pints chicken stock	4¼ cups chicken stock
sea salt and black pepper	sea salt and black pepper
squeeze of lemon juice	squeeze of lemon juice

Break the eggs into a bowl and beat with the chopped chervil. Heat the stock in a saucepan to boiling point and pour a few spoonfuls on to the beaten eggs. Stir vigorously, then return the egg mixture to the pan containing the rest of the stock. Stir over a gentle heat until slightly thickened, without allowing it to boil. Add salt and pepper and a squeeze of lemon juice. Serve immediately.

CURRIED CORIANDER SOUP

Metric/Imperial	American
25g/1oz butter	2 tablespoons butter
1 teaspoon ground coriander	1 teaspoon ground coriander
½ teaspoon ground cumin	½ teaspoon ground cumin
2 tablespoons flour	2 tablespoons flour
900ml/1½ pints strong chicken stock	3¾ cups strong chicken stock
juice of ½ lemon	juice of ½ lemon
sea salt and black pepper	sea salt and black pepper
150ml/¼ pint thin cream	⅔ cup light cream
50g/2oz cooked rice	⅓ cup cooked rice
2 tablespoons chopped coriander leaves	2 tablespoons chopped coriander leaves

Heat the butter in a saucepan and stir in the ground coriander and cumin. Stir over a low heat for 1 minute before adding the flour. Continue to stir for 2 minutes, then add the heated stock. Stir until blended, then simmer for 4 minutes. Add lemon juice to taste, and salt and pepper. Stir in the cream and the cooked rice. When the soup is heated through, add the chopped coriander leaves and stand for a moment or two before serving.

DUCK SOUP WITH PURSLANE AND GINGER

Metric/Imperial
1 small duckling
1.5 litres/2½ pints cold
 water
1 onion
1 carrot
2 sticks celery
1 bay leaf
3 sprigs parsley
1 bunch purslane or
 watercress
sea salt and black peppercorns
25g/1oz root ginger
2 tablespoons tarragon or
 dill vinegar
2 tablespoons chopped
 chives

American
1 small duckling
6¼ cups cold water
1 onion
1 carrot
2 stalks celery
1 bay leaf
3 sprigs parsley
1 bunch purslane or
 watercress
sea salt and black peppercorns
1oz ginger root
2 tablespoons tarragon or
 dill vinegar
2 tablespoons chopped
 chives

Start to make this soup the day before you plan to serve it. Put the duckling in a pan with the cold water. Add the halved onion, sliced carrot and celery, bay leaf and parsley. Pick the tips off the purslane (or watercress), set them aside and add the stalks to the pan. Throw in some salt and 8 or 9 black peppercorns. Bring to the boil and simmer gently for 1 hour, or a little longer, until the duckling is just cooked. Lift it out and cut off the best meat. Wrap the meat in cling film (Saran wrap) and set aside. Return the carcass to the pan. Continue to cook for another hour, adding more water if necessary. Strain the liquid and discard the vegetables. Leave the soup to cool before putting it in the refrigerator.

The next day, remove all fat from the surface and taste the soup. If the flavour is too weak, reduce the quantity of liquid by fast boiling. If the flavour is satisfactory, reheat the soup in a clean pan, adding the roughly chopped purslane (or watercress) tips, the sliced root ginger, the diced meat of the bird, and more salt and pepper as needed. Stir in the vinegar and the chopped chives and serve.

If you do not have any tarragon or dill vinegar, substitute a tablespoonful each of lemon juice and white wine vinegar. A cheaper version of this soup can be made using a joint of duck and some chicken wings.

Above: Chervil Soup; Duck soup with purslane and ginger

LENTIL AND HERB SOUP

Metric/Imperial
100g/4oz lentils, red or
    brown
1.2 litres/2 pints stock:
    veal, chicken, game or
    beef
1 small onion
1½ tablespoons olive oil
1 clove garlic
100g/4oz spinach beet,
    or spinach
sea salt and black pepper
50g/2oz chopped mixed
    herbs: sorrel, parsley,
    chervil, tarragon,
    lovage and lemon
    thyme
juice of ½ small lemon
150ml/¼ pint natural
    yogurt or buttermilk

American
½ cup lentils, red or
    brown
5 cups stock: veal
    chicken, game or
    beef
1 small onion
1½ tablespoons olive oil
1 clove garlic
¼lb spinach
sea salt and black pepper
1½ cups chopped mixed
    herbs: sorrel, parsley,
    chervil, tarragon,
    lovage and lemon
    thyme
juice of ½ small lemon
⅔ cup unflavored yogurt
    or buttermilk

Wash the lentils and pick over carefully, removing any small stones. Put them in a large pan with the stock. Bring to the boil and simmer until they are soft – 30 minutes for red lentils, and 45 minutes for brown.

Peel and chop the onion. Heat the oil in a frying pan (skillet) and sauté the onion until soft and golden, adding the finely minced garlic halfway through. Wash the spinach beet (or spinach), cut in slices and add to the lentils when they are soft, with salt and pepper to taste. Simmer until the spinach is cooked, about 8 minutes, then add the onion and garlic and the roughly chopped herbs. Simmer for a further 2 to 3 minutes, then cool slightly. Purée in a blender and add a little lemon juice – about 1 tablespoon – and the yogurt or buttermilk. Serve immediately, or, if it is necessary to reheat, do so very carefully, without allowing it to boil. This soup is also good served cold.

TARRAGON CONSOMMÉ

Metric/Imperial	American
900ml/1½ pints chicken stock	3¾ cups chicken stock
1½ tablespoons chopped tarragon	1½ tablespoons chopped tarragon
sea salt and black pepper	sea salt and black pepper

Heat the stock in a saucepan. Put the chopped tarragon in a mortar and pound. Add 150ml/¼ pint/⅔ cup of the boiling stock gradually, pounding all the time, then leave to stand for 5 minutes. Pour the contents of the mortar (or blender) back into the remaining stock in the saucepan and reheat, adding salt and pepper as required. Serve in cups, either plain, or with a tarragon dumpling in each cup (see page 195).

VARIATIONS

Follow the recipe for *Tarragon Consommé*, substituting 1 tablespoon of chopped lovage and ½ tablespoon of chopped parsley for the chopped tarragon. Serve alone, or with a lovage dumpling in each cup (see page 195).

Follow the recipe for *Tarragon Consommé*, substituting 1½ tablespoons of chopped chervil for the tarragon, and using veal stock instead of chicken stock. Serve alone, or with a chervil dumpling (see page 195).

Follow the recipe for *Tarragon Consommé*, substituting 1½ tablespoons of chopped dill for the tarragon, and beef stock for the chicken stock. Serve alone, or with a dill dumpling in each cup (see page 195).

BUTTERMILK AND DILL SOUP

Metric/Imperial	American
50g/2oz butter	¼ cup butter
4 leeks	4 leeks
275g/10oz potatoes	10oz potatoes
600ml/1 pint chicken stock	2½ cups chicken stock
sea salt and black pepper	sea salt and black pepper
600ml/1 pint buttermilk	2½ cups buttermilk
6 tablespoons chopped dill	6 tablespoons chopped dill

Heat the butter in a saucepan. Wash and slice the leeks and cook them gently for 8 minutes. Add the peeled and thickly sliced potatoes. Stir well to mix, then add the heated stock with salt and pepper to taste. Cover and simmer for 25 to 30 minutes, until soft. Cool slightly, then purée in a blender in batches with the buttermilk. Adjust the seasoning and chill. Stir in the chopped dill shortly before serving.

Left: Lentil and herb soup

Above: Preparation for vegetable soup

VEGETABLE SOUP WITH CHERVIL

Metric/Imperial	American
225g/8oz carrots	½lb carrots
1.2 litres/2 pints chicken stock	5 cups chicken stock
225g/8oz turnips	½lb turnips
350g/12oz courgettes	¾lb zucchini
sea salt and black pepper	sea salt and black pepper
4 tablespoons thick cream	¼ cup heavy cream
2 tablespoons chopped chervil	2 tablespoons chopped chervil

Peel the carrots, cut them in thick slices and put them in a saucepan with the stock. Bring to the boil and simmer for 5 minutes. Add the turnips, peeled and cut in chunks, and cook for a further 10 minutes. Add the courgettes (zucchini), unpeeled and cut in thick slices, and cook for 12 to 15 minutes more, or until all the vegetables are soft. Push through a coarse food mill or purée very briefly in a blender. Reheat, adding salt and pepper. Stir in the cream and the chopped chervil and serve. (When chervil is not available, parsley can be substituted.)

FENNEL CONSOMMÉ WITH LOVAGE

Metric/Imperial	American
1 large head Florence fennel	1 large root fennel
900ml/1½ pints game or chicken stock	3¾ cups game or chicken stock
1 tablespoon lemon juice	1 tablespoon lemon juice
sea salt and black pepper	sea salt and black pepper
2 tablespoons chopped lovage	2 tablespoons chopped lovage

Scrub the fennel and cut it in thin slices. Put it in a saucepan with the stock. Bring to the boil and simmer for 25 to 30 minutes, or until the fennel is soft. Strain the soup and reheat, adding lemon juice if needed, and salt and pepper to taste. Stir in the chopped lovage and stand for 3 to 4 minutes before serving.

FISH SOUP WITH FENNEL

Metric/Imperial	American
450g/1lb plaice or lemon sole, filleted	1lb flounder, filleted
bones from the fish	bones from the fish
1 bay leaf	1 bay leaf
4 stalks parsley	4 stalks parsley
2 stalks lovage	2 stalks lovage
1.5 litres/2½ pints cold water	6¼ cups cold water
sea salt and 6 black peppercorns	sea salt and 6 black peppercorns
1 small onion	1 small onion
1 carrot	1 carrot
1 leek	1 leek
225g/8oz hake or monkfish	½lb hake
25g/1oz butter	2 tablespoons butter
1 tablespoon flour	1 tablespoon flour
2 tablespoons sour cream	2 tablespoons sour cream
2 tablespoons chopped fennel leaves	2 tablespoons chopped fennel leaves

Put the fish bones in a pan with the bay leaf, parsley and lovage. Cover with the cold water, add salt and peppercorns, and bring to the boil. Simmer for 30 minutes. Peel and chop the onion and carrot. Trim and chop the leek. Put them in a saucepan. Pour the fish stock over the vegetables through a sieve (strainer). Bring to the boil and simmer for another 30 minutes, then put in the hake. Simmer for 15 minutes, or until the hake is cooked. Remove the hake and put the plaice (flounder) fillets into the pan. Simmer for 5 minutes, then remove them. Cool the soup slightly, then purée it in a blender.

Melt the butter in a clean pan, stir in the flour and cook for 1 minute. Stir in the blended soup and simmer for 3 minutes, stirring. Add salt and pepper to taste. Take the hake off the bone and chop it; skin the plaice (flounder) fillets and chop them. Put both sorts of fish into the soup and stir in the sour cream. When all is hot, add the chopped fennel and stand, covered, for 3 to 4 minutes before serving. Serve as it is, or with a fennel dumpling (see page 195) in each bowl.

MUSHROOM SOUP WITH CHERVIL

Metric/Imperial	American
225g/8oz mushrooms	½lb mushrooms
900ml/1½ pints chicken stock	3¾ cups chicken stock
150ml/¼ pint sour cream	⅔ cup sour cream
juice of ½ lemon	juice of ½ lemon
sea salt and black pepper	sea salt and black pepper
3 tablespoons chopped chervil	3 tablespoons chopped chervil

Wipe the mushrooms clean on a damp cloth. Do not peel. Chop them, stalks and all. Heat the stock in a saucepan and put in the chopped mushrooms. Simmer for 15 minutes, then cool slightly. Purée in a blender and add the sour cream. Blend until really smooth, then add about 1½ tablespoons lemon juice to taste, and salt and black pepper. Pour into a clean pan and reheat, adding the chopped chervil a few moments before serving.

NETTLE SOUP

Metric/Imperial	American
450g/1lb potatoes	1lb potatoes
225g/8oz young nettles	½lb young nettles
50g/2oz butter	¼ cup butter
900ml/1½ pints chicken stock	3¾ cups chicken stock
sea salt and black pepper	sea salt and black pepper
4 tablespoons sour cream	¼ cup sour cream

Peel the potatoes and cut them in thick slices. Wash the nettles and chop them coarsely. (Only the top 5 to 6cm/2 to 3in of the young nettles must be used.)

Cook the potatoes for 10 minutes in salted water; drain. Melt the butter in a saucepan, add the nettles and stew gently for 10 minutes. Heat the stock. Add the parboiled potatoes and the stock, bring to the boil, and simmer for another 10 minutes. When all is soft, cool slightly then purée in a blender. After blending, return the soup to a clean pan. Add salt and pepper to taste and stir in the sour cream.

This soup can only be made for a few weeks in the spring, when the nettles are very young and tender.

PARSLEY CHOWDER

Metric/Imperial	American
25g/1oz butter	2 tablespoons butter
1 onion	1 onion
675g/1½lb haddock, filleted	1½lb haddock, filleted
450g/1lb potatoes	1lb potatoes
sea salt and black pepper	sea salt and black pepper
300ml/½ pint thin cream	1¼ cups light cream
6 tablespoons chopped parsley	6 tablespoons chopped parsley

Heat the butter in a heavy pan. Peel the onion and chop it quite finely. Stir it around in the butter until coated with fat. Cut the skinned fillets of fish into neat pieces and lay them on top of the onion. Peel the potatoes and cut them in slices about 0.5cm/¼in thick. Put them in layers over the fish, sprinkling with salt and pepper.

Add enough hot water to come level with the potatoes, and bring to the boil. Cover the pan and simmer for 40 minutes. When the potatoes are soft, heat the cream and add it to the pan. Stir very gently without breaking up the potatoes. Add salt and pepper to taste, and stir in the chopped parsley. Serve with water biscuits (crackers) or matzos.

Opposite: Fish soup with fennel

Below: Parsley chowder

PARSLEY SOUP

Metric/Imperial	American
1 large onion	1 large onion
2 large carrots	2 large carrots
50g/2oz butter	¼ cup butter
150g/5oz potato	1 large potato
900ml/1½ pints chicken stock	3¾ cups chicken stock
sea salt and black pepper	sea salt and black pepper
25g/1oz parsley, heads only	¾ cup parsley, heads only

Peel the onion, clean the carrots and slice them all very thinly; there should be roughly equal amounts of each. Heat the butter in a pan and stew the onion and carrot gently for about 6 minutes. Add the peeled and thinly sliced potato. After 3 more minutes pour on the heated stock. Add salt and pepper and simmer, covered, for 35 minutes, then leave to cool slightly. Purée in a blender with the parsley, then reheat, adding extra seasoning as required.

GREEN PEA SOUP WITH MINT

Metric/Imperial	American
450g/1lb shelled peas	3 cups shelled peas
300ml/½ pint chicken stock	1¼ cups chicken stock
300ml/½ pint thin cream	1¼ cups light cream
sea salt and black pepper	sea salt and black pepper
2 tablespoons finely chopped mint	2 tablespoons finely chopped mint

Cook the peas in a saucepan of very little lightly salted water, then purée them in a blender. Add the chicken stock and cream and blend until smooth. Add salt and pepper to taste. For a hot soup, reheat and stir in the chopped mint a few minutes before serving. For a cold soup, chill well and add the mint 5 to 10 minutes prior to serving.

PROVENÇAL SOUP WITH PISTOU

Metric/Imperial	American
1 medium onion	1 medium onion
2 small leeks	2 small leeks
2 small carrots	2 small carrots
175g/6oz courgettes	1 cup sliced zucchini
175g/6oz string beans	1½ cups diced snap beans
225g/8oz tomatoes	½lb tomatoes
6 tablespoons olive oil	6 tablespoons olive oil
1.2 litres/2 pints hot water	5 cups hot water
100g/4oz cooked haricot beans	⅔ cup cooked navy beans
sea salt and black pepper	sea salt and black pepper
50g/2oz short macaroni	½ cup short macaroni
PISTOU:	PISTOU:
3 cloves garlic	3 cloves garlic
40g/1½oz finely chopped basil leaves	1 cup finely chopped basil leaves
50g/2oz freshly grated Parmesan cheese	½ cup freshly grated Parmesan cheese
4 tablespoons olive oil	¼ cup olive oil

Chop the onion, leeks and carrots, keeping them all in separate piles. Cut the unpeeled courgettes (zucchini) in slices 1cm/½in thick. Cut the string (snap) beans in 2.5cm/1in pieces; skin and chop the tomatoes.

Heat the oil in a heavy pan and cook the onion and leeks until softened and pale golden. Add the hot water, carrots and haricot (navy) beans. (Canned haricot beans may be used as an alternative, in which case add them when the other vegetables are cooked.) Bring to the boil, add salt and pepper, and simmer for 45 minutes. Add the courgettes (zucchini), string (snap) beans and tomatoes and simmer for a further 20 minutes. Add the macaroni and cook for about 15 minutes longer, until tender.

While the soup is cooking, make the pistou: peel the garlic and chop it very finely. Pound it to a pulp in a mortar. Add the basil leaves to the garlic. Pound again until the garlic and basil are amalgamated. Add the grated cheese and continue pounding. When all is smooth, beat in the oil drop by drop. When all has blended into a smooth paste, put the pistou in a warm tureen and pour the boiling soup over it. Cover and stand for 5 minutes. Serves 8 to 10.

PUMPKIN SOUP WITH BASIL

Metric/Imperial	American
450g/1lb pumpkin	1lb pumpkin
225g/8oz carrots	½lb carrots
900ml/1½ pints chicken stock	3¾ cups chicken stock
1 onion	1 onion
50g/2oz butter	¼ cup butter
225g/8oz tomatoes	½lb tomatoes
sea salt and black pepper	sea salt and black pepper
pinch of sugar	pinch of sugar
3 tablespoons thick cream (optional)	3 tablespoons heavy cream (optional)
2 tablespoons chopped basil	2 tablespoons chopped basil

Peel the pumpkin and cut it in cubes about 2cm/1in square. Clean the carrots and cut them in 0.5cm/¼in slices. Put the pumpkin and the carrots in a pan with the stock and bring to the boil. Simmer, covered, for 20 minutes, until soft.

Peel the onion and chop it quite finely. Heat the butter in a saucepan and stew the onions for 4 to 5 minutes. Skin the tomatoes and chop them coarsely before adding to the onion. Cook gently for 6 minutes, until slightly mushy.

Put the pumpkin and carrots through a medium food mill, or purée briefly in a blender, reserving about 300ml/½ pint/1¼ cups of the liquid. Add as much of the reserved liquid as is needed to give a consistency of thin (light) cream. Stir in the onion and tomato mixture with its juice. Add salt and pepper and a pinch of sugar. Add the cream, if used, and the basil. Stand, covered, for 5 minutes.

ROOT VEGETABLES WITH LOVAGE

Metric/Imperial	American
1 onion	1 onion
50g/2oz butter	¼ cup butter
175g/6oz carrots	6oz carrots
175g/6oz parsnips	6oz parsnips
175g/6oz turnips	6oz turnips
1 litre/1¾ pints chicken stock	4¼ cups chicken stock
sea salt and black pepper	sea salt and black pepper
4 tablespoons sour cream	¼ cup sour cream
3 tablespoons chopped lovage	3 tablespoons chopped lovage

Slice the onion thinly and stew gently in the butter, adding the other vegetables, also thinly sliced, after 4 minutes. Cook

gently for a further 8 minutes, then add the heated stock. Season to taste with salt and pepper and simmer, covered, for 30 minutes, or until all are soft.

Purée briefly in a blender, or push through a medium food mill, and return to the pan. Reheat, adjust the seasoning and stir in the sour cream. Stir in the chopped lovage and stand for a few moments before serving.

SAFFRON SOUP WITH CHIVES

Metric/Imperial	American
fish bones, heads, tails, etc	fish bones, heads, tails, etc
1.5 litres/2½ pints cold water	6¼ cups cold water
3 onions	3 onions
1 carrot	1 carrot
1 leek	1 leek
1 bay leaf	1 bay leaf
3 sprigs parsley	3 sprigs parsley
6 black peppercorns	6 black peppercorns
1 tablespoon sea salt	1 tablespoon sea salt
1½ tablespoons white wine vinegar	1½ tablespoons white wine vinegar
300ml/½ pint lager	1¼ cups lager
2 packets saffron	2 envelopes saffron
4 tablespoons olive oil	¼ cup olive oil
450g/1lb halibut steak	1lb halibut steak
4 tablespoons cooked rice	¼ cup cooked rice
4 tablespoons chopped chives	¼ cup chopped chives

Provençal soup with pistou; Root vegetables with lovage

Put the fish trimmings in a pan with the cold water. Slice one of the onions, the carrot and the leek and add them to the pan with the bay leaf, parsley, peppercorns and sea salt. Bring slowly to the boil and simmer for 30 minutes, skimming when required. Strain, discarding all the solid ingredients, add vinegar to the clear liquid and cool. Mix with the lager and heat, adding saffron, and salt and pepper to taste. Simmer for 15 minutes.

Chop the two remaining onions. Heat the olive oil and cook the onions gently until golden. Grill (broil) the halibut steak, then flake the flesh, removing all skin and bone. Stir the fried onions, the cooked rice, and the flaked fish into the soup, and scatter with chopped chives. Serves 6 to 8.

SORREL AND LETTUCE SOUP

Metric/Imperial	American
100g/4oz sorrel	¼lb sorrel
100g/4oz lettuce	¼lb lettuce
50g/2oz parsley	1½ cups parsley
50g/2oz butter	¼ cup butter
100g/4oz potato	¼lb potato
600ml/1 pint chicken stock	2½ cups chicken stock
sea salt and black pepper	sea salt and black pepper
4 tablespoons thin cream	¼ cup light cream

Wash the sorrel, lettuce and parsley and shake them dry, then pat in a cloth. Chop roughly. Heat the butter in a heavy pan and put in the three green vegetables. Stew gently for 6 minutes, then add the peeled and sliced potato. Stir around until well mixed, then pour on the heated stock. Add salt and simmer, covered, for 25 minutes. Push through a food mill or coarse sieve (strainer) – a blender will not do – and reheat in the clean pan. Add more salt and some black pepper, stir in the cream and serve.

TOMATO SOUP WITH BASIL

Metric/Imperial	American
1 large mild onion	1 large mild onion
50g/2oz butter	¼ cup butter
675g/1½lb tomatoes	1½lb tomatoes
600ml/1 pint chicken stock	2½ cups chicken stock
sea salt and black pepper	sea salt and black pepper
pinch of sugar	pinch of sugar
3 tablespoons chopped basil	3 tablespoons chopped basil

Peel and chop the onion. Melt the butter in a saucepan and cook the onion gently until soft but not coloured. Skin the tomatoes, chop them and add to the onion. Stir for a few minutes in the butter, then pour on the heated stock. Bring to the boil, then lower the heat and simmer for 20 minutes, adding salt, pepper and a pinch of sugar.

Purée briefly in a blender, or pass through a medium food mill. Adjust the seasoning, cool, and chill well. Ten minutes before serving, stir in the chopped basil.

JELLIED CUCUMBER AND MINT SOUP

Metric/Imperial	American
1 shallot	1 shallot
1 cucumber	1 cucumber
900ml/1½ pints chicken stock	3¾ cups chicken stock
sea salt and black pepper	sea salt and black pepper
2 tablespoons lemon juice	2 tablespoons lemon juice
1 packet gelatine	1 envelope gelatine
3 tablespoons chopped mint	3 tablespoons chopped mint
lemon quarters to serve	lemon quarters to serve

Chop the peeled shallot finely. Remove about half the skin of the cucumber and discard. Grate the remaining cucumber coarsely, squeezing out the juice. Heat the stock and cook the chopped shallot for 4 minutes. Add the grated cucumber and salt and pepper to taste. Stir in the lemon juice.

Dissolve the gelatine in a little of the stock; when dissolved, strain and return to the rest of the soup. Leave to cool. When half-set, stir in the finely chopped mint. Chill again.

To serve, spoon into cups – it is not meant to be a firm jelly – and serve with lemon quarters.

TARRAGON SOUP

Metric/Imperial	American
6 sprigs tarragon	6 sprigs tarragon
900ml/1½ pints strong chicken stock	3¾ cups strong chicken stock
25g/1oz butter	2 tablespoons butter
1 tablespoon flour	1 tablespoon flour
1 egg yolk	1 egg yolk
4 tablespoons thin cream	¼ cup light cream
1½ tablespoons lemon juice	1½ tablespoons lemon juice
sea salt and black pepper	sea salt and black pepper

Pick most of the best leaves off the tarragon sprigs and set aside. Heat the stock and add the stalks with the remaining leaves. Bring to boiling point, then cover the pan and remove from the heat for 20 minutes.

Melt the butter in a pan, add the flour and stir until blended to a smooth paste. Pour on the stock through a sieve (strainer) and simmer for 3 to 4 minutes, stirring all the time. When smooth and blended, beat the egg yolk in a bowl with the cream and stir in a few spoonfuls of the hot soup. Return the egg mixture to the pan and stir until amalgamated, without allowing it to boil. Add the lemon juice and salt and pepper to taste. Chop the reserved tarragon leaves and scatter over the top. Stand for a few minutes before serving.

Above: Tomato soup with basil; Jellied cucumber and mint soup

Opposite: Herb pâté

Pâtes, Sausages & Stuffings

All pâtés, without exception, are improved by the addition of fresh herbs. The smooth pâtés made from fish or shellfish are good with chopped tarragon, dill or burnet, while a chicken pâté is improved by adding lovage, tarragon or chervil. A liver pâté is enhanced by the careful addition of a very little chopped sage; this is one of the few herbs that is almost as good dried as fresh, but the dried form must be treated with great caution, for it can be overpowering. A little sage is also good in a pâté made from pork sausagemeat, while some of the other strong herbs – marjoram, savory and hyssop – are also good used in moderation in coarse country-style pâtés and terrines. All game pâtés, whether based on birds, venison, or rabbit, are greatly improved by the addition of juniper berries. I like to crush them in a mortar together with coarse salt, black peppercorns, and a clove or two of garlic, before adding to the pâté. Since fresh herbs are still available during the start of the game season, they can also be added in the form of thyme, lemon thyme, summer savory, marjoram and tarragon.

Homemade sausages can be made by those enterprising enough to find a butcher who will supply the casings, and possibly even fill them for you with your own mixture. Gadgets for filling sausages are available, either on their own or as attachments for a mixer. They are surprisingly easy to make and exceptionally good. Since the actual ingredients are very similar to those of a pâté, the same herbs are good with both. Plenty of juniper berries and black peppercorns, a little garlic, together with chopped sage or basil combined with a generous amount of chopped parsley will make a very fresh-tasting sausage, far removed from most commercial brands. The traditional sausagemeat flavourings of sage and thyme may be varied according to personal taste: I prefer a lighter one made with lovage, chervil and tarragon. The best filling in my opinion is based on pure pork, although good sausages can also be made from a mixture of pork and beef, or pork and venison.

For hundreds of years, and in many different countries, fresh herbs have been added to stuffings for poultry, game, boned joints of meat, and whole fish. The basic mixture of breadcrumbs, rice or mashed potato makes a bland background which is ideally suited to sharp herby flavours. Dried herbs can also be used in stuffings, although I prefer to use the seeds of dill and fennel during the winter months, when the leaves are unavailable. Fortunately fresh parsley is available the year round, and this is one of the best herbs for stuffings.

HERB PÂTÉ

Metric/Imperial	American
450g/1lb belly of pork	1lb fatty pork
225g/8oz unsmoked bacon	½lb salt pork
100g/4oz pig's liver	¼lb pork liver
1 medium onion	1 medium onion
2 cloves garlic	2 cloves garlic
sea salt and black pepper	sea salt and black pepper
6 juniper berries	6 juniper berries
225g/8oz spinach	½lb spinach
100g/4oz sorrel	¼lb sorrel
50g/2oz chopped parsley	1½ cups chopped parsley
50g/2oz chopped mixed herbs: chervil, dill, tarragon, lovage, marjoram, lemon thyme and sage	1½ cups chopped mixed herbs: chervil, dill, tarragon, lovage, marjoram, lemon thyme and sage
1 large egg	1 large egg
juice of ½ lemon	juice of ½ lemon

Ask your butcher to mince (grind) the pork, bacon and liver for you. Put all the meats together in a large bowl and add the peeled and chopped onion and crushed garlic. Add salt and pepper to taste, and the crushed juniper berries. Blanch the spinach and sorrel for 4 minutes in boiling salted water; drain in a colander (strainer), pressing out as much moisture as possible, then chop and stir into the meat mixture. Stir the chopped parsley and the chopped mixed herbs into the mixture. Beat the egg lightly and stir it in, adding the lemon juice.

Turn into an ovenproof dish or tin mould and cover with foil. Put in a roasting pan half full of hot water and cook for approximately 1 hour 20 minutes in a moderate oven (180°C/350°F or Gas Mark 4). When done, the pâté will have shrunk away from the edges of the container. Cool for 1 hour, then lay a 1kg/2lb weight on top and leave until completely cold. Store in the refrigerator. Turn out on a flat dish to serve, with toast or French bread and butter.

CHICKEN AND TARRAGON PÂTÉ

Metric/Imperial
1 roasting chicken,
  about 1.5kg/3½lb
350g/12oz belly of pork
350g/12oz unsalted
  streaky bacon
1 medium onion
225g/8oz pork or bacon fat
2 teaspoons sea salt
1 teaspoon black pepper
1½ tablespoons green
  peppercorns
1 clove garlic (optional)
3 tablespoons brandy
3 tablespoons medium dry
  vermouth or dry white
  wine
3 tablespoons chopped
  tarragon
1 large egg

American
1 roasting chicken,
  about 3½lb
¾lb fatty pork
¾lb salt pork
1 medium onion
½lb pork or bacon fat
2 teaspoons sea salt
1 teaspoon black pepper
1½ tablespoons green
  peppercorns
1 clove garlic (optional)
3 tablespoons brandy
3 tablespoons medium dry
  vermouth or dry white
  wine
3 tablespoons chopped
  tarragon
1 large egg

Cut the raw chicken off the bones and chop the meat by hand. Keep the carcass for making stock. Mince (grind) the belly of pork (fatty pork), streaky bacon (salt pork) and the peeled onion. Cut a few long strips of pork or bacon fat and set aside. Cut the remainder in dice. Mix all the meat and the onion together, adding salt and black pepper, green peppercorns drained of their juice, and the crushed clove of garlic, if liked. Stir in the brandy and the vermouth (or white wine). Fry a tiny ball of the mixture in a frying pan (skillet) to test the seasoning – it should be quite highly seasoned. Stir in the tarragon and the lightly beaten egg.

Line an ovenproof dish with the strips of fat laid diagonally across the bottom. Pile in the mixture and cover with foil and then a lid. Place in a roasting pan half full of hot water and cook in a moderate oven (160°C/325°F or Gas Mark 3) for 2 hours 10 minutes. Remove from the oven and cool for about 1 hour. Remove the lid and place a weight (1.5kg/3 to 3½lb is about right) on the foil until the pâté is completely cold. Store in the refrigerator.

Make the pâté 1 or 2 days before eating; it will keep for 8 to 9 days. Alternatively, make in two dishes and cook for 1¾ hours. One can be eaten soon after making, the other sealed with an airtight layer of melted lard (pork fat) after cooling, and kept for several weeks under refrigeration. One large pâté will serve 10 to 12 people; the small pâtés will serve 5 to 6.

Above: Rabbit pâté with herbs; Chicken and tarragon pâté

GAME PÂTÉ WITH JUNIPER BERRIES

Metric/Imperial	American
1 casserole pheasant	1 casserole pheasant
0.75kg/1½lb belly of pork	1½lb fatty pork
100g/4oz fat unsmoked bacon	¼lb mild bacon
2 cloves garlic	2 cloves garlic
½ tablespoon sea salt	½ tablespoon sea salt
15 black peppercorns	15 black peppercorns
15 juniper berries	15 juniper berries
150ml/¼ pint chicken stock or game stock	⅔ cup chicken stock or game stock
2 tablespoons brandy	2 tablespoons brandy
few thin strips bacon fat	few thin strips bacon fat

Put the bird to roast for 15 minutes only in a moderately hot oven (200°C/400°F or Gas Mark 6). Take out and leave to cool, then strip the carcass of its meat. Use the bones to make a game soup, or stock. Chop the meat by hand if you have the time, otherwise put it through the mincer (grinder). Mince (grind) the pork and the bacon and mix all together in a large bowl.

Peel and chop the garlic and put it in a mortar with the salt, peppercorns and juniper berries. Pound all together until coarsely crushed, then stir into the pâté mixture. Add the stock and the brandy and mix well.

Lay a few strips of bacon fat across the bottom of an ovenproof dish or tin mould, then pile the pâté mixture on top of it. Cook uncovered, standing in a roasting pan half full of hot water, for about 1¾ hours in a moderate oven (160°C/325°F or Gas Mark 3). Alternatively, make two smaller pâtés and cook for 1¼ hours. Cool for 1 hour, then weigh down with a 1kg/2lb weight on a piece of foil. When completely cold, remove the weight and store the pâté in the refrigerator. Make 1 to 2 days before eating. One large pâté will serve 10 to 12 people; the small pâtés will serve 5 to 6.

LIVER PÂTÉ WITH SAGE

Metric/Imperial	American
350g/12oz calves' liver	¾lb calf liver
350g/12oz pigs' liver	¾lb pork liver
100g/4oz chicken livers	¼lb chicken livers
175g/6oz rindless streaky bacon rashers	9 bacon slices
4 shallots	4 shallots
1 clove garlic	1 clove garlic
sea salt and black pepper	sea salt and black pepper
4 tablespoons vermouth or dry white wine	¼ cup vermouth or dry white wine
2 tablespoons chopped sage or 2 teaspoons dried sage	2 tablespoons chopped sage or 2 teaspoons dried sage
1 egg	1 egg

Ask your butcher to put the livers through the mincer (grinder) for you, or do it at home. Cut 5 or 6 thin strips of bacon fat to line the dish. Chop the rest of the bacon into small dice and mix it with the livers. Peel the shallots and garlic and chop them finely. Stir into the pâté, adding salt and black pepper. Stir in the vermouth (or wine), and the sage. Beat the egg lightly and stir in. Fry a tiny ball of the mixture in a pan (skillet) to test for seasoning. Adjust as necessary.

Line an ovenproof dish or tin mould with the strips of fat, then pile in the mixture. Cover with foil and stand in a roasting pan half full of hot water and cook for about 1½ hours in a moderate oven (160°C/325°F or Gas Mark 3). Cool for 1 hour, then lay a 1kg/2lb weight on top and leave until completely cold. Store in the refrigerator for 1 to 2 days before serving. Serve with toasted brown bread.

RABBIT PÂTÉ WITH HERBS

Metric/Imperial	American
225g/8oz boneless rabbit	½lb boneless rabbit
225g/8oz belly of pork	½lb fatty pork
100g/4oz pie veal	¼lb boneless veal
100g/4oz fat unsmoked bacon	¼lb mild bacon
1 clove garlic	1 clove garlic
2 teaspoons sea salt	2 teaspoons sea salt
1 teaspoon black peppercorns	1 teaspoon black peppercorns
12 juniper berries	12 juniper berries
¼ teaspoon mace	¼ teaspoon mace
1½ tablespoons chopped parsley	1½ tablespoons chopped parsley
1 teaspoon chopped sage	1 teaspoon chopped sage
1 teaspoon chopped thyme	1 teaspoon chopped thyme
1 egg	1 egg
2 tablespoons brandy	2 tablespoons brandy
150ml/¼ pint white wine	⅔ cup white wine

Put the rabbit through the mincer (grinder) with the pork, veal and bacon. Mix them all together in a big bowl. Peel the garlic and crush it in a mortar with the salt, peppercorns, juniper berries and mace. Add to the meat. Stir in the chopped herbs and the lightly beaten egg, then the brandy and the wine.

Pile into an ovenproof dish or tin mould and stand in a roasting pan half full of hot water. Bake for 1¾ hours in a moderate oven (160°C/325°F or Gas Mark 3). Alternatively, cook in 2 small dishes, allowing 1 hour 20 minutes. When half cooled, weigh down with a 1kg/2lb weight (for the large pâté). Chill in the refrigerator for 2 to 3 days before serving. One small pâté can be stored for future use by sealing with a layer of melted lard (pork fat) after cooling; once sealed, they can be kept in a cool place for up to 8 weeks. Turn out to serve, cutting away the fat surround. One large pâté will serve 6 to 8, the smaller ones 3 to 4 each.

VARIATION
Follow the recipe for *Rabbit Pâté*, substituting venison for rabbit.

PORK AND SAGE PÂTÉ

Metric/Imperial	American
450g/1lb pure pork sausagemeat	1lb pure pork sausagemeat
1 medium onion	1 medium onion
2 cloves garlic	2 cloves garlic
100g/4oz rindless streaky bacon	6 bacon slices
1 teaspoon sea salt	1 teaspoon sea salt
½ teaspoon black peppercorns	½ teaspoon black peppercorns
10 juniper berries	10 juniper berries
8 sage leaves	8 sage leaves
6 lovage leaves	6 lovage leaves
4 sprigs marjoram	4 sprigs marjoram
4 sprigs thyme or lemon thyme	4 sprigs thyme or lemon thyme
1 large egg	1 large egg
6 tablespoons vermouth or dry white wine	6 tablespoons vermouth or dry white wine
2 tablespoons brandy	2 tablespoons brandy

Put the sausagemeat in a large bowl and break it up with wooden spoons. Peel the onion and chop it quite finely, peel and chop the garlic, and mix them both with the meat. Chop the bacon and add it to the pork. Crush the sea salt, peppercorns and juniper berries in a mortar and stir them into the meat mixture. Add the chopped herbs, the lightly beaten egg, the vermouth (or wine), and brandy; mix well.

Turn into a rectangular tin or ovenproof dish, and stand in a roasting pan half full of hot water. Cover with foil and cook for 1½ hours in a moderate oven (160°C/325°F or Gas Mark 3). Take out of the oven and leave to cool for 1 hour, before putting a weight on top. When completely cold, remove the weight and store the pâté in the refrigerator.

PRAWN (SHRIMP) PÂTÉ WITH DILL

Metric/Imperial	American
350g/12oz peeled prawns	2 cups shelled shrimp
175g/6oz medium-fat cheese	6oz ricotta or diet cheese
3 tablespoons sour cream	3 tablespoons sour cream
2 tablespoons lemon juice	2 tablespoons lemon juice
sea salt and black pepper	sea salt and black pepper
2½ tablespoons chopped dill	2½ tablespoons chopped dill
dash of Tabasco sauce	dash of Tabasco sauce

Purée the prawns (shrimp), the cream cheese (ricotta or diet cheese), sour cream and lemon juice in a blender. Add salt and pepper to taste and blend again. Add the dill, reserving ½ tablespoon for the garnish, and a dash of Tabasco. Blend again, taste, pile into a dish and chill in the refrigerator. Scatter the remaining dill over the top, and a few extra prawns (shrimps), if you like.

HERBY PORK SAUSAGES

Metric/Imperial	American
225g/8oz belly of pork	½lb fatty pork
225g/8oz lean pork, from the leg	½lb lean pork, from the leg
6 tablespoons milk	6 tablespoons milk
75g/3oz soft brown breadcrumbs	1½ cups soft brown breadcrumbs
1 clove garlic	1 clove garlic
1 teaspoon black peppercorns	1 teaspoon black peppercorns
2 teaspoons sea salt	2 teaspoons sea salt
12 juniper berries	12 juniper berries
¼ teaspoon mace	¼ teaspoon mace
¼ teaspoon allspice	¼ teaspoon allspice
1 tablespoon chopped parsley	1 tablespoon chopped parsley
1 teaspoon chopped sage	1 teaspoon chopped sage
1 teaspoon chopped thyme	1 teaspoon chopped thyme

Put the lean part of the belly of pork (fatty pork) through the mincer (grinder) with the lean pork. Cut the fat in small squares by hand. Pour the milk over the breadcrumbs and leave for 10 minutes. Squeeze them in your hands and add to the meat. Mix the fat and lean meat and the breadcrumbs together thoroughly.

Peel and chop the garlic and put it in a mortar with the peppercorns, coarse salt, juniper berries, mace and allspice. Pound all together until crushed and mixed, then stir into the meat mixture. Finally stir in the herbs.

The filling is now ready for forcing into the casings. If the sausages are hung in the air for a couple of days, the flavour will grow stronger. The taste is fresher if the sausages are cooked the same day as they are made. The sausages can be fried, grilled (broiled), or placed on a greased baking sheet and cooked for 30 minutes in a moderate oven (180°C/350°F or Gas Mark 4). Alternatively, the filling can be made into two long sausages weighing about 350g/¾lb each and poached for 40 minutes in simmering water. Since these can be eaten hot or cold, they are useful for taking on picnics. They can also be wrapped in pastry after poaching and made into a giant sausage roll.

VARIATIONS

Follow the recipe for *Herby Pork Sausages*, substituting 1½ tablespoons of chopped basil and 1½ tablespoons of chopped parsley for the sage, thyme and parsley.

Follow the recipe for *Herby Pork Sausages*, substituting 225g/8oz of boneless brisket of beef for the lean pork.

FENNEL STUFFING

Metric/Imperial	American
1 small onion	1 small onion
25g/1oz butter	2 tablespoons butter
50g/2oz soft breadcrumbs	1 cup soft breadcrumbs
sea salt and black pepper	sea salt and black pepper
2 tablespoons chopped fennel leaves	2 tablespoons chopped fennel leaves
1 egg	1 egg

Peel and chop the onion. Melt the butter in a frying pan (skillet) and cook the onion until it turns light brown. Remove from the heat and stir in the breadcrumbs. Add salt and black pepper to taste, then stir in the chopped fennel. (In winter time, fennel seed can be used, or dried fennel; in these cases, use 2 teaspoonsful only.) Beat the egg and stir it in. Use to stuff fish before baking or grilling (broiling).

VARIATION

Follow the recipe for *Fennel Stuffing*, substituting 3 tablespoons of chopped parsley for the chopped fennel. Use to stuff small fish such as trout and mackerel before grilling (broiling) or baking.

PARSLEY AND BREAD STUFFING

Metric/Imperial	American
175g/6oz shallots	6oz shallots
50g/2oz butter	¼ cup butter
175g/6oz soft white breadcrumbs	3 cups soft white breadcrumbs
8 tablespoons chopped parsley	½ cup chopped parsley
sea salt and black pepper	sea salt and black pepper

Peel the shallots and chop them finely. Melt the butter in a frying pan (skillet) and fry the shallots until golden. Add the breadcrumbs and stir around until well mixed. Remove from the heat and stir in the chopped parsley. Add salt and black pepper to taste. Leave to cool completely before using to stuff a large chicken. (A boiling fowl as well as a roasting bird will benefit enormously from stuffing.) To stuff a turkey, make in double quantities.

Herby pork sausages; Prawn (shrimp) pâté with dill; Pork and sage pâté; Fennel stuffing; Parsley and bread stuffing

RICE STUFFING WITH HERBS

Metric/Imperial	American
200g/7oz long-grain rice	*1 cup long-grain rice*
1 medium onion	*1 medium onion*
40g/1½oz butter	*3 tablespoons butter*
100g/4oz streaky bacon	*6 bacon slices*
sea salt and black pepper	*sea salt and black pepper*
6 tablespoons chopped	*6 tablespoons chopped*
mixed herbs: chervil,	*mixed herbs: chervil,*
tarragon, dill, mint,	*tarragon, dill, mint,*
parsley and chives	*parsley and chives*

Cook the rice in a saucepan of boiling salted water until almost tender; drain. Peel and chop the onion. Melt the butter in a frying pan (skillet). Cook the onion until softened and pale golden. Add the chopped bacon and stir until lightly coloured. Remove from the heat and stir in the rice, adding salt and pepper to taste. Stir in the chopped herbs. Use as a stuffing for vegetables such as red or green peppers, tomatoes, cucumber, custard marrow (squash), or cabbage leaves, or for a roasting chicken or guinea fowl (guinea hen).

SAGE AND ONION STUFFING

Metric/Imperial	American
1 medium onion	*1 medium onion*
50g/2oz butter	*¼ cup butter*
75g/3oz soft breadcrumbs	*1½ cups soft breadcrumbs*
sea salt and black pepper	*sea salt and black pepper*
3 tablespoons chopped	*3 tablespoons chopped*
sage or 2 teaspoons	*sage or 2 teaspoons*
dried sage	*dried sage*
1 large egg	*1 large egg*
4 tablespoons milk	*¼ cup milk*

Peel and chop the onion. Melt the butter in a frying pan (skillet) and cook the onion until slightly coloured. Remove the pan from the heat and stir in the breadcrumbs. Add salt and pepper to taste and stir in the chopped sage. Beat the egg lightly and stir into the breadcrumb mixture. Add the milk and mix thoroughly. Use to stuff a duck, a goose or a joint of pork, boned and rolled.

POTATO AND PARSLEY STUFFING

Metric/Imperial	American
1 medium onion	*1 medium onion*
15g/½oz beef dripping	*1 tablespoon beef drippings*
225g/8oz pure pork sausagemeat	*½lb pure pork sausagemeat*
225g/8oz freshly mashed potatoes	*½lb freshly mashed potatoes*
sea salt and black pepper	*sea salt and black pepper*
8 tablespoons chopped parsley	*½ cup chopped parsley*

Peel and chop the onion. Melt the dripping in a frying pan (skillet) and fry the onion until pale golden. Stir in the sausagemeat, breaking it up with two wooden spoons. Brown lightly and remove from the heat. Stir in the freshly mashed potato and season well with salt and black pepper. Stir in the chopped parsley and mix thoroughly. Use to stuff a gosling or a large duck or chicken. For a large goose or a turkey, make in double quantities.

Above: Rice stuffing with herbs; Potato and parsley stuffing

Opposite: Scrambled (buttered) eggs with tarragon

Eggs

Eggs make an ideal vehicle for herbs; their bland flavour and smooth consistency can be used to advantage with the more delicate summer herbs. The tart acidity of sorrel makes a pleasing contrast, while the sharp oniony flavour of chives is another obvious choice. Poached eggs can be laid on a purée of nettles, or of sorrel, or on a bed of hop tips, which are the thinnings of young hops, cut before the first spraying. Poached or soft-boiled eggs can be served cold, encased in a herb-flavoured jelly. Hot poached eggs make a good winter dish, served on a creamy purée of potato, flecked with the green of mixed chopped herbs.

Hard-boiled eggs also make an excellent luncheon dish, covered in a thin purée of vegetables with added herbs, or in a saffron sauce with a border of rice. Cold hard-boiled eggs look very pretty laid on a bed of shredded lettuce and covered with a cold herb sauce, based either on mayonnaise or on yogurt. Stuffed eggs are made by taking the yolks of hard-boiled eggs and mashing them to a smooth paste with a little mayonnaise or sour cream. Chopped herbs are then added to the mixture, which is piled back into the halved whites.

An omelette aux fines herbes is a classic herb dish, and one of the best. Other more unusual omelettes can be made using purslane, sorrel, or garlic-flavoured croûtons. I find it better to make 2 omelettes of 5 eggs each for 4 people, rather than one large omelette. Scrambled eggs are delicious with added herbs, especially chives, tarragon, chervil or dill. Baked eggs, in little china cocotte dishes, are greatly improved by a spoonful of cream mixed with chopped tarragon, added at the very end of the cooking.

Many different sauces can be used in conjunction with eggs. There are the creamy hot sauces, flavoured with chopped herbs and flecked with green. Then there are the uncooked sauces, made with mixtures of sour cream, yogurt and cream cheese; these also make an ideal background for fresh herb flavours. The classic French sauces – hollandaise, béarnaise and mayonnaise – are exquisite with herbs added, although this is not strictly orthodox. Thin purées of cooked vegetables – onions, cucumbers, spinach, sorrel or watercress – can be used as sauces for poached or hard-boiled eggs, with suitable herbs added. The combination of eggs and fresh herbs is both appetizing and nutritious, and in every way suited to the life most of us live today, which demands light meals that are not too lengthy to prepare.

SCRAMBLED (BUTTERED) EGGS WITH CHIVES

Metric/Imperial	American
75g/3oz butter	6 tablespoons butter
8 eggs	8 eggs
sea salt and black pepper	sea salt and black pepper
4 thick slices wholemeal bread	4 thick slices wholewheat bread
63g/2½oz can tomato purée	2 tablespoons tomato paste
3 tablespoons chopped chives	3 tablespoons chopped chives

Melt 25g/1oz/2 tablespoons of butter in a pan over a gentle heat. Beat the eggs lightly, add salt and pepper, and scramble (cook) as usual in the butter. Toast the slices of bread and spread them with the remaining butter and a layer of tomato purée (paste). Pile the scrambled (buttered) eggs on top and scatter with the chopped chives. This makes a delicious snack, or a light lunch served with a green salad.

SCRAMBLED (BUTTERED) EGGS WITH TARRAGON

Metric/Imperial	American
8 large eggs	8 large eggs
sea salt and black pepper	sea salt and black pepper
40g/1½oz butter	3 tablespoons butter
2 tablespoons thick cream	2 tablespoons heavy cream
2 tablespoons chopped tarragon	2 tablespoons chopped tarragon
4 slices pumpernickel bread (optional)	4 slices pumpernickel bread (optional)

Beat the eggs lightly and season with salt and pepper. Melt the butter in a shallow pan and tip in the eggs. Scramble (cook) very slowly, scraping the bottom of the pan with a metal spoon. When they are just set, remove from the heat and stir in the cream and most of the chopped tarragon, keeping back a little to scatter over the top. Tip the eggs into a shallow dish, garnish with the remaining tarragon and leave to cool. Alternatively, pile on to 4 lightly buttered slices of pumpernickel just before serving, and accompany with a green salad for a light lunch.

GARLIC OMELETTE

Metric/Imperial	American
2 slices dry bread	2 slices dry bread
1 large clove garlic	1 large clove garlic
50g/2oz butter	¼ cup butter
5 eggs	5 eggs
sea salt and black pepper	sea salt and black pepper
½ tablespoon finely chopped parsley	½ tablespoon finely chopped parsley

Trim the crusts off the bread, and cut each slice into small cubes. Peel and crush the garlic. Heat most of the butter in a frying pan (skillet), leaving just enough to cook the omelette, and fry the bread until golden, stirring constantly and adding the crushed garlic. Remove from the pan and set aside. Break the eggs into a bowl. Beat lightly with a fork and season with salt and black pepper. Heat the remaining butter in an omelette pan and tip in the eggs. As the eggs start to set, tip in the garlic-flavoured croûtons and continue to cook quickly, turning the omelette out on to a flat dish before the eggs have completely set. Sprinkle with chopped parsley and serve immediately.

One omelette will serve 2 people. Large omelettes are awkward to make: it is better to prepare 2 smaller ones for 4 people.

OMELETTE AUX FINES HERBES

Metric/Imperial	American
5 eggs	5 eggs
sea salt and black pepper	sea salt and black pepper
1 teaspoon chopped chervil	1 teaspoon chopped chervil
1 teaspoon chopped parsley	1 teaspoon chopped parsley
1 teaspoon chopped tarragon	1 teaspoon chopped tarragon
1 teaspoon chopped chives	1 teaspoon chopped chives
15g/½oz butter	1 tablespoon butter

Beat the eggs lightly in a bowl, adding salt and pepper. Have the chopped herbs mixed together in a saucer. Heat the butter in a hot frying pan (skillet), pour in the eggs and add most of the herbs after a moment's cooking. Make the omelette swiftly, lifting the cooked edges with a spatula and allowing the uncooked eggs to run underneath. Turn out on a hot dish and scatter a few chopped herbs over the top. One omelette will serve 2 people.

PURSLANE OMELETTE

Metric/Imperial	American
2 bunches purslane	2 bunches purslane
40g/1½oz butter	3 tablespoons butter
5 eggs	5 eggs
sea salt and black pepper	sea salt and black pepper

Pick the top 5cm/2in off the purslane, wash the leaves and pat dry in a cloth. Melt the butter in a frying pan (skillet)

Garlic omelette; Herb soufflé; Baked eggs with tarragon

and put in the purslane. Cook for 3 to 4 minutes, until it is softened. Beat the eggs in a bowl with salt and pepper and pour them over the purslane. Cook like a flat omelette, lifting the edges with a spatula to allow the uncooked eggs to run underneath, but without attempting to fold it. Turn out on a flat plate to serve. One omelette will serve 2 people.

SORREL OMELETTE

Metric/Imperial	American
5 eggs	5 eggs
sea salt and black pepper	sea salt and black pepper
15g/½oz butter	1 tablespoon butter
4 tablespoons chopped sorrel	¼ cup chopped sorrel

Beat the eggs lightly in a bowl, adding salt and pepper to taste. Heat a frying pan (skillet) until it is very hot. Drop in all but a tiny piece of the butter and, when it sizzles, pour in the eggs. As soon as the bottom layer has set, scatter the chopped sorrel evenly over the whole surface. Continue to cook as usual, lifting the cooked edges with a spatula and allowing the uncooked eggs to run underneath.

As soon as the eggs are almost cooked, which will take only a matter of moments, turn the omelette out on to a hot dish, folding it in half as you do it. Put the remaining piece of butter on top and serve immediately. One omelette will serve 2 people.

HERB SOUFFLÉ

Metric/Imperial	American
40g/1½oz butter	3 tablespoons butter
2 tablespoons flour	2 tablespoons flour
200ml/⅓ pint milk	⅞ cup milk
sea salt and black pepper	sea salt and black pepper
½ teaspoon Dijon mustard	½ teaspoon Dijon mustard
50g/2oz Gruyère cheese, grated	½ cup grated Gruyère cheese
1 tablespoon chopped burnet	1 tablespoon chopped burnet
3 egg yolks	3 egg yolks
4 egg whites	4 egg whites

Melt the butter in a small saucepan, stir in the flour and cook over a low heat for 1 minute, stirring until smooth. Heat the milk and add it to the pan. Continue to cook over a low heat, stirring all the time, until the ingredients have blended into a smooth creamy sauce. Simmer gently for 3 minutes. Add salt and pepper to taste, and stir in the mustard, grated cheese and burnet.

Take off the heat and cool for a moment, then stir in the lightly beaten egg yolks. Cool for 5 minutes, then fold in the stiffly beaten whites. Turn into a buttered 900ml/1½ pint/3¾ cup ovenproof soufflé dish and bake for 20 minutes in a moderately hot oven (200°C/400°F or Gas Mark 6). Serve immediately.

VARIATIONS

Follow the recipe for *Herb Soufflé*, substituting dill for basil.

Follow the recipe for *Herb Soufflé*, substituting burnet for basil.

Follow the recipe for *Herb Soufflé*, substituting chervil for basil.

BAKED EGGS WITH TARRAGON

Metric/Imperial	American
3 sprigs tarragon	3 sprigs tarragon
150ml/¼ pint thin cream	⅔ cup light cream
sea salt and black pepper	sea salt and black pepper
4 large eggs	4 large eggs

Strip 1 teaspoon of the best leaves from the tarragon sprigs and chop them. Put the rest in a small pan with the cream and bring to the boil. Remove from the heat, cover the pan, and leave for 20 minutes. Strain the cream and add salt and black pepper to taste. Break each egg into a buttered individual ramekin and stand them in a roasting pan with enough hot water in it to come halfway up the sides of the dishes.

Cook in a moderate oven (160°C/325°F or Gas Mark 3) until the whites are almost set. Pour a little cream over each one, just enough to cover the surface, then return to the oven for another 2 minutes. Sprinkle with the chopped tarragon and serve immediately.

EGGS WITH YOGURT AND HERBS

Metric/Imperial	American
800–900g/1½–2lb potatoes	1½–2lb potatoes
25g/1oz butter	2 tablespoons butter
sea salt and black pepper	sea salt and black pepper
150ml/¼ pint natural yogurt	⅔ cup unflavored yogurt
6 tablespoons chopped mixed herbs: parsley, chives, dill and chervil	6 tablespoons chopped mixed herbs: parsley, chives, dill and chervil
4 eggs	4 eggs

Boil the potatoes in salted water. When they are cooked, drain them and push them through a food mill. Dry out the purée by stirring it for a few minutes in a pan over a gentle heat. When most of the moisture has been eliminated, stir in the butter and salt and pepper to taste. Beat the yogurt until smooth, then stir it into the potato purée. Next add the chopped herbs. Pour the purée into a shallow dish. Poach or soft-boil the eggs and put them on the purée. (To cook soft-boiled eggs, put them in a saucepan of boiling salted water for exactly 5 minutes, then shell them carefully, holding them under a cold tap.)

EGGS IN HERB SAUCE

Metric/Imperial	American
6–8 eggs	6–8 eggs
1 lettuce	1 head lettuce
HERB SAUCE:	HERB SAUCE:
1 egg yolk	1 egg yolk
150ml/¼ pint olive oil	⅔ cup olive oil
1½ tablespoons white wine vinegar	1½ tablespoons white wine vinegar
½ tablespoon lemon juice	½ tablespoon lemon juice
150ml/¼ pint thin cream	⅔ cup light cream
40g/1½oz chopped mixed herbs: parsley, chives, chervil, dill, tarragon, and marjoram	1 cup chopped mixed herbs: parsley, chives, chervil, dill, tarragon, and marjoram

Hard-boil the eggs or, if you prefer them soft-boiled, boil them for exactly 5 minutes, then place in cold water before shelling. Make a mayonnaise with the egg yolk, olive oil, vinegar and lemon juice (see method page 190). Mix it with the cream and stir in the chopped herbs. These should be so finely chopped that they are almost reduced to a purée.

Make a bed of shredded lettuce leaves on a flat dish and lay the shelled eggs on it. If hard-boiled, they should be cut in half and laid cut side down; if soft-boiled, leave them whole. Pour the green sauce over all and serve as a first course.

If using hard-boiled eggs, 6 will probably be enough as this allows 3 halves for each person; if soft-boiled, allow 2 eggs each.

POACHED EGGS ON SORREL PURÉE

Metric/Imperial	American
675g/1½lb sorrel	1½lb sorrel
25g/1oz butter	2 tablespoons butter
2 teaspoons flour	2 teaspoons flour
sea salt and black pepper	sea salt and black pepper
4 eggs	4 eggs
CREAM SAUCE:	CREAM SAUCE:
25g/1oz butter	2 tablespoons butter
1 tablespoon flour	1 tablespoon flour
150ml/¼ pint chicken stock	⅔ cup chicken stock
150ml/¼ pint thin cream	⅔ cup light cream
3 tablespoons grated Gruyère cheese	3 tablespoons grated Gruyère cheese
sea salt and black pepper	sea salt and black pepper

Cook the sorrel in boiling salted water and drain well. (If you do not have enough sorrel, it can be mixed with spinach.) Chop it, and purée it in a blender or by pushing through a fine food mill. Melt the butter in a saucepan, stir in the flour to make a smooth paste and add the sorrel purée. Cook gently for 3 minutes, stirring often. Add salt and black pepper to taste, and pour into a shallow dish. Poach the eggs, drain them on a cloth, and put them on the purée.

Keep the eggs and purée warm while you make the sauce. Melt the butter in a saucepan, stir in the flour to make a smooth paste and cook for 1 minute. Heat the stock and cream together and add them to the roux. Stir until smooth. Simmer for 3 minutes, then add the grated cheese and salt and black pepper to taste. Pour a little of the sauce over the eggs without covering them completely. Serve the remaining sauce separately.

POACHED EGGS ON GREEN POTATO PURÉE

Metric/Imperial	American
1kg/2lb potatoes	2lb potatoes
200ml/⅓ pint milk	⅞ cup milk
75g/3oz butter	6 tablespoons butter
sea salt and black pepper	sea salt and black pepper
6 spring onions	6 scallions
2 tablespoons chopped dill	2 tablespoons chopped dill
2 tablespoons chopped parsley	2 tablespoons chopped parsley
4 eggs	4 eggs

Boil the potatoes, mash them and dry out over a gentle heat. Keep them warm. Heat the milk in a saucepan with the butter, adding salt and pepper to taste. Chop the white parts and the tender green leaves of the spring onions (scallions) and add them to the milk with the chopped herbs. Gradually stir this mixture into the hot potatoes, and beat until smooth. Pour into a shallow serving dish.

Poach the eggs, drain them, and put them on top of the potato. This light dish is suitable for lunch or supper.

EGGS ON HOPS WITH HOLLANDAISE SAUCE

Metric/Imperial	American
450g/1lb hop tips or asparagus tips	1lb hop tips or asparagus tips
sea salt and black pepper	sea salt and black pepper
4 poached eggs	4 poached eggs
hollandaise sauce with herbs (see page 186)	hollandaise sauce with herbs (see page 186)

Cut the hop tips (or asparagus tips) to an equal length, tie in 2 or 3 bundles, and lower them into a pan of boiling water. Cook until tender when pierced with a skewer, lift out and drain well. Unfasten the bundles and lay the hop tips on a flat dish. Sprinkle them with salt and pepper, and put the poached eggs on top. Pour over the hollandaise sauce and serve immediately.

EGGS ON NETTLE PURÉE

Metric/Imperial	American
4 large eggs	4 large eggs
675g/1½lb young nettle tops	1½lb young nettle tops
40g/1½oz butter	3 tablespoons butter
4 tablespoons thick cream	¼ cup heavy cream
sea salt and black pepper	sea salt and black pepper

Bring a pan of lightly salted water to the boil and put in the eggs. Cook them for exactly 5 minutes, then hold them under the cold tap and shell carefully. Place them in a bowl of hot water until the nettle purée is ready.

Throw the nettles into a large pan of fast boiling water, lightly salted. Cook briskly until tender; 5 to 6 minutes should be enough if they are really young. Drain thoroughly in a colander (strainer), forcing out as much water as possible. Chop them finely, preferably in a food processor or by hand, and return them to a clean pan. Reheat, adding the butter and the cream, and salt and pepper to taste. Spoon the purée into 4 individual dishes. Dry the soft-boiled eggs and put one in each of the dishes of purée.

Left: Hard-boiled eggs with cucumber

Opposite: Eggs with saffron sauce; Stuffed eggs; Eggs in tarragon jelly

HARD-BOILED EGGS WITH CUCUMBER

Metric/Imperial	American
1 cucumber	1 cucumber
40g/1½oz butter	3 tablespoons butter
1 teaspoon flour	1 teaspoon flour
150ml/¼ pint chicken stock	⅔ cup chicken stock
½ tablespoon chopped dill	½ tablespoon chopped dill
sea salt and black pepper	sea salt and black pepper
4 tablespoons thick cream	¼ cup heavy cream
4 hard-boiled eggs	4 hard-boiled eggs

Peel the cucumber and chop it roughly. Melt the butter in a saucepan and stew the cucumber gently for 5 minutes. Sprinkle in the flour, and add the heated stock. Simmer for 10 minutes, then add the dill, salt and pepper to taste, and stir in the cream. Put a hard-boiled egg in each of 4 small bowls and spoon the cucumber over them. This makes a good light vegetarian dish.

EGGS WITH NUTS AND HERBS

Metric/Imperial	American
4 eggs	4 eggs
heart of 1 Cos lettuce	heart of 1 Romaine lettuce
2 tablespoons chopped hazelnuts	2 tablespoons chopped filberts
1 tablespoon chopped dill	1 tablespoon chopped dill
1 tablespoon chopped chervil or parsley	1 tablespoon chopped chervil or parsley
200ml/⅓ pint thin cream	⅞ cup light cream
2 tablespoons lemon juice	2 tablespoons lemon juice
sea salt and black pepper	sea salt and black pepper

Hard-boil the eggs and remove the shells when they are cold. Wash the lettuce, dry it on a cloth and cut it in strips. Lay the shredded lettuce on a flat dish with the eggs on top. Stir the chopped nuts and herbs into the cream; add the lemon juice and a little salt and black pepper. Spoon the sauce over the eggs. Serve as a first course.

EGGS WITH ONIONS AND SAGE

Metric/Imperial	American
450g/1lb onions	1lb onions
75g/3oz butter	6 tablespoons butter
1 teaspoon flour	1 teaspoon flour
450ml/¾ pint chicken stock	2 cups chicken stock
12 large sage leaves	12 large sage leaves
6 tablespoons thick cream	6 tablespoons heavy cream
sea salt and black pepper	sea salt and black pepper
4 hard-boiled eggs	4 hard-boiled eggs

Peel the onions and chop them quite coarsely. Melt the butter in a saucepan and stew the onions for 10 minutes. Stir in the flour, then add the heated stock. Chop the sage and add it to the pan; cover and simmer slowly for a further 10 to 15 minutes, until the onions are soft. Stir in the cream, and add salt and pepper to taste.

Put a hard-boiled egg in each of 4 bowls, and spoon the sauce over them. This good simple dish is ideal for those on a vegetarian diet.

EGGS IN TARRAGON JELLY

Metric/Imperial	American
4 eggs	4 eggs
4 sprigs tarragon	4 sprigs tarragon
450ml/¾ pint chicken stock	2 cups chicken stock
2½ teaspoons gelatine	2½ teaspoons gelatine
4 lettuce leaves to garnish	4 lettuce leaves to garnish

Bring a saucepan of lightly salted water to the boil. Put the eggs into the pan and cook them for exactly 5 minutes. Cool the eggs immediately under cold water, and shell them carefully.

Strip 4 of the best leaves from the tarragon sprigs and reserve them. Heat the stock, which must be of a good flavour and totally free from fat, with the tarragon sprigs. When it boils, draw the pan to the side of the fire and cover it. Leave for 15 minutes to infuse. If the flavour still seems weak, bring back to the boil and leave to cool once more. Lift out the tarragon and stir in the gelatine. Stir the stock over a very low heat until the gelatine has melted. Pour through a strainer to make a thin layer in each of 4 *oeufs en gelée* moulds, or use ramekin dishes.

Put in the refrigerator to set. When firm, lay a tarragon leaf on the bottom of each one, then an egg. Pour the remaining stock through a strainer to cover the eggs. Chill until set. To serve, turn out on individual plates and surround with shredded lettuce. Garnish with thin slices of stuffed (Spanish) olive, if you like.

EGGS WITH SAFFRON SAUCE

Metric/Imperial	American
225g/8oz long-grain rice	1 cup long-grain rice
pinch of saffron	pinch of saffron
4 eggs	4 eggs
saffron sauce (see page 187)	saffron sauce (see page 187)

Wash and drain the rice. Bring a saucepan of salted water to the boil, add the saffron, and cook the rice until tender. Drain it well, and keep it warm in a shallow serving dish. Hard-boil the eggs, shell them and lay them in the middle of the rice.

Prepare the saffron sauce and pour some over the warm eggs, handing the remainder separately. This makes an unusual and delicious dish; for a more substantial meal, allow 2 eggs per person.

STUFFED EGGS

Metric/Imperial	American
6 eggs	6 eggs
sea salt and black pepper	sea salt and black pepper
2 tablespoons sour cream	2 tablespoons sour cream
2 tablespoons chopped chives	2 tablespoons chopped chives
1 tablespoon chopped dill	1 tablespoon chopped dill
1 tablespoon chopped tarragon	1 tablespoon chopped tarragon
few sprigs of dill to garnish	few sprigs of dill to garnish

Boil the eggs for 12 minutes then cool them quickly in a bowl of cold water. Shell them, cut them in half lengthwise and scoop out the yolks, being careful not to damage the whites. Mash them to a paste, adding salt and pepper and the sour cream to make a smooth mixture. (Do not do this in a blender, or the result will be too smooth.) Stir in the chopped herbs. Pile the mixture back into the egg whites, and arrange them on a flat dish, with feathery sprigs of dill curling among them.

Vegetarian Dishes

Most of the dishes described here are based on starch, grain and cereals. Strict vegetarians may substitute vegetable stock for the chicken stock designated in some of the recipes. They may be used as first courses, as main dishes for a light meal, or as part of a selection of vegetable dishes. In vegetarian cooking, herbs acquire an importance unequalled in other fields. When neither meat nor fish is present in a dish, there is often a feeling of something lacking, some dominant flavour to pull all the others together. Herbs do this in a totally successful way; when used with understanding and sensitivity, they can give a focal point to a dish without in any way overpowering the other ingredients.

The subdued flavour of farinaceous and leguminous foods makes a good background for herbs; pastry dishes can be made with fresh herbs incorporated in the filling, while rice is good with almost all herbs, especially saffron, tarragon, chervil, dill, chives and parsley. Saffron must be the most expensive of herbs and spices. It is irreplaceable by any other substance: although its colour can be simulated by the use of turmeric as a cheaper substitute, nothing can duplicate its elusive and fascinating fragrance. It makes the best of all flavourings for a risotto. Dried vegetables – haricot (navy) beans, lentils and chick peas (garbanzos) – make nourishing and inexpensive meals, whether served hot with garlic and herb butter, or cold, mixed with a herb-flavoured vinaigrette or a yogurt and mint sauce.

Herb koulibiac

HERB KOULIBIAC

Metric/Imperial	American
175g/6oz cooked rice	1 cup cooked rice
4 hard-boiled eggs	4 hard-boiled eggs
2 bunches spring onions	2 bunches scallions
100g/4oz mushrooms	$\frac{1}{4}$lb mushrooms
25g/1oz butter	2 tablespoons butter
2 tablespoons chopped parsley	2 tablespoons chopped parsley
2 tablespoons chopped chives	2 tablespoons chopped chives
2 tablespoons chopped chervil	2 tablespoons chopped chervil
675g/1½lb short pastry, made with 450g/1lb flour	1½lb basic pie dough, made with 4 cups flour
75g/3oz butter, melted	6 tablespoons butter, melted
sea salt and black pepper	sea salt and black pepper
1 egg yolk	1 egg yolk

Have freshly cooked and well-drained rice. Shell the eggs and cut them into thick slices. Trim the spring onions (scallions) and slice them thinly. Wipe the mushrooms with a clean damp cloth and slice them. Heat the butter in a saucepan and cook the mushrooms briefly, until softened. Mix the chopped herbs with the rice.

Divide the pastry in half and roll out one piece to form a rectangle, about 25 × 20cm/10 × 8in. Mix the rice with the melted butter and lay half of it in a layer on the pastry, leaving the edges uncovered. Sprinkle with salt and pepper and lay the sliced eggs over it. Cover with the sliced spring onions (scallions), the sliced mushrooms, and the remaining rice. Roll out the remaining pastry and cover the first piece exactly, trimming the edges to fit. Dampen the inner edges and squeeze together to seal. Brush all over with beaten egg yolk and bake for 25 minutes in a moderately hot oven (200°C/400°F or Gas Mark 6). Serve hot, with a creamy herb sauce. This makes a good vegetarian main course.

HERB QUICHE

Metric/Imperial	American
350g/12oz short pastry, made with 225g/8oz flour	¾lb basic pie dough, made with 2 cups flour
1 egg yolk	1 egg yolk
FILLING:	FILLING:
100g/4oz sorrel	¼lb sorrel
100g/4oz spinach	¼lb spinach
50g/2oz parsley	1½ cups parsley
1 bunch watercress	1 bunch watercress
4 tablespoons chopped mixed herbs: tarragon, chervil, burnet and dill	¼ cup chopped mixed herbs: tarragon, chervil, burnet and dill
2 eggs	2 eggs
450ml/¾ pint thin cream	2 cups light cream
sea salt and black pepper	sea salt and black pepper
50g/2oz freshly grated Parmesan cheese	½ cup freshly grated Parmesan cheese

Line a 23–25cm/9–10in flan tin (pie pan) with the pastry. Weigh down with foil and the pastry trimmings and bake for 10 minutes in a moderately hot oven (200°C/400°F or Gas Mark 6). Remove the foil and trimmings, brush the pastry all over with beaten egg yolk and put it back in the oven for a further 5 minutes. Take out and cool.

Wash and drain the sorrel, spinach, parsley and watercress. Put them all into a large pan of boiling water and boil for 4 minutes. Drain well, pressing out the moisture with the back of a wooden spoon. When the greens are cool enough to handle, squeeze out the liquid between your hands. Chop the drained greens and add the mixed herbs to them. Beat the eggs in a bowl, add the cream and beat until blended, adding salt and pepper to taste and most of the grated Parmesan, reserving a little to scatter over the top. Mix the egg mixture with the chopped greenstuffs and pour into the pastry case (pie shell). Scatter the reserved cheese over the top and bake for 30 minutes in a moderate oven (180°C/350°F or Gas Mark 4). Serve immediately.

Herb quiche; Mushrooms in pastry cases

MUSHROOMS IN PASTRY CASES

Metric/Imperial	American
350g/12oz short pastry, made with 225g/8oz flour	¾lb basic pie dough, made with 2 cups flour
450g/1lb flat mushrooms	1lb flat mushrooms
50g/2oz butter	¼ cup butter
½ tablespoon flour	½ tablespoon flour
200ml/⅓ pint chicken stock	⅞ cup chicken stock
6 tablespoons sour cream	6 tablespoons sour cream
sea salt and black pepper	sea salt and black pepper
lemon juice to taste	lemon juice to taste
½ tablespoon chopped parsley	½ tablespoon chopped parsley
½ tablespoon chopped chives	½ tablespoon chopped chives
½ tablespoon chopped tarragon	½ tablespoon chopped tarragon
1 egg yolk	1 egg yolk

Chill the pastry for 30 minutes before using. Roll it out thinly and line four 7.5–10cm/3–4in round tin moulds. Lay a small piece of greased foil in each one, with a few pastry trimmings on it. Bake for 10 minutes in a moderately hot oven (190°C/375°F or Gas Mark 5). Remove the foil and pastry and put the pans back in the oven for a further 5 minutes. Remove from the oven and leave to cool.

Wipe the mushrooms with a clean damp cloth and cut off the stalks. Slice the caps. Melt 40g/1½oz/3 tablespoons of butter in a covered pan. Cook the mushroom caps gently, stirring once or twice. When they are soft, drain off the juice and remove the pan from the heat. Melt the remaining butter in a saucepan and stir in the flour. Cook for 1 minute, stirring all the time. Add the heated stock and the sour cream, and cook for 3 minutes, stirring often. Add salt and pepper and lemon juice to taste, then mix in the drained mushrooms. Reheat the mixture and stir in the herbs.

Brush the pastry cases (pie shells) all over with beaten egg yolk and bake them for a further 5 minutes in a moderately hot oven (190°C/375°F or Gas Mark 5). Remove them from the oven, fill with the hot mushroom mixture and serve immediately.

PIZZA WITH DRIED HERBS

Metric/Imperial
300ml/½ pint thick tomato
   sauce (see page 188)
1 teaspoon dried oregano
½ teaspoon dried thyme
175–200g/6–7oz mozzarella
   cheese
2 tablespoons freshly
   grated Parmesan cheese
2 tablespoons olive oil
DOUGH:
1 teaspoon dried yeast
150ml/¼ pint warm water
pinch of sugar
225g/8oz strong flour
½ teaspoon salt
1 tablespoon olive oil

American
1¼ cups thick tomato
   sauce (see page 188)
1 teaspoon dried oregano
½ teaspoon dried thyme
6–7oz mozzarella
   cheese
2 tablespoons freshly
   grated Parmesan cheese
2 tablespoons olive oil
DOUGH:
½ package active dry yeast
⅔ cup warm water
pinch of sugar
2 cups bread or
   all-purpose flour
½ teaspoon salt
1 tablespoon olive oil

To make the dough, put the yeast in a cup with 2 table-spoons of the warm water, and a pinch of sugar. Leave in a warm place for 10 minutes until frothy. Sift the flour with the salt into a large bowl. Make a depression in the centre of the flour and pour in the yeast liquid, the remaining lukewarm water, and the olive oil. Beat with a wooden spoon until it all clings together, adding a drop more water if required, then turn out on to a floured surface and knead for 5 minutes.

Put the dough back in a clean bowl, lightly oiled, and cover it with cling film (Saran wrap). Stand the bowl in a warm place for 1 to 2 hours until the dough has roughly doubled in volume. (Meanwhile make the tomato sauce.) When the dough has risen sufficiently, knock it back (punch it down), and turn out on to a floured board. Knead again briefly for about 2 to 3 minutes, and divide it in 2 pieces.

Roll each piece out fairly thinly. Pick up each one and pull it gently between the hands to make a large thin round, roughly 25cm/10in across. Lay the 2 circles of dough on oiled baking sheets and cover each one with 150ml/ ¼ pint/⅔ cup thick tomato sauce, spreading it evenly almost up to the edge. Sprinkle over each one ½ teaspoon of dried oregano and ¼ teaspoon of dried thyme or, better still, wild thyme. Grate the mozzarella cheese coarsely and scatter half over each pizza. Sprinkle the grated Parmesan on top, and pour a thin trickle of olive oil, about 1 tablespoon, over each. Bake them for about 12 minutes in a hot oven (220°C/425°F or Gas Mark 7) or until the edges of the dough are browned and the centre lightly coloured.

BROWN RICE WITH HERBS

Metric/Imperial
2 leeks
25g/1oz butter
1 tablespoon oil
200g/7oz brown rice
1 bunch spring onions
approx. 450ml/¾ pint
   chicken stock
sea salt and black pepper
1 tablespoon chopped
   chives
1 tablespoon chopped
   parsley
1 tablespoon chopped dill
1 tablespoon chopped
   basil
300ml/½ pint natural
   yogurt to serve

American
2 leeks
2 tablespoons butter
1 tablespoon oil
1 cup brown rice
1 bunch scallions
approx. 2 cups chicken
   stock
sea salt and black pepper
1 tablespoon chopped
   chives
1 tablespoon chopped
   parsley
1 tablespoon chopped dill
1 tablespoon chopped
   basil
1¼ cups unflavored
   yogurt to serve

Trim, wash and slice the leeks. Heat the butter and oil in a heavy saucepan and cook the sliced leeks slowly for 6 to 8 minutes. Wash and drain the rice and add it to the leeks. Stir around for a minute or two, until the rice is coated with fat. Add the sliced spring onions (scallions) and pour on 450ml/¾ pint/2 cups heated chicken stock. Add salt and pepper, cover the pan and simmer for 45 minutes, stirring occasionally.

By the end of the cooking time, the rice should be tender and the stock absorbed; if not, add a little more stock and cook for a further 5 minutes. If there is still some liquid left, cook for a few minutes uncovered. Stir in the herbs, and serve with a bowl of yogurt on the table as a sauce.

GREEN RICE

Metric/Imperial	American
100g/4oz long-grain rice	½ cup long-grain rice
sea salt and black pepper	sea salt and black pepper
3 tablespoons olive oil	3 tablespoons olive oil
2 teaspoons white wine vinegar	2 teaspoons white wine vinegar
squeeze of lemon juice	squeeze of lemon juice
2 tablespoons chopped parsley	2 tablespoons chopped parsley
2 tablespoons chopped chives	2 tablespoons chopped chives
1 tablespoon chopped dill	1 tablespoon chopped dill
1 tablespoon chopped tarragon	1 tablespoon chopped tarragon

Cook the rice in a saucepan of boiling salted water until tender; drain well. While the rice is still hot, stir in some sea salt and black pepper, the olive oil, vinegar, and lemon juice. When the rice has cooled, stir in the chopped herbs. This can be served with cold fish dishes, cold meat and hard-boiled eggs, as well as other vegetarian dishes.

Pizza with dried herbs; Brown rice with herbs; Green rice; Herb risotto

HERB RISOTTO

Metric/Imperial	American
1 shallot	1 shallot
40g/1½oz butter	3 tablespoons butter
225g/8oz Italian medium-grain rice	1 cup Italian medium-grain rice
approx. 750ml/1¼ pints chicken stock	approx. 3 cups chicken stock
pinch of saffron	pinch of saffron
1 bay leaf	1 bay leaf
12 leaves sage	12 leaves sage
12 sprigs thyme	12 sprigs thyme
12 leaves tarragon	12 leaves tarragon
12 leaves marjoram	12 leaves marjoram
sea salt and black pepper	sea salt and black pepper

Peel and chop the shallot. Melt the butter in a heavy saucepan and cook the shallot until soft. Wash and thoroughly drain the rice and add to the pan. Stir around until coated with fat, then pour on 400ml/14fl oz/1¾ cups of heated stock. Cover the pan and simmer gently until almost all the liquid is absorbed.

Add the saffron, crushed bay leaf and the finely chopped herbs to 175ml/6fl oz/¾ cup of the stock and pour it into the rice. Cover again, and cook gently until the stock is absorbed. If the rice is tender, season with salt and pepper and serve, otherwise add the remaining stock and continue to simmer until cooked.

RICE WITH YOGURT

Metric/Imperial	American
200g/7oz long-grain rice	1 cup long-grain rice
1 bunch spring onions	1 bunch scallions
3 tablespoons sunflower-seed oil	3 tablespoons sunflower-seed oil
225g/8oz tomatoes	½lb tomatoes
150ml/¼ pint natural yogurt	⅔ cup unflavored yogurt
4 tablespoons chopped mixed herbs: chervil, chives, dill, tarragon or basil and parsley	¼ cup chopped mixed herbs: chervil, chives, dill, tarragon or basil and parsley
sea salt and black pepper	sea salt and black pepper
lemon juice to taste	lemon juice to taste

Wash and drain the rice and cook it in a saucepan of boiling salted water. Drain well. Slice the spring onions (scallions). Heat the oil in a frying pan (skillet) and cook the sliced onions (scallions) gently until soft and pale golden. Skin the tomatoes and slice them quite thinly, draining off any juice. Mix the cooked onions and the raw sliced tomatoes with the rice, working gently so as not to break up the tomatoes. Beat the yogurt and stir into the rice mixture with the chopped herbs. Add salt and pepper to taste, and a little lemon juice.

SAFFRON RICE

Metric/Imperial	American
200g/7oz Italian medium-grain rice	1 cup Italian medium-grain rice
6 tablespoons olive oil	6 tablespoons olive oil
25g/1oz pine kernels	2 tablespoons pine nuts (pignoli)
1 medium onion	1 medium onion
approx. 900ml/1½ pints chicken stock	approx. 3¾ cups chicken stock
pinch of saffron	pinch of saffron
1 teaspoon sea salt	1 teaspoon sea salt

Wash the rice well and drain. Heat the oil in a large frying pan (skillet) and cook the pine kernels (nuts) until pale golden. Lift them out with a slotted spoon and keep warm. Peel the onion, slice it thinly and cook it in the same oil until soft and nicely coloured. Lift out and keep warm.

Put the rice in the same pan and stir around in the hot oil for 2 to 3 minutes. Heat the stock and dissolve the saffron and the salt in 300ml/½ pint/1¼ cups. Pour this on to the rice, cover the pan, and simmer until the stock is absorbed. Add more boiling stock and continue to cook gently. Continue adding stock until the rice is tender, by which time all the stock will probably have been absorbed. Pile on a shallow dish and scatter over the fried onions and pine kernels (nuts). This useful dish goes well with grilled (broiled) meat or fish, as well as other vegetarian dishes.

RICE WITH CHICK PEAS

Metric/Imperial	American
50g/2oz dried chick peas or 200g/7oz canned chick peas	⅓ cup dried chick peas (garbanzos) or 1 cup canned chick peas
200g/7oz long-grain rice	1 cup long-grain rice
100g/4oz chopped Spanish onion	1 cup chopped Bermuda onion
sea salt and black pepper	sea salt and black pepper
3 tablespoons olive oil	3 tablespoons olive oil
3 tablespoons lemon juice	3 tablespoons lemon juice
198g/7oz can tuna fish (optional)	7oz can tuna fish (optional)
2 tablespoons chopped chervil	2 tablespoons chopped chervil

If using dried chick peas soak them for 3 to 4 hours, or overnight. Drain them and put them in a saucepan with cold water to cover and bring slowly to the boil. Simmer until the peas are soft when crushed between the fingers; this will take anything from 1 to 2 hours. Add salt only towards the end of the cooking. Drain and leave to cool. Alternatively, use canned chick peas, drained.

Wash and drain the rice and cook it in a saucepan of salted boiling water; drain well. While it is still hot, put the rice in a bowl with the drained chick peas and stir in the finely sliced onion with salt and black pepper to taste. Stir in the olive oil and lemon juice. Non-vegetarians may like to add some tuna fish at this stage. Drain the can of tuna fish and break the fish into flakes. Fork into the rice. Stir in the chopped chervil, and leave to cool completely before serving. Do not chill.

VINE LEAVES WITH HERB STUFFING

Metric/Imperial	American
225g/8oz onions	½lb onions
150ml/¼ pint olive oil	⅔ cup olive oil
100g/4oz Italian medium-grain rice	½ cup Italian medium-grain rice
600ml/1 pint boiling water	2½ cups boiling water
2 tablespoons pine kernels	2 tablespoons pine nuts (pignoli)
2 tablespoons seedless raisins	2 tablespoons seedless raisins
sea salt and black pepper	sea salt and black pepper
juice of 1 lemon	juice of 1 lemon
3 tablespoons chopped mixed herbs: dill, tarragon and parsley	3 tablespoons chopped mixed herbs: dill, tarragon and parsley
225g/8oz preserved vine leaves or 24 fresh vine leaves	½lb preserved vine leaves or 24 fresh vine leaves

Peel and chop the onions. Heat half the oil in a frying pan (skillet) and cook the onion until softened and pale golden. Wash and drain the rice and add it to the pan. Stir around for 2 to 3 minutes. Pour on 300ml/½ pint/1¼ cups boiling water. Add the pine kernels (nuts) and the raisins, and salt and pepper to taste. Simmer gently until the water is absorbed, about 8 to 10 minutes. Add more salt and pepper

if needed, 1 tablespoon lemon juice and the chopped herbs.

Turn out on to a plate to cool while you prepare the vine leaves. (These can be bought in packets or cans from Greek and Cypriot shops.) Soak them in a sink full of cold water for a minute or two, then gently separate them and lay on a wire rack to drain. If using fresh vine leaves, blanch them for 3 minutes in boiling water, then drain. When the stuffing has cooled, place a heaped tablespoon in the centre of each leaf, then roll them up loosely into a cigar shape leaving room for the rice to swell.

Put a layer of unused leaves in the bottom of a broad pan and lay the filled leaves on them. Pour over the remaining olive oil, 2 tablespoons lemon juice, and 300ml/½ pint/1¼ cups hot water. Lay a flat plate on top of the vine leaves to press them down lightly, and cover the pan. Bring to the boil and simmer gently for 45 minutes. Leave to cool in the pan. To serve, lay the little rolls on a flat dish and sprinkle with a little more lemon juice. Serve as a first course, or with cocktails.

Opposite: Rice with yogurt; Rice with chick peas

Below: Vine leaves with herb stuffing

GREEN PANCAKES WITH CREAM CHEESE

Metric/Imperial	American
100g/4oz sorrel or spinach	¼lb sorrel or spinach
100g/4oz plain flour	1 cup all-purpose flour
pinch of sea salt	pinch of sea salt
1 egg	1 egg
150ml/¼ pint milk	⅔ cup milk
lard for frying	lard for frying
FILLING:	FILLING:
450g/1lb cream cheese	2 cups cream cheese
sea salt and black pepper	sea salt and black pepper
4 tablespoons chopped chives	¼ cup chopped chives

Wash and drain the sorrel (or spinach). Push the leaves through a juice extractor; you should have about 4 tablespoons (¼ cup) of juice. If you do not have a juice extractor, cook the leaves in a saucepan with a little water and push through a sieve (strainer) to make a thin purée.

Sift the flour into a bowl with the salt. Beat in the egg and the milk, then the sorrel juice or purée. Allow the batter to stand for a little before using. Season the cream cheese with salt and pepper, and mix in the chopped chives. Melt a little lard in a frying pan (skillet) and use the batter to make 8 small pancakes. Put about 2 tablespoons of the cheese filling in each pancake and roll them up.

HERB GNOCCHI

Metric/Imperial	American
225g/8oz spinach	½lb spinach
100g/4oz sorrel	¼lb sorrel
1 bunch watercress	1 bunch watercress
50g/2oz parsley	1½ cups parsley
1 tablespoon chopped chervil	1 tablespoon chopped chervil
1 tablespoon chopped tarragon	1 tablespoon chopped tarragon
1 tablespoon chopped dill	1 tablespoon chopped dill
25g/1oz butter	2 tablespoons butter
175g/6oz ricotta cheese	6oz ricotta cheese
sea salt and black pepper	sea salt and black pepper
75g/3oz freshly grated Parmesan cheese	¾ cup freshly grated Parmesan cheese
2 eggs	2 eggs
2½ tablespoons flour	2½ tablespoons flour
melted butter to serve (optional)	melted butter to serve (optional)

Start the day before. Wash and drain the spinach, sorrel, watercress and parsley. Throw them into a large pan of boiling water and boil for 4 minutes, then drain. (If sorrel is not available, use extra spinach.) When cool enough to handle, squeeze out as much moisture as possible in the hands, then chop finely, by hand or in a food processor. Add the chopped herbs and stir the purée in a saucepan over a low heat for several minutes, to dry it out.

Cut the butter into small bits, beat the ricotta cheese to a smooth consistency, and add to the purée with salt and pepper. Stir in one-third of the Parmesan cheese. Take the pan off the heat. Beat the eggs, and stir them into the mixture. Finally, stir in the sifted flour and beat until smooth. Pour into a shallow dish and leave to cool. Place in the refrigerator, uncovered, and leave overnight. (It can be left for 2 days if preferred.)

After chilling, the mixture should have become firm enough to handle; if not, this is because the green purée was too moist. In this case, stir in a little extra flour – but not too much, or the gnocchi will be heavy.

Have a large pan of lightly salted water on the boil, and form the green mixture into egg-shaped gnocchi, using 2 teaspoons and rolling them very lightly on a floured board. Drop them in batches into the pan; do not crowd them. When they float to the surface, after 4 to 5 minutes, lift them out with a slotted spoon and drain on a cloth. Test one to make sure they are cooked through, then transfer to a hot serving dish while you cook the others. Sprinkle the gnocchi with a little Parmesan cheese and serve with a bowl of the remaining grated Parmesan on the table and a small jug (pitcher) of melted butter, if you like.

BEANS WITH GARLIC AND HERBS

Metric/Imperial	American
200g/7oz dried haricot beans	1 cup navy beans
1 Spanish onion	1 Bermuda onion
1 carrot	1 carrot
1 stick celery	1 stalk celery
sea salt and black pepper	sea salt and black pepper
1 clove garlic	1 clove garlic
3 tablespoons olive oil	3 tablespoons olive oil
1 tablespoon white wine vinegar	1 tablespoon white wine vinegar
2 tablespoons chopped chervil	2 tablespoons chopped chervil
1 tablespoon chopped chives	1 tablespoon chopped chives
1 teaspoon chopped lovage	1 teaspoon chopped lovage
1 teaspoon chopped summer savory	1 teaspoon chopped summer savory

Soak the beans in cold water for 3 to 4 hours or overnight. Drain them, and put them in a saucepan with plenty of fresh cold water. Bring to the boil slowly. Add half the peeled onion, the cleaned carrot and celery and cook until tender, adding salt towards the end of the cooking.

As soon as the beans are soft, but not yet broken, drain them and discard the vegetables (or keep them with the stock for making soup). Add more salt, as necessary, and lots of black pepper. While the beans are still hot, stir in the remaining half onion, thinly sliced, and the peeled and crushed garlic. Stir in the oil and vinegar and the chopped herbs. Serve soon after cooling; on no account chill.

NOODLES WITH MARROW (SQUASH) AND DILL

Metric/Imperial	American
450g/1lb vegetable marrow or *large courgettes*	1lb summer squash or *large zucchini*
50g/2oz butter	¼ cup butter
sea salt and black pepper	sea salt and black pepper
2 tablespoons chopped dill	2 tablespoons chopped dill
350g/12oz noodles	¾lb noodles

Peel the marrow (squash) or courgettes (zucchini). It will probably be necessary to discard the seeds and soft interior of the marrow (summer squash), but not if you are using courgettes (zucchini).

Cut the flesh into small cubes, about 1cm/½in square. Heat the butter in a saucepan and cook the marrow (squash) gently until just tender but still crisp, without allowing the butter to burn. Add salt and pepper to taste, and stir in the dill. Leave to stand, covered, while you boil the noodles. Drain them well and return them to the pan. Reheat gently, and stir in the marrow (squash) with its juice. Serve immediately.

HERB PUDDING

Metric/Imperial	American
50g/2oz pearl barley	⅓ cup pearl barley
100g/4oz nettles	¼lb nettles
100g/4oz sorrel or *spinach*	¼lb sorrel or *spinach*
1 bunch spring onions	1 bunch scallions
25g/1oz parsley	¾ cup parsley
20g/¾oz chopped mixed herbs: summer savory, marjoram, burnet, tarragon, chervil and dill	½ cup chopped mixed herbs: summer savory, marjoram, burnet, tarragon, chervil and dill
sea salt and black pepper	sea salt and black pepper
1 egg	1 egg

Soak the pearl barley in cold water for 2 to 4 hours. Drain well. Wash the nettles, sorrel or spinach, spring onions (scallions) and parsley. Chop them quite finely (quickly done in a food processor), and mix into the drained barley with the mixed herbs. Add salt and pepper, then turn into a colander (strainer) lined with muslin (cheesecloth). Tie it up so that it forms a round shape and lower into a pan of boiling water, or stock. Simmer for 1 hour, or cook for 20 minutes in a pressure cooker.

Lift out and drain for a moment in a colander (strainer). Untie the pudding and turn it into a bowl. Break it up, and stir in 1 beaten egg. Add more salt and black pepper, to taste, then turn into an ovenproof dish and bake for 15 to 20 minutes in a moderate oven (180°C/350°F or Gas Mark 4), until firm and lightly browned on top. This old-fashioned English country recipe makes an excellent vegetarian dish. It is also good with boiled bacon, sausages, or game.

Above: Green pancakes with cream cheese; Herb gnocchi

LENTILS WITH MINT

Metric/Imperial	American
225g/8oz brown lentils	1 cup brown lentils
sea salt and black pepper	sea salt and black pepper
1 clove garlic	1 clove garlic
150ml/¼ pint natural yogurt	⅔ cup unflavored yogurt
½ bunch watercress	½ bunch watercress
1½ tablespoons chopped mint	1½ tablespoons chopped mint

Pour boiling water over the lentils in a bowl and leave them to soak for 4 hours. Alternatively, soak them overnight in cold water. Drain the lentils and put them in a saucepan with enough fresh cold water to cover. Bring to the boil slowly and simmer for 20 minutes, or until just tender but not mushy.

Drain the lentils reserving the liquid. Stir in salt and pepper to taste, and the peeled and crushed clove of garlic. Measure 150ml/¼ pint/⅔ cup of the lentil stock and mix it with the yogurt. Stir into the lentils. Pick the tips off the watercress and stir them into the lentil mixture. Mix well, finally adding the chopped mint. Do not chill but serve cold with cold sausage dishes, cold lamb, cold boiled ham or bacon, or other vegetable dishes.

Fish

Herbs have many different uses in fish cookery, according to the type of fish in question, and the manner of cooking it. For flavouring a fish stock or court-bouillon, for instance, herbs very similar to those used in a meat stock would be suitable, such as bay, parsley, thyme and possibly lovage. The same applies to poaching fish, or making fish aspic, although in the latter case the aspic jelly is sometimes flavoured by infusion with one herb only. Tarragon is often used in this way, and the stock is then strained and mixed with gelatine to form a herb-flavoured jelly.

Baked fish can be scattered with herbs and sprinkled with olive oil and lemon juice before being wrapped in foil and laid on the oven rack. Since the more delicate herbs would lose their flavour if used in this way, the stronger ones like rosemary, thyme, lovage and fennel are more appropriate. A large piece of halibut, turbot or hake can be poached and served hot, with a herb sauce, while fillets of firm fish are good when left to cool and coated with a chaud-froid sauce made from the fish stock flavoured with fines herbes, enriched with cream and set with gelatine. A plainly grilled (broiled) fish served with herb butter can hardly be bettered; the best is the most expensive, alas: a Dover sole on the bone, with a pat of parsley butter melting over it. Trout are good fried quickly in butter (with a little oil added to prevent it burning), with chopped parsley and lemon juice added to the juices and poured over the fish. Mackerel, on the other hand, are better stuffed with a fennel stuffing, then deeply scored on each side and basted with olive oil and lemon juice while grilling (broiling). A fish pie can be improved by mixing the cooked flaked haddock in a herb sauce, with a layer of sliced hard-boiled eggs under its covering of mashed potato. A mixture of fresh and smoked haddock makes a more unusual dish, flaked and mixed together in a creamy parsley sauce flavoured with Parmesan cheese, and served with croûtons of toast or poached eggs for a luncheon dish.

Dill seems especially suited to cold fish dishes, shell-fish in particular. I like to make a salad of mixed white fish and shellfish in a lemon-flavoured vinaigrette, and serve a creamy dill sauce separately. A seviche of raw scallops, cut very thin and marinated for 24 hours in citrus fruit juice is enhanced by finely chopped feathery dill leaves. (Mexican in origin, a seviche is a dish of shellfish or fillets of tender white fish marinated in lemon or lime juice, and eaten uncooked.) Both scallops and mussels are delicious when taken out of their shells after poaching and served, either hot or cold, in a delicate sauce flavoured with chopped herbs or with saffron.

COLD POACHED BASS WITH HERBS

Metric/Imperial	American
1 sea bass, about 1kg/2lb	1 sea bass, about 2lb
1 onion	1 onion
1 carrot	1 carrot
1 stick celery	1 stalk celery
1 bay leaf	1 bay leaf
3 stalks parsley	3 stalks parsley
3 sprigs lovage	3 sprigs lovage
2 tablespoons white wine vinegar	2 tablespoons white wine vinegar
1 tablespoon sea salt	1 tablespoon sea salt
10 black peppercorns	10 black peppercorns
225g/8oz tomatoes	½lb tomatoes
1 bunch spring onions	1 bunch scallions
1 tablespoon olive oil	1 tablespoon olive oil
3 tablespoons lemon juice	3 tablespoons lemon juice
3 tablespoons chopped mixed herbs: chervil, dill, tarragon, parsley and chives	3 tablespoons chopped mixed herbs: chervil, dill, tarragon, parsley and chives
hollandaise sauce with herbs (see page 186) or 2 lemons	hollandaise sauce with herbs (see page 186) or 2 lemons

Put the fish in a pan that fits it as neatly as possible and cover with cold water. Lift out the bass. Peel and halve the onion, clean and halve the carrot and celery. Put them in the pan with the bay leaf, parsley, lovage, vinegar, salt and peppercorns. Bring slowly to the boil and simmer for 30 minutes. Leave to cool.

Return the bass to the pan and bring back to the boil. Simmer for 20 minutes. Remove the pan from the heat and leave the fish to cool in the liquid. An hour or two later, lift out the fish and remove the skin. Lay the bass on a platter.

Skin the tomatoes and chop them, discarding any juice. Slice the spring onions (scallions) and mix them with the

chopped tomatoes in a bowl. Add a little salt and pepper, the olive oil and 1 tablespoon lemon juice. Mix lightly then lay all around the fish. Pour the remaining lemon juice over the fish, and scatter the dish with the chopped herbs. Serve with hollandaise sauce with herbs, or simply with lemons cut into quarters.

Above: Cold poached bass with herbs

Opposite: Eel in green sauce

EEL IN GREEN SAUCE

Metric/Imperial
1kg/2lb small freshwater
  eel, skinned
4 shallots
3 tablespoons olive oil
225g/8oz mixed sorrel,
  watercress and spinach
50g/2oz celery leaves or
  celery and lovage mixed
2 tablespoons chopped
  parsley
1 tablespoon chopped
  chervil
½ tablespoon chopped
  tarragon
fish stock or water
dry white wine
1 bay leaf
sea salt and black pepper

American
2lb small freshwater eel,
  skinned
4 shallots
3 tablespoons olive oil
½lb mixed sorrel,
  watercress and spinach
1½ cups celery leaves or
  celery and lovage mixed
2 tablespoons chopped
  parsley
1 tablespoon chopped
  chervil
½ tablespoon chopped
  tarragon
fish stock or water
dry white wine
1 bay leaf
sea salt and black pepper

Cut the eel in 5cm/2in chunks. Peel and chop the shallots. Heat the oil in a saucepan and gently fry the shallots, making sure they do not turn brown. Wash and chop all the leaf vegetables and herbs, except the bay leaf, and add them to the shallots. Cook slowly in the oil for 10 to 12 minutes. Add the eel, and cover with roughly equal amounts of fish stock (or water) and wine. The liquid should only just cover the fish, otherwise it will be too thin to set to a jelly later. Add the bay leaf, salt and pepper, and cover the pan. Bring quickly to the boil and boil fast for 1 minute. Lower the heat, and simmer for 20 minutes.

Remove the bay leaf and tip the contents of the pan into a deep serving dish or tureen. As a hot dish, serve straight away, in soup plates, accompanied by a dish of plain boiled potatoes. To serve cold (which I prefer), allow to cool, then chill in the refrigerator overnight. Serve with brown bread and butter. A generous amount for 4 people, this interesting dish is a Belgian speciality.

BROCHETTE OF FISH WITH HERBS

Metric/Imperial	American
675g/1½lb halibut or conger eel	1½lb halibut or swordfish
3 tablespoons olive oil	3 tablespoons olive oil
1 tablespoon lemon juice	1 tablespoon lemon juice
1 tablespoon chopped tarragon	1 tablespoon chopped tarragon
1 tablespoon chopped dill	1 tablespoon chopped dill
1 tablespoon chopped parsley	1 tablespoon chopped parsley
2 lemons to serve	2 lemons to serve

Skin and bone the fish, cut in neat cubes and put them in a bowl. Pour over the olive oil and lemon juice, and stir in the chopped herbs. Leave for 3 to 4 hours, then thread the cubes on to 4 skewers. Grill (broil) slowly, turning often and basting with the oil and lemon juice. Serve with lemon quarters.

HADDOCK IN PARSLEY SAUCE

Metric/Imperial	American
350g/12oz fresh haddock fillet	¾lb fresh haddock fillet
300ml/½ pint milk	1¼ cups milk
1 smoked haddock on the bone, about 450g/1lb	¾lb finnan haddie fillets
2 hard-boiled eggs	2 hard-boiled eggs
PARSLEY SAUCE:	PARSLEY SAUCE:
40g/1½oz butter	3 tablespoons butter
3 tablespoons flour	3 tablespoons flour
150ml/¼ pint thin cream	⅔ cup light cream
sea salt and black pepper	sea salt and black pepper
4 tablespoons chopped parsley	¼ cup chopped parsley
2 tablespoons freshly grated Parmesan cheese	2 tablespoons freshly grated Parmesan cheese

Put the fresh haddock in a broad pan with the milk. Add enough water almost to cover the fish. Cover and cook gently for about 8 minutes, or until the fish flakes easily. Lift out the fish and discard any skin and bone, breaking the flesh into large flakes. Keep it warm. Put the smoked fish in the same liquid, adding a little more water if needed, and simmer for 12 minutes, or until tender. Lift out the fish and flake the flesh, removing all skin and bone. Keep warm with the fresh haddock.

To make the parsley sauce, strain the liquid and measure out 450ml/¾ pint/2 cups. Melt the butter in a clean pan, stir in the flour and cook for 1 minute. Pour on the strained fish stock and simmer for 3 minutes, stirring as it thickens. Stir in the cream and add salt and pepper to taste. (It is unlikely that much salt will be necessary.) Stir in the chopped parsley and the grated Parmesan cheese.

Chop the hard-boiled eggs and add them to the fish. Mix the eggs and fish with the sauce. Reheat the mixture briefly if necessary, and pour into a serving dish.

HALIBUT SALAD

Metric/Imperial	American
575g/1¼lb halibut	1¼lb halibut
4 tablespoons olive oil	¼ cup olive oil
2 tablespoons lemon juice	2 tablespoons lemon juice
sea salt and black pepper	sea salt and black pepper
1 bunch spring onions	1 bunch scallions
4 tablespoons chopped mixed herbs: tarragon, chervil, chives and dill	¼ cup chopped mixed herbs: tarragon, chervil, chives and dill

Have the fish in 1 thick piece if possible. Brush a piece of foil with 1 tablespoon of the olive oil and lay the fish on it. Sprinkle the fish with 1 tablespoon of the lemon juice and some salt and black pepper. Wrap up the fish in the foil and lay on a rack in a roasting pan. Bake in a moderate oven (180°C/350°F or Gas Mark 4) for 35 minutes. When it is cooked, allow the foil to cool before unwrapping it.

Break the fish into large flakes, discarding skin and bone, and put it into a bowl. Mix the fish very gently with the remaining oil and lemon juice. Slice the spring onions (scallions) and add them to the fish. Try not to break up the fish more than you can help. Add plenty of salt and black pepper and stir in the chopped herbs.

This pretty green and white dish makes a light main course for a summer meal, or a first course. It can also be served in conjunction with other cold dishes, such as scrambled eggs with tarragon, whole tomatoes with chopped herbs, green rice, and a lettuce salad.

BAKED HALIBUT WITH ROSEMARY

Metric/Imperial	American
olive oil	olive oil
4 halibut steaks, about 225g/8oz each	4 halibut steaks, about ½lb each
sea salt and black pepper	sea salt and black pepper
100g/4oz shallots	¼lb shallots
675g/1½lb tomatoes	1½lb tomatoes
2 tablespoons chopped rosemary	2 tablespoons chopped rosemary

Brush four pieces of foil with olive oil. Sprinkle the fish steaks with salt and pepper on each side and lay them on the foil. Peel the shallots, chop them very finely and scatter them over the fish. Skin the tomatoes, chop them quite finely and lay them over the shallots. Sprinkle the chopped rosemary over the tomatoes. Dribble a little olive oil over each steak and wrap up the foil.

Put the parcels of foil on a rack in a roasting pan and bake in a moderate oven (180°C/350°F or Gas Mark 4) for 25 minutes. Serve with new potatoes and a green salad.

MACKEREL WITH FENNEL STUFFING

Metric/Imperial	American
4 small mackerel	4 small mackerel
fennel stuffing (see page 109)	fennel stuffing (see page 109)
olive oil	olive oil
3 lemons to serve	3 lemons to serve

Have the mackerel left whole, but with their heads and tails cut off. This leaves a neat pocket to fill with the stuffing. Make the fennel stuffing and press it into the cavity in each of the fish. Make three diagonal cuts on each side of the fish, and pour over each one a little olive oil and lemon juice.

Grill (broil) under a fierce heat to start with, then lower the heat to finish cooking. They will take about 8 minutes on each side, basting with more oil and lemon juice a few times. Serve with plenty of cut lemons. This dish needs no accompaniment.

Brochette of fish with herbs; Halibut salad; Baked halibut with rosemary

MARINATED MACKEREL WITH FENNEL

Metric/Imperial
2 medium mackerel
yolks of 2 hard-boiled eggs
1 tablespoon chopped
    fennel or dill leaves
MARINADE:
300ml/½ pint dry white
    wine
4 tablespoons white wine
    vinegar
1 shallot
1 carrot
1 clove garlic
1 bay leaf
6 black peppercorns
3 stalks parsley
2 sprigs thyme

SOUR CREAM SAUCE:
6 tablespoons sour cream
pinch of dry mustard
sea salt and black pepper

American
2 medium mackerel
yolks of 2 hard-boiled eggs
1 tablespoon chopped
    fennel or dill leaves
MARINADE:
1¼ cups dry white
    wine
¼ cup white wine
    vinegar
1 shallot
1 carrot
1 clove garlic
1 bay leaf
6 black peppercorns
3 stalks parsley
2 sprigs thyme

SOUR CREAM SAUCE:
6 tablespoons sour cream
pinch of mustard powder
sea salt and black pepper

Have the mackerel left whole but with the heads and tails cut off. Put all the ingredients for the marinade in a small pan and bring to the boil. Cook for 20 minutes, then pour it over the mackerel in a narrow pan. Bring back to the boil and simmer, covered, for about 10 minutes. Leave the fish to cool in the marinade, then lift them out and cut them into 8 fillets, free from all skin and bone. Lay them on a shallow dish.

To make the sauce, mix the sour cream with 2 table-spoons of the strained marinade in a bowl and add the mustard, salt and black pepper. Beat until smooth and pour over the fillets.

Chop the egg yolks very finely and scatter them evenly over the dish. Chop the fennel (or dill leaves) and sprinkle them over all. Chill for an hour or two before serving. Herring or trout may be substituted for the mackerel. Serve as a first course, with brown bread and butter.

Opposite: Mussels in dill sauce; Marinated mackerel with fennel

Below: Red mullet (snapper) with fennel

MUSSELS IN DILL SAUCE

Metric/Imperial	American
2.25 litres/2 quarts mussels	5 pints mussels
1 stick celery	1 stalk celery
3 stalks parsley	3 stalks parsley
1 shallot	1 shallot
4 tablespoons dry white wine	¼ cup dry white wine
DILL SAUCE:	DILL SAUCE:
3 tablespoons Dijon mustard	3 tablespoons Dijon mustard
300ml/½ pint thin cream	1¼ cups light cream
juice of ½ lemon	juice of ½ lemon
sea salt and black pepper	sea salt and black pepper
4 tablespoons chopped dill leaves	¼ cup chopped dill leaves

Clean the mussels and put them in a deep saucepan with the cleaned and sliced celery, the parsley, and the peeled and sliced shallot. Add the wine and cover the pan. Bring to the boil and cook gently for 4 to 5 minutes, until all the shells have opened. (Discard any that do not open.) Take off the lid and leave to cool.

Put the mustard in a small bowl and gradually beat the cream into it. Add the lemon juice and salt and pepper to taste – not much salt will be needed. When the mussels are cool, lift them out of their shells and stir them into the creamy sauce. (Keep their cooking stock for a fish soup.) Stir in the dill and serve soon after cooling. Serve alone as a first course, or with a bowl of cooled boiled rice as a light main course.

COLD MACKEREL FILLETS

Metric/Imperial	American
2 large mackerel	2 large mackerel
olive oil	olive oil
juice of 2 lemons	juice of 2 lemons
½ mild onion	½ mild onion
2 tablespoons chopped parsley	2 tablespoons chopped parsley

Remove the heads from the fish and clean them without splitting them. Score the mackerel on each side 2 or 3 times. Brush them with olive oil and lemon juice and cook them under a grill (broiler) for about 8 minutes each side. When they are done, leave them to get quite cold. (Do not chill.)

Remove the skin and divide each fish into 4 neat fillets; lay them on a flat serving dish. Chop the onion finely and scatter it over the fish. Dribble a little olive oil and some lemon juice over each fillet. Scatter the chopped parsley over all and serve with a tomato salad.

RED MULLET (SNAPPER) WITH FENNEL

Metric/Imperial	American
4 red mullet	4 red snapper
6–8 sprigs fennel	6–8 sprigs fennel
olive oil	olive oil
juice of 1 lemon	juice of 1 lemon
lemon quarters to garnish	lemon quarters to garnish

Score the fish lightly on each side with a sharp knife. Reserve 2 tablespoons of chopped fennel leaves. Chop up the remaining leaves finely with the stalks. Lay the fish on a grill pan (broiler) and stuff them with some of the fennel, laying the rest of it between the fish. Sprinkle with olive oil and some of the lemon juice. Grill (broil) under a fairly fierce heat for 4 to 5 minutes on each side, then a further 4 to 5 minutes at a gentler heat. Baste with more oil and lemon juice as needed.

To serve hot: simply lay the whole fish on a flat dish and scatter the chopped fennel leaves over them. Surround with lemon quarters. To serve cold: after cooling, skin and fillet the fish and lay the fillets on a flat dish. Sprinkle with lemon juice and scatter the chopped fennel leaves over them. Garnish with cut lemons.

PLAICE (FLOUNDER) IN TARRAGON ASPIC

Metric/Imperial	American
2 fillets plaice, with bones	*2 fillets flounder, with bones*
1 carrot	*1 carrot*
1 onion	*1 onion*
1 stick celery	*1 stalk celery*
1 bay leaf	*1 bay leaf*
sea salt and black peppercorns	*sea salt and black peppercorns*
150ml/¼ pint white wine or 3 tablespoons white wine vinegar	*⅔ cup white wine or 3 tablespoons white wine vinegar*
4 sprigs tarragon	*4 sprigs tarragon*
lemon juice, to taste	*lemon juice, to taste*
½ tablespoon gelatine	*½ tablespoon gelatine*
2 tomatoes	*2 tomatoes*
herb mayonnaise (see page 190) to serve (optional)	*herb mayonnaise (see page 190) to serve (optional)*

Skin the fillets and cut each one in half. Peel and halve the carrot and onion and put them in a saucepan with the fish bones and skins, the cleaned and chopped celery and the bay leaf. Add some salt and a few black peppercorns. Cover with cold water and dry white wine (or vinegar). Bring to the boil and simmer for 30 minutes.

Strain the liquid into a clean pan and put in the rolled fillets of fish. Strip 4 of the best leaves from the tarragon, then add the remaining leaves and stalks to the pan. Poach very gently for 5 to 6 minutes, then lift out the fish and leave it to cool. Strain the stock again and measure 300ml/½ pint/1¼ cups. If the flavour is weak reduce the stock first by fast boiling. Add lemon juice to taste.

Dissolve the gelatine in a cup in a little of the hot stock. When it is dissolved, mix it with the rest of the liquid. Strain the stock again and pour a thin layer into each of 4 tin moulds, or cocotte dishes. Cool, then chill in the refrigerator until set. Lay a tarragon leaf in the centre of each, then a rolled fillet of fish. Skin the tomatoes and chop them finely, discarding the seeds and juice. Scatter the chopped tomato round the fish. Fill each cocotte dish with the remaining fish jelly and chill until set. To serve, turn out onto small flat plates and surround with a little shredded lettuce. Serve alone, or with a herb mayonnaise, if liked. This makes an appetizing first course for a dinner party, or summer luncheon.

PLAICE (FLOUNDER) WITH HERB STUFFING

Metric/Imperial	American
8 fillets plaice	*8 small fillets flounder*
225g/8oz ricotta or low-fat cream cheese	*½lb ricotta or diet cheese*
25g/1oz chopped parsley	*¾ cup chopped parsley*
1 egg yolk	*1 egg yolk*
sea salt and black pepper	*sea salt and black pepper*
juice of 1 lemon	*juice of 1 lemon*
8 large spinach leaves	*8 large spinach leaves*
hollandaise sauce with herbs (see page 186) (optional)	*hollandaise sauce with herbs (see page 186) (optional)*

Skin the fillets, wash them and pat them dry. Put the ricotta (or low-fat or diet cheese) in a blender with the parsley and the egg yolk. Blend until smooth, adding salt and pepper to taste. Sprinkle each fillet with salt and pepper and a little lemon juice. Lay 2 teaspoons of the stuffing on each fillet and roll up.

Blanch the spinach leaves by throwing them into boiling water for 3 minutes. Drain them, plunge into cold water and drain again. Spread them out and lay a rolled fillet in each leaf. Wrap them up and cook in a steamer for 8 minutes over rapidly boiling water. Serve with boiled new potatoes and hollandaise sauce with herbs, if liked.

Scallops in herb sauce; Plaice (flounder) with herb stuffing; Plaice (flounder) in tarragon aspic; Prawns (shrimp) and melon in dill sauce

PRAWNS (SHRIMP) AND MELON IN DILL SAUCE

Metric/Imperial
1 small honeydew melon
225g/8oz peeled prawns
juice of ½ lemon
DILL SAUCE:
100g/4oz medium-fat
  cream cheese
6–8 tablespoons buttermilk
sea salt and black pepper
1 teaspoon dill vinegar or
  lemon juice
2½ tablespoons chopped
  dill

American
1 small honeydew melon
1¼ cups shelled shrimp
juice of ½ lemon
DILL SAUCE:
½ cup ricotta or diet
  cheese
6–8 tablespoons buttermilk
sea salt and black pepper
1 teaspoon dill vinegar or
  lemon juice
2½ tablespoons chopped
  dill

Cut the flesh of the melon into small cubes and mix it with the prawns (shrimp). Sprinkle with the lemon juice.

Purée the cream cheese (ricotta or diet cheese) in a blender with 2 tablespoons of the buttermilk, adding up to 8 tablespoons of buttermilk until the mixture reaches the consistency of medium thick cream. The quantity of buttermilk needed will depend on the consistency of the cheese. Add salt and pepper to taste, the dill vinegar (or lemon juice) and 2 tablespoons of the chopped dill, reserving the rest for garnish.

Mix the sauce with the prawns (shrimp) and melon, and chill for 1 hour before serving. Mix again just before serving, and sprinkle with the remaining dill. Serve as a first course.

SCALLOPS IN HERB SAUCE

Metric/Imperial
12 scallops
150ml/¼ pint white wine
150ml/¼ pint water
sea salt and black pepper
25g/1oz butter
1 tablespoon flour
150ml/¼ pint thin cream
1 tablespoon chopped
  tarragon
1 tablespoon chopped dill
1 tablespoon chopped
  chives
1 tablespoon chopped
  parsley

American
12 scallops
⅔ cup white wine
⅔ cup water
sea salt and black pepper
2 tablespoons butter
1 tablespoon flour
⅔ cup light cream
1 tablespoon chopped
  tarragon
1 tablespoon chopped dill
1 tablespoon chopped
  chives
1 tablespoon chopped
  parsley

Cut the scallops off their shells, discarding the beard-like fringe and intestinal thread. Wash the white part and the coral, pat dry, and cut them into quarters. Put the wine and the water in a shallow lidded pan. Add a pinch of salt and some freshly ground black pepper. Bring to the boil, then put in the scallops. Cover, and simmer for 8 minutes, or until tender. Lift out the scallops with a slotted spoon and keep warm.

Keep the cooking liquid warm in the saucepan. Mix the butter and flour together in a cup until they form a smooth paste. Drop the paste, bit by bit, into the cooking liquid and stir until smooth, simmering very gently to make a sauce. Add the cream and stir again, then stir in the chopped herbs. Put the scallops back into the sauce for a moment to reheat, then pour it all into a shallow serving dish.

Serve alone, with crusty bread and butter, as a first course, or with boiled rice as a light main course. When scallops are expensive, fewer of them may be used and the quantities made up with new potatoes, skinned, boiled, and cut into thick slices. In this case, do not serve with rice.

SEVICHE OF SCALLOPS WITH HERBS

Metric/Imperial	American
10 large scallops	*10 large scallops*
4 scallop shells	*4 scallop shells*
150ml/¼ pint lemon juice	*⅔ cup lemon juice*
1½ tablespoons chopped shallot	*1½ tablespoons chopped shallot*
½ tablespoon chopped tarragon	*½ tablespoon chopped tarragon*
½ tablespoon chopped dill	*½ tablespoon chopped dill*
½ tablespoon chopped chives	*½ tablespoon chopped chives*
½ tablespoon chopped parsley	*½ tablespoon chopped parsley*
1½ tablespoons sunflower-seed oil	*1½ tablespoons sunflower-seed oil*

Detach the scallops from their shells and scrape off the beard-like fringe and intestinal thread. Cut away the orange flesh. Wash the white parts and pat dry. Cut in slices about 5mm/¼in thick. Wash and prepare the coral in the same way, if you like. Choose 4 medium shells, scrub them well and leave to drain. Put the sliced scallops in a bowl and pour over the lemon juice. (There should be enough almost to cover them.) Cover with cling film (Saran wrap) and put in the refrigerator for 24 hours, stirring occasionally.

When ready to serve, chop the shallots and the herbs very finely indeed. Drain off the lemon juice from the scallops and stir in the oil. Add the shallots and herbs and mix well. Spoon on to the shells and serve immediately as a first course, with brown bread and butter.

SHELLFISH SALAD WITH TARRAGON

Metric/Imperial	American
450g/1lb hake or halibut	*1lb hake or halibut*
juice of 2 lemons	*juice of 2 lemons*
6 scallops	*6 scallops*
6 giant prawns	*6 jumbo shrimp*
225g/8oz prawns	*½lb shrimp*
1 Cos lettuce	*1 head Romaine lettuce*
1 green pepper	*1 green pepper*
½ cucumber	*½ cucumber*
4 hard-boiled eggs (optional)	*4 hard-boiled eggs (optional)*
HERB SAUCE:	HERB SAUCE:
100g/4oz medium-fat cream cheese	*½ cup ricotta or diet cheese*
150ml/¼ pint buttermilk	*⅔ cup buttermilk*
squeeze of lemon juice	*squeeze of lemon juice*
sea salt and black pepper	*sea salt and black pepper*
3 tablespoons chopped tarragon	*3 tablespoons chopped tarragon*

Put the hake or halibut in a large saucepan and just cover with cold water. Bring to the boil and poach gently until the fish is cooked. Remove the pan from the heat and allow the fish to cool in the cooking liquor. When cool, drain the fish, remove all skin and bone and break the flesh into large flakes. Pour the juice of 1 lemon over the fish and set it aside while preparing the other ingredients.

Poach the prepared scallops for 4 to 5 minutes in the same water as the fish. Drain them, discarding the liquor, moisten with lemon juice and set aside. Shell all the prawns (shrimp) and soak them for 10 minutes in cold, slightly salty water. Wash the lettuce and cut it into strips. Deseed the pepper and peel the cucumber. Cut them into sticks like thick matchsticks. Put the shredded lettuce in a large bowl and cover with the pepper and the cucumber. Pile the flaked hake (or halibut) in the centre, and surround with the halved hard-boiled eggs, if used. Scatter the prawns (shrimp) and sliced scallops on top.

Make the herb sauce by puréeing the cheese and buttermilk together in a blender, adding a drop of lemon juice and salt and pepper to taste. Stir in the chopped tarragon. Pour the sauce over the salad and mix well before serving. This makes a light main course for a summer meal.

Opposite: Shellfish salad with tarragon

Left: Seviche of scallops with herbs

TROUT WITH PARSLEY STUFFING

Metric/Imperial	American
4 trout	4 trout
parsley stuffing for fish	parsley stuffing for fish
(see page 109)	(see page 109)
50g/2oz butter	¼ cup butter
1 tablespoon lemon juice	1 tablespoon lemon juice
2 lemons to serve	2 lemons to serve

Clean the fish and fill them with the stuffing. Make three shallow diagonal cuts on each side. Melt the butter in a small saucepan. Add the lemon juice to it and use this liquid to baste the fish as they cook. Grill (broil) for 5 minutes close to a fierce heat, then a further 6 to 8 minutes further away. Serve with lemon quarters. Accompany with new potatoes and a green vegetable, or green salad.

TURBOT (SEA BASS) STEAMED WITH SORREL

Metric/Imperial	American
225g/8oz sorrel	½lb sorrel
4 steaks turbot	4 steaks sea bass
sea salt and black pepper	sea salt and black pepper
50g/2oz butter	¼ cup butter

Cut the stalks off the sorrel. Take enough large leaves to line a steamer, and lay the fish steaks on it. Sprinkle them with salt and pepper and cover with another layer of sorrel leaves. Place over boiling water and steam for 10 minutes, or until the flesh flakes easily away from the bone.

Meanwhile cut the remaining sorrel into strips. Melt the butter in a pan and cook the shredded sorrel very briefly, just long enough for it to soften and change colour. When the steaks are ready, take off the sorrel leaves and lay the fish on a platter. Cover each steak with buttered sorrel, with its juice. Serve with boiled potatoes; no other vegetable is necessary.

FISH STOCK

Metric/Imperial	American
675–900g/1½–2lb fish	1½–2lb fish bones, heads,
bones, heads, etc	etc
1 onion	1 onion
1 carrot	1 carrot
1 leek	1 leek
1 stick celery	1 stalk celery
3 stalks parsley	3 stalks parsley
1 bay leaf	1 bay leaf
2 sprigs thyme or	2 sprigs thyme or
lemon thyme	lemon thyme
2 sprigs lovage	2 sprigs lovage
1 tablespoon sea salt	1 tablespoon sea salt
10–12 black peppercorns	10–12 black peppercorns
2 tablespoons white wine	2 tablespoons white wine
vinegar	vinegar

Wash the fish bones and trimmings and put in a deep pan. Peel the onion and carrot and clean the leek and celery. Add the vegetables to the pan with the herbs, and the salt and peppercorns. Cover with cold water. Add 2 tablespoons of white wine vinegar, or a drop of white wine, and bring to the boil slowly. Simmer gently for 45 minutes, then strain the stock, discarding all the solid ingredients, and leave it to cool before using. If the flavour is weak, reduce the stock by fast boiling.

Poultry & Game

Many delicious dishes combine the delicate taste of chicken with summer herbs. One of my favourites is *poulet à l'estragon*, a poached chicken in a creamy sauce flecked with green and imbued with the subtle taste of tarragon. This can be served either hot or cold, and has always seemed to me one of the most perfect of summer dishes. A chicken salad can be an excellent dish, or a very dull one, depending on the care with which it is made. When the soft flesh of the bird is contrasted with crisp salad vegetables – Cos (Romaine) lettuce, cucumber, green pepper, fennel and spring onions (scallions) – first marinated in lemon juice and then served in a cream dressing flavoured with lovage, dill, or chervil, it is ideal for a summer luncheon party. Creamed chicken is much improved by the addition of burnet or chervil; it can be served as it stands, or on toast, or with poached eggs laid on top.

Hyssop is a herb which helps to counteract the high fat content of certain foods like duck, goose and pork. Both goose and duck are delicious when served with the classic sage and onion stuffing, or with a sage and apple sauce. A young duckling can be split in half, basted with honey and orange juice, and cooked in a hot oven with a mixture of robust herbs: marjoram, rosemary, and thyme. Guinea fowl (guinea hen) tends to be a dry bird, and is best braised on a bed of flavouring vegetables and herbs which are later puréed and enriched with sour cream to make a sauce. Pheasant is also good cooked in this way, while the small game birds, quail, partridge and squab, are best cooked on a spit and served with a herb risotto.

Juniper berries have a particular affinity for game, and should always be included in stuffings and marinades. Both venison and hare benefit from a marinade, which is later used as a basting liquid. Rabbit, on the other hand, is better treated like chicken; it is excellent served in a mustardy sauce with dill, or cooked with saffron and thyme. Lovage is a herb which goes especially well with rabbit and game birds of milder flavour; it combines the fresh parsley taste with that of celery, and its own special warm peppery flavour: stronger than chervil or parsley, it is still more delicate than sage or rosemary, both of which I use with caution.

CHICKEN WITH HERBS AND ORANGE

Metric/Imperial	American
50g/2oz butter	$\frac{1}{4}$ cup butter
1.5kg/3½lb chicken	3½lb chicken
juice of 1 orange	juice of 1 orange
2 sprigs marjoram	2 sprigs marjoram
2 sprigs lemon thyme	2 sprigs lemon thyme
2 sprigs parsley	2 sprigs parsley
4 sprigs chervil	4 sprigs chervil
4 large leaves basil	4 large leaves basil
sea salt and black pepper	sea salt and black pepper

Heat the butter in a flameproof casserole, put the chicken in and let it brown all over. Pour over the juice of the orange and surround the chicken with the herbs. Add salt and pepper. Lay the bird on its side and cover the pot. Cook in a cool oven (150°C/300°F or Gas Mark 2), for 1½ hours, turning the chicken over once or twice.

When cooked, remove the bird from the casserole, carve it, and arrange the pieces on a hot serving dish. Strain the cooking juices, discarding the herbs. Pour over the chicken pieces and serve with noodles and a green salad. If liked, garnish the chicken with orange slices.

CHICKEN BREASTS IN GREEN SAUCE

Metric/Imperial	American
1 onion	1 onion
1 carrot	1 carrot
1 leek	1 leek
4 chicken breasts	4 chicken breasts
4 sprigs parsley	4 sprigs parsley
4 sprigs lovage	4 sprigs lovage
1 small bay leaf	1 small bay leaf
1 teaspoon sea salt	1 teaspoon sea salt
10 black peppercorns	10 black peppercorns
225g/8oz noodles	½lb noodles
25g/1oz butter	2 tablespoons butter
HERB SAUCE:	HERB SAUCE:
100g/4oz sorrel or 1 small packet frozen chopped spinach	¼lb sorrel or 1 small package frozen chopped spinach
1 bunch watercress	1 bunch watercress
40g/1½oz butter	3 tablespoons butter
2 tablespoons flour	2 tablespoons flour
150ml/¼ pint thin cream	⅔ cup light cream
1½ tablespoons chopped tarragon	1½ tablespoons chopped tarragon
1½ tablespoons chopped parsley	1½ tablespoons chopped parsley
sea salt and black pepper	sea salt and black pepper

Peel and slice the onion, clean and chop the carrot and leek. Choose a saucepan large enough to hold the chicken breasts and put the vegetables in it with the parsley, lovage and bay leaf. Cover with cold water, add the salt and peppercorns, and bring to the boil. When boiling point is reached, put in the chicken and lower the heat. Cover the pan and simmer for 35 minutes. When the chicken breasts are tender, lift them out, remove the skin, and keep them warm. Strain the stock and measure 300ml/½ pint/1¼ cups. Cook the noodles as usual, drain and keep them warm.

To make the herb sauce, cook the sorrel briefly in boiling water, drain it and chop it to a fine purée. (Alternatively cook the spinach and drain it well.) Throw the tips of the watercress into boiling water and cook for 4 minutes; drain them well and chop to a fine purée. (This can be done quickly in a food processor.) Melt the butter in a small saucepan over a low heat. Stir in the flour and cook together for 2 minutes, stirring all the time. Pour on the strained stock and stir until blended. Add the cream and simmer for 3 minutes, still stirring. Allow the sauce to cool slightly, then put it into a blender with the puréed sorrel (or 2 table-spoons puréed spinach) and watercress, the chopped tarragon and parsley. Blend all together then reheat in a clean saucepan, adding salt and pepper to taste.

Put the noodles in a shallow serving dish. Dot them with butter, and sprinkle with salt and pepper. Lay the chicken breasts on top, pour the sauce over them and serve. If necessary, the dish may be reheated for 20 minutes in a moderate oven (180°C/350°F or Gas Mark 4). Serve with a tomato salad.

CREAMED CHICKEN WITH BURNET

Metric/Imperial	American
450g/1lb cooked chicken, chopped	2 cups chopped cooked chicken
2 shallots or 1 small onion	2 shallots or 1 small onion
50g/2oz butter	¼ cup butter
3 tablespoons flour	3 tablespoons flour
300ml/½ pint chicken stock	1¼ cups chicken stock
300ml/½ pint thin cream	1¼ cups light cream
sea salt and black pepper	sea salt and black pepper
2 tablespoons chopped burnet	2 tablespoons chopped burnet

Have the chicken chopped into small square pieces. Peel and chop the shallots (or onion). Melt the butter in a saucepan and fry the shallots (or onion) gently until pale golden. Remove from the heat and add the flour, stirring for 1 minute. Stir in the heated stock, return the saucepan to the heat, and cook until smooth. Add the cream and simmer for 3 minutes, stirring. Add salt and pepper to taste. Mix in the chopped chicken. Stir until all is well-mixed and heated through, then stir in the chopped burnet. Stand, covered, for 5 minutes before serving. Serve with rice, or on toast, or with poached eggs on top.

Above: Chicken with herbs and orange;
Chicken breasts in green sauce

BRAISED CHICKEN WITH CHERVIL

Metric/Imperial	American
25g/1oz butter	2 tablespoons butter
1 tablespoon oil	1 tablespoon oil
1.5kg/3½lb chicken, jointed	3½lb chicken, cut into serving pieces
2 Spanish onions	2 Bermuda onions
100g/4oz carrots	¼lb carrots
6 sprigs chervil	6 sprigs chervil
150ml/¼ pint chicken stock	⅔ cup chicken stock
2 tablespoons vermouth or dry white wine	2 tablespoons vermouth or dry white wine
sea salt and black pepper	sea salt and black pepper
2 tablespoons thick cream	2 tablespoons heavy cream
1–2 tablespoons lemon juice	1–2 tablespoons lemon juice

Heat the butter and oil in a shallow, lidded pan and brown the chicken joints. Lift them out with a slotted spoon and keep warm. Peel the onions and clean the carrots. Slice the vegetables thinly and put them into the pan, stirring them round until well-coated with fat. Strip a few of the best leaves from the chervil sprigs and set aside. Lay the rest on top of the sliced vegetables. Heat the stock and vermouth (or wine) in a small saucepan and pour over. Lay the chicken joints on top, and sprinkle them with salt and pepper. Cover the pan and simmer for 40 minutes, or until tender, stirring now and then.

Lift out the chicken and keep hot on a serving dish. Skim off the fat from the surface of the sauce and cool slightly. Purée the cooking liquid and vegetables in a blender. Add cream and salt and pepper and blend again. Add lemon juice to taste; the quantity will depend on the sweetness of the carrots. Pour the sauce over the chicken and garnish with the reserved chervil leaves. Serve with new potatoes or boiled rice, and a green salad.

CHICKEN WITH HERBS IN FOIL

Metric/Imperial	American
2 tablespoons Dijon mustard	2 tablespoons Dijon mustard
2 tablespoons natural yogurt	2 tablespoons unflavored yogurt
4 chicken breasts	4 chicken breasts
sea salt and black pepper	sea salt and black pepper
olive oil	olive oil
6 tablespoons chopped mixed herbs: parsley, chervil, tarragon and dill	6 tablespoons chopped mixed herbs: parsley, chervil, tarragon and dill
juice of 1 lemon	juice of 1 lemon

Mix the mustard and yogurt together and coat the chicken pieces with it on both sides. Sprinkle with salt and pepper. Brush 4 pieces of foil with olive oil and lay the chicken breasts on them. Scatter a thick layer of herbs on top of each piece and sprinkle with lemon juice. Wrap in the foil, folding the ends tightly so that no juice can escape. Lay the packets on a rack in a moderately hot oven (190°C/375°F or Gas Mark 5) and cook for 30 minutes. Serve with rice and a green salad.

CURRIED CHICKEN WITH CORIANDER

Metric/Imperial

1 onion
1 carrot
1 stick celery
1.5kg/3½lb roasting
   chicken
1 bay leaf
3 sprigs parsley
3 sprigs lovage
1 teaspoon sea salt
6 black peppercorns
CURRY SAUCE:
3 tablespoons desiccated
   coconut
1 large onion
2 cloves garlic
50g/2oz butter
1 tablespoon mild curry
   powder
¼ teaspoon ground
   turmeric
¼ teaspoon ground cumin
   seed
¼ teaspoon ground
   coriander
pinch of ground chilli
1 tablespoon red currant
   jelly
juice of 1 lime or ½ lemon
1 tablespoon flour
4 tablespoons natural
   yogurt
2 tablespoons chopped
   almonds
2 tablespoons chopped
   coriander or
   3 tablespoons chopped
   basil

American

1 onion
1 carrot
1 stalk celery
3½lb roasting chicken
1 bay leaf
3 sprigs parsley
3 sprigs lovage
1 teaspoon sea salt
6 black peppercorns
CURRY SAUCE:
3 tablespoons shredded
   coconut
1 large onion
2 cloves garlic
¼ cup butter
1 tablespoon mild curry
   powder
¼ teaspoon ground
   turmeric
¼ teaspoon ground cumin
   seed
¼ teaspoon ground
   coriander
pinch of ground chili
1 tablespoon red currant
   jelly
juice of 1 lime or ½ lemon
1 tablespoon flour
¼ cup unflavored yogurt
2 tablespoons chopped
   almonds
2 tablespoons chopped
   coriander or
   3 tablespoons chopped
   basil

Peel and halve the onion; clean the carrot and celery and chop coarsely. Put the vegetables in a saucepan with the chicken, bay leaf, parsley, lovage, salt and peppercorns. Pour in enough cold water just to cover the chicken and poach for 1 hour, or 20 minutes in a pressure cooker. Lift out the chicken when it is tender. When the chicken is cool enough to handle, remove all the skin and bones and cut the meat into neat small pieces. Set aside.

Strain the liquid in which the chicken was cooked, discarding the vegetables and herbs. Taste the stock: if it is too weak, reduce it by fast boiling until it has a good flavour. Measure out 600ml/1 pint/2½ cups.

To make the curry sauce, pour half of the stock over the desiccated (shredded) coconut in a bowl and leave for 15 minutes to form a coconut 'milk'. Peel the onion and chop it finely. Peel the garlic cloves and crush them. Melt the butter in a large saucepan and cook the chopped onion gently until pale golden, adding the garlic halfway through. Sprinkle on the curry powder and spices, stirring all the time. Pour on the remaining 300ml/½ pint/1¼ cups stock and stir until blended. Simmer gently for 15 minutes, then add the red currant jelly through a sieve (strainer) and the lime or lemon juice. Pour the coconut 'milk' through a sieve (strainer) into the curry sauce, pushing lightly with the back of a wooden spoon to extract all the liquid. Stir the flour into the yogurt to make a smooth paste and add it to the curry sauce, continuing to stir until all is blended.

Add the chicken pieces to the sauce. Reheat, stirring, and finally add the chopped nuts and the coriander (or basil). Stand, covered, for 5 minutes before serving. Accompany with plain boiled rice.

Braised chicken with chervil; Chicken with herbs in foil; Curried chicken with coriander

POACHED CHICKEN WITH HERB SAUCE

Metric/Imperial	American
1.5–1.75kg/3½–4lb roasting chicken	3½–4lb roasting chicken
1 onion	1 onion
1 carrot	1 carrot
1 bay leaf	1 bay leaf
3 sprigs lovage	3 sprigs lovage
3 sprigs parsley	3 sprigs parsley
3 sprigs thyme	3 sprigs thyme
sea salt and 12 black peppercorns	sea salt and 12 black peppercorns
HERB SAUCE:	HERB SAUCE:
25g/1oz butter	2 tablespoons butter
2 tablespoons flour	2 tablespoons flour
150ml/¼ pint thick cream	⅔ cup heavy cream
sea salt and black pepper	sea salt and black pepper
1 tablespoon chopped tarragon	1 tablespoon chopped tarragon
1 tablespoon chopped dill	1 tablespoon chopped dill
1 tablespoon chopped chervil	1 tablespoon chopped chervil
1 tablespoon chopped chives	1 tablespoon chopped chives

Put the bird in a saucepan just large enough to hold it. Add cold water to almost cover it, then remove the bird. Peel the onion and carrot and put them in the pan with the bay leaf, lovage, parsley, thyme, some salt and about 12 black peppercorns. Bring to the boil and simmer, covered, for 30 minutes.

Return the chicken to the pan, bring back to the boil, cover and simmer very gently for about 1 hour, or until it is just cooked. Take it out and carve into neat slices. Lay the slices in a shallow serving dish, cover with foil, and keep warm while you make the sauce.

If the pot was only just big enough to hold the bird, you should have a small amount of good stock; otherwise reduce it by fast boiling to 300ml/½ pint/1¼ cups. Strain, and remove as much fat as possible from the surface. Melt the butter in a small pan, add the flour and cook for 1 minute, stirring, then pour on the strained stock. Stir until blended, then add the cream. Simmer gently for 4 minutes, add salt and pepper to taste, and stir in the chopped herbs. (Any mixture of suitable herbs can be used according to what you have; this is only a suggestion.) Pour some of the sauce over the chicken slices, and serve the rest in a sauce-boat. Accompany with new potatoes and young carrots, or boiled rice and a green salad. Serves 5 to 6.

VARIATION

Follow the recipe for *Poached Chicken with Herb Sauce*, substituting 3 tablespoons chopped dill for the 4 tablespoons mixed herbs. Serve with new potatoes and carrots.

Opposite: Cold chicken with herb dressing

Right: Preparation for Poached chicken with herb sauce; Chicken in mustard and dill sauce

CHICKEN IN MUSTARD AND DILL SAUCE

Metric/Imperial	American
1 medium onion	1 medium onion
25g/1oz butter	2 tablespoons butter
1 tablespoon sunflower-seed oil	1 tablespoon sunflower-seed oil
1 chicken, jointed	1 chicken, cut into serving pieces
seasoned flour	seasoned flour
300ml/½ pint chicken stock	1¼ cups chicken stock
1 tablespoon Dijon mustard	1 tablespoon Dijon mustard
sea salt and black pepper	sea salt and black pepper
1½ tablespoons chopped dill	1½ tablespoons chopped dill

Peel and chop the onion. Melt the butter and oil in a saucepan and cook the onion until pale golden. Toss the chicken joints in seasoned flour and add to the onion. Turn the chicken over until all the pieces are evenly coloured on all sides. Heat the chicken stock and pour it on, stirring until blended. Stir in the mustard with salt and pepper to taste. Cover the pan and simmer gently.

After 35 minutes test a white piece of chicken to see if it is tender. If so, lift out the breasts, wings and all white meat and keep warm in a serving dish. Leave the legs and thighs to cook for a further 5 minutes. Lift out the dark joints and add to the white in the serving dish.

Taste the sauce for seasoning, adding salt and pepper as needed, then stir in the chopped dill and pour over the chicken. Stand for 4 to 5 minutes before serving. Serve with new potatoes and string (snap) beans.

COLD CHICKEN WITH HERB DRESSING

Metric/Imperial
1.5kg/3½lb roasting
  chicken
1 onion
1 carrot
1 leek
1 bay leaf
3 sprigs parsley
3 sprigs lovage
2 sprigs thyme
sea salt
HERB DRESSING:
1 egg yolk
pinch of sea salt
150ml/¼ pint olive oil
1 teaspoon white wine
  vinegar
1 teaspoon lemon juice
1 tablespoon Dijon
  mustard
4 tablespoons natural
  yogurt
2 tablespoons chopped dill
2 tablespoons chopped
  chervil

American
3½lb roasting
  chicken
1 onion
1 carrot
1 leek
1 bay leaf
3 sprigs parsley
3 sprigs lovage
2 sprigs thyme
sea salt
HERB DRESSING:
1 egg yolk
pinch of sea salt
⅔ cup olive oil
1 teaspoon white wine
  vinegar
1 teaspoon lemon juice
1 tablespoon Dijon
  mustard
¼ cup unflavored yogurt
2 tablespoons chopped
  dill
2 tablespoons chopped
  chervil

Start to prepare this dish the day before you plan to serve it.

Put the chicken in a saucepan that will just hold it nicely and cover with cold water. Remove the bird. Peel and halve the onion, peel the carrot, and clean the leek, slicing it lengthwise. Add the vegetables to the cold water with the herbs and some salt. Bring almost to the boil and cover the pan. Cook for 30 minutes, then replace the chicken, bring back to the boil, and simmer for 1 hour. Lift out the chicken and leave to cool.

Continue to boil the remaining contents of the pan until you have a small amount of strongly flavoured stock, tasting frequently to see that it does not get too salty. Strain and leave to cool, then chill in the refrigerator overnight.

Make the dressing the next day. Remove all fat from the surface of the stock. Make a mayonnaise with the egg yolk, salt, oil, vinegar and lemon juice (see method page 192). Stir in the mustard, then mix with the yogurt. Stir in 4 tablespoons (¼ cup) chicken stock which will have set to a jelly. Beat until smooth, or purée briefly in a blender, then stir in the chopped herbs. Carve the chicken into joints or slices free from bone, as you prefer. Lay them on a flat dish and spoon the dressing over them. Chill for 1 hour before serving. Serve with a potato salad in a vinaigrette dressing and a lettuce salad.

POULET À L'ESTRAGON I

To prepare a hot *Poulet à l'Estragon*, follow the recipe for *Poached Chicken with Herb Sauce* (see page 140), substituting 3 tablespoons chopped tarragon for the 4 tablespoons mixed herbs. Serve with new potatoes and a lettuce salad.

POULET À L'ESTRAGON II

Metric/Imperial	American
1 onion	1 onion
1 carrot	1 carrot
1 leek	1 leek
1.5kg/3½lb roasting chicken	3½lb roasting chicken
½ bay leaf	½ bay leaf
3 sprigs parsley	3 sprigs parsley
3 sprigs lovage	3 sprigs lovage
1 teaspoon sea salt	1 teaspoon sea salt
6 black peppercorns	6 black peppercorns
4 branches tarragon	4 branches tarragon
½ tablespoon gelatine	½ tablespoon gelatine
300ml/½ pint thick cream	1¼ cups heavy cream

Peel and halve the onion and carrot. Clean the leek and chop it coarsely. Put the vegetables in a saucepan with the chicken, bay leaf, parsley, lovage, salt and peppercorns. Pour in enough cold water just to cover the chicken and poach for 1 hour, or until the bird is tender. Lift out the chicken, and when it is cool enough to handle cut it into joints and remove the skin. Arrange the joints on a flat dish and leave in a cool place.

Strain the cooking liquid, discarding the vegetables and herbs. Leave overnight, or until completely cold, then remove all fat from the surface. Take 9 or 10 of the best leaves from the tarragon and reserve them to use as a garnish. Reheat the clear stock with the tarragon branches, and boil it up until it is reduced to 300ml/½ pint/1¼ cups, tasting it occasionally to make sure it is not too salty. Pour through a sieve (strainer) into a bowl and discard the tarragon branches.

Pour a little of the hot stock over the gelatine in a cup and stir until dissolved. Pour it back into the stock, mix together and strain the stock into a clean bowl. Set the bowl in a larger one holding ice, and stir the stock as it cools until it is on the point of setting. Whip the cream lightly and fold it into the stock. Continue to stir over the ice until almost set, then start to spoon this sauce over the chicken joints. Allow the first layer of sauce to set, then spoon a second layer over it, smoothing carefully with a palette knife dipped in hot water, to make the surface even. Chill the joints in the refrigerator for 1 hour, then trim the edges of each one carefully, with a sharp, pointed knife. Transfer the joints to a clean dish, and lay a few tarragon leaves on top of each one before serving.

CHICKEN PANCAKES WITH CHERVIL

Metric/Imperial	American
1.5kg/3lb roasting chicken	3lb roasting chicken
1 onion	1 onion
1 carrot	1 carrot
1 stick celery	1 stalk celery
1 bay leaf	1 bay leaf
3 stalks parsley	3 stalks parsley
sea salt and black pepper	sea salt and black pepper
BATTER:	BATTER:
175g/6oz plain flour	1½ cups all-purpose flour
pinch of sea salt	pinch of sea salt
1 egg	1 egg
1 egg yolk	1 egg yolk
250–300ml/8–10fl oz milk	1–1¼ cups milk
lard for frying	lard for frying
SAUCE:	SAUCE:
50g/2oz butter	¼ cup butter
3½ tablespoons flour	3½ tablespoons flour
150ml/¼ pint thin cream	⅔ cup light cream
sea salt and black pepper	sea salt and black pepper

Chicken pancakes with chervil;
Poulet à l'estragon II

1 tablespoon chopped chervil	1 tablespoon chopped chervil
1 tablespoon chopped tarragon	1 tablespoon chopped tarragon
25g/1oz Gruyère cheese, grated	$\frac{1}{4}$ cup grated Gruyère cheese

Put the chicken in a close-fitting flameproof casserole. Peel the onion and carrot and scrub the celery. Chop the vegetables coarsely and tuck them around the chicken with the bay leaf and parsley. Add salt and pepper and enough cold water to come halfway up the side of the pot. Cover the casserole and bring to the boil slowly. Simmer gently for 50 minutes. At the end of the cooking time, test a leg with a skewer to make sure the meat is tender. Continue cooking for 10 minutes if necessary. When the chicken is cooked, lift it out of the casserole, drain it and leave to cool. Strain the cooking liquid into a bowl and leave to cool. Cut the chicken meat into small neat pieces, discarding the skin. Remove all fat from the surface of the cold stock. Measure out 450ml/$\frac{3}{4}$ pint/2 cups and reserve.

To make the batter, put the flour in a mixing bowl with the salt. Make a well in the centre with a wooden spoon and drop in the egg and egg yolk, beaten together, and 250ml/8fl oz/1 cup of milk. Beat vigorously until it has the consistency of thick (heavy) cream, adding a little more milk if necessary. Leave the batter to stand for 1 hour before use.

To make the sauce, melt the butter in a pan, stir in the flour, and cook for 1 minute, stirring. Heat the reserved stock and pour it into the pan, stirring all the time to blend as the sauce thickens. Stir in the cream and cook gently for 3 minutes. Add salt and pepper to taste. Mix half the sauce with the chopped chicken in a bowl and stir in the chopped herbs. Add most of the grated cheese to the other half of the sauce and keep it warm.

Melt a little lard in a frying pan (skillet) and use the batter to make 10 to 12 pancakes. Divide the chicken filling evenly among the pancakes, rolling them up into a cigar shape and laying them side by side in a buttered gratin dish. Pour the reserved sauce over the pancakes and scatter the remaining cheese on top. Cook in a moderate oven (180°C/350°F or Gas Mark 4) for 20 minutes or until the cheese has melted and the top is golden brown. This dish can be made in advance if reheated in a moderate oven for 30 minutes before serving.

Ten to twelve pancakes will serve 4 to 6 as a light main course. Serve with a lettuce salad.

CHICKEN SMOTHERED IN HERBS

Metric/Imperial	American
1 onion	1 onion
1 carrot	1 carrot
1 leek	1 leek
4 stalks parsley	4 stalks parsley
3 stalks lovage	3 stalks lovage
$\frac{1}{2}$ bay leaf	$\frac{1}{2}$ bay leaf
sea salt and 6 black peppercorns	sea salt and 6 black peppercorns
4 chicken breasts	4 chicken breasts
1 teaspoon gelatine	1 teaspoon gelatine
4 tablespoons thick cream	$\frac{1}{4}$ cup heavy cream
50g/2oz cream cheese	$\frac{1}{4}$ cup cream cheese
$1\frac{1}{2}$ tablespoons chopped chervil	$1\frac{1}{2}$ tablespoons chopped chervil
$1\frac{1}{2}$ tablespoons chopped dill	$1\frac{1}{2}$ tablespoons chopped dill
$1\frac{1}{2}$ tablespoons chopped tarragon	$1\frac{1}{2}$ tablespoons chopped tarragon
$1\frac{1}{2}$ tablespoons chopped chives	$1\frac{1}{2}$ tablespoons chopped chives

Peel and slice the onion and carrot, clean and slice the leek and put them in a saucepan with the parsley, lovage, bay leaf, salt and peppercorns. Cover generously with cold water and bring to the boil. Simmer for 30 minutes, then add the chicken breasts. Cover the pan and simmer gently for 30 minutes, or until the breasts are tender. Lift them out, and strain the stock, discarding the vegetables and herbs. Reduce the stock by fast boiling until 150ml/$\frac{1}{4}$ pint/$\frac{2}{3}$ cup remains. Cool quickly by standing the pan in iced water, and remove the fat from the surface.

Take 2 tablespoons of the stock and dissolve the gelatine in it in a cup. Purée the remaining stock in a blender with the cream and the cream cheese. Add the dissolved gelatine and blend again. Pour into a small bowl and stand in iced water, stirring often, until it starts to thicken. Remove the skin from the chicken breasts and lay them on a flat, shallow dish. Spoon the thickening sauce over them, leaving each layer to set before adding another. Chill for 30 minutes, until firm. Then cut each piece out carefully with a sharp, pointed knife and lay on a flat serving dish.

Shake the chopped herbs carefully over each chicken breast so that they form a thick green covering. Serve immediately, or chill again until ready. If preferred, this dish can be made with a whole chicken, poached. In this case, make double the quantity of sauce, to coat the different joints, but the same amount of herbs should suffice. Serve with salads: rice or potato, lettuce and tomato.

Chicken smothered in herbs; Chicken in terracotta;
Duck with honey and herbs

CHICKEN IN TERRACOTTA

Metric/Imperial	American
1.5kg/3lb chicken	3lb chicken
about 3 tablespoons Dijon mustard	about 3 tablespoons Dijon mustard
1 clove garlic	1 clove garlic
sea salt and black pepper	sea salt and black pepper
3 sprigs chervil	3 sprigs chervil
3 sprigs tarragon	3 sprigs tarragon
3 sprigs dill	3 sprigs dill
3 sprigs parsley	3 sprigs parsley
2 sprigs lemon thyme	2 sprigs lemon thyme
1 sprig marjoram	1 sprig marjoram
1 tablespoon olive oil	1 tablespoon olive oil

Thick terracotta pots ('chicken bricks' or 'romertopf') especially for baking chickens in can be bought now in many kitchen shops; they are foolproof to use, and keep the oven clean.

Paint the bird all over with mustard and lay it in the bottom half of the terracotta pot. Cut the peeled clove of garlic in half and rub it over the inside of the pot. Rub the skin of the bird with salt and pepper. Scatter the herbs over the bird, tucking some inside it. Pour the olive oil over the chicken and close the pot.

Place in a cold oven, turn up the heat as high as it will go and leave for 1–$1\frac{1}{2}$ hours. Take the pot out of the oven and remove the bird. Carve the chicken and arrange the pieces on a serving platter. Strain the cooking juices from the pot, discarding the herbs, and pour the juices over the carved chicken. Serve with rice or noodles and a green salad.

CHICKEN STOCK

Metric/Imperial	American
1–2 chicken carcasses, or 675g/1½lb chicken wings, necks, feet, etc.	1–2 chicken carcasses, or 1½lb chicken wings, necks, feet, etc.
1 large onion	1 large onion
3 cloves	3 cloves
1 large carrot	1 large carrot
1 leek	1 leek
1 stick celery	1 stalk celery
1 bay leaf	1 bay leaf
3 stalks parsley	3 stalks parsley
3 sprigs lovage	3 sprigs lovage
1 tablespoon sea salt	1 tablespoon sea salt
10 black peppercorns	10 black peppercorns

Put the carcasses (or wing tips, necks etc.) in a deep saucepan and cover generously with cold water. Add the halved onion, still in its skin and stuck with the cloves, and the cleaned and halved carrot, leek and celery. Put in the herbs, salt and peppercorns and bring to the boil slowly. Cover the pan, lower the heat, and simmer for 3 hours or 1 hour in a pressure cooker. Strain, discarding the vegetables and herbs, and leave the stock to cool. Chill in the refrigerator overnight.

The next day remove all fat from the surface. If weak in flavour, reduce by fast boiling. The strained stock will keep for 3 to 4 days in the refrigerator.

DUCK WITH HONEY AND HERBS

Metric/Imperial	American
2.5kg/5½lb duck	5½lb duck
4 tablespoons clear honey	¼ cup clear honey
1 tablespoon chopped rosemary	1 tablespoon chopped rosemary
1 tablespoon chopped marjoram	1 tablespoon chopped marjoram
1 tablespoon chopped thyme	1 tablespoon chopped thyme
½ tablespoon chopped summer savory	½ tablespoon chopped summer savory
½ tablespoon chopped hyssop	½ tablespoon chopped hyssop
black pepper	black pepper
4 tablespoons orange juice	¼ cup orange juice

Halve the duck and brush on both sides with the honey. (If it is too thick, warm it slightly.) Mix the chopped herbs together. Lay the duck, skin side uppermost, on an oiled roasting pan, and sprinkle with the chopped herbs and some black pepper. Pour over a little of the orange juice and prick the duck pieces here and there with a sharp skewer.

Leave for 1 to 2 hours to absorb the flavour, then bake in a moderately hot oven (200°C/400°F or Gas Mark 6), for 50 minutes, basting with the remaining orange juice. Move the halves around once or twice, so that they brown evenly all over. They should be well browned, almost charred, on the outside, and nicely cooked inside.

To serve, cut into quarters and lay on a flat dish. Throw away the juice as it will be too fatty to serve with the duck. Serve with rice, noodles, or new potatoes and a green salad.

Opposite: *Rabbit in mustard and herb sauce;*
Quail with herb risotto
Left: *Braised guinea fowl with lovage*

BRAISED GUINEA FOWL WITH LOVAGE

Metric/Imperial	American
1 guinea fowl	1 guinea hen
40g/1½oz butter	3 tablespoons butter
1 Spanish onion	1 Bermuda onion
4 sticks celery	4 stalks celery
175g/6oz carrots	6oz carrots
2 leeks	2 leeks
6 sprigs lovage	6 sprigs lovage
150ml/¼ pint chicken stock	⅔ cup chicken stock
2 tablespoons vermouth or dry white wine	2 tablespoons vermouth or dry white wine
sea salt and black pepper	sea salt and black pepper
4 tablespoons sour cream	¼ cup sour cream
squeeze of lemon juice (optional)	squeeze of lemon juice (optional)

Cut the guinea fowl (guinea hen) in half. Heat the butter in a flameproof casserole and brown the bird on both sides. Take it out and put the cleaned and thinly sliced vegetables – onion, celery, carrots and leeks – in the casserole. Stir around until well mixed, then cook gently for 4 minutes. Lay the sprigs of lovage on top of the vegetables, replace the bird, and pour over the heated stock and the vermouth (or wine). Sprinkle with salt and pepper, cover the pan, and cook gently for 1 hour 10 minutes, stirring once or twice.

When the bird is tender, remove it from the casserole and cut each piece in half. Lay the four quarters in a shallow dish and keep them warm. Skim off the fat from the surface of the cooled stock and throw away the lovage. Purée the stock and the vegetables in a blender, adding the sour cream and salt and pepper to taste. If it is a little too sweet (this will depend on the carrots) add a little lemon juice. Reheat the sauce and pour it over the bird. Serve with boiled or puréed potatoes and a green vegetable.

PHEASANT WITH HERBS

Metric/Imperial	American
marinade I (see page 150)	marinade I (see page 150)
1 pheasant	1 pheasant
1 onion	1 onion
1 carrot	1 carrot
1 leek	1 leek
1 stick celery	1 stalk celery
40g/1½oz beef dripping	3 tablespoons beef drippings
300ml/½ pint game stock or chicken stock	1¼ cups game stock or chicken stock
3 sprigs thyme	3 sprigs thyme
3 sprigs lovage	3 sprigs lovage
3 sprigs summer savory	3 sprigs summer savory
1 sprig rosemary	1 sprig rosemary
sea salt and black pepper	sea salt and black pepper
1 teaspoon flour	1 teaspoon flour
150ml/¼ pint sour cream	⅔ cup sour cream
1 tablespoon chopped parsley to garnish	1 tablespoon chopped parsley to garnish

Make the marinade and pour it over the pheasant in a close-fitting deep dish. Leave overnight.

Next day lift out the bird and wipe it dry. Strain and reserve the marinade. Peel the onion and carrot and trim the leek and celery. Slice the vegetables and cook them gently in the dripping in a flameproof casserole, stirring occasionally. After about 6 minutes, put in the bird and brown it lightly on all sides. Heat the stock in a saucepan with the strained marinade and pour it over the bird. Tuck the herbs around it and add salt and black pepper. Cover the casserole and transfer it to a moderate oven (160°C/325°F or Gas Mark 3). If the pheasant is a roasting bird, it will be ready in 1 hour; if an old bird, allow 2 to 2½ hours. Turn the bird over from time to time. When tender, take it out and carve it. Lay the pieces in a serving dish and keep them warm while you make the sauce.

Take the herbs out of the casserole and discard them. Purée the vegetables and the cooled cooking liquid together in a blender, or push through a food mill. Pour back into a clean pan and reheat gently. Beat the flour into the sour cream in a small bowl, until smooth, then stir it bit by bit into the sauce. Cook gently for 3 minutes, stirring constantly, then add more salt and pepper as required. Pour over the pheasant in its dish and sprinkle with finely chopped parsley. If there is too much sauce for the meat, serve some separately in a sauceboat.

RABBIT IN MUSTARD AND HERB SAUCE

Metric/Imperial	American
575g/1¼lb boneless rabbit	1¼lb boneless rabbit
225g/8oz shallots or	½lb shallots or
tiny onions	tiny onions
1 clove garlic	1 clove garlic
40g/1½oz butter	3 tablespoons butter
seasoned flour	seasoned flour
300ml/½ pint chicken stock	1¼ cups chicken stock
6 sprigs thyme	6 sprigs thyme
sea salt and black pepper	sea salt and black pepper
1 tablespoon Dijon	1 tablespoon Dijon
mustard	mustard
150ml/¼ pint thick cream	⅔ cup heavy cream
2 tablespoons chopped dill	2 tablespoons chopped dill

Cut the rabbit in neat pieces; peel the shallots or small onions. (If none are available, simply chop large onions.) Peel and chop the garlic. Melt the butter in a saucepan and cook the onions until pale golden, adding the chopped garlic halfway through. Toss the rabbit pieces in seasoned flour and add them to the pan. Stir until lightly coloured all over, then pour on the heated stock. Put in the thyme, salt and pepper and the mustard. Cover the pan and cook very gently for 1½ hours, until tender, stirring occasionally.

Lift out the rabbit and the whole onions and keep warm in a serving dish. Push the sauce through a sieve (strainer),

throwing away the thyme. Reheat the sauce in a clean pan, adding the cream and stirring until blended. Adjust the seasoning, stir in the dill and pour over the rabbit. The sauce is really delicious, so serve this dish with plenty of boiled potatoes or crusty French bread to mop it up, and a green salad.

QUAIL WITH HERB RISOTTO

Metric/Imperial	American
4–8 quail	4–8 quail
600ml–1.2 litres/1–2 pints	2½–5 cups milk
milk	¼–½ cup butter,
50–100g/2–4oz butter,	melted
melted	2–3 sprigs rosemary
2–3 sprigs rosemary	sea salt and black pepper
sea salt and black pepper	herb risotto (see page 121)
herb risotto (see page 121)	

Put the quail in a large saucepan and cover with milk. Bring to the boil and simmer for 7 minutes. Drain them and pat dry. Put the birds on a spit or on a rack in a roasting pan. Pour the melted butter over them and lay the rosemary in the pan. Sprinkle with salt and black pepper. Roast for 8 minutes, either on the spit or in a moderately hot oven (200°C/400°F or Gas Mark 6), basting them once or twice with the butter. Serve with herb risotto. Allow 1 to 2 birds per person according to appetite.

RABBIT IN SAFFRON SAUCE

Metric/Imperial	American
1 farm rabbit, jointed	1 domestic rabbit, cut into
marinade 1 (see page 150)	serving pieces
seasoned flour	marinade 1 (see page 150)
25g/1oz butter	seasoned flour
2 tablespoons olive oil	2 tablespoons butter
3 shallots or 1 medium	2 tablespoons olive oil
onion	3 shallots or 1 medium
1 clove garlic	onion
150ml/¼ pint chicken	1 clove garlic
stock	⅔ cup chicken stock
pinch of saffron	pinch of saffron
sea salt and black pepper	sea salt and black pepper
3 sprigs thyme	3 sprigs thyme

Wipe the rabbit joints and put them in a bowl. Make the marinade and tip it over them. Leave overnight, or for several hours, turning over now and then.

When you are ready to cook, take out the rabbit pieces and wipe them dry. Strain and reserve the marinade. Toss the joints in seasoned flour. Heat the butter and oil in a saucepan and brown the rabbit pieces. Peel and slice the shallots (or onion). Lift the rabbit pieces out of the pan and keep them warm. Put the shallots into the pan and brown them slowly. Peel and crush the garlic and add it halfway through. Put the rabbit back in the pan. Heat the stock with the saffron and pour it over the rabbit. Add the strained marinade and salt and pepper to taste. Put in the fresh thyme, cover the pan, and simmer for 1½ hours, or until the rabbit is very tender.

Stand for a few minutes before serving, then skim off any fat from the surface and throw away the thyme. Garnish with sprigs of parsley, if you like, and serve with boiled potatoes and a green salad.

SADDLE OF HARE IN DILL SAUCE

Metric/Imperial	American
marinade 1 (see page 150)	marinade 1 (see page 150)
made with 300ml/½ pint	made with 1¼ cups
white wine	white wine
2 saddles of hare	2 saddles of hare
about 3 tablespoons	about 3 tablespoons
Dijon mustard	Dijon mustard
25g/1oz butter	2 tablespoons butter
2 tablespoons olive oil	2 tablespoons olive oil
300ml/½ pint chicken stock	1¼ cups chicken stock
or game stock	or game stock
1 bay leaf	1 bay leaf
2 sprigs rosemary	2 sprigs rosemary
4 sprigs thyme	4 sprigs thyme
sea salt and black pepper	sea salt and black pepper
1 teaspoon flour	1 teaspoon flour
150ml/¼ pint sour cream	⅔ cup sour cream
1½ tablespoons chopped	1½ tablespoons chopped
dill	dill

Pour the marinade over the saddles of hare in a deep bowl and stand for 24 hours, basting now and then.

Lift out the saddles and pat them dry; paint them with Dijon mustard on the skinned side. Heat the butter and oil in an oval flameproof casserole and brown the saddles all over. Heat the stock with the strained marinade and pour over. Add the herbs and salt and pepper to taste. Cook slowly for 1½ hours, basting often. When tender, lift out the saddles and carve into thin strips, parallel to the backbone. Put the slices of hare on a serving dish and keep them warm.

Strain the cooking liquid into a bowl and leave it to stand for a minute or two. Take off the fat from the surface of the sauce and measure 300ml/½ pint/1¼ cups. Beat the flour into the sour cream until smoothly amalgamated. Reheat the strained sauce in a pan. When it is almost boiling, stir in the flour and sour cream gradually. Stir until boiling point is reached, then simmer for 3 minutes, stirring. Stir in the dill, adding salt and pepper if required. Pour some of the sauce over the hare, serving the rest separately. Serve with mashed potatoes or beef marrow and chervil dumplings (see page 195), carrots or leeks, and some herb jelly.

VENISON STEAKS WITH SAGE BUTTER

Metric/Imperial	American
4 tablespoons olive oil	¼ cup olive oil
marinade 1 (see page 150)	marinade 1 (see page 150)
4 steaks venison, from	4 steaks venison, from
the leg	the leg
1 Spanish onion	1 Bermuda onion
3 tablespoons oil for	3 tablespoons oil for
frying	frying
1 large green pepper	1 large green pepper
1 large red pepper	1 large red pepper
sea salt and black pepper	sea salt and black pepper
1–2 cloves garlic	1–2 cloves garlic
25g/1oz butter	2 tablespoons butter
sage butter (see page 194)	sage butter (see page 194)

Add the olive oil to the marinade and pour it over the steaks in a deep dish. Leave them for 24 hours, basting now and then.

Take the steaks out of the marinade and pat them dry before cooking. Peel and slice the onion. Heat the oil in a saucepan and stew the onion slowly for 5 minutes. Add the peppers, deseeded and cut into strips. Add salt and black pepper and cook slowly for 10 minutes, adding the peeled and crushed garlic towards the end. When all the vegetables are soft, pour them into a serving dish and keep warm.

Heat the butter in a frying pan (skillet) and cook the steaks slowly, allowing about 4 minutes each side. Lay them on top of the vegetables and put a piece of chilled sage butter on top of each one.

Saddle of hare in dill sauce; Rabbit in saffron sauce

BRAISED VENISON WITH HERBS

Metric/Imperial	American
marinade II (see below)	marinade II (see below)
1kg/2lb rolled leg of venison	2lb rolled leg of venison
25g/1oz beef dripping	2 tablespoons beef drippings
1 onion	1 onion
2 carrots	2 carrots
2 leeks	2 leeks
3 rashers streaky bacon	3 slices fatty bacon
300ml/½ pint game or chicken or beef stock	1¼ cups game or chicken or beef stock
1 bay leaf	1 bay leaf
3 leaves sage	3 leaves sage
3 sprigs thyme	3 sprigs thyme
2 sprigs rosemary	2 sprigs rosemary
6 black peppercorns	6 black peppercorns
6 juniper berries	6 juniper berries
sea salt	sea salt

Pour the marinade over the venison in a deep dish. Leave for 12 to 14 hours, or up to 2 days if you prefer. Baste now and then.

Take out the meat and wipe it dry. Melt the dripping in a flameproof casserole or large saucepan and brown the venison all over. Take it out of the pan and keep it warm. Add the peeled and sliced onion, carrots and leeks. Cook the vegetables slowly for 8 to 10 minutes with the lid on, then wrap the venison in the bacon and lay it on the vegetables. Strain the marinade. Heat it with the stock in a saucepan and pour it over the meat. Tuck the fresh herbs around the meat with the peppercorns and juniper berries. Add salt, cover the pan, and simmer for anything from 1½ to 2½ hours, depending on the age of the venison and the length of time it has been hung. Allow the maximum, for

it can be easily kept hot, or reheated without harm.

Lift out the meat and carve it in quite thick slices. Lay them in a shallow dish and cover with the vegetables, discarding the herbs. Strain the sauce and leave for a few moments to cool a little, keeping the meat warm meanwhile. Skim off the fat from the surface of the sauce and pour some of it over the meat, serving the rest separately. Serve with mashed potatoes and Brussels sprouts.

MARINADE I

Metric/Imperial	American
1 onion	1 onion
1 bay leaf	1 bay leaf
6 sprigs thyme	6 sprigs thyme
3 sprigs marjoram	3 sprigs marjoram
3 sprigs summer savory	3 sprigs summer savory
2 sprigs hyssop	2 sprigs hyssop
1 sprig rosemary	1 sprig rosemary
150ml/¼ pint dry white wine	⅔ cup dry white wine

Peel and slice the onion. Crumble the bay leaf. Scatter both over the food to be marinated, then lay the sprigs of different herbs over as well. Pour over the wine and leave for 12 to 24 hours, basting occasionally with a wooden spoon. The game is usually dried before cooking, and the marinade strained and used as cooking liquid, either alone or mixed with stock.

MARINADE II

Metric/Imperial	American
1 onion	1 onion
1 carrot	1 carrot
1 stick celery	1 stalk celery
4 tablespoons olive oil	¼ cup olive oil
300ml/½ pint red wine	1¼ cups red wine
1 clove garlic, lightly crushed	1 clove garlic, lightly crushed
1 bay leaf	1 bay leaf
3 sprigs thyme	3 sprigs thyme
3 sprigs parsley	3 sprigs parsley
3 sprigs lovage	3 sprigs lovage
2 sprigs marjoram	2 sprigs marjoram
2 sprigs summer savory	2 sprigs summer savory
2 sprigs hyssop	2 sprigs hyssop
1 sprig rosemary	1 sprig rosemary
6 black peppercorns, lightly crushed	6 black peppercorns, lightly crushed
6 juniper berries, lightly crushed	6 juniper berries, lightly crushed

Peel and slice the onion. Clean and slice the carrot and celery. Heat the oil in a saucepan and cook the vegetables gently for 6 to 8 minutes, stirring. Add the wine, garlic, herbs, peppercorns and juniper berries. Bring to the boil and simmer, covered, for 30 minutes. Cool before using.

This is good for all game, birds or animals; it can be strained after marinating and used as the cooking liquid, either alone or mixed with stock.

Meat

Each different meat seems to have its own herb, or group of herbs, which complements it. The bland flavour of veal, for instance, is best combined with the sharp acidity of sorrel, or the subtle tastes of tarragon, chervil or dill. Pork also goes well with these three, as it does with the stronger sage. Sage, however, must be used with caution if it is not to dominate the dish. Combined with onions, sage makes a delicious dish with sliced calves' (calf) liver, *fegato alla Veneziana*; with breadcrumbs added, it gives us the traditional English stuffing for roast goose, duck, or joints of pork. It can also be mixed with apple sauce for serving with the same meats.

Boiled beef is good served with a dill sauce, as is done in Central European countries, or with a *salsa verde*, a vinaigrette thickened with quantities of chopped onion, garlic and herbs. This excellent green sauce is also served in its native Italy as the accompaniment to a platter of mixed boiled meats, comprising beef, tongue, chicken and cooked ham. Robust dishes of roast and braised beef need stronger flavours such as horse-radish, garlic and bay. French *daubes* of beef are invariably flavoured with garlic, rosemary and thyme, while the English beef stew relies on parsley, thyme and bay.

Lamb has strong affinities with rosemary, mint and garlic. A leg of lamb spiked with slivers of garlic and roasted with 2 or 3 sprigs of rosemary in the pan is a classic French dish, while the traditional English leg of lamb is plainly roasted and served with mint sauce or mint jelly. Cubes of lean lamb, threaded on skewers and grilled (broiled), are good first marinated and later basted with olive oil, lemon juice and fresh herbs.

Dishes made from minced (ground) meat are much improved by adding fresh herbs; lamb meat balls are good with chopped mint added, while a meat loaf makes a good background for mixtures of marjoram, thyme and rosemary.

Cold meat dishes, particularly those in aspic, benefit from the use of herbs, both as flavouring and as a garnish. Plump lamb cutlets, cooked until just tender and trimmed of all fat, can be encased in a transparent mint-flavoured aspic. A joint of braised veal can be carved and covered with a sauce made from mayonnaise mixed with yogurt and flavoured with chopped herbs. Sliced cold boiled beef can be set in a dill-flavoured aspic, while a classic French dish, *jambon persillé*, consists of cubes of ham suspended in a green jelly made from the ham liquor thickened with parsley.

Above: Boiled beef with dill sauce

Opposite: Braised venison with herbs

BOILED BEEF WITH DILL SAUCE

Metric/Imperial	American
1.5kg/3lb fresh silverside beef	3lb boneless rump beef
1 large onion	1 large onion
3 cloves	3 cloves
1 large carrot	1 large carrot
1 leek	1 leek
3 sprigs parsley	3 sprigs parsley
3 sprigs lovage	3 sprigs lovage
3 sprigs thyme	3 sprigs thyme
1 bay leaf	1 bay leaf
1 tablespoon sea salt	1 tablespoon sea salt
12 black peppercorns	12 black peppercorns
dill sauce I (see page 185) to serve	dill sauce I (see page 185) to serve

Put the meat in a saucepan that fits it nicely and cover with cold water. Lift out the meat and bring the water to the boil. Return the meat to the saucepan and bring back to the boil. Skim off the scum that rises to the surface, until only a white foam remains.

Peel and halve the onion and stick the cloves into it. Clean and halve the carrot and leek. Add these vegetables to the saucepan with the herbs, salt and peppercorns. Bring back to the boil, then lower the heat. Simmer gently for 2 hours, then lift out the beef and strain the stock. Keep the meat hot while you make the dill sauce, using the beef stock. Carve the beef and serve with boiled potatoes and carrots, with the dill sauce in a separate bowl.

VARIATION

Follow the recipe for *Boiled Beef with Dill Sauce*, substituting *Salsa Verde* (see page 192) for the dill sauce.

BRAISED BEEF WITH HORSE-RADISH

Metric/Imperial	American
1.25kg/2½lb rolled topside	2½lb boneless rump roast
1 onion	1 onion
1 carrot	1 carrot
1 stick celery	1 stalk celery
40g/1½oz lard	3 tablespoons lard
300ml/½ pint beef stock	1¼ cups beef stock
sea salt and black pepper	sea salt and black pepper
2 tablespoons chopped parsley	2 tablespoons chopped parsley
horse-radish sauce (see page 191) to serve	horse-radish sauce (see page 191) to serve
MARINADE:	MARINADE:
1 onion	1 onion
1 carrot	1 carrot
1 stick celery	1 stalk celery
1 bay leaf	1 bay leaf
3 sprigs parsley	3 sprigs parsley
3 sprigs thyme	3 sprigs thyme
2 sprigs lovage	2 sprigs lovage
900ml/1½ pints water	3¾ cups water
4 tablespoons red wine vinegar	¼ cup red wine vinegar

Start the day before. To make the marinade: peel and slice the onion, carrot and celery and put them in a pan with the herbs, water and vinegar. Boil for 30 minutes, then leave to cool. When cold, pour over the meat, vegetables and all, in a deep bowl. Leave overnight, turning occasionally.

The next day, lift out the beef and wipe it dry. Strain the marinade into a jug (pitcher), discarding the cooked vegetables. Clean and slice the fresh vegetables. Melt the lard in a broad heavy saucepan and let the chopped vegetables brown slightly. Put in the meat and let it brown on all sides. Heat the stock and the strained marinade and pour them on. Add salt and pepper, cover the pan, and simmer gently for 2½ hours.

Lift out the meat and carve it into neat slices. Lay the slices in a shallow dish and spoon the vegetables over it. Take off as much fat as possible from the surface of the sauce, and spoon some over the meat. Serve the rest separately. Accompany with the horse-radish sauce.

BEEF STEW WITH MARIGOLDS

Metric/Imperial	American
1 large onion	1 large onion
1 large carrot	1 large carrot
2 sticks celery	2 stalks celery
1 large green pepper	1 large green pepper
1 head Florence fennel	1 root fennel
25g/1oz butter	2 tablespoons butter
2 tablespoons olive oil	2 tablespoons olive oil
1.25kg/2½lb stewing beef	2½lb stewing beef
seasoned flour	seasoned flour
300ml/½ pint stock	1¼ cups stock
150ml/¼ pint wine, red or white	⅔ cup wine, red or white
pinch of saffron or 1 tablespoon tomato purée	pinch of saffron or 1 tablespoon tomato paste
1 orange	1 orange
sea salt and black pepper	sea salt and black pepper
1 bay leaf	1 bay leaf
3 sprigs thyme	3 sprigs thyme
6 leaves sage	6 leaves sage
4 sprigs marjoram	4 sprigs marjoram
4 sprigs parsley	4 sprigs parsley
GARNISH:	GARNISH:
2 marigold flowers, fresh or dried, or 2 tablespoons chopped parsley	2 marigold flowers, fresh or dried, or 2 tablespoons chopped parsley

Clean all the vegetables and cut them into sticks like thick matchsticks. Heat the butter and oil in a heavy flameproof casserole and brown the vegetables lightly.

Cut the meat into rectangles about 4cm/1½in by 2.5cm/1in, quite thin. Toss in seasoned flour and add to the pan. Stir around until browned. Heat the stock and wine in a saucepan with the saffron or tomato purée (paste). Add the stock to the casserole and stir until blended with the flour. Add the juice of the orange, a small slice of the peel and salt and pepper. Cover the pan, and cook in a cool oven (150°C/300°F or Gas Mark 2) for 2 hours, or until the beef is tender. Add the herbs 15 minutes before the end of the cooking.

To serve, turn into a warmed serving dish and scatter with marigold petals. (Failing marigold petals, garnish with freshly chopped parsley.)

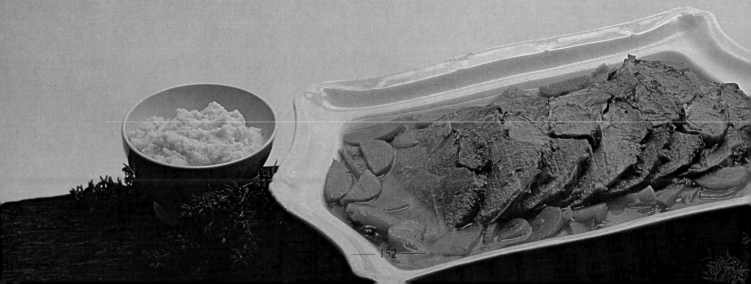

BEEF IN DILL JELLY

Metric/Imperial	American
1.75kg/4lb rolled topside of beef	4lb round of beef
2 cloves garlic	2 cloves garlic
1 large onion	1 large onion
1 large carrot	1 large carrot
2 sticks celery	2 stalks celery
2 bay leaves	2 bay leaves
1 bottle dry white wine	1 bottle dry white wine
3 tablespoons olive oil	3 tablespoons olive oil
3 tablespoons brandy	3 tablespoons brandy
1.5kg/3lb veal bones	3lb veal bones
1 chicken carcass	1 chicken carcass
white of 1 egg	white of 1 egg
2½ tablespoons chopped dill leaves (reserve the stalks)	2½ tablespoons chopped dill leaves (reserve the stalks)
675g/1½lb small carrots	1½lb small carrots

Make small slits in the beef with a sharp knife. Peel the garlic cloves, cut them in thin spikes and stick them into the slits. Put the beef in a deep bowl and strew over it the peeled and sliced onion, carrot and celery. Add the bay leaves and pour over the wine. Leave in the marinade for 12 to 24 hours, turning the piece of meat over from time to time.

When ready to cook, lift out the meat and wipe dry with soft paper towels. Heat the oil in a heavy flameproof casserole and brown the meat on all sides. Warm the brandy, ignite, and pour it, flaming, over the beef. When the flames have died down, put in the veal bones and chicken carcass, and pour over the marinade with its flavouring vegetables and herbs.

Bring to the boil on top of the stove, then cover the casserole and transfer it to the oven, pre-heated to 150°C/300°F or Gas Mark 2, and cook for 4 hours.

Remove the beef and leave to cool. Strain the stock and discard the chicken and veal bones and vegetables. Leave the stock to cool. When cold, remove all the fat from the surface. Beat the egg white until frothy. Heat the stock in a saucepan and whisk the egg white into it over the heat. When the stock boils, draw the pan to one side and allow the foam to subside. Boil it up once more and pour the stock through a sieve (strainer) lined with muslin (cheesecloth). The egg white will retain the impurities, leaving a clear liquid which, on cooling, will set to a clear jelly. Reheat the stock in a clean saucepan with the stalks of the dill, and as it reaches boiling point, draw the pan away from the fire and cover it. Leave for 15 minutes to infuse.

Meanwhile clean the small carrots and cook them whole. Carve the beef into neat slices. Strain the stock once more and discard the dill stalks. Pour a thin layer of stock into a round or oval dish. Put in the refrigerator to set. When firm, scatter a layer of chopped dill over the jelly, then arrange a layer of carrots cut in half lengthwise. Pour on a thin layer of jelly then set again in the refrigerator. Next make a layer of sliced beef, then more jelly, dill, carrots, and so on continuing these alternate layers until the dish is full. Press down lightly so that the jelly covers the contents of the dish, weighing down lightly with a plate if necessary. Leave for several hours in the refrigerator to set.

The next day, turn out by running a thin knife round the edge of the dish, and standing it in a shallow bowl of hot water for a few moments only to loosen the bottom. Turn out on to a flat dish. Accompany with potato salad, tomatoes in horse-radish sauce, a lettuce salad, or celery rémoulade. Serves 6 to 8.

Braised beef with horse-radish; Beef stew with marigolds; Beef in dill jelly

BEEF STOCK

Metric/Imperial	American
1.5kg/3lb beef bones, cracked	3lb beef bones, cracked
450g/1lb shin of beef	1lb beef shank
1 onion, with its skin	1 onion, with its skin
1 carrot	1 carrot
1 stick celery	1 stalk celery
1 bay leaf	1 bay leaf
3 sprigs parsley	3 sprigs parsley
3 sprigs lovage	3 sprigs lovage
3 sprigs thyme	3 sprigs thyme
1 tablespoon sea salt	1 tablespoon sea salt

Put the beef bones in a deep pan, cover with cold water and bring slowly to the boil. Skim off the scum which rises to the surface until only a white foam remains. Put in the shin of beef (beef shank) cut in several pieces, the halved onion, the cleaned and chopped carrot and celery, and the herbs. Add salt and cover the pan. Simmer gently for 3 hours (or 1 hour in a pressure cooker), then strain and cool.

Chill overnight in the refrigerator, and next day remove all the fat from the surface before using. (Keep the fat for frying.) The strained stock will keep for 3 to 4 days in the refrigerator.

LAMB WITH FENNEL

Metric/Imperial	American
675g/1½lb boned shoulder of lamb	1½lb boneless shoulder of lamb
seasoned flour	seasoned flour
1 mild onion	1 mild onion
1 large green pepper	1 large green pepper
1–2 heads Florence fennel	1–2 roots fennel
3 tablespoons olive oil	3 tablespoons olive oil
450ml/¾ pint veal stock or *chicken stock*	2 cups veal stock or *chicken stock*
pinch of saffron	pinch of saffron
sea salt and black pepper	sea salt and black pepper

Cut the lamb into neat rectangular pieces and toss in seasoned flour. Peel the onion and slice it thinly; cut the pepper in strips, discarding the seeds, and slice the fennel thinly. Heat the oil in a saucepan and brown the lamb pieces. Lift them out of the pan with a slotted spoon and put in the vegetables. Cook gently until lightly coloured, stirring often.

Return the meat to the saucepan and add the heated stock. Stir in the saffron and add salt and pepper to taste. Cover and simmer for 1¼ hours, or until the meat is tender. Serve with boiled rice or couscous.

MEAT BALLS WITH MINT

Metric/Imperial	American
575g/1¼lb minced lamb	1¼lb ground lamb
sea salt and black pepper	sea salt and black pepper
1 tablespoon oil	1 tablespoon oil
50g/2oz onion, finely chopped	½ cup finely chopped onion
3 tablespoons chopped parsley	3 tablespoons chopped parsley
3 tablespoons chopped mint	3 tablespoons chopped mint

Put the minced (ground) lamb in a large bowl and add salt and pepper. Heat the oil in a saucepan and sauté the onion until lightly coloured. Stir the onion into the meat. Add the chopped herbs and mix well. Form into small balls, place on a greased baking sheet and bake for 25 minutes in a moderate oven (180°C/350°F or Gas Mark 4), turning over once or twice. Alternatively, the meat balls may be cooked in a frying pan (skillet). Serve with yogurt and mint sauce (see page 193).

SKEWERS OF LAMB WITH HERBS

Metric/Imperial	American
½ leg of lamb, boned	½ leg of lamb, boned
½ medium onion	½ medium onion
1 clove garlic	1 clove garlic
6 sprigs lemon thyme	6 sprigs lemon thyme
6 sprigs marjoram	6 sprigs marjoram
3 sprigs lovage	3 sprigs lovage
3 sprigs rosemary	3 sprigs rosemary
3 sprigs parsley	3 sprigs parsley
4 tablespoons olive oil	¼ cup olive oil
4 tablespoons red wine	¼ cup red wine

Cut the meat into cubes about 2.5cm/1in square and put them in a bowl. Peel the onion, slice it thinly and mix with the meat. Stir in the peeled and crushed garlic. Pick the leaves of the herbs off their branches and chop. Mix with the meat. Stir in the oil and the wine. Leave for 4 to 6 hours or overnight.

Thread the pieces of meat loosely on to skewers. Cook over charcoal or an open fire, or grill (broil). Use the remaining marinade for basting. If you have plenty of rosemary, burn some sprigs under the skewers and use a little branch as a basting brush. Serve immediately, with fried rice and a mixed salad.

Opposite: Lamb with fennel; Meat balls with mint; Yogurt and mint sauce (page 193); Skewers of lamb with herbs

Right: Lamb with mint crust

LAMB WITH MINT CRUST

Metric/Imperial	American
1 shoulder of lamb	1 shoulder of lamb
MINT CRUST:	MINT CRUST:
3 tablespoons soft white breadcrumbs	3 tablespoons soft white breadcrumbs
3 tablespoons mint sauce (see page 191)	3 tablespoons mint sauce (see page 191)
1 tablespoon chopped parsley	1 tablespoon chopped parsley
1 clove garlic	1 clove garlic
sea salt and black pepper	sea salt and black pepper

Put the shoulder of lamb on a rack in a roasting pan and cook in a moderate oven (180°C/350°F or Gas Mark 4) for 25 minutes per 0.5kg/1lb.

To make the mint crust, mix the breadcrumbs to a paste with the mint sauce, adding the chopped parsley and the finely chopped garlic. Add the salt and pepper to taste.

Thirty minutes before the end of the roasting time, take out the joint and spread the mint mixture over the fat surface, pressing it down well with a palette knife. Baste once with the pan juices and return to the oven to finish cooking. The crust should be golden brown when the cooking time is up.

Lamb steaks with thyme; Braised veal with herbs;
Veal with rosemary; Veal with tarragon

LAMB STEAKS WITH THYME

Metric/Imperial	American
4 *slices leg of lamb, about* *2.5cm/1in thick*	4 *slices leg of lamb, about* *1in thick*
2 *tablespoons olive oil*	2 *tablespoons olive oil*
1 *tablespoon lemon juice*	1 *tablespoon lemon juice*
24 *small sprigs lemon* *thyme or ordinary* *thyme*	24 *small sprigs lemon* *thyme or ordinary* *thyme*
sea salt and black pepper	*sea salt and black pepper*
herb butter to serve	*herb butter to serve*

Ask the butcher to cut a leg of lamb for you, sawing through the bone. Rub each steak on each side with olive oil and lemon juice. Pull the leaves off the thyme and scatter over the meat, on both sides. Leave for 1 to 2 hours. Grill (broil) the steaks, preferably over charcoal or an open fire. Sprinkle with salt and pepper after cooking. Serve with a herb butter flavoured with tarragon, basil, or mixed herbs.

VEAL WITH TARRAGON

Metric/Imperial	American
6 *sprigs tarragon*	6 *sprigs tarragon*
300ml/½ *pint thick cream*	1¼ *cups heavy cream*
40g/1½oz *butter*	3 *tablespoons butter*
4 *veal escalopes*	4 *veal scallops*
juice of ½ small lemon	*juice of ½ small lemon*
sea salt and black pepper	*sea salt and black pepper*

Strip about 12 large leaves from the sprigs of tarragon and reserve. Heat the cream in a small pan with the sprigs. Bring slowly to boiling point and draw the pan to the side of the fire. Cover the pan, and leave for 20 minutes to infuse, stirring occasionally.

Melt the butter in a flat frying pan (skillet). When it is very hot, cook the escalopes (scallops) quickly; 2 minutes on each side should be enough. Remove them to a flat dish and keep hot.

Pour the cream through a sieve (strainer) into the frying pan (skillet) and stir well to mix with the juices. Add about 1 tablespoon lemon juice to taste, and plenty of salt and black pepper. Pour over the veal and scatter with the reserved tarragon leaves, chopped. Serve with new potatoes or rice, and a greed salad.

VEAL IN MUSTARD AND DILL SAUCE

Metric/Imperial	American
675g/1½lb *pie veal*	1½lb *boneless veal*
1 *large onion*	1 *large onion*
25g/1oz *butter*	2 *tablespoons butter*
1 *tablespoon olive oil*	1 *tablespoon olive oil*
seasoned flour	*seasoned flour*
300ml/½ *pint veal stock* *or chicken stock*	1¼ *cups veal stock* *or chicken stock*
4–5 *sprigs dill*	4–5 *sprigs dill*
sea salt and black pepper	*sea salt and black pepper*
1 *tablespoon Dijon* *mustard*	1 *tablespoon Dijon* *mustard*
150ml/¼ *pint thick cream*	½ *cup heavy cream*

Trim the veal into neat even pieces. Peel and chop the onion quite finely. Heat the butter and oil in a flameproof casserole and cook the onion until golden. Toss the veal in seasoned flour and add to the onion. Cook until lightly browned, stirring, then add the heated stock. Stir until blended. Remove enough leaves from the sprigs of dill to give 2 tablespoons when chopped. Set aside the leaves. Add the sprigs, salt, pepper and mustard to the casserole and cover. Simmer gently for 1¼ hours or until the veal is tender.

Lift out the dill sprigs and throw away. Add the cream, stir until blended, then add the chopped dill and stand for a few moments before serving. Serve with new potatoes or rice and a green salad.

BRAISED VEAL WITH HERBS

Metric/Imperial	American
1.25kg/2½lb boned and rolled shoulder of veal	2½lb boneless shoulder roast of veal
25g/1oz butter	2 tablespoons butter
1 tablespoon oil	1 tablespoon oil
2 onions	2 onions
2 carrots	2 carrots
3 sprigs parsley	3 sprigs parsley
3 sprigs lovage	3 sprigs lovage
150ml/¼ pint dry white wine	⅔ cup dry white wine
150ml/¼ pint veal stock or *chicken stock*	⅔ cup veal stock or *chicken stock*
sea salt and black pepper	sea salt and black pepper
1 teaspoon flour	1 teaspoon flour
4 tablespoons sour cream	¼ cup sour cream
squeeze of lemon juice	squeeze of lemon juice
1½ tablespoons chopped burnet	1½ tablespoons chopped burnet
1½ tablespoons chopped chervil	1½ tablespoons chopped chervil

Choose a saucepan that fits the veal closely. Melt the butter and the oil in the pan and brown the meat on all sides. Lift out the meat and put the peeled and sliced onions and carrots in the pan. Stir for 5 to 6 minutes, until lightly coloured, then replace the meat, lay the parsley and lovage around it and cover with the heated wine and stock. Sprinkle with salt and black pepper, cover the pan and simmer gently for 1½ hours, or until the meat is tender. Open the pan several times during the cooking to baste the meat, and turn it from side to side.

When cooked, lift out the veal and keep warm. Skim the fat from the surface of the cooled cooking liquid and put it in a blender with the braised vegetables, discarding the herbs. After blending, pour into a clean pan and reheat. Stir the flour into the sour cream in a bowl. When the sauce boils, pour it slowly on to the sour cream and stir until smooth. Return to the pan and stir over a low heat until blended and slightly thickened. Add a squeeze of lemon juice, to taste, and more salt and pepper as needed, then stir in the chopped burnet and chervil. (If only one of the two herbs is available, use 3 tablespoons of it on its own.)

Carve the meat in thin slices, lay on a warmed platter, and pour the sauce over all. Serve with boiled potatoes and a green vegetable.

VEAL WITH ROSEMARY

Metric/Imperial	American
1 onion	1 onion
3 tablespoons olive oil	3 tablespoons olive oil
2 cloves garlic	2 cloves garlic
1kg/2lb lean veal, from the leg	2lb lean veal, from the leg
sea salt and black pepper	sea salt and black pepper
225g/8oz fresh tomatoes or *a 400g/14oz can tomatoes, drained*	½lb fresh tomatoes or *a 14oz can tomatoes, drained*
150ml/¼ pint dry white wine	⅔ cup dry white wine
3 sprigs rosemary	3 sprigs rosemary

Peel and chop the onion. Heat the oil in a saucepan and cook the onion gently until pale golden. Peel and crush the garlic and add it to the onion while it is cooking. Cut the meat into neat rectangular pieces and add them to the pan. Stir around until browned on all sides. Add salt and black pepper. Peel and deseed the tomatoes; chop them quite finely and add to the pan. (If using canned tomatoes, drain off the juice, chop the tomatoes roughly, and add to the meat.) Pour on the wine, put in the sprigs of rosemary and cover the pan. Cook gently for 1½ hours, stirring occasionally. To serve the veal stew, take out the rosemary and accompany with rice and a green salad.

COLD VEAL IN HERB SAUCE

Metric/Imperial	American
1.25kg/2½lb boned and rolled shoulder of veal	2½lb boneless shoulder roast of veal
25g/1oz butter	2 tablespoons butter
1 tablespoon oil	1 tablespoon oil
2 onions	2 onions
2 carrots	2 carrots
3 sprigs parsley	3 sprigs parsley
3 sprigs lovage	3 sprigs lovage
sea salt and black pepper	sea salt and black pepper
150ml/¼ pint dry white wine	⅔ cup dry white wine
150ml/¼ pint veal stock or *chicken stock*	⅔ cup veal stock or *chicken stock*
HERB SAUCE:	HERB SAUCE:
1 egg yolk	1 egg yolk
pinch of salt	pinch of salt
150ml/¼ pint olive oil	⅔ cup olive oil
1 teaspoon white wine vinegar	1 teaspoon white wine vinegar
1 teaspoon lemon juice	1 teaspoon lemon juice
1 teaspoon Dijon mustard	1 teaspoon Dijon mustard
4 tablespoons natural yogurt	¼ cup unflavored yogurt
1 tablespoon chopped dill	1 tablespoon chopped dill
1 tablespoon chopped tarragon	1 tablespoon chopped tarragon
1 tablespoon chopped chervil	1 tablespoon chopped chervil
1 tablespoon chopped chives	1 tablespoon chopped chives

Start to prepare this dish the day before you plan to serve it. Choose a saucepan that fits the veal closely. Melt the butter and oil in the pan and brown the meat on all sides. Lift out the meat and put in the peeled and sliced onions and carrots. Cook gently for about 6 minutes before returning the meat to the pan. Lay the parsley and lovage around it and sprinkle with salt and black pepper. Pour over the wine and the stock and bring to the boil. Cover closely and simmer for 1½ hours, or until the meat is tender. During the cooking, open the pan several times to baste the meat thoroughly and turn it over once or twice. When the meat is tender, lift out and leave to cool overnight. Strain the juices and chill in the refrigerator. Use the braised vegetables for another dish.

Next day make the sauce: prepare a mayonnaise with the egg yolk, salt, olive oil, vinegar and lemon juice (see method page 190). Stir in the mustard, then mix with the yogurt. Remove all fat from the surface of the veal juices, and stir 4 tablespoons (¼ cup) into the sauce; they will have set to a light jelly, so it will need some beating or a brief purée in a blender to make a smooth sauce. Stir in the chopped herbs.

Carve the veal in thin slices, trim off any fat, and lay them on a flat dish. Spoon over the sauce and chill for an hour or two before serving. Serve with new potatoes and string (snap) beans, or a potato salad, a lettuce salad and a tomato salad.

VEAL IN SORREL SAUCE

Metric/Imperial	American
675g/1½lb pie veal	1½lb boneless veal
1 large onion	1 large onion
1 large carrot	1 large carrot
25g/1oz butter	2 tablespoons butter
1 tablespoon oil	1 tablespoon oil
300ml/½ pint hot water	1¼ cups hot water
sea salt and black pepper	sea salt and black pepper
6 sprigs thyme	6 sprigs thyme
3 sprigs marjoram	3 sprigs marjoram
2 sprigs lovage	2 sprigs lovage
1 bay leaf	1 bay leaf
SORREL SAUCE:	SORREL SAUCE:
50g/2oz chopped sorrel	1½ cups chopped sorrel
150ml/¼ pint chicken stock or *veal stock*	⅔ cup chicken stock or *veal stock*
25g/1oz butter	2 tablespoons butter
1 tablespoon flour	1 tablespoon flour
150ml/¼ pint thin cream	⅔ cup light cream
juice of ½ lemon	juice of ½ lemon

Cut the veal into neat pieces about 2.5cm/1in square. Peel and chop the onion; clean the carrot, cut it in half lengthwise, then into slices. Heat the butter and oil together in a saucepan, and cook the meat with the vegetables until lightly coloured, stirring frequently. Add the hot water, salt and pepper and the herbs, cover the pan and simmer for 1¼ to 1½ hours, until the veal is tender.

While the veal is cooking, prepare the sorrel sauce. Simmer the sorrel in the stock for 5 minutes; cool slightly, then purée in a blender. Melt the butter in a small saucepan, stir in the flour and cook for 1 minute, stirring. Add the sorrel purée and stir until blended. Put to one side until the veal is cooked. Take out the herbs and add the sorrel purée gradually, stirring constantly until it is blended with the veal. Add the cream and the lemon juice and more salt and pepper, if needed. Serve with new potatoes and carrots.

VEAL STOCK

Metric/Imperial	American
1.5kg/3lb veal bones, including some knuckle bones	3lb veal bones, including some from the shank
1 large onion, with its skin	1 large onion, with its skin
1 carrot	1 carrot
1 leek	1 leek
1 stick celery	1 stalk celery
3 sprigs parsley	3 sprigs parsley
3 sprigs lovage	3 sprigs lovage
1 tablespoon sea salt	1 tablespoon sea salt
450g/1lb pie veal	1lb boneless veal

Put the veal bones in a deep pan and cover generously with cold water. Bring slowly to the boil, skimming off the scum that rises to the surface. When no more forms, add the halved onion, the cleaned and sliced carrot, leek and celery and the herbs. Throw in the salt and simmer, partially covered, for 2 hours.

Cut the pie veal (boneless veal) into chunks and add it to the pan. After simmering for another hour, take out the veal and use it for another dish. Strain the stock and leave to cool. The next day it will have set to a firm jelly which can be used as aspic, with added flavourings. Remove all fat from the surface before using.

If using a pressure cooker, allow 40 minutes cooking before adding the chopped veal, and 20 minutes afterwards. This stock will keep for 3 or 4 days in the refrigerator.

PORK CHOPS WITH HONEY AND HERBS

Metric/Imperial	American
4 pork chops	4 pork chops
3 tablespoons clear honey	3 tablespoons clear honey
3 tablespoons chopped marjoram	3 tablespoons chopped marjoram
3 tablespoons chopped thyme	3 tablespoons chopped thyme
sea salt and black pepper	sea salt and black pepper
juice of ½ lemon	juice of ½ lemon

Brush the chops on each side with the honey. (If the honey is thick, it may be slightly warmed.) Mix the 2 chopped herbs and coat the chops with them evenly. Sprinkle with salt and pepper and a little lemon juice. Grill (broil) for 5 minutes on each side close to the heat, then a further 5 to 10 minutes on each side, depending on the thickness, further away from the heat. Serve immediately, with new potatoes and a green salad.

Opposite: Veal in sorrel sauce

Right: Pork chops with honey and herbs

LIVER WITH ONIONS

Metric/Imperial	American
450g/1lb calves' liver	1lb calf liver
225g/8oz mild onions	½lb mild onions
6 tablespoons olive oil	6 tablespoons olive oil
25g/1oz butter	2 tablespoons butter
sea salt and black pepper	sea salt and black pepper
1 teaspoon chopped sage	1 teaspoon chopped sage
½ tablespoon white wine vinegar	½ tablespoon white wine vinegar
2 tablespoons chopped parsley to garnish	2 tablespoons chopped parsley to garnish

Have the liver cut as thinly as possible. Then cut it into small pieces, about 3cm/1½in square. Peel the onions and slice them thinly. Heat 4 tablespoons (¼ cup) olive oil with the butter in a frying pan (skillet) and cook the onions gently until soft and pale golden. Do not let them colour too much.

Heat the remaining oil in another frying pan (skillet) and cook the liver briskly, turning often. It will only take about 2 to 3 minutes. Tip the onions into the pan with the liver and cook both together for 1 minute. Add salt and pepper and the chopped sage and turn into a serving dish. Pour the vinegar into the pan and swirl around, then pour over the liver and onions. Sprinkle with chopped parsley and serve immediately.

PORK BAKED IN FOIL

Metric/Imperial	American
olive oil	olive oil
1 large pork fillet, about 450g/1lb	1 pork tenderloin, about 1lb
6 sprigs marjoram	6 sprigs marjoram
6 sprigs lemon thyme	6 sprigs lemon thyme
6 small sprigs tarragon	6 small sprigs tarragon
3 sprigs rosemary	3 sprigs rosemary
sea salt and black pepper	sea salt and black pepper
juice of ½ lemon	juice of ½ lemon

Heat a little olive oil in a frying pan (skillet) and brown the fillet (tenderloin) very quickly on all sides. Lay a piece of foil on a work surface, rub it lightly all over with oil, and arrange the sprigs of herbs over it. Sprinkle with salt and pepper. Put the fillet (tenderloin) on top, sprinkle with salt and pepper and the juice of half a lemon.

Wrap up in the foil, sealing the ends so that no juice can escape. Put the foil parcel on a rack on a baking sheet and cook for 30 minutes in a moderately hot oven (190°C/375°F or Gas Mark 5). Unwrap the parcel and pour the cooking juice carefully into a small jug (pitcher) to serve with the meat. Discard the herbs and foil. Carve the meat into diagonal slices and serve with rice, noodles, or boiled potatoes and a green vegetable. This will serve 3; or double the quantities for 6.

ROAST PORK WITH SAGE AND ONION STUFFING

Metric/Imperial	American
a hand of pork, about 1.75kg/4lb	a fresh picnic shoulder, about 4lb
olive oil	olive oil
sea salt	sea salt
sage and onion stuffing (see page 110)	sage and onion stuffing (see page 110)

Have the skin of the joint scored to give a crisp crackling. (This is only possible in England, where the skin is left on joints of pork for roasting.)

Lay the pork in a roasting pan and pour a little olive oil over the skin, then sprinkle it with sea salt. Heat the oven to 230°C/450°F or Gas Mark 8. Put the joint in, and turn the oven down to 180°C/350°F or Gas Mark 4. Allow 30 minutes per 0.5kg/1lb, plus 30 minutes. One hour before the pork is ready, spoon the stuffing around it in the pan. Baste from time to time with the juices, and add a little extra oil occasionally.

To serve, put the joint on a carving dish and surround with the stuffing. Serve the cooking juices in a small jug (pitcher). Serve with apple sauce, roast or puréed potatoes, and a green vegetable.

JAMBON PERSILLÉ

Metric/Imperial	American
2.5–3kg/6lb ham or gammon	6lb smoked ham (rump or shank)
450g/1lb knuckle of veal	1lb veal shank
4 calves' feet or pigs' feet	4 calves' feet or pigs' feet
1 bay leaf	1 bay leaf
2 sprigs parsley	2 sprigs parsley
1 stick celery	1 stalk celery
10 shallots or 6 small onions	10 shallots or 6 small onions
2 cloves	2 cloves
12 black peppercorns	12 black peppercorns
1.5 litres/2 bottles dry white wine	2 bottles (6¼ cups) dry white wine
3 tablespoons white wine vinegar	3 tablespoons white wine vinegar
50g/2oz finely chopped parsley	1½ cups finely chopped parsley

Soak the ham (or gammon) in cold water for 24 hours, changing the water two or three times. Put in a large pot and cover with fresh cold water. Bring to the boil and simmer for 30 minutes. Cool, then cut out the bone. Keep the water. Cook the knuckle of veal (veal shank) and the calves' or pigs' feet for 10 minutes in boiling salted water, then drain and rinse them well under cold running water.

Clean the pot the ham was cooked in and put back the ham with the veal, feet, bay leaf, parsley sprigs, celery, shallots, cloves and peppercorns. Do not add salt. Pour over the wine and vinegar and add enough of the reserved cooking water to just cover the ham. Bring to the boil and carefully remove all scum that floats to the surface. Cover and simmer very gently indeed for 3 hours.

Remove the ham, discard the veal, feet, vegetables and herbs, and strain the liquid into a bowl through a double layer of muslin (cheesecloth). Cool the liquid by sitting the bowl in a sink half full of very cold water. Cut the ham into cubes about 3cm/1 to 1½in square, and crush lightly with a fork. Press the pieces of ham into a shallow round bowl or pudding bowl, mixing the fat and lean as evenly as possible. When the strained liquid has cooled, remove all the fat from the surface and stir in the finely chopped parsley. Pour the liquid over the ham, making sure that it penetrates to the bottom of the bowl. Cool overnight in the refrigerator.

To serve, turn out on a large platter. This pretty dish is worth making for a party; it will serve 12 easily, and can be made a few days in advance.

Vegetables

The horticultural connection between herbs and vegetables is very close. In many cases, they even belong to the same family. Lovage is so similar in appearance to the celery leaf that the two are difficult to tell apart, while two closely related varieties of fennel are cultivated, one for its leaf and seed which are used as herbs, and the other, Florence fennel, for its bulbous root, which is classified as a vegetable.

The flavours of certain vegetables and herbs have such a strong affinity for each other as to defy all attempts to improve upon their partnership; new potatoes cooked with mint can hardly be bettered, although the Scandinavians tend to use dill, which also makes an exquisite combination. The English have always cooked green peas with mint, while the French add savory to almost all bean dishes. The Italians are great lovers of basil, and add it to tomato dishes all summer long, where its warm sweet flavour brings out the taste of sun-ripened tomatoes to perfection. Beetroot (beet) and dill make a good combination, especially when served in a sour cream sauce, and mushrooms go well with almost all the delicate herbs, especially chervil. Potato salad is one of my favourite summer dishes, either dressed in a mayonnaise-type sauce, or in a vinaigrette. In either case, it is vastly improved in flavour and appearance by generous additions of chopped parsley and chives.

The root vegetables of autumn and winter are delicious when garnished with lovage; turnips, carrots, swedes (rutabagas) and parsnips all go well with this herb, and with parsley, which is available all through the winter. On the whole I think the more delicate herbs go best with vegetables, and prefer to keep the stronger-flavoured woody ones, like rosemary, bay and thyme for use in meat dishes. The exception is sage, which also blends well with all onion dishes.

I tend to use one herb at a time in vegetable cookery, for the taste of each vegetable is so subtle that it does not need complex additions. In most cases, the herb is simply sprinkled on at the end of the cooking, acting both as a flavouring and a garnish. In other instances, a herb sauce is all that is needed to complement the vegetable, which has been boiled, steamed or baked. A baked potato needs only a spoonful of sour cream with chopped herbs, while grilled (broiled) tomatoes are enormously improved by the last-minute addition of herb butter.

BEETROOT (BEET) WITH DILL

Metric/Imperial	American
675g/1½lb small beetroot, cooked	1½lb small beet, cooked
25g/1oz butter	2 tablespoons butter
150ml/¼ pint sour cream	⅔ cup sour cream
sea salt and black pepper	sea salt and black pepper
2 tablespoons chopped dill	2 tablespoons chopped dill

Skin the beetroot (beet) and cut into quite thick slices. Melt the butter in a pan and cook the sliced beetroot (beet) gently until heated through. Add the sour cream and simmer for 2 to 3 minutes, adding salt and pepper to taste. Stir in the chopped dill and stand for a few moments, covered, before serving. Serve with roast chicken or veal escalopes (scallops).

Jambon persillé; Beetroot (beet) with dill

CABBAGE STUFFED WITH HERBS

Metric/Imperial	American
5 large cabbage leaves	5 large cabbage leaves
225g/8oz spinach	½lb spinach
1 bunch watercress	1 bunch watercress
1 lettuce	1 head lettuce
100g/4oz sorrel	¼lb sorrel
100g/4oz long-grain rice	½ cup long-grain rice
1 bunch spring onions	1 bunch scallions
100g/4oz cooked ham	½ cup chopped cooked ham
100g/4oz mushrooms	1 cup sliced mushrooms
50g/2oz chopped parsley	1½ cups chopped parsley
50g/2oz chopped mixed herbs: chervil, cress, dill, tarragon, mint, lemon balm, marjoram and lovage	1½ cups chopped mixed herbs: chervil, garden cress, dill, tarragon, mint, lemon balm, marjoram and lovage
sea salt and black pepper	sea salt and black pepper
stock	stock

Choose 5 perfect cabbage leaves and throw them into a large pan of boiling water. Boil for 5 minutes, then drain, reserving the water. Wash and drain the spinach, watercress, lettuce and sorrel and put them into the same pan. Blanch for 3 minutes. Drain, forcing out excess water in a colander (strainer). When cool enough to handle, squeeze between the hands to press out as much water as possible, then chop.

Wash the rice, drain it, and put in a large bowl. Stir in the sliced spring onions (scallions), the chopped ham, the sliced mushrooms, and the chopped greens and herbs. Add plenty of salt and pepper and mix well.

Line a pudding bowl first with a piece of muslin (cheesecloth) and then the blanched cabbage leaves. Spoon in the stuffing, and tie up the muslin (cheesecloth) so that the stuffing is completely enclosed in cabbage leaves. Do not tie too tightly; leave room for the rice to swell as it cooks. Lift the parcel out of the bowl, lower it into a large pan of boiling stock and cook for 1 hour. Lift out and stand for a moment or two in a colander (strainer) to drain, then untie and turn out on to a serving dish. Serve with a tomato sauce. This substantial dish makes a good main course.

CARROTS WITH MINT

Metric/Imperial	American
675g/1½lb young carrots	1½lb young carrots
sea salt	sea salt
50g/2oz butter	¼ cup butter
1 tablespoon sugar	1 tablespoon sugar
2 tablespoons chopped mint	2 tablespoons chopped mint

Clean the carrots. If they are tiny, leave them whole, otherwise cut in halves or quarters lengthwise. Cook in lightly salted boiling water until tender. Drain, return the carrots to the pan, and add butter and sugar. Stir over a very low heat for 3 to 4 minutes, until faintly caramelized. Cover and leave over the flame for 2 minutes longer. Add the mint, stir to mix well, and serve. Delicious with chicken, duck, veal or lamb.

CAULIFLOWER WITH CHERVIL

Metric/Imperial	American
1 medium cauliflower	1 medium cauliflower
MAYONNAISE:	MAYONNAISE:
1 egg yolk	1 egg yolk
150ml/¼ pint olive oil	⅔ cup olive oil
½ tablespoon lemon juice	½ tablespoon lemon juice
3–4 tablespoons thin cream	3–4 tablespoons light cream
3 tablespoons chopped chervil	3 tablespoons chopped chervil

Clean the cauliflower, divide it into sprigs and cook in boiling water until barely tender; drain. Make the mayonnaise in advance (this dish is only worth making with homemade mayonnaise – see method page 190), and thin it with a little thin (light) cream. Stir the chopped chervil into the mayonnaise and mix lightly with the cooked cauliflower. Allow to cool. Serve soon after cooling; do not chill. This is best served as an hors d'oeuvre.

COURGETTES (ZUCCHINI) WITH TOMATOES

Metric/Imperial	American
450g/1lb courgettes	1lb zucchini
40g/1½oz butter	3 tablespoons butter
225g/8oz tomatoes	½lb tomatoes
sea salt and black pepper	sea salt and black pepper
pinch of sugar	pinch of sugar
2 tablespoons chopped basil	2 tablespoons chopped basil

Wash the courgettes (zucchini) but do not peel them. Trim the ends and cut them into slices about 1cm/½in thick. Melt the butter in a pan and stew the courgettes (zucchini) gently for about 8 minutes. Peel the tomatoes and chop coarsely. Add them to the pan and simmer for a further 7 to 8 minutes, stirring occasionally. Season with salt, pepper, and a pinch of sugar. Stir in the chopped basil and serve.

COURGETTES (ZUCCHINI) WITH DILL

Metric/Imperial	American
675g/1½lb courgettes	1½lb zucchini
40g/1½oz butter	3 tablespoons butter
sea salt and black pepper	sea salt and black pepper
2 tablespoons chopped dill	2 tablespoons chopped dill

Do not peel the courgettes (zucchini). Simply wash them, cut off the ends, and cut in 1cm/½in slices. Melt the butter in a pan, add the sliced courgettes (zucchini), and stew gently, covered, for about 12 minutes, shaking the pan occasionally. When tender, season with salt and pepper and stir in the chopped dill and serve.

COURGETTES (ZUCCHINI) WITH CHIVES

Metric/Imperial	American
450g/1lb courgettes	1lb zucchini
sea salt	sea salt
4 tablespoons sour cream	¼ cup sour cream
2 tablespoons chopped chives	2 tablespoons chopped chives

Wash and trim the unpeeled courgettes (zucchini) and cut into slices about 1cm/½in thick. Drop them into a saucepan containing a little boiling salted water and cook, covered, for 12 minutes. Drain and return to the pan. Stir over a gentle heat to dry out, then add the sour cream. Stir until well mixed and heated, add the chopped chives, and serve.

Cauliflower with chervil; Cabbage stuffed with herbs; Courgettes (zucchini) with tomatoes

STUFFED COURGETTE (ZUCCHINI) FLOWERS

Metric/Imperial	American
10–12 large courgette flowers	10–12 large zucchini flowers
oil for deep frying	oil for deep frying
lemon quarters to serve	lemon quarters to serve
BATTER:	BATTER:
100g/4oz plain flour	1 cup all-purpose flour
pinch of sea salt	pinch of sea salt
2 tablespoons sunflower-seed oil	2 tablespoons sunflower-seed oil
150ml/¼ pint warm water	⅔ cup warm water
1 egg white	1 egg white
FILLING:	FILLING:
25g/1oz butter	2 tablespoons butter
1 shallot or small onion	1 shallot or small onion
100g/4oz medium-grain rice	½ cup medium-grain rice
450ml/¾ pint chicken stock	2 cups chicken stock
sea salt and black pepper	sea salt and black pepper
1½ tablespoons chopped basil	1½ tablespoons chopped basil

Wash the flowers carefully, and shake dry in a soft cloth.

To make the batter, sift the flour with the salt into a large bowl. Stir in the oil and the lukewarm water. The consistency should be like fairly thick cream; you may need to add a little extra water. Stand for 1 to 2 hours in a cool place. Just before using, whip the egg white and fold in.

To make the filling, heat the butter in a deep frying pan (skillet) and fry the chopped shallot (or onion) gently until pale golden. Rinse the rice well in a colander and drain. Add the rice to the pan. Stir around for a minute or two, then pour on half the heated stock. Cover the pan and simmer until the stock is almost absorbed; reheat the remaining stock and add most of it to the pan. When the stock is absorbed for the second time, the rice should be tender; if not, add a little extra stock. When cooked, add salt and pepper and stir in the chopped basil. Leave to cool.

To fill the flowers, separate the petals carefully and spoon into each one a little filling – only about 2 or 3 teaspoonsful – and fold the petals over it. Dip each one in the batter, and scrape off excess batter on the edge of the bowl. Heat a pan of oil to 185°C/360°F and drop in the stuffed flowers, a few at a time. Cook for about 4 minutes, turning once, until golden brown on each side. Drain while the rest cook, then serve immediately, with lemon quarters. Serve as a first course, unaccompanied.

FENNEL AND TOMATOES WITH DILL

Metric/Imperial	American
4 small heads Florence fennel	4 small roots fennel
sunflower-seed oil or ground-nut oil for frying	sunflower-seed oil or peanut oil for frying
sea salt and black pepper	sea salt and black pepper
450g/1lb tomatoes	1lb tomatoes
3 tablespoons chopped dill	3 tablespoons chopped dill

Cut the fennel into very thin vertical slices. Heat enough oil to cover the bottom of a heavy pan and stew the fennel gently, stirring often, until almost soft. Add plenty of salt and pepper. Skin and slice the tomatoes. Add them to the fennel and continue to cook gently for 5 minutes, stirring very carefully now and again with a spatula, to avoid breaking up the tomatoes. When ready, stir in the chopped dill and turn into a dish to cool. Serve cold, but do not chill.

This dish is better made a day in advance, for the flavour seems to improve on standing. Serve as a first course, either alone, or with one or two other vegetable dishes.

Fennel and tomatoes with dill

KOHLRABI WITH BASIL

Metric/Imperial	American
675g/1½lb kohlrabi	1½lb kohlrabi
50g/2oz beef dripping	¼ cup beef drippings
300ml/½ pint beef stock	1¼ cups beef stock
or game stock	or game stock
sea salt and black pepper	sea salt and black pepper
2 tablespoons chopped	2 tablespoons chopped
basil	basil

Skin the kohlrabi finely and cut into thin slices. Melt the dripping in a pan and cook the kohlrabi gently, stirring now and then, for 8 to 10 minutes. Heat the stock and add it to the pan; cover and simmer for about 15 minutes, until just soft. Add the salt and pepper and chopped basil, turn off the heat, cover the pan and leave for 4 minutes.

To serve, lift the sliced kohlrabi into a serving dish and pour the juices with the chopped basil over it. Serve with roast or grilled (broiled) lamb.

MUSHROOMS WITH DILL

Metric/Imperial	American
450g/1lb mushrooms	1lb mushrooms
50g/2oz butter	¼ cup butter
300ml/½ pint sour cream	1¼ cups sour cream
sea salt and black pepper	sea salt and black pepper
2 tablespoons chopped dill	2 tablespoons chopped dill

Cut the stalks off the mushrooms, wipe the caps, and slice them. Heat the butter in a pan and stew the mushrooms gently for about 8 minutes, stirring occasionally. Add the sour cream and simmer for a further 2 to 3 minutes. Add salt and pepper to taste, and finally the chopped dill. Stand, covered, for a few moments before serving. This dish is excellent served with veal escalopes (scallops), steaks, or grilled (broiled) chicken.

Stuffed mushrooms; Mushrooms with dill

STUFFED MUSHROOMS

Metric/Imperial	American
8 flat mushrooms,	8 flat mushrooms,
about 6cm/2½in across	about 2½in across
3–4 tablespoons olive oil	3–4 tablespoons olive oil
350g/12oz tomatoes	¾lb tomatoes
1 clove garlic	1 clove garlic
1 bunch spring onions	1 bunch scallions
3 tablespoons chopped	3 tablespoons chopped
chives	chives
sea salt and black pepper	sea salt and black pepper
pinch of sugar	pinch of sugar
½ tablespoon lemon juice	½ tablespoon lemon juice

Wipe the mushrooms and cut the stalks off level with the caps. Oil a baking sheet and lay the mushrooms on it, stalk side uppermost. Pour a teaspoon of olive oil over each one and bake for 20 minutes in a moderate oven (180°C/350°F or Gas Mark 4). Remove and cool.

Skin the tomatoes and chop very finely. Peel and crush the garlic and slice the spring onions (scallions) thinly. Pile the tomatoes, garlic and spring onions (scallions) together on a chopping board and chop until reduced to a purée. Put in a bowl and stir in the chopped chives, salt, pepper and a pinch of sugar. Add 1 tablespoon olive oil and the lemon juice. Pile a little of the mixture on top of each of the cooled mushroom caps. Serve as a first course, or as part of a selection of vegetable dishes.

Onions in sage sauce; Potato cakes with parsley; Potatoes with rosemary; Tomatoes with herb butter

ONIONS IN SAGE SAUCE

Metric/Imperial	American
350g/12oz tiny onions	¾lb tiny onions
25g/1oz butter	2 tablespoons butter
1 tablespoon flour	1 tablespoon flour
150ml/¼ pint chicken stock	⅔ cup chicken stock
sea salt and black pepper	sea salt and black pepper
½ teaspoon chopped sage	½ teaspoon chopped sage
or 6 sage leaves	or 6 sage leaves
2 tablespoons thick cream	2 tablespoons heavy cream
1 tablespoon chopped	1 tablespoon chopped
parsley	parsley

Peel the onions and leave them whole. Heat the butter in a saucepan and brown the onions gently, allowing 5 minutes, stirring often. Blend in the flour and cook for 1 minute, then add the heated stock and stir until smooth. Add salt and pepper to taste, and the chopped sage or sage leaves. Cover the pan and simmer for 20 to 30 minutes, stirring occasionally.

When the onions are soft right through, stir in the cream and the chopped parsley and serve. This is excellent with lamb cutlets, roast lamb, pork chops, liver or roast duck.

ONION PURÉE WITH SAGE

Metric/Imperial	American
675g/1½lb onions	1½lb onions
25g/1oz beef	2 tablespoons beef
dripping	drippings
100g/4oz carrots	¼lb carrots
300ml/½ pint chicken stock	1¼ cups chicken stock
sea salt and black pepper	sea salt and black pepper
1 tablespoon chopped sage	1 tablespoon chopped sage
squeeze of lemon juice	squeeze of lemon juice
2 tablespoons sour cream	2 tablespoons sour cream

Peel and slice the onions and cook slowly in the beef dripping in a shallow lidded pan. After about 8 minutes add the cleaned and thinly sliced carrots. Four minutes later, pour on the heated stock. Add salt and pepper and the chopped sage. Cover the pan and simmer for 15 minutes, stirring occasionally. Cool, then purée in a blender. Return to a clean pan, and reheat, adding more salt and pepper as needed, a squeeze of lemon juice and the sour cream.

If necessary, a little more chopped sage may be added at this stage, but this is a very powerful herb which must be used with a light touch. The flavour of the sage should be quite faint, so that it blends with the other ingredients rather than overpowering them. This purée is delicious served with game, especially pheasant and grouse, pork, veal, duck, and pure pork sausages.

PEASE PUDDING

Metric/Imperial	American
1–1.5kg/2–3lb maincrop	2–3lb maincrop peas,
peas, in the pod	in the pod
sea salt and black pepper	sea salt and black pepper
pinch of sugar	pinch of sugar
3 tablespoons chopped	3 tablespoons chopped
mint	mint
40g/1½oz butter	3 tablespoons butter

Shell the peas and tip them into a pudding basin (bowl) lined with a piece of muslin (cheesecloth). Add salt and pepper and a pinch of sugar. Stir in 2 tablespoons chopped mint and tie up the muslin (cheesecloth) with string. Bring a large pan of water or light stock to the boil and lower in the muslin (cheesecloth) bag. Cover the pan, and cook for 1 hour.

When the time is up, lift the bag out of the pan and stand in a colander (strainer) for a few minutes to drain. Untie the bag and tip the peas into a food processor, or a vegetable mill with a coarse mesh. Purée roughly, and tip back into the muslin (cheesecloth) to reform into a round ball. Turn out on a serving dish. Heat the butter in a pan with the remaining mint and pour it over the pudding. Serve with boiled ham, roast pork, or sausages.

This pudding is also good cold: leave to cool in its muslin (cheesecloth) after puréeing, then turn out on a dish and cut into slices. Do not cover with melted butter. This is good with cold cooked ham, pork and bacon.

POTATOES WITH ROSEMARY

Metric/Imperial	American
675g/1½lb potatoes	1½lb potatoes
3 tablespoons olive oil	3 tablespoons olive oil
1 clove garlic (optional)	1 clove garlic (optional)
2 sprigs rosemary	2 sprigs rosemary
sea salt and black pepper	sea salt and black pepper

Cook the potatoes in their skins in boiling salted water until they are three-quarters cooked. When they are cool enough to handle, peel them and cut into thick slices. Heat the oil in a frying pan (skillet) and add the potatoes with the peeled and crushed garlic, if used. Pull the leaves off the rosemary and stir them into the potatoes. Fry gently for about 15 to 20 minutes, stirring often, until the potatoes are nicely browned. Scatter over some black pepper before serving. These potatoes are delicious served with all lamb dishes, grilled (broiled) steaks, or pork chops.

POTATO CAKES WITH PARSLEY

Metric/Imperial	American
350g/12oz freshly mashed potato	1½ cups freshly mashed potato
100g/4oz flour	1 cup flour
sea salt	sea salt
freshly ground black pepper	freshly ground black pepper
50g/2oz butter	¼ cup butter
2 tablespoons chopped parsley	2 tablespoons chopped parsley

Have the hot mashed potato in a large bowl and gradually work in the flour, sprinkling it on and beating with a wooden spoon. Add salt and freshly ground black pepper to taste. Cut the butter into tiny pieces and stir into the potato mixture, at room temperature. Stir in the parsley, and continue to beat until all is smooth.

Turn out on a floured board and roll out very lightly, using plenty of flour, until about 5mm/¼in thick. Cut into rounds and cook on a hot griddle, lightly greased, until golden brown on each side. These potato cakes are very good with bacon and eggs, or cooked ham.

VARIATION

Follow the recipe for *Potato Cakes with Parsley*, substituting 1 teaspoon of caraway seeds for the parsley. Serve with pork fillet (tenderloin), grilled (broiled) chicken, or veal escalopes (scallops).

TOMATOES WITH HERB BUTTER

Metric/Imperial	American
4 large ripe tomatoes	4 large ripe tomatoes
25g/1oz herb butter (see pages 193–5)	2 tablespoons herb butter (see pages 193–5)

Cut the tomatoes in half and grill (broil) until soft and nicely browned. Have the herb butter prepared beforehand; put ½ teaspoon on top of each tomato half and return to the grill (broiler) for a moment to melt. Serve immediately.

These are delicious with scrambled (buttered) eggs, fried slices of ham, sausages, grilled (broiled) white fish, and grilled (broiled) lamb cutlets. Any of the herb butters described on pages 193–5 are suitable; basil and garlic butter is particularly good.

RATATOUILLE WITH BASIL

Ratatouille with basil; Turnips with parsley sauce; Stuffed tomatoes III

Metric/Imperial	American
1 Spanish onion	1 Bermuda onion
2 aubergines	2 eggplant
sea salt	sea salt
1 green pepper	1 green pepper
1 red pepper	1 red pepper
225g/8oz small courgettes	½lb small zucchini
225g/8oz tomatoes	½lb tomatoes
2 cloves garlic	2 cloves garlic
approx. 150ml/¼ pint sunflower-seed oil	approx. ⅔ cup sunflower-seed oil
freshly ground black pepper	freshly ground black pepper
3 tablespoons chopped basil	3 tablespoons chopped basil

Chop the onion finely. Cut the unpeeled aubergine (eggplant) into cubes and sprinkle with salt; leave for 20 minutes to drain. Chop the peppers, discarding the stalks and seeds, slice the unpeeled courgettes (zucchini) and chop the skinned tomatoes. Peel and crush the garlic. Heat the oil in a broad heavy pan. Cook the onion gently for about 6 minutes. Pat the aubergine (eggplant) dry with paper towels and add it to the onion with the peppers. Stew gently, adding more oil as necessary, for 10 minutes, then add the courgettes (zucchini) and cook for a further 5 minutes. Finally add the tomatoes and the garlic and cook for 10 minutes more until all is soft and slightly mushy. Add plenty of salt and black pepper and stir in the chopped basil.

This dish is equally good served hot or cold. If serving hot, leave for 4 or 5 minutes after adding the basil to allow the flavour to permeate the whole. Serve as an hors d'oeuvre or as part of a selection of vegetable dishes.
Serves 6.

TOMATOES WITH YOGURT AND BASIL

Metric/Imperial	American
450g/1lb tomatoes	1lb tomatoes
50g/2oz butter	¼ cup butter
sea salt and black pepper	sea salt and black pepper
pinch of sugar	pinch of sugar
300ml/½ pint natural yogurt	1¼ cups unflavored yogurt
2 tablespoons chopped basil	2 tablespoons chopped basil
25g/1oz pine kernels	2 tablespoons pine nuts (pignoli)
1 flat bread, or pitta, to garnish (optional)	1 Euphrates bread to garnish (optional)

Skin the tomatoes and chop coarsely, allowing excess juice to drain away by leaving them on a sloping board for 10 minutes. Melt the butter in a shallow pan and cook the tomatoes gently for a few minutes, until just softened without becoming mushy. Remove the pan from the heat. Add salt and pepper to taste, and a pinch of sugar. Have the yogurt at room temperature, beat it until smooth, and stir into the pan. Stir in the chopped basil, pour into a shallow serving dish and scatter the pine kernels (nuts) over the top. If you like, garnish the tomatoes with triangles of flat bread, toasted until crisp and light golden.

Serve immediately, or keep warm for a little, but do not attempt to reheat after adding the yogurt. This dish is meant to be warm rather than hot. It is excellent served with grilled (broiled) skewers of lamb.

STUFFED TOMATOES I

Metric/Imperial	American
4 large tomatoes	4 large tomatoes
6 eggs	6 eggs
sea salt and black pepper	sea salt and black pepper
25g/1oz butter	2 tablespoons butter
1½ tablespoons thick cream	1½ tablespoons heavy cream
1 tablespoon chopped chervil	1 tablespoon chopped chervil

Cut the tops off the tomatoes and hollow out the insides with a small teaspoon. Stand them upside down to drain for about 15 minutes. Dry them with soft paper towels.

Beat the eggs in a bowl with salt and pepper. Melt the butter in a saucepan, add the eggs and scramble them slowly, removing the pan from the heat just before the eggs are set. Stir in the cream and the chopped chervil and turn into a dish to cool. As soon as the eggs are cool, spoon them into the tomatoes and serve immediately: if left to stand a skin will form on the surface of the egg.

Serve as a first course, or as part of a selection of vegetable dishes for a light lunch.

STUFFED TOMATOES II

Metric/Imperial	American
4 large tomatoes	4 large tomatoes
100g/4oz cream cheese	½ cup cream cheese
4 tablespoons natural yogurt	¼ cup unflavored yogurt
2 tablespoons very finely chopped cucumber	2 tablespoons very finely chopped cucumber
sea salt and black pepper	sea salt and black pepper
1 tablespoon chopped burnet	1 tablespoon chopped burnet

Cut a thin slice off the top of each tomato and hollow out the inside with a teaspoon. Discard the seeds and juice, and cut the flesh into tiny dice. Beat the cream cheese with the yogurt until smooth, or purée in a blender. Stir in the chopped tomato and cucumber. Add salt and pepper to taste and stir in the chopped burnet. Fill the tomatoes with the mixture and serve soon after.

Serve as a first course, or as part of a selection of vegetable dishes for a main course.

STUFFED TOMATOES III

Metric/Imperial	American
4 large tomatoes	4 large tomatoes
75g/3oz long-grain rice	½ cup long-grain rice
15g/½oz butter	1 tablespoon butter
1 tablespoon chopped onion	1 tablespoon chopped onion
300–450ml/½–¾ pint chicken stock	1¼–2 cups chicken stock
sea salt and black pepper	sea salt and black pepper
1 tablespoon chopped basil	1 tablespoon chopped basil

Cut the tops off the tomatoes and hollow out the insides with a small teaspoon. Stand upside down to drain while you make the filling.

Wash and drain the rice. Melt the butter in a saucepan and brown the onion. Add the rice and stir around for 2 minutes. Pour on half of the heated stock. Simmer gently until the stock is absorbed, then add half the remainder. Continue to simmer until the stock is absorbed. Test to see if the rice is tender and, if not, add the rest of the stock and cook a little longer. When the liquid is absorbed and the rice just cooked, remove from the heat and stir in salt and pepper to taste and the chopped basil. Leave to cool. Dry the inside of the tomatoes with paper towels and fill them with the rice mixture. Leave to cool before serving. Serve as a first course, or as a light main dish with a green salad.

TURNIPS WITH PARSLEY SAUCE

Metric/Imperial	American
675g/1½lb small turnips	1½lb small turnips
50g/2oz butter	¼ cup butter
1 tablespoon Dijon mustard	1 tablespoon Dijon mustard
150ml/¼ pint thick cream	⅔ cup heavy cream
sea salt and black pepper	sea salt and black pepper
6 tablespoons finely chopped parsley	6 tablespoons finely chopped parsley

Scrub the turnips clean. If they are really tiny, leave them whole. Otherwise cut them in halves or quarters. Cook until tender in lightly salted water, and drain. Dry out over a very gentle heat, then stir in the butter, mustard, and cream, adding salt and pepper to taste. Stir in the chopped parsley and serve with lamb, duck, beef or chicken.

Tomatoes with yogurt and basil

MARROW (SQUASH) STUFFED WITH HERBS

Metric/Imperial	American
1 vegetable marrow	1 summer squash
sea salt	sea salt
1½ tablespoons chopped basil	1½ tablespoons chopped basil
STUFFING:	STUFFING:
100g/4oz long-grain rice	½ cup long-grain rice
1 onion	1 onion
40g/1½oz butter	3 tablespoons butter
100g/4oz cooked ham	½ cup chopped cooked ham
100g/4oz sorrel	¼lb sorrel
50g/2oz chopped parsley	1½ cups chopped parsley
12 leaves tarragon	12 leaves tarragon
3 sprigs marjoram	3 sprigs marjoram
6 leaves lemon balm	6 leaves lemon balm
3 sprigs mint	3 sprigs mint
2 sprigs rosemary	2 sprigs rosemary
sea salt and black pepper	sea salt and black pepper
TOMATO SAUCE:	TOMATO SAUCE:
1 small onion	1 small onion
25g/1oz butter	2 tablespoons butter
1 tablespoon olive oil	1 tablespoon olive oil
1 clove garlic	1 clove garlic
450g/1lb tomatoes or a 400g/14oz can tomatoes	1lb tomatoes or a 14oz can tomatoes
sea salt and black pepper	sea salt and black pepper
½ teaspoon sugar	½ teaspoon sugar

To make the stuffing, cook the rice until nearly tender; drain. Peel and chop the onion. Melt the butter in a pan and cook the onion until pale golden. Chop the ham. Cut out the central stalks of the sorrel and chop the leaves. Chop all the herbs. Mix all the stuffing ingredients together, adding salt and pepper to taste.

Cut the skin off the marrow, leaving a few thin strips of dark green skin to give a stripy effect. Cut in half horizontally and scoop out the soft interior. Sprinkle with salt and leave upside down to drain for 20 to 30 minutes.

To make the tomato sauce, peel and chop the onion. Melt the butter in a pan with the oil and cook the onion until soft, adding the crushed garlic halfway through. Add the skinned and chopped (or canned) tomatoes and simmer for 12 minutes, adding salt and pepper and a little sugar.

Dry the marrow (squash) with soft paper towels. Pile the stuffing carefully into one half and put the other half back on top so that the inner cavity is filled with stuffing. Lay the marrow (squash) in an oiled piece of foil in a flameproof dish and pour the tomato sauce over it. Wrap the foil round it, sealing the ends tightly and cook for about 1 hour in a moderate oven (180°C/350°F or Gas Mark 4), basting 2 or 3 times with the sauce. If the marrow (squash) is not fresh it will take much longer than 1 hour to cook; if, on the other hand, it has come straight from the garden it may be soft in 45 minutes. When it is ready, open the foil, scatter over the chopped basil and close the foil again for 2 to 3 minutes before serving. Serve as a main course.

MARROW (SQUASH) WITH MINT

Metric/Imperial	American
1 vegetable marrow, about 1kg/2lb	1 summer squash, about 2lb
sea salt	sea salt
40g/1½oz butter	3 tablespoons butter
freshly ground black pepper	freshly ground black pepper
4 tablespoons orange juice	¼ cup orange juice
2 tablespoons chopped mint	2 tablespoons chopped mint

Peel the vegetable marrow (squash), using a sharp knife in preference to a potato peeler as a thicker layer needs to be removed than with potatoes. Cut into slices about 2cm/¾in thick, then in sections, discarding the seeds and soft interior. Sprinkle with salt and leave to drain for about 20 minutes. Pat dry with soft paper towels.

Heat the butter in a saucepan and put in the marrow (squash). Cover and cook gently for about 8 minutes, stirring 2 or 3 times. It should be just soft without being mushy. Add salt and pepper, orange juice and the chopped mint. Serve with roast chicken, veal escalopes (scallops), or grilled (broiled) lamb cutlets.

PURÉE OF MARROW (SQUASH) AND TOMATO WITH MINT

Metric/Imperial	American
1 vegetable marrow, about 1kg/2lb	1 summer squash, about 2lb
sea salt	sea salt
50g/2oz butter	¼ cup butter
225g/8oz tomatoes	½lb tomatoes
3 tablespoons chopped mint	3 tablespoons chopped mint
freshly ground black pepper	freshly ground black pepper

Cut the marrow (squash) into slices about 2cm/¾in thick. Peel, and cut each slice into sections, discarding the pulpy interior. Sprinkle with salt and leave for about 20 minutes to drain. Pat dry with soft paper towels.

Heat the butter in a shallow lidded pan and cook the marrow (squash) gently, covered, for 8 to 10 minutes, until just soft. Cool slightly. Skin the tomatoes and purée, raw, in a blender with the marrow (squash) and the chopped mint. Add salt and pepper to taste. Reheat for a hot vegetable dish, or chill and serve icy cold. This refreshing purée is especially good served cold with fish, chicken or veal.

Opposite: Avocado salad with oregano

Salads

Almost all the summer herbs, that is to say the annuals which are more delicate in flavour than the woody perennials, are good when added to salads. The mellow flavour of olive oil seems to bring out their full flavour, while for the acid element I like to use a mild white wine vinegar, or wine vinegar mixed with lemon juice.

In the Middle East, in Greece and in Italy, dried herbs are often added to salads in preference to fresh. Dried mint, for instance, adds a special character to a dish of thinly sliced cucumber and garlic in yogurt, while dried oregano makes an excellent addition to mixed salads containing cheese, whether the Greek feta or the Italian mozzarella. Dried thyme, particularly the wild variety commonly used in Mediterranean countries, is also good when added to salads, and in some ways better than our garden variety, even when fresh. These dried herbs are of course especially valuable during the winter months, as are the range of flavoured oils and vinegars which have been made during the summer, with garlic, basil, dill, tarragon, burnet and chervil.

A delicious way of serving many vegetables is to cook them lightly, then dress them while still warm with oil and vinegar or lemon juice. String (snap) beans, leeks, cauliflower, courgettes (zucchini) and small whole onions are all good served in this way, and even better when garnished with an appropriate herb. Other vegetables are better served raw, like tomatoes, cucumber, fennel and mushrooms. Mushrooms absorb an enormous quantity of oil, which makes a rather extravagant dish, but they are so good when really fresh, and flavoured with plenty of garlic, parsley and chives that they repay the cost. Small tomatoes make a pretty dish when peeled, left whole, and piled in a pyramid on a flat dish, with a herb sauce poured over them. Some of the root vegetables, notably celeriac, kohlrabi and turnips, are excellent raw if coarsely grated and mixed lightly with a sauce rémoulade with added herbs. All of these dishes are highly nutritious, rich in vitamins and, when made with a minimum of oil, useful for those on slimming diets. They can be served as the first course for a meal, or, with a few added ingredients, as a light main course. Hard-boiled eggs go well with many of them, especially vinaigrettes of cauliflower, potato and tomato. Cubes of hard cheese also mix well with oil and vinegar and with vegetables, and add nourishment without much extra effort. Little bits of crisp fried bacon and croûtons of fried bread are delicious when added to a potato salad, or one of dandelion leaves.

AVOCADO SALAD WITH OREGANO

Metric/Imperial	American
2 avocados	2 avocados
4 large lettuce leaves	4 large lettuce leaves
4 tomatoes	4 tomatoes
175–200g/6–7oz mozzarella cheese	6–7oz mozzarella cheese
sea salt and black pepper	sea salt and black pepper
6 tablespoons olive oil	6 tablespoons olive oil
2 tablespoons white wine vinegar	2 tablespoons white wine vinegar
1 teaspoon dried oregano	1 teaspoon dried oregano

Cut the avocados in half, peel them and remove the stones (pits). Lay a lettuce leaf on each plate and put half an avocado on it cut side down. Run a knife lengthwise down the centre of the avocado, then cut it across in slices. Skin the tomatoes and cut them in half. Slice each half, and lay the slices on either side of the avocados. Cut the mozzarella cheese in thin slices and lay them between the tomato slices. Sprinkle with salt and pepper. Mix the oil and vinegar together and dribble over the salad, then scatter a pinch of dried oregano over each plate. Serve as a first course.

CABBAGE SALAD WITH DILL

Metric/Imperial	American
¼ Chinese cabbage or ¼ hard white cabbage	¼ head Chinese cabbage or ¼ head hard white cabbage
½ cucumber	½ cucumber
½ bunch spring onions	½ bunch scallions
sea salt and black pepper	sea salt and black pepper
3 tablespoons sunflower-seed oil	3 tablespoons sunflower-seed oil
1 tablespoon white wine vinegar	1 tablespoon white wine vinegar
4 hard-boiled eggs	4 hard-boiled eggs
2 tablespoons chopped dill	2 tablespoons chopped dill

Wash and drain the cabbage and cut it across in thin strips. Pile it into a salad bowl. Peel the cucumber and cut it in half lengthwise, then in semi-circular slices. Slice the spring onions (scallions), using the white bulb and the best of the green leaves.

Mix all together and add salt and black pepper. Stir in the oil and vinegar and mix thoroughly. Shell the eggs, cut in half lengthwise, then in semi-circular slices. Mix lightly into the salad, adding the chopped dill at the same time.

KOHLRABI WITH HERB SAUCE

Metric/Imperial	American
675g/1½lb kohlrabi	1½lb kohlrabi
quick herb sauce (see page 190)	quick herb sauce (see page 190)

Choose 2 small kohlrabi rather than 1 enormous one. The flavour will be more delicate and the texture finer. Peel the kohlrabi and grate them coarsely. Make the sauce and mix it lightly with the grated kohlrabi. Serve as a first course.

CELERIAC WITH HERB SAUCE

Metric/Imperial	American
675g/1½lb celeriac	1½lb celery root
quick herb sauce (see page 190)	quick herb sauce (see page 190)

Peel the celeriac (celery root) and grate it coarsely. Mix it lightly with the herb sauce and serve as a first course.

CUCUMBER SALAD WITH MINT

Metric/Imperial	American
½ cucumber	½ cucumber
600ml/1 pint natural yogurt	2½ cups unflavored yogurt
1–2 cloves garlic	1–2 cloves garlic
sea salt and black pepper	sea salt and black pepper
½ teaspoon dried mint	½ teaspoon dried mint

Peel the cucumber and cut it into thin slices. Beat the yogurt until it is smooth. Peel and crush the garlic and stir it into the yogurt. Fold in the sliced cucumber, adding a little salt and pepper. Pour into a serving bowl and scatter the dried mint over the top. Chill for an hour or two before serving. This is particularly good with hot roast lamb.

DANDELION SALAD

Metric/Imperial	American
175g/6oz dandelion leaves	6oz dandelion leaves
100g/4oz streaky bacon	6 slices bacon
2 slices bread	2 slices bread
1 clove garlic	1 clove garlic
25g/1oz butter	2 tablespoons butter
sea salt and black pepper	sea salt and black pepper
3 tablespoons olive oil	3 tablespoons olive oil
1 tablespoon white wine vinegar	1 tablespoon white wine vinegar

Wash and dry the dandelion leaves. If they are past their first youth, cut out the central core along with the stalk. Cut the leaves into slices and pile them onto a salad bowl.

Cut the bacon into strips and fry in a frying pan (skillet) until crisp. Take the bacon out of the pan. Cut the crusts off the bread, and cut each slice into cubes. Peel and crush the garlic. Heat the butter in the bacon fat and fry the bread with the crushed garlic until golden brown. Lift the bread cubes out of the pan and drain on paper towels.

Season the dandelion leaves with salt and black pepper, and turn them gently but thoroughly in the olive oil and vinegar. Add the bacon and croûtons and mix again. Serve soon after mixing.

GREEK SALAD

Metric/Imperial	American
225g/8oz tomatoes	½lb tomatoes
½ cucumber	½ cucumber
1 green pepper	1 green pepper
1 large mild onion	1 large mild onion
sea salt and black pepper	sea salt and black pepper
3 tablespoons olive oil	3 tablespoons olive oil
1 tablespoon white wine vinegar	1 tablespoon white wine vinegar
100g/4oz Greek feta cheese	¼ lb Greek feta cheese
1 teaspoon dried oregano	1 teaspoon dried oregano

Skin the tomatoes and cut them into quite thick slices. Peel the cucumber and cut it into thick slices. Halve the pepper, discarding the stalk and seeds, and cut it into strips. Peel the onion and cut it in half, then slice each half thinly. Mix all these ingredients together in a salad bowl, adding salt and black pepper to taste. Stir in the oil and vinegar and mix well. Chop the *feta* cheese roughly and scatter the pieces over the top. Sprinkle the dried oregano over all and mix briefly before serving.

Cabbage salad with dill; Greek salad; Celeriac in herb sauce

GREEN SALAD WITH HERB SAUCE

Metric/Imperial	American
1 round lettuce	1 head Boston lettuce
1 batavia	1 escarole
100g/4oz corn salad (mâche)	¼lb (1 bunch) lamb's lettuce (corn or field salad)
HERB SAUCE:	HERB SAUCE:
2 hard-boiled eggs	2 hard-boiled eggs
2 tablespoons thick cream	2 tablespoons heavy cream
2 tablespoons olive oil	2 tablespoons olive oil
2 teaspoons white wine vinegar	2 teaspoons white wine vinegar
sea salt and black pepper	sea salt and black pepper
1 tablespoon chopped chives	1 tablespoon chopped chives
1 tablespoon chopped dill	1 tablespoon chopped dill
1 tablespoon chopped tarragon	1 tablespoon chopped tarragon

Break the lettuce leaves in pieces and pile in a salad bowl. Using only the pale green inner leaves of the batavia (escarole), scatter them over the lettuce and put the corn salad (lamb's lettuce) on top.

Separate the whites and yolks of the hard-boiled eggs. Chop the egg whites and scatter over the green salad. Mash the egg yolks to a paste with the cream, and stir in the oil very gradually. Then add the vinegar slowly and stir until blended. Add the salt and pepper to taste, and stir in the herbs. Pour the herb sauce over the greens and mix well.

MUSHROOM SALAD WITH HERBS

Metric/Imperial	American
225g/8oz very fresh button mushrooms	2 cups very fresh button mushrooms
sea salt and black pepper	sea salt and black pepper
2 tablespoons finely chopped onion	2 tablespoons finely chopped onion
1 clove garlic	1 clove garlic
4 tablespoons olive oil	¼ cup olive oil
1 tablespoon white wine vinegar	1 tablespoon white wine vinegar
½ tablespoon lemon juice	½ tablespoon lemon juice
2 tablespoons chopped chervil	2 tablespoons chopped chervil
2 tablespoons chopped chives	2 tablespoons chopped chives

Wipe the mushrooms with a damp cloth; remove the stalks and cut the caps into thin slices. Put them in a serving bowl and add lots of coarse salt and black pepper. Stir in the chopped onion and crushed garlic. Stir in the oil and vinegar, then the lemon juice and the chopped herbs. Serve soon after making, or the mushrooms will dry up and need yet more oil.

Opposite Above: Tomato and mozzarella salad with basil

Below: Green salad with herb sauce; Parsley and mint salad; Mushroom salad with herbs

PARSLEY AND MINT SALAD

Metric/Imperial	American
2 bunches spring onions	2 bunches scallions
½ small Florence fennel, about 100g/4oz	½ small root fennel, about ¼lb
350g/12oz tomatoes	¾lb tomatoes
25g/1oz chopped parsley	¾ cup chopped parsley
5 tablespoons chopped mint	⅓ cup chopped mint
2 tablespoons olive oil	2 tablespoons olive oil
1 tablespoon lemon juice	1 tablespoon lemon juice

Slice the spring onions (scallions) thinly and place in a bowl. Cut the fennel horizontally into very thin slices and add them to the spring onions (scallions). Skin and chop the tomatoes; add them to the other vegetables. Chop the parsley and mint quite coarsely and mix with the other ingredients. Pour over the oil and lemon juice and mix again. This is a very nutritious salad, full of vitamins.

TOMATO AND MOZZARELLA SALAD WITH BASIL

Metric/Imperial	American
450g/1lb tomatoes	1lb tomatoes
225g/8oz mozzarella	½lb mozzarella
sea salt and black pepper	sea salt and black pepper
3 tablespoons olive oil	3 tablespoons olive oil
1 tablespoon white wine vinegar	1 tablespoon white wine vinegar
1½ tablespoons chopped basil	1½ tablespoons chopped basil

Skin the tomatoes and slice them thinly and evenly. Lay them on one half of a flat serving dish. Cut the cheese into thin slices and lay them on the other half of the same dish. Season the tomatoes with salt and black pepper, the mozzarella with pepper only. Pour over the oil and vinegar and scatter the chopped basil over all. Allow the salad to stand for a little before serving.

POTATO SALAD I

Metric/Imperial	American
675g/1½lb new or waxy potatoes	1½lb new or waxy potatoes
4 tablespoons thin cream	¼ cup light cream
150ml/¼ pint homemade mayonnaise	⅔ cup homemade mayonnaise
sea salt and black pepper	sea salt and black pepper
3 tablespoons chopped chervil	3 tablespoons chopped chervil

Wash the potatoes and cook them in their skins in boiling salted water. As soon as they are cool enough to handle, skin them and slice thickly into a bowl. Add the cream to the mayonnaise to thin it, and stir into the potatoes while they are still warm. Add salt and pepper to taste, and stir in the chopped chervil. Serve soon after making.

Potato salad I

PARSLEY SALAD

Metric/Imperial	American
50g/2oz chopped parsley	1½ cups chopped parsley
2 tablespoons sunflower-seed oil	2 tablespoons sunflower-seed oil
1 tablespoon lemon juice	1 tablespoon lemon juice
freshly ground black pepper	freshly ground black pepper

Parsley can be chopped quickly in a food processor. Tip it into a bowl and stir in the oil and lemon juice. Add a little freshly ground black pepper. Serve soon after making.

This nutritious salad is delicious served with yogurt cheeses (see pages 182–3), with rye bread (see page 198), or wholewheat bread. It makes a small bowl, but a little goes a long way.

POTATO SALAD II

Metric/Imperial	American
675g/1½lb new or waxy potatoes	1½lb new or waxy potatoes
3 tablespoons olive oil	3 tablespoons olive oil
1 tablespoon white wine vinegar	1 tablespoon white wine vinegar
sea salt and black pepper	sea salt and black pepper
2 tablespoons chopped parsley	2 tablespoons chopped parsley
2 tablespoons chopped chives	2 tablespoons chopped chives

Wash the potatoes and cook them in their skins in boiling salted water. Drain and skin them as soon as they are cool enough to handle. Cut them into thick slices or quarters, according to size. Pour over the oil and vinegar while they are still hot, and add black pepper and more salt as needed. Stir in the chopped herbs and serve soon after cooling; do not chill.

HOT POTATO SALAD

Metric/Imperial	American
675g/1½lb new or waxy potatoes	1½lb new or waxy potatoes
2 tablespoons finely chopped onion	2 tablespoons finely chopped onion
3 tablespoons olive oil	3 tablespoons olive oil
1 tablespoon white wine vinegar	1 tablespoon white wine vinegar
sea salt and black pepper	sea salt and black pepper
4 tablespoons chopped chives	¼ cup chopped chives

Wash the potatoes and cook them in their skins in boiling salted water. Peel them as soon as they are cool enough to handle. Cut into quarters or thick slices and stir in the chopped onion. Pour over the oil and vinegar, and mix gently, trying not to break the potatoes. Add salt and pepper. Stir in 3 tablespoons of chives. Turn the salad into a serving dish and scatter the remaining chives over the top.

SORREL, EGG AND POTATO SALAD

Metric/Imperial	American
1 round lettuce	1 head lettuce
225g/8oz new potatoes	½lb new potatoes
4 tablespoons olive oil	¼ cup olive oil
4 hard-boiled eggs	4 hard-boiled eggs
4 tablespoons shredded sorrel	¼ cup shredded sorrel
sea salt and black pepper	sea salt and black pepper
pinch of sugar	pinch of sugar
½ teaspoon Dijon mustard	½ teaspoon Dijon mustard
1 tablespoon white wine vinegar	1 tablespoon white wine vinegar

Wash and dry the lettuce. Break it into pieces and place in a salad bowl. Wash the potatoes and boil them in their skins. Peel and slice them thickly as soon as they are cool enough to handle. Pour 1 tablespoon olive oil over them while they are still hot. Shell the eggs and slice them thickly. When the potatoes have cooled, pile them in the centre of the lettuce and surround with the sliced eggs. Cut the sorrel into shreds and scatter over the salad. Make a dressing with salt and black pepper, sugar, mustard, vinegar and the remaining oil. Pour over the salad just before serving.

TOMATO, CUCUMBER AND FENNEL SALAD

Metric/Imperial	American
350g/12oz tomatoes	¾lb tomatoes
½ cucumber	½ cucumber
½ small Florence fennel, about 100g/4oz	½ small root fennel, about ¼lb
sea salt and black pepper	sea salt and black pepper
2 tablespoons olive oil	2 tablespoons olive oil
½ tablespoon white wine vinegar	½ tablespoon white wine vinegar
½ tablespoon lemon juice	½ tablespoon lemon juice

Skin the tomatoes and slice them thinly. Lay them on a flat dish. Peel the cucumber, slice it thinly and lay over the tomatoes. Cut the fennel in thin horizontal slices and scatter over the cucumber, reserving the feathery leaves. Sprinkle with salt and black pepper. Mix the oil, vinegar and lemon juice in a bowl and pour over all. Chop the fennel leaves and scatter them over the salad.

TOMATO MOULDS WITH DILL SAUCE

Metric/Imperial	American
300ml/½ pint tomato juice	1¼ cups tomato juice
1½ tablespoons gelatine	1 tablespoon gelatine
300ml/½ pint V8 vegetable juice	1¼ cups V8 vegetable juice
225g/8oz medium-fat cheese	1 cup cream cheese
150ml/¼ pint sour cream	⅔ cup sour cream
2 tablespoons lemon juice	2 tablespoons lemon juice
lettuce leaves	lettuce leaves
450ml/¾ pint dill sauce II (see page 188)	2 cups dill sauce II (see page 188)

Take 2 tablespoons tomato juice and dissolve the gelatine in it. Mix the remaining tomato juice and the V8 juice with the cream cheese and sour cream in a blender. Stir in the lemon juice and the dissolved gelatine. Pour through a strainer into small tin moulds, *oeuf en cocotte* or ramekin dishes; this amount will fill 6 to 8 dishes, depending on their capacity. Chill in the refrigerator until set. To serve, turn each one out on a lettuce leaf on a plate and serve with dill sauce. Alternatively, garnish with sprigs of watercress and tomato quarters. This is a useful dish for a buffet. Serves 6 to 8.

Hot potato salad; Sorrel, egg and potato salad; Tomato, cucumber and fennel salad; Tomato moulds with dill sauce

VEGETABLE SALAD WITH HERB SAUCE

Metric/Imperial	American
175g/6oz new potatoes	1 cup new potatoes (cooked and sliced)
2 tablespoons olive oil	2 tablespoons olive oil
175g/6oz courgettes	1 cup sliced zucchini
175g/6oz string beans	1½ cups diced snap beans
1 bunch spring onions	1 bunch scallions
1 lettuce	1 head lettuce
HERB SAUCE:	HERB SAUCE:
2 hard-boiled eggs	2 hard-boiled eggs
2 tablespoons thick cream	2 tablespoons heavy cream
2 tablespoons olive oil	2 tablespoons olive oil
2 teaspoons white wine vinegar	2 teaspoons white wine vinegar
sea salt and black pepper	sea salt and black pepper
1 tablespoon chopped chives	1 tablespoon chopped chives
1 tablespoon chopped dill	1 tablespoon chopped dill
1 tablespoon chopped tarragon	1 tablespoon chopped tarragon

Wash the potatoes and boil them in their skins. Peel them while they are still hot and cut them into slices. Pour over 1 tablespoon olive oil and leave to cool. Cut the washed but unpeeled courgettes (zucchini) into slices about 1cm/½in thick. Drop them into a saucepan containing a little boiling salted water. Cover the pan and cook for 12 minutes; drain and sprinkle with ½ tablespoon olive oil. Cut the string (snap) beans into 2.5cm/1in pieces. Boil them until just tender, drain and sprinkle with ½ tablespoon olive oil. Trim the spring onions (scallions), leaving the bulbs whole. Break the lettuce leaves into pieces and put them in a salad bowl. Cover with the potatoes, courgettes (zucchini) string (snap) beans and spring onions (scallions).

To make the sauce, separate the yolks from the whites of the hard-boiled eggs. Chop the whites and sprinkle over the salad. Crush the yolks and mix to a paste with the cream. Stir in 2 tablespoons olive oil very gradually, then the vinegar. Add salt and pepper to taste, and the chopped herbs. Pour over the salad and mix well.

WATERCRESS SALAD WITH CHIVES

Metric/Imperial	American
1 bunch watercress	1 bunch watercress
450g/1lb tomatoes	1lb tomatoes
4 Petit Suisse cheeses	½ cup Philadelphia cheese
4 tablespoons chopped chives	¼ cup chopped chives
sea salt and black pepper	sea salt and black pepper
pinch of sugar	pinch of sugar
½ teaspoon mustard	½ teaspoon mustard
1 tablespoon white wine vinegar	1 tablespoon white wine vinegar
3 tablespoons olive oil	3 tablespoons olive oil

Wash the watercress well and dry on a clean cloth. Pick off the tender sprigs of the watercress and lay them around the rims of 4 individual plates. Skin and slice the tomatoes and lay them in the centre of the watercress. Unwrap the *Petits Suisses* and roll each one in the chopped chives. (Cut the chilled Philadelphia cheese into quarters, and roll each piece in the chopped chives.) Lay them on top of the tomatoes. Sprinkle all with salt and black pepper.

Make a dressing by mixing together the sugar, mustard, vinegar and oil. Serve the dressing separately, or pour over each plate just before serving. This salad can be arranged on 1 large dish if preferred.

Desserts & Cheeses

Most herbs are best used in conjunction with savoury tastes, but there are some whose own character merges well with the sweet/sour flavour of certain fruits. Mint, for instance, makes a refreshing addition to many fruit dishes, especially those containing lemon juice. Mint can also be added to a grapefruit ice, or to a compote of melon. Delicious sorbets (sherbets) can be based on a lemon-flavoured syrup, and infused with different leaves. Elder flowers and black currant leaves make two of the most delicate, while the various different mints, especially pineapple mint, are also well worth trying. The scented leaves of certain geraniums – Pelargonium × fragrans – also make a subtle water ice, while elder flowers can be dipped in batter and deep fried, to make an unusual fritter. A frothy summer dessert can be made by folding red or black currants or blueberries into a light mixture of yogurt, cream and egg white; the final touch is achieved by adding a little finely chopped mint. Sweet Cicely is another herb which can be used successfully in sweet dishes, for it goes well with cooked fruit and seems to add its own sweetness. I add it to compotes and mousses of apples, pears and apricots, and to mixed fruit salads. It is especially good with apples. Another is angelica, whose leaves can be chopped and added to compotes of fruit either raw or cooked, while the crystallized (candied) stalks can be used for decorating sweet dishes.

I have included a recipe using rose hips, the decorative fruit of the wild or dog rose, and of the Rosa rubiginosa. *They are rich in Vitamin C, and can by long cooking be made into syrups and sauces. Very valuable as a food for babies, they are also enjoyed by those adults with a sweet tooth, for much sugar is needed to make them palatable.*

Cream cheese and herbs make a particularly delicious combination. A light form of cream cheese can be made from drained yogurt; this can then be mixed with chopped fresh herbs, or in the Middle Eastern way, with a mixture of dried wild thyme and sesame seeds. A firm cream cheese like the French Petit Suisse, or the American Philadelphia, can be rolled in chopped parsley and chives, or a mixture of cheeses – Gruyère, Parmesan and Demi-sel – can be combined and coated with freshly chopped herbs. Small dishes of chopped herbs can be put on the table at the same time as a platter of cheeses, for sprinkling on cream cheese, or little sprigs of burnet, parsley or chervil can be served to munch with hard cheese like Cheddar, Gruyère and Parmesan.

Opposite: Vegetable salad with herb sauce;
Watercress salad with chives

Above: Red currant snow with mint

APPLES WITH SWEET CICELY

Metric/Imperial	American
675g/1½lb cooking apples	1½lb cooking apples
sugar to taste	sugar to taste
2 teaspoons chopped Sweet Cicely	2 teaspoons chopped Sweet Cicely

Peel the apples, cut out the cores, and cut into slices. Put them in a heavy pan with enough water to cover the bottom. Add some sugar, depending on the sweetness of the apples, and cook slowly with the lid on until they are soft. Stir in the Sweet Cicely and leave to cool. (Alternatively, the apples can be sieved (strained) or put in a blender if a smooth purée is preferred.) Serve cold, with whipped cream.

RED CURRANT SNOW WITH MINT

Metric/Imperial	American
150ml/¼ pint thick cream	⅔ cup heavy cream
2 egg whites	2 egg whites
150ml/¼ pint natural yogurt	⅔ cup unflavored yogurt
2 tablespoons caster sugar	2 tablespoons sugar
450g/1lb red currants or blueberries	4 cups red currants or blueberries
2 tablespoons chopped mint	2 tablespoons chopped mint

Whip the cream until thick but not dry. Beat the egg whites until stiff. Beat the yogurt until smooth. Mix the egg whites and then the yogurt into the cream, folding them in lightly. Stir in the sugar. Wash and drain the red currants or blueberries. Pull the berries off the stalks and fold into the cream. Stir in the chopped mint and serve soon after making.

ELDER FLOWER FRITTERS

Metric/Imperial	American
12 elder flower heads	12 elder flower heads
oil for deep frying	oil for deep frying
caster sugar for dredging	sugar for dredging
BATTER:	BATTER:
100g/4oz plain flour	1 cup all-purpose flour
pinch of sea salt	pinch of sea salt
2 tablespoons sunflower- seed oil	2 tablespoons sunflower- seed oil
150ml/¼ pint warm water	⅔ cup warm water
1 egg white	1 egg white

To make the batter, sift the flour into a bowl and add the salt. Stir in the oil and mix in enough lukewarm water to give the consistency of fairly thick cream. Leave to stand for 1 to 2 hours in a cool place. Just before using, beat the egg white in a bowl until it is stiff and fold it into the batter.

Rinse the elder flower heads and shake them dry in a cloth. Dip each one in the batter, shaking off any excess, and drop into a large pan of oil heated to 180°C/360°F. Do not try to fry them all at once as they must not be crowded. When each batch is done, drain briefly on crumpled paper towels then lay them on a serving dish in a warm place until the others are done. Sprinkle with sugar and serve straight away.

ELDER FLOWER SORBET

Metric/Imperial	American
900ml/1½ pints water	3¾ cups water
350g/12oz caster sugar	1½ cups sugar
16 elder flower heads	16 elder flower heads
juice of 2 lemons	juice of 2 lemons
white of 1 large egg	white of 1 large egg
red currants or sprigs of mint to decorate	red currants or sprigs of mint to decorate

Put the water in a pan with the sugar. Bring to the boil and simmer until the sugar has dissolved. Wash the elder flowers and shake them dry. Put them in the pan, cover it and remove it from the heat. Leave for 30 minutes to infuse. Strain, and stir in the lemon juice. Turn into a rigid container and cool. Freeze for 1 hour, until semi-frozen.

Beat the egg white in a bowl until it is firm though not stiff. Fold it into the sorbet (sherbet) and freeze it again until firm, about 1 hour. To serve, spoon into wine glasses. Each glass may be decorated with a few red currants, or a tiny sprig of mint. Serves 6.

VARIATION

Follow the recipe for *Elder Flower Sorbet*, substituting 24 young black currant leaves for the elder flowers. Decorate with a tiny black currant leaf, or a few red currants.

GERANIUM LEAF SORBET

Metric/Imperial	American
12 scented geranium leaves	12 scented geranium leaves
75g/3oz caster sugar	6 tablespoons sugar
300ml/½ pint water	1¼ cups water
juice of 1 large lemon	juice of 1 large lemon
1 egg white	1 egg white
4 tiny geranium leaves to decorate	4 tiny geranium leaves to decorate

Wash the geranium leaves and shake them dry. Put the sugar and water in a pan and boil until the sugar has dissolved. Put the leaves in the pan, cover it, and turn off the heat. Leave for 20 minutes then taste. If the flavour is too weak, bring the liquid to the boil once more, turn off the heat, cover the pan and leave it for a further 10 minutes.

When the flavour is satisfactory, strain the syrup into a rigid container, add the lemon juice, and leave to cool. Freeze until semi-frozen, about 45 minutes to 1 hour, then fold in the stiffly beaten egg white. Continue to freeze until a firm mush, about 1 hour. Serve in glasses, each one decorated with a tiny geranium leaf.

MINT SORBET

Metric/Imperial	American
6 large sprigs mint: spearmint, apple mint, eau-de-cologne mint or peppermint	6 large sprigs mint: spearmint, apple mint, eau-de-cologne mint or peppermint
75g/3oz caster sugar	6 tablespoons sugar
300ml/½ pint water	1¼ cups water
juice of 1 large lemon	juice of 1 large lemon
1 egg white	1 egg white
4 tiny sprigs mint to decorate	4 tiny sprigs mint to decorate

Wash the mint and shake it dry. Put the sugar and water in a pan and boil until the sugar has dissolved. Put in the mint, cover the pan and turn off the heat. Leave for 20 minutes, then taste. If the flavour is weak, bring the liquid to the boil again, cover the pan, turn off the heat and leave for a further 10 minutes.

When the flavour is satisfactory, strain the liquid into a rigid container, add the lemon juice and leave to cool. Freeze until semi-frozen, about 45 minutes to 1 hour. Beat the egg white in a bowl until it is stiff. Fold it into the sorbet (sherbet) and return it to the freezer until frozen to a firm mush, about 1 hour. To serve, spoon into four glasses and decorate each one with a tiny sprig of mint.

GRAPEFRUIT AND MINT SORBET

Metric/Imperial	American
juice of 2 large grapefruit	juice of 2 large grapefruit
50g/2oz caster sugar	¼ cup sugar
150ml/¼ pint water	⅔ cup water
3 sprigs mint	3 sprigs mint
1 egg white	1 egg white
4 small mint leaves to decorate	4 small mint leaves to decorate

Squeeze the juice from the grapefruit and strain it. Boil the sugar and water together in a pan until the sugar has dissolved. Put the mint into the sugar syrup, cover the pan and leave it off the heat for 20 minutes. Strain and leave to cool. Mix the cooled syrup with the grapefruit juice and pour into a rigid container. Freeze until semi-frozen, about 45 minutes to 1 hour.

Beat the egg white in a bowl until it is stiff. Fold it into the sorbet (sherbet) and return it to the freezer until frozen to a firm mush, about 1 hour. Serve in glasses, each one decorated with a small mint leaf.

MELON WITH RASPBERRIES AND MINT

Metric/Imperial	American
1 honeydew melon	1 honeydew melon
225g/8oz raspberries	1⅔ cups raspberries
2 tablespoons caster sugar	2 tablespoons sugar
1 tablespoon chopped mint	1 tablespoon chopped mint

Cut a slice off the top of the melon and scoop out the seeds. Cut out the flesh with a sharp-edged spoon and cut it into cubes or balls. Hull and wash the raspberries. Mix them lightly in a bowl with the melon cubes or balls. Mix the sugar and mint together in a cup. Tip them into the fruit and fold in carefully. Return the fruit to the melon shell to serve, or put it in a glass bowl. Serve soon after making or the fruit will become soft.

ROSE HIP SAUCE

Metric/Imperial	American
225g/8oz rose hips	2 cups rose hips
450ml/¾ pint water	2 cups water
225g/8oz sugar	1 cup sugar

The best rose hips for cooking are the plump ones from varieties of *Rosa rubiginosa*. Cut each hip in half with a sharp knife. Put the water in a pan with the sugar. Boil gently until the sugar has melted, then put in the rose hips. Half cover the pan and cook gently for 1 hour, adding more boiling water from time to time as needed.

Pour through a sieve (strainer), pressing the pulp with the back of a spoon, then leave to cool. You should have 200 to 300ml/⅓ to ½ pint/⅞ to 1¼ cups of syrup. This is rich in vitamin C, and is a valuable food for babies and small children. Older children and adults with a sweet tooth may like it poured over vanilla ice cream.

MIXED CHEESE WITH HERBS

Metric/Imperial	American
175g/6oz Philadelphia cheese	¾ cup Philadelphia cheese
25g/1oz Gruyère cheese, grated	¼ cup grated Gruyère cheese
25g/1oz freshly grated Parmesan cheese	¼ cup freshly grated Parmesan cheese
pinch of dry mustard	pinch of mustard powder
sea salt and black pepper	sea salt and black pepper
pinch of cayenne pepper	pinch of cayenne pepper
4–6 tablespoons chopped burnet or chervil	4–6 tablespoons chopped burnet or chervil

Mash the soft cheese until smooth, then beat in the two grated hard cheeses. Add a pinch of mustard and salt and black pepper to taste. Stir in a pinch of cayenne pepper, then chill for 2 hours, until firm. Form the cheese into balls, and roll each one in the chopped herb. Lay them on a small flat plate and serve with warm water biscuits (crackers).

YOGURT CHEESE WITH FRESH HERBS

Metric/Imperial	American
600ml/1 pint natural yogurt	2½ cups unflavored yogurt
sea salt and black pepper	sea salt and black pepper
1 tablespoon thin cream or sour cream	1 tablespoon light cream or sour cream
¼ clove garlic	¼ clove garlic
½ tablespoon chopped tarragon	½ tablespoon chopped tarragon
½ tablespoon chopped dill	½ tablespoon chopped dill
½ tablespoon chopped chervil or parsley	½ tablespoon chopped chervil or parsley

Line a colander or strainer with muslin (cheesecloth). Stand it over a bowl. Tip the yogurt into the muslin (cheesecloth) and tie it up with string so that it forms a bag. Lift it out of the colander and leave it to drain overnight, tying the string to a tap (faucet) over a sink.

The next day, tip the drained curds from the bag into a bowl. Beat until smooth, adding a little salt and pepper and the cream or sour cream. Crush the garlic and stir it in with most of the chopped herbs, keeping some back to scatter over the top. Pile into a small dish, level off with a palette knife, and sprinkle the remaining herbs on top. Chill for an hour or two before serving.

YOGURT CHEESE WITH DRIED HERBS

Metric/Imperial
600ml/1 pint natural
   yogurt
sea salt and black pepper
2 teaspoons olive oil
1 teaspoon dried thyme
   (wild thyme if possible)
1 teaspoon sesame seeds

American
2½ cups unflavored
   yogurt
sea salt and black pepper
2 teaspoons olive oil
1 teaspoon dried thyme
   (wild thyme if possible)
1 teaspoon sesame seeds

Line a colander or strainer with muslin (cheesecloth). Stand it over a bowl. Tip the yogurt into the muslin (cheesecloth) and tie it up with string, to form a bag. Lift it out of the colander. Tie the strings to a tap (faucet) over a sink and leave to drain overnight.

The next day, tip the drained curds into a bowl and beat until smooth, adding a little salt and pepper and the olive oil. Form into a flat round shape. Pound the dried thyme and sesame seeds together in a mortar, then tip them on to a piece of greaseproof paper or nonstick parchment. Lay the cheese in the paper, turning it over so that it is coated all over with the pounded herbs. Chill in the refrigerator before serving.

Serve with rye bread (see page 198), or any good whole-wheat bread. This makes a delicious light meal served with a parsley salad (see page 175).

FRUIT SALAD WITH SWEET CICELY

Metric/Imperial
1 small melon
1 pear
3 plums
1 peach
100g/4oz green grapes
100g/4oz strawberries
juice of 2 oranges
juice of 1 lime (optional)
juice of ½ lemon
1½ tablespoons caster
   sugar
1½ tablespoons chopped
   sweet Cicely

American
1 small melon
1 pear
3 plums
1 peach
1 cup white grapes
¾ cup strawberries
juice of 2 oranges
juice of 1 lime (optional)
juice of ½ lemon
1½ tablespoons
   sugar
1½ tablespoons chopped
   sweet Cicely

Cut the top off the melon and scoop out the seeds. Cut the flesh into small cubes. Peel the pear and remove the core. Wash and stone (pit) the plums. Skin and stone (pit) the peach. Cut the pear, plums and peach into cubes. Peel the grapes and remove any seeds. Cut the strawberries in half.

Mix all the small neat pieces of fruit together in a glass bowl. Mix the juice of the citrus fruits together, sweeten it with the sugar and pour over the fruit. Stir in the chopped sweet Cicely and serve soon after making.

Sauces, Butters & Garnishes

The enormous range of herb sauces provides one of the simplest ways of incorporating herbs into our diet. First come the cooked sauces, made usually with stock, which may be chicken, veal, or fish according to the dish the sauce is to accompany, and sometimes enriched with cream. It is sometimes thickened with a purée of chopped herbs, sometimes merely flavoured with a garnish of chopped herbs added at the very end of the cooking. Cooked sauces include some of the classics of haute cuisine such as hollandaise sauce, delicious variations of which may be made with a handful of chopped herbs stirred in at the last moment, and sauce béarnaise, flavoured with tarragon.

The range of uncooked sauces is even wider. It includes all those based on an emulsion of oil and egg yolk, such as mayonnaise and rémoulade, and the vinaigrette family with added mixtures of chopped herbs. In some cases, other green leaves are added, together with chopped hard-boiled eggs, as in the Italian salsa verde, the traditional accompaniment to boiled meat. The scope of English cookery includes the simple mint sauce to eat with roast lamb and horseradish sauce to accompany roast beef, as well as a more unusual sauce made from a combination of mustard and dill which is excellent with chicken, veal and rabbit. There are many good sauces which can be quickly made in a blender using mixtures of yogurt, cream cheese and buttermilk, all of which combine perfectly with the fresh taste of herbs to make light summery sauces.

Many foreign countries, whose use of herbs is based upon long and delicious tradition, have unusual sauces based largely on one individual herb. The Lebanese, for instance, make a sauce of chopped parsley and sesame seed paste to serve with fish, while the French and Italians from regions bordering the Mediterranean, love to make pistou or pesto, a sauce composed of large quantities of fresh basil, which is served with noodles, or stirred at the last moment into a vegetable soup.

Fresh herbs are also ideal for adding to garnishes, which may take many different forms. In central European countries, small dumplings incorporating fresh herbs are made; these are delicious when added to soups of meat or fish, or to a meat stew or chicken fricassée. In the same countries, small pancakes are often made with chopped herbs incorporated in the batter. These are left to cool after cooking, then cut into strips for adding to clear soups. All these little-known dishes are worth trying, but for simplicity and charm, my favourite is the garnish of fried parsley, an old-fashioned accompaniment to fried fillets of fish.

APPLE SAUCE WITH SAGE

Metric/Imperial	American
2 cooking apples	2 cooking apples
½ teaspoon sugar	½ teaspoon sugar
black pepper	black pepper
1 teaspoon chopped sage	1 teaspoon chopped sage

Peel and core the apples and cut them in slices. Put them in a small pan with just enough water to cover the bottom of the pan. Stew gently until soft. Add sugar and a sprinkling of black pepper. Stir in the chopped sage and stand, covered, for 5 minutes before serving. If preferred, the sauce can be sieved (strained) before adding the sage. Serve with roast duck and roast pork.

CHERVIL SAUCE I

Metric/Imperial	American
6 sprigs chervil	6 sprigs chervil
150ml/¼ pint thin cream	⅔ cup light cream
25g/1oz butter	2 tablespoons butter
1 tablespoon flour	1 tablespoon flour
300ml/½ pint chicken stock	1¼ cups chicken stock
sea salt and black pepper	sea salt and black pepper

Pick the best leaves – about 2 tablespoons – off the chervil and chop finely. Put the chervil stalks and remaining leaves in a small pan with the cream. Bring to boiling point, then cover the pan and draw away from the heat; leave for 20 minutes to infuse. Strain before using.

Melt the butter in a pan, stir in the flour and cook for 1 minute. Add the heated stock and stir until blended. Pour on the strained cream and cook gently for 4 minutes. Add salt and pepper to taste, stir in the chopped chervil leaves and serve.

This delicate sauce is good with poached chicken, white fish, hard- or soft-boiled eggs, or with a chicken salad.

DILL SAUCE I

Metric/Imperial	American
25g/1oz butter	2 tablespoons butter
1 tablespoon flour	1 tablespoon flour
300ml/½ pint beef stock	1¼ cups beef stock
or chicken stock	or chicken stock
150ml/¼ pint thin cream	⅔ cup light cream
1 teaspoon Dijon mustard	1 teaspoon Dijon mustard
sea salt and black pepper	sea salt and black pepper
3 tablespoons chopped dill	3 tablespoons chopped dill

Melt the butter in a pan, stir in the flour and cook for 1 to 2 minutes, stirring. Heat the stock with the cream and pour on; blend and simmer gently for about 4 minutes. Stir in the mustard and add salt and pepper to taste. Add the chopped dill just before serving.

Serve hot with boiled beef, soft-boiled eggs and cooked vegetables; serve cold with skinned tomatoes and salads.

Opposite: Apple sauce with sage

Below: Chervil sauce I; Dill sauce I;
Cucumber and dill sauce

CUCUMBER AND DILL SAUCE

Metric/Imperial	American
½ cucumber	½ cucumber
small bunch dill	small bunch dill
15g/½oz butter	1 tablespoon butter
150ml/¼ pint chicken stock	⅔ cup chicken stock
or fish stock	or fish stock
100g/4oz low-fat cream	½ cup ricotta or diet
cheese	cheese
sea salt and black pepper	sea salt and black pepper

Peel the cucumber and chop it. Strip 1 tablespoon of leaves from the dill, chop them and set aside. Chop the rest of the dill and stew it gently in the butter with the cucumber. Cook in a covered pan for 5 minutes. Add the heated stock, using one that is appropriate to the dish with which it will be served, and simmer for another 5 minutes. Cool slightly, then purée in a blender with the cream cheese. Reheat, adding salt and pepper to taste. At the last moment, stir in the chopped dill leaves.

If made with chicken stock, serve with poached chicken, veal escalopes (scallops) or soft-boiled eggs. If made with fish stock, serve with poached white fish or salmon steaks.

BÉARNAISE SAUCE WITH HERBS

Metric/Imperial	American
150ml/¼ pint white wine vinegar	⅔ cup white wine vinegar
1 tablespoon chopped shallots	1 tablespoon chopped shallots
2 sprigs tarragon	2 sprigs tarragon
1 sprig chervil	1 sprig chervil
1 sprig parsley	1 sprig parsley
2 leaves lovage	2 leaves lovage
3 black peppercorns	3 black peppercorns
175g/6oz butter	¾ cup butter
4 egg yolks	4 egg yolks
1 teaspoon chopped chives (optional)	1 teaspoon chopped chives (optional)
1 teaspoon chopped chervil (optional)	1 teaspoon chopped chervil (optional)
1 teaspoon chopped tarragon (optional)	1 teaspoon chopped tarragon (optional)

Put the vinegar in a small pan with the shallots, tarragon, chervil, parsley, lovage and peppercorns. Boil until the liquid is reduced to 4 tablespoons; strain. Return to the pan and add the butter, cut into small pieces, stirring.

Have the container of a food processor or blender heated by filling it with hot water beforehand. Empty it and put in the egg yolks. Process briefly, not more than 30 seconds, then pour on the boiling vinegar and butter mixture in a steady stream through the hole in the lid. Stop processing immediately it has all been poured in.

Pour into a double boiler and stir over hot water until very slightly thickened. If you like, stir in the chopped herbs (a classic *sauce béarnaise* does not have any garnish) and serve immediately. This exquisite sauce is delicious with steaks and roast beef.

HOLLANDAISE SAUCE WITH HERBS

Metric/Imperial	American
3 egg yolks	3 egg yolks
pinch of sea salt	pinch of sea salt
100g/4oz butter	½ cup butter
1 tablespoon lemon juice	1 tablespoon lemon juice
3 tablespoons chopped mixed herbs: chervil, dill, tarragon and chives	3 tablespoons chopped mixed herbs: chervil, dill, tarragon and chives

This tricky sauce is quickly made in a food processor or blender. Have the container heated by filling with hot water and standing for a few minutes; drain and dry.

Break in the egg yolks with the salt. Heat the butter until almost boiling, then add the lemon juice. Turn on the food processor, and pour in the butter slowly through the lid. Stop as soon as it is amalgamated. Spoon into a bowl, stir in the chopped herbs and serve immediately.

The sauce can be kept warm for a short time, if absolutely necessary, by standing the bowl over hot water, but do not attempt to reheat it. Serve with poached fish, shellfish, poached eggs, asparagus, broccoli or artichokes.

PARSLEY AND EGG SAUCE

Metric/Imperial	American
25g/1oz butter	2 tablespoons butter
1½ tablespoons flour	1½ tablespoons flour
300ml/½ pint chicken stock or fish stock	1¼ cups chicken stock or fish stock
4 tablespoons thin cream	¼ cup light cream
sea salt and black pepper	sea salt and black pepper
3 tablespoons finely chopped parsley	3 tablespoons finely chopped parsley
1 hard-boiled egg	1 hard-boiled egg

Melt the butter in a saucepan, stir in the flour and cook for 1 to 2 minutes. Pour on the heated stock and stir until blended, allowing to simmer for about 3 minutes. Stir in the cream and add salt and pepper to taste. When smooth and well seasoned, stir in the chopped parsley and the chopped hard-boiled egg.

Made with chicken stock, this sauce is good with boiled bacon. Made with fish stock, serve with boiled white fish, smoked haddock or smoked cod.

VARIATION

Follow the recipe for *Parsley and Egg Sauce*, omitting the egg and increasing the chopped parsley to 5 tablespoons.

SAFFRON SAUCE

Metric/Imperial	American
25g/1oz butter	2 tablespoons butter
1 tablespoon finely chopped shallot	1 tablespoon finely chopped shallot
1 tablespoon flour	1 tablespoon flour
300ml/½ pint chicken stock or fish stock	1¼ cups chicken stock or fish stock
pinch of saffron	pinch of saffron
sea salt and black pepper	sea salt and black pepper
2 tablespoons sour cream	2 tablespoons sour cream

Melt the butter in a small saucepan and cook the shallot very gently for 3 minutes, without allowing it to brown. Add the flour and stir until blended. Cook for 1 minute. Heat the stock and pour it on; stir until blended and simmer for 3 to 4 minutes, adding the saffron and salt and pepper to taste. Stir in the sour cream and serve. This unusual sauce is good with poached white fish, hard-boiled eggs, rice, and cauliflower. (Use chicken stock for all, except fish.)

SORREL SAUCE I

Metric/Imperial	American
100g/4oz sorrel	¼lb sorrel
300ml/½ pint chicken stock or fish stock	1¼ cups chicken stock or fish stock
15g/½oz butter	1 tablespoon butter
1 tablespoon flour	1 tablespoon flour
4 tablespoons cream	¼ cup cream
sea salt and black pepper	sea salt and black pepper

Cut out and discard the central stalks of the sorrel and chop the leaves. Simmer for 5 minutes in the stock; cool slightly, then purée in a blender. Melt the butter in a pan, add the flour and stir over a low heat until blended. Pour on the sorrel purée, stirring, and simmer for 4 minutes. Add the cream, and salt and pepper to taste. Serve with veal, poached white fish, hard-boiled eggs, or noodles. (Use chicken stock for all dishes, except fish.)

Béarnaise sauce with herbs; Hollandaise sauce with herbs; Sorrel sauce I; Parsley and egg sauce

TOMATO SAUCE WITH MIXED HERBS

Metric/Imperial	American
1 small onion	1 small onion
25g/1oz butter	2 tablespoons butter
1 tablespoon olive oil	1 tablespoon olive oil
1 clove garlic	1 clove garlic
450g/1lb tomatoes	1lb tomatoes
sea salt and black pepper	sea salt and black pepper
1 teaspoon sugar	1 teaspoon sugar
1 teaspoon chopped lemon thyme	1 teaspoon chopped lemon thyme
1 teaspoon chopped marjoram or oregano	1 teaspoon chopped marjoram or oregano
1 teaspoon chopped chervil or parsley	1 teaspoon chopped chervil or parsley
1 teaspoon chopped dill	1 teaspoon chopped dill
1 teaspoon chopped tarragon or basil	1 teaspoon chopped tarragon or basil
½ teaspoon chopped lovage	½ teaspoon chopped lovage

Peel and chop the onion finely. Melt the butter in a pan with the oil. Add the onion and cook gently for 5 minutes, adding the crushed clove of garlic halfway through. Skin the tomatoes and chop; add them to the pan with salt and pepper to taste, and the sugar. Simmer for 10 to 12 minutes, until most of the juice has evaporated but the tomatoes still retain their fresh taste.

Stir in all the chopped herbs, cover the pan, and stand for 5 minutes before serving. Serve with pasta, gnocchi, steamed courgettes (zucchini) and vegetable timbales.

THICK TOMATO SAUCE

Metric/Imperial	American
2 tablespoons olive oil	2 tablespoons olive oil
1 medium onion	1 medium onion
1 clove garlic	1 clove garlic
1½ medium (400g/14oz) cans Italian plum tomatoes	1½ medium (14oz) cans peeled tomatoes
4 tablespoons tomato purée	¼ cup tomato paste
sea salt and black pepper	sea salt and black pepper
1 teaspoon sugar	1 teaspoon sugar
½ bay leaf	½ bay leaf
2 teaspoons chopped basil	2 teaspoons chopped basil

Heat the oil in a broad pan. Peel and chop the onion and cook it slowly until softened. Do not let the onion colour more than a pale yellow. Peel and crush the garlic and add it towards the end. Pour in the canned tomatoes with their juice and the tomato purée (paste). Chop roughly in the pan with the edge of a palette knife. Add the salt and pepper, sugar, and bay leaf. Simmer slowly for 1 hour with the lid off, until reduced to a thick sauce, stirring now and then. Add the chopped basil for the last few minutes only.

Use for making pizzas (see page 120), or for freezing. This recipe makes approximately 450ml/¾ pint/2 cups.

DILL SAUCE II

Metric/Imperial	American
6 sprigs dill	6 sprigs dill
150ml/¼ pint thin cream	⅔ cup light cream
1 egg yolk	1 egg yolk
1 teaspoon Dijon mustard	1 teaspoon Dijon mustard
pinch of salt	pinch of salt
150ml/¼ pint olive oil	⅔ cup olive oil
2 teaspoons white wine vinegar	2 teaspoons white wine vinegar

Strip about a tablespoonful of the best leaves from the dill, chop them and set aside. Put the cream in a small pan, with the remaining dill stalks and leaves. Bring to boiling point, cover the pan, and remove from the heat. Leave for 15 minutes to infuse. Strain and cool.

Meanwhile, make a mayonnaise (see method for herb mayonnaise page 190). Break the egg yolk into a bowl, add the mustard and salt, and add the oil very gradually, drop by drop, stirring all the time. When all is amalgamated, stir in the vinegar.

Stir the cooled cream into the mayonnaise and add the chopped dill leaves. Serve with soft-boiled eggs, cooked vegetables, new potatoes and salads.

VARIATION

Follow the recipe for *Dill Sauce II*, substituting 6 sprigs tarragon for the dill.

EGG AND HERB SAUCE

Metric/Imperial	American
2 hard-boiled egg yolks	2 hard-boiled egg yolks
2 tablespoons thick cream	2 tablespoons heavy cream
2 tablespoons olive oil	2 tablespoons olive oil
2 teaspoons white wine vinegar	2 teaspoons white wine vinegar
sea salt and black pepper	sea salt and black pepper
1 tablespoon chopped chives	1 tablespoon chopped chives
1 tablespoon chopped dill	1 tablespoon chopped dill
1 tablespoon chopped tarragon	1 tablespoon chopped tarragon

Mash the egg yolks to a paste with the cream. Add the oil very gradually, stirring all the time, then the vinegar. Add salt and pepper to taste, then the chopped herbs. Serve with salads of all sorts; the egg whites can be chopped and added to the salad.

GARLIC AND HERB SAUCE

Metric/Imperial	American
1 large clove garlic	1 large clove garlic
pinch of sea salt	pinch of sea salt
150ml/¼ pint natural yogurt	⅔ cup unflavored yogurt
black pepper	black pepper
2 tablespoons chopped mixed herbs: parsley, chives, dill and tarragon	2 tablespoons chopped mixed herbs: parsley, chives, dill and tarragon

Crush the chopped garlic to a paste in a mortar. Add a pinch of salt and continue to pound. Beat in the yogurt gradually, pounding all the time. When all is amalgamated, taste for seasoning, adding more salt and black pepper as required. Stir in the chopped herbs and chill until ready to serve.

Serve with grilled (broiled) chicken, grilled (broiled) skewers of lamb, pork chops, stuffed green peppers or tomatoes, or grilled (broiled) fish.

Thick tomato sauce; Egg and herb sauce; Garlic and herb sauce

HERB RÉMOULADE

Metric/Imperial	American
2 hard-boiled egg yolks	2 hard-boiled egg yolks
2 raw egg yolks	2 raw egg yolks
sea salt and black pepper	sea salt and black pepper
1 tablespoon Dijon mustard	1 tablespoon Dijon mustard
300ml/½ pint olive oil	1¼ cups olive oil
2 tablespoons white wine vinegar	2 tablespoons white wine vinegar
1 tablespoon tarragon vinegar	1 tablespoon tarragon vinegar
1 tablespoon dill vinegar	1 tablespoon dill vinegar
6 tablespoons sour cream or *natural* yogurt	6 tablespoons sour cream or *unflavored* yogurt
4–6 tablespoons chopped mixed herbs: chervil, dill, chives, cress and parsley	4–6 tablespoons chopped mixed herbs: chervil, dill, chives, garden cress and parsley
1 tablespoon chopped capers (optional)	1 tablespoon chopped capers (optional)
1 tablespoon chopped gherkins (optional)	1 tablespoon chopped dill pickle (optional)

Mash the hard-boiled egg yolks in a bowl with a fork, and beat in the raw yolks to make a paste. Add a pinch of salt, some black pepper and the mustard, and beat until smooth. Start adding the oil drop by drop, beating all the time. Thin with a teaspoon of the vinegar if it gets too thick. Continue to beat until all the oil is used up, then add the remaining vinegars. (If you have no tarragon or dill vinegar, simply substitute white wine vinegar.) When the sauce is smooth, stir in the sour cream (or yogurt), and the chopped herbs.

Strictly speaking, a rémoulade should contain chopped capers and gherkins (sweet dill pickle) but this version is more subtle. Serve with *crudités*, vegetable salads, hard-boiled eggs, cold meat or cold fish.

HERB MAYONNAISE

Metric/Imperial	American
2 egg yolks	2 egg yolks
pinch of salt	pinch of salt
½ teaspoon Dijon mustard	½ teaspoon Dijon mustard
300ml/½ pint olive oil	1¼ cups olive oil
1½ tablespoons white wine vinegar	1½ tablespoons white wine vinegar
½ tablespoon lemon juice	½ tablespoon lemon juice
4 tablespoons chopped mixed herbs: chervil, dill, chives, tarragon, cress and parsley	¼ cup chopped mixed herbs: chervil, dill, chives, tarragon, garden cress and parsley

The first six ingredients should be at room temperature before you start. Break the egg yolks into a bowl. Beat with a wooden spoon, adding a pinch of salt. Add the mustard and beat again. Put the oil in a small jug (pitcher), and start to add it to the egg yolks very slowly, literally drop by drop to start with, beating continuously. After a few moments an emulsion will have been formed and you can start to add the oil in a very thin trickle.

When half the oil has been amalgamated, it can be added more quickly, but continue beating all the time. If it gets too thick to work easily, add a very little of the vinegar, not more than a teaspoonful. When all the oil is finished, add the remaining vinegar and lemon juice, tasting as you do it and stopping when you feel it is tart enough. (If at any point the sauce separates, start again either with a third egg yolk, into which you beat the curdled sauce very, very slowly, or with a teaspoon of Dijon mustard in place of the egg yolk.) When the sauce is finished, stir in the chopped herbs.

This lovely green sauce is the best possible accompaniment to cold poached salmon or salmon trout, hard-boiled eggs, or cold fish in aspic.

QUICK HERB SAUCE

Metric/Imperial	American
150ml/¼ pint mayonnaise	⅔ cup mayonnaise
150ml/¼ pint natural yogurt	⅔ cup unflavored yogurt
2 hard-boiled egg yolks	2 hard-boiled egg yolks
1 teaspoon Dijon mustard	1 teaspoon Dijon mustard
sea salt and black pepper	sea salt and black pepper
1 tablespoon chopped dill	1 tablespoon chopped dill
1 tablespoon chopped chives	1 tablespoon chopped chives
1 tablespoon chopped parsley	1 tablespoon chopped parsley

The mayonnaise for this sauce does not have to be home-made; a good commercial variety will do perfectly well.

Mix the mayonnaise and yogurt together until smooth; mash the egg yolks with the mustard and stir the yogurt and mayonnaise mixture into them. When smooth, add salt and pepper to taste and stir in the chopped herbs. Serve with grated raw vegetables, *crudités* or mixed salads.

HORSE-RADISH SAUCE

Metric/Imperial	American
300ml/½ pint sour cream	1¼ cups sour cream
1½–2 tablespoons grated horse-radish	1½–2 tablespoons grated horse-radish
sea salt and black pepper	sea salt and black pepper
1–2 teaspoons lemon juice	1–2 teaspoons lemon juice

Beat the cream in a bowl until smooth, then stir in the grated horse-radish bit by bit, until you have the desired strength. Add salt and black pepper and lemon juice to taste. Serve with hot or cold roast beef, and smoked fish of all kinds.

LEBANESE PARSLEY SAUCE

Metric/Imperial	American
150ml/¼ pint tahini	⅔ cup tahini
2–3 cloves garlic	2–3 cloves garlic
150ml/¼ pint lemon juice	⅔ cup lemon juice
4 tablespoons water	¼ cup water
pinch of salt	pinch of salt
40g/1½oz chopped parsley	1 cup chopped parsley

Tahini is a paste made from sesame seeds and oil; it can be bought in health food shops and Eastern stores.

Beat the tahini in a bowl until smooth. Peel and crush the garlic and add it to the tahini with the lemon juice, water and salt. It should be like a fairly thick cream; if necessary, thin with a little more water. Stir in the chopped parsley and serve with fried fish, grilled (broiled) lamb, or *crudités*.

PISTOU

Metric/Imperial	American
1 large ripe tomato	1 large ripe tomato
40g/1½oz chopped basil	1 cup chopped basil
2 cloves garlic	2 cloves garlic
4 tablespoons pine kernels	¼ cup pine nuts (pignoli)
50g/2oz freshly grated Parmesan cheese	½ cup freshly grated Parmesan cheese
150ml/¼ pint olive oil	⅔ cup olive oil

Cut the tomato in half horizontally and grill (broil) until soft and quite blackened on the surface. Remove the skin and chop the flesh. Put the chopped basil in a mortar and pound until crushed. Peel and crush the garlic, chop the nuts and add both to the basil. Pound again. Add the chopped tomato and continue to pound, finally adding the freshly grated cheese. When all is smooth, pour on the oil drop by drop, as if making a mayonnaise, continuing to pound constantly.

When finished, this marvellous sauce should have the consistency of creamed butter. Serve with spaghetti, gnocchi, noodles, or in a minestrone-type soup.

Opposite: Herb rémoulade

Right: Pistou

MINT SAUCE

Metric/Imperial	American
4 tablespoons finely chopped mint	¼ cup finely chopped mint
1 teaspoon sugar	1 teaspoon sugar
2 tablespoons lemon juice	2 tablespoons lemon juice
1 tablespoon white wine vinegar	1 tablespoon white wine vinegar
4 tablespoons boiling water	¼ cup boiling water

Put the chopped mint in a mortar and pound with the sugar until completely crushed and well mixed. Stir in the lemon juice and vinegar, then the boiling water. Mix well and leave to cool. Serve with roast lamb.

MUSTARD AND DILL SAUCE

Metric/Imperial	American
½ tablespoon Dijon mustard	½ tablespoon Dijon mustard
½ tablespoon olive oil	½ tablespoon olive oil
4 tablespoons natural yogurt	¼ cup unflavored yogurt
juice of ½ lemon	juice of ½ lemon
2 tablespoons chopped dill	2 tablespoons chopped dill

Put the mustard in a bowl and stir in the oil drop by drop, as if making a mayonnaise. When the mustard and oil have blended together smoothly, stir in the yogurt. Add lemon juice to taste and stir in the chopped dill. If at any stage the sauce separates, purée it in a blender to emulsify. Serve with grilled (broiled) pork chops, meat loaf, white fish, or grilled (broiled) chicken.

SALSA VERDE

Metric/Imperial	American
1 egg yolk	1 egg yolk
1 tablespoon Dijon mustard	1 tablespoon Dijon mustard
1 teaspoon sugar	1 teaspoon sugar
sea salt and black pepper	sea salt and black pepper
2 cloves garlic	2 cloves garlic
½ large mild onion	½ large mild onion
40g/1½oz chopped mixed herbs: parsley, chives, dill and tarragon	1 cup chopped mixed herbs: parsley, chives, dill and tarragon
3 tablespoons white wine vinegar	3 tablespoons white wine vinegar
150ml/¼ pint olive oil	⅔ cup olive oil
2 hard-boiled eggs	2 hard-boiled eggs

If you have a food processor, all the ingredients can be put in together and blended.

Alternatively, they can be mixed by hand as follows: break the egg yolk into a bowl and beat with a wooden spoon until smooth. Stir in the mustard, sugar, a good pinch of sea salt and several turns of the pepper mill. Add the peeled and crushed garlic, finely chopped onion, and the chopped herbs. Stir in the vinegar and the olive oil, then the chopped hard-boiled eggs.

A good accompaniment to hot or cold boiled beef, artichokes, asparagus, poached white fish, new potatoes, *haricots verts* (green beans) and many other vegetables.

VINAIGRETTE WITH MIXED HERBS

Metric/Imperial	American
pinch of sea salt	pinch of sea salt
freshly ground black pepper	freshly ground black pepper
½ teaspoon Dijon mustard	½ teaspoon Dijon mustard
½ teaspoon sugar	½ teaspoon sugar
1½ tablespoons white wine vinegar	1½ tablespoons white wine vinegar
6 tablespoons olive oil	6 tablespoons olive oil
½ tablespoon lemon juice	½ tablespoon lemon juice
½ teaspoon chopped tarragon	½ teaspoon chopped tarragon
½ teaspoon chopped borage (optional)	½ teaspoon chopped borage (optional)
½ teaspoon chopped lemon balm (optional)	½ teaspoon chopped lemon balm (optional)
1 teaspoon chopped chervil	1 teaspoon chopped chervil
1 teaspoon chopped dill	1 teaspoon chopped dill
2 teaspoons chopped chives	2 teaspoons chopped chives
1 clove garlic	1 clove garlic

It is easier to mix this salad dressing directly in the salad bowl, but it can be made in a separate bowl if you prefer.

Put a pinch of salt, preferably sea salt, in first, then a few turns of the pepper mill. Add the mustard and sugar, then pour on the vinegar and stir to dissolve the seasonings.

Add the oil gradually, beating well with a wooden spoon to make an emulsion.

Finally add the lemon juice and stir in the chopped herbs. Any suitable mixture can be used. Borage and lemon balm, for instance, are optional; not much used in England and America, they are traditional herbs for flavouring salads in Germany and other central European countries. Add a peeled clove of garlic and stand for 1 hour; before using, discard the garlic. Serve with salads of all sorts.

VARIATION

Follow the recipe for *Vinaigrette with Mixed Herbs*, substituting 1 tablespoon chopped basil for the chopped mixed herbs. Serve with lettuce or tomato salads.

SORREL SAUCE II

Metric/Imperial	American
10 young sorrel leaves (about 20g/¾oz when chopped)	10 young sorrel leaves (about ½ cup when chopped)
2 tablespoons medium-fat cream cheese	2 tablespoons cream cheese
4 tablespoons natural yogurt	¼ cup unflavored yogurt
4 tablespoons thick cream	¼ cup heavy cream
1 teaspoon lemon juice	1 teaspoon lemon juice
sea salt and black pepper	sea salt and black pepper

Cut the central stalk out of the sorrel leaves, and chop the leaves in a blender with the cream cheese, yogurt, cream and lemon juice. Add salt and pepper if needed. Transfer to a serving bowl and chill.

This tart and delicious sauce is good with cold fillets of white fish, hard- or soft-boiled eggs, or poured over a mixed, green, or chicken salad.

YOGURT AND MINT SAUCE

Metric/Imperial	American
300ml/½ pint natural yogurt	1¼ cups unflavored yogurt
1 cucumber	1 cucumber
1–2 cloves garlic	1–2 cloves garlic
sea salt and black pepper	sea salt and black pepper
24 mint leaves	24 mint leaves

Beat the yogurt in a bowl until smooth. Peel the cucumber and grate it coarsely. Squeeze out excess moisture from the cucumber between the hands. Peel and crush the garlic. Purée the yogurt, cucumber and garlic in a blender with salt and pepper and the mint leaves. Chill before serving.

This makes a generous amount to serve with hot or cold roast lamb, grilled (broiled) skewers of lamb, poured over a dish of hot boiled new potatoes, or spread over a dish of cold sliced lamb. The sauce can be made in half quantities if preferred.

BASIL AND GARLIC BUTTER

Metric/Imperial	American
1 clove garlic	1 clove garlic
2 tablespoons chopped basil	2 tablespoons chopped basil
75g/3oz butter	6 tablespoons butter
sea salt and black pepper	sea salt and black pepper

Peel and chop the garlic and pound in a mortar. Add the chopped basil and pound again. Add the butter, cut in small pieces, and pound again. (The butter should be cool and firm, but not hard.) Add salt and pepper to taste. (Alternatively, the mixture can be quickly made in a food processor or blender.) Chill before serving. Serve with steaks, lamb cutlets, or grilled (broiled) fish.

CHIVE BUTTER

Metric/Imperial	American
75g/3oz butter	6 tablespoons butter
3 tablespoons chopped chives	3 tablespoons chopped chives
1 tablespoon lemon juice	1 tablespoon lemon juice
sea salt and black pepper	sea salt and black pepper

Use butter that is firm and cool, but not taken straight from the refrigerator. Pound the butter in a mortar until smooth. Add the chopped chives and pound again until they are amalgamated. Beat in the lemon juice, and add salt and pepper to taste. (Alternatively, prepare the butter in a food processor or blender.) Chill until ready to serve. Serve with grilled (broiled) lamb cutlets, grilled (broiled) sole (flounder) or other white fish.

MIXED HERB BUTTER

Metric/Imperial	American
75g/3oz butter	6 tablespoons butter
½ tablespoon chopped tarragon	½ tablespoon chopped tarragon
½ tablespoon chopped chervil	½ tablespoon chopped chervil
½ tablespoon chopped dill	½ tablespoon chopped dill
½ tablespoon chopped chives	½ tablespoon chopped chives
½ tablespoon chopped mint	½ tablespoon chopped mint
1 tablespoon lemon juice	1 tablespoon lemon juice
sea salt and black pepper	sea salt and black pepper

Pound the butter with a pestle in a mortar until smooth. Add the chopped herbs in turn gradually, pounding after each addition. When smooth, add lemon juice, and salt and pepper to taste. (Alternatively, prepare the butter in a food processor or blender.) Chill until firm. Serve with grilled (broiled) meats, grilled (broiled) fish, noodles, or grilled (broiled) tomatoes.

A mixed salad tossed in Vinaigrette with mixed herbs; Skewers of lamb served with Yogurt and mint sauce

MINT BUTTER

Metric/Imperial	American
75g/3oz butter	6 tablespoons butter
2 tablespoons chopped mint	2 tablespoons chopped mint
½ tablespoon lemon juice	½ tablespoon lemon juice
sea salt and black pepper	sea salt and black pepper

Pound the butter until smooth in a mortar. Add the chopped mint and pound again, until thoroughly mixed. Add the lemon juice and continue to pound. Add salt and pepper to taste. (Alternatively, make the butter in a food processor or blender.) Chill until firm. Serve with grilled (broiled) lamb – cutlets or chops – with new potatoes, carrots, or green peas.

PARSLEY BUTTER

Metric/Imperial	American
75g/3oz butter	6 tablespoons butter
1 clove garlic	1 clove garlic
3 tablespoons chopped parsley	3 tablespoons chopped parsley
1 tablespoon lemon juice	1 tablespoon lemon juice
sea salt and black pepper	sea salt and black pepper

Use butter that is cool and firm, but not taken straight out of the refrigerator. Pound the butter in a mortar until it has the consistency of smooth cream. Crush the peeled clove of garlic. Add it to the butter and continue to pound so that the garlic is thoroughly incorporated. Add the parsley and pound again, finally adding the lemon juice and salt and pepper to taste. (Alternatively, prepare the butter in a food processor or blender.) Chill until firm. Serve with steaks, grilled (broiled) fish, or grilled (broiled) tomatoes.

SAGE BUTTER

Metric/Imperial	American
75g/3oz butter	6 tablespoons butter
12 leaves sage (about 1 tablespoon when chopped)	12 leaves sage (about 1 tablespoon when chopped)
sea salt and black pepper	sea salt and black pepper
1 teaspoon onion juice	1 teaspoon onion juice
2 teaspoons lemon juice	2 teaspoons lemon juice

Cut the butter into small pieces and pound in a mortar until smooth. Chop the sage and add to the butter. Pound again until mixed to a paste, flecked with green. Add salt and pepper to taste, and a teaspoon of onion juice, made by crushing a piece of onion in a garlic press. Add the lemon juice and pound again. (Alternatively, make the butter in a food processor or blender.) Chill until firm. Serve with lamb cutlets, veal chops, or grilled (broiled) tomatoes.

TARRAGON AND PARSLEY BUTTER

Metric/Imperial	American
75g/3oz butter	6 tablespoons butter
1½ tablespoons chopped tarragon	1½ tablespoons chopped tarragon
1 tablespoon chopped parsley	1 tablespoon chopped parsley
1 tablespoon lemon juice	1 tablespoon lemon juice
sea salt and black pepper	sea salt and black pepper

Use butter that is cool, but not too cold. Pound the butter in a mortar until smooth. Add the chopped herbs and pound again. Add lemon juice to taste and salt and pepper. (Alternatively, make the butter in a food processor or blender.) Chill until firm. Serve with grilled (broiled) steaks or lamb cutlets, grilled sole (broiled flounder), noodles, or grilled (broiled) tomatoes.

FRIED PARSLEY

Metric/Imperial	American
1 large bunch very fresh parsley sprigs	1 large bunch very fresh parsley sprigs
oil for frying	oil for frying

Wash the parsley sprigs in cold water and dry thoroughly with a soft cloth. Heat the oil in a frying pan (skillet) to 170°C/335°F. Drop in the sprigs, a few at a time, and let them cook for about 3 minutes, turning once. They will frizzle and turn a bright emerald green. Lift out, drain on paper towels, and serve as soon as possible while they are still very crisp and brittle.

This is a most delicious old-fashioned garnish for fried fillets of fish, preferably Dover sole, and is rarely seen nowadays.

PARSLEY DUMPLINGS

Metric/Imperial	American
50g/2oz self-raising flour	½ cup all-purpose flour
pinch of salt	pinch of salt
15g/½oz butter	1 tablespoon butter
1 large egg	1 large egg
1 tablespoon chopped parsley	1 tablespoon chopped parsley

Sift the flour into a bowl with the salt. Cut in the butter in small pieces. Beat the egg with the chopped parsley and stir in. Beat until smooth. If using an electric mixer, put all ingredients in the bowl together and beat at medium speed until well mixed.

Drop small teaspoonsful of the mixture into a broad pan of boiling salted water. Cover and boil gently for 10 minutes, turning halfway through. Lift out with a slotted spoon and serve, either in a clear soup or with a beef stew, or with boiled beef.

VARIATIONS

Follow the recipe for *Parsley Dumplings*, substituting chervil for parsley. Serve with *Chervil Consommé* (page 99).

Follow the recipe for *Parsley Dumplings*, substituting dill for parsley. Serve with *Dill Consommé* (see page 99), or *Chicken in Mustard and Dill Sauce* (see page 140).

Follow the recipe for *Parsley Dumplings*, substituting fennel for parsley. Serve with *Fish Soup with Fennel* (see page 100).

Follow the recipe for *Parsley Dumplings*, substituting ½ tablespoon chopped lovage and ½ tablespoon chopped parsley for the tablespoon of chopped parsley. Serve with *Lovage Consommé* (see page 99).

Follow the recipe for *Parsley Dumplings*, substituting tarragon for parsley. Serve with *Tarragon Consommé* (see page 99), or *Poulet à l'Estragon* (see page 142).

BEEF MARROW AND CHERVIL DUMPLINGS

Metric/Imperial
40g/1½oz beef marrow
1 egg
pinch of salt
approx. 50g/2oz soft white
    breadcrumbs
1 tablespoon finely
    chopped chervil

American
3 tablespoons beef marrow
1 egg
pinch of salt
approx. 1 cup soft white
    breadcrumbs
1 tablespoon finely
    chopped chervil

In a pan, warm the marrow slightly, until semi-melted, and beat until smooth with a wooden spoon. Add the beaten egg and beat again, adding a pinch of salt. Add the breadcrumbs and the chervil by degrees, mixing until you have a soft firm dough. Stand for 30 minutes, then form into tiny balls, not much bigger than your thumbnail.

Drop the dumplings into a pan of boiling water, lightly salted, and simmer for 4 to 5 minutes with the lid on. (Alternatively, they can be simmered in beef or chicken stock, made from the marrow bones, a chicken carcass and some flavouring vegetables.) The dumplings will float to the top when cooked. Test one by cutting it in half to make sure it is cooked through. Drain briefly, then serve in a clear soup, or with a game dish like saddle of hare (see page 148).

HERB PANCAKE STRIPS

Metric/Imperial
75g/3oz plain flour
pinch of salt
1 egg
150ml/¼ pint milk
2 tablespoons finely
    chopped chervil
lard for frying

American
¾ cup all-purpose flour
pinch of salt
1 egg
⅔ cup milk
2 tablespoons finely
    chopped chervil
lard for frying

Sift the flour into a large bowl and make a hole in the middle. Add a pinch of salt and break in the egg. With a wire whisk, start beating in the egg incorporating the flour from round the edges. At the same time, pour on the milk slowly. When all is amalgamated, beat hard until very smooth, then stand in a cool place for 1 hour before using.

Beat again thoroughly before making the pancakes and stir in the chopped chervil. Melt a little lard in a frying pan (skillet) and use the batter to make 8 small thin pancakes. Roll them up and cut them in strips. Serve in clear soup. Alternatively, serve the pancakes whole, as a dish on their own, spread with cream cheese and rolled up.

Beef marrow and chervil dumplings; Herb pancake strips

Breads, Sandwiches & Biscuits

The part of herbs most valuable for bread-making is the seeds. Both caraway and anise seeds give a most unusual and delicious flavour to a bread, that is equally good eaten with butter and jam, with cream cheese, or toasted and served with fish or meat pâtés. Both these seeds also go well with rye bread, but since this is a difficult bread to make, the recipe given here uses only a small proportion of rye flour mixed with white bread flour. Garlic bread is simply a thick French loaf, cut in diagonal slices and spread with garlic butter, then wrapped in foil and heated in the oven. It is extremely fattening, but delicious served with fish soups, minestrone, or with oily vegetable dishes like ratatouille. Saffron bread, on the other hand, is an English medieval bread sometimes made in a sweet form almost like a cake, or as given here, unsweetened. It is excellent eaten with a Mediterranean fish soup, with thick vegetable soups, or with fish hors d'oeuvre. It is also good with vegetable dishes, and even better toasted. Any remains can be made into crumbs, and used as a tasty coating for fried fillets of fish.

The green leaves of herbs are best used in sandwiches, either alone or in conjunction with cream cheese. Both the purslane sandwich and the burnet and cheese sandwich given here have become two of my favourite snacks, perfect for a light lunch, while the small and elegant parsley sandwiches and herb sandwiches are ideal for serving at tea-time, or with smoked fish hors-d'oeuvre. The little cheese-flavoured biscuits (cookies) with dried herbs are delicious served with any of the herb consommés on pages 99–100, while the herb scones (biscuits) make a good dish for a substantial tea.

ANISE SEED BREAD

Metric/Imperial	American
450g/1lb strong flour	1lb white bread flour
pinch of sea salt	pinch of sea salt
1 tablespoon dried yeast	1 package active dry yeast
1 tablespoon sugar	1 tablespoon sugar
just under 300ml/½ pint milk	just under 1¼ cups milk
1 egg	1 egg
2 teaspoons anise seed	2 teaspoons anise seed

Put the flour in a large bowl with the salt. Stand in a warm place. Put the yeast into a cup with the sugar. Warm the milk to blood heat and add 2 tablespoons of it to the yeast. Leave to stand in a warm place for 10 minutes or until frothy. Beat the egg in a bowl and stir into it the remaining warm milk. Add the anise seeds.

Make a well in the centre of the flour with a wooden spoon and pour in the yeast mixture. Cover with flour and pour on the egg and milk, stirring vigorously with a wooden spoon. As soon as it starts to hold together, start to knead by hand, turning it out on a floured surface. Knead for 6 to 8 minutes, until smooth and elastic.

Wash the bowl and dry it, rub with a little oil and put back the dough, turning it over so that it is lightly coated with oil. Cover with a cloth and stand in a warm place to rise. Leave for 1 hour, or until doubled in volume. Knock back (punch down), turn out and knead again for 4 to 5 minutes.

Form into a roll and turn into an oiled loaf tin, 25 × 10 × 7.5cm/10 × 4 × 3in. Leave in a warm place for about 40 minutes, covered with a cloth, to rise again. Bake for 40 minutes in a moderately hot oven (200°C/400°F or Gas Mark 6). This unusual bread is very good with butter and honey, with cream cheese or toasted and eaten with pâté.

VARIATION

Follow the recipe for *Anise Seed Bread*, substituting caraway seeds for anise seeds.

GARLIC BREAD

Metric/Imperial	American
1 French loaf	1 French loaf
2 cloves garlic	2 cloves garlic
½ teaspoon sea salt	½ teaspoon sea salt
75g/3oz butter	6 tablespoons butter

Make wide diagonal cuts in the bread, stopping just before you slice right through it. Peel the garlic, crush it with the salt and beat it into the butter until smooth. Spread the garlic butter on each side of each slice of bread, then squeeze together and spread any remaining butter over the crust. Wrap in foil and bake for 5 minutes in a moderately hot oven (200°C/400°F or Gas Mark 6).

Anise seed bread

RYE BREAD

Metric/Imperial	American
275g/10oz strong flour	2½ cups white bread flour
50g/2oz rye flour	½ cup rye flour
1 tablespoon dried yeast	1 package active dry yeast
1 tablespoon sugar	1 tablespoon sugar
120ml/4fl oz water	½ cup water
½ tablespoon sea salt	½ tablespoon sea salt
120ml/4fl oz milk	½ cup milk
1 teaspoon caraway seeds	1 teaspoon caraway seeds
1 teaspoon anise seed	1 teaspoon anise seed
1 teaspoon grated orange rind	1 teaspoon grated orange rind

Mix the two flours together. Put the yeast and the sugar in a cup. Warm 3 tablespoons of the water to blood heat and add it to the yeast. Leave to stand in a warm place for 10 minutes or until frothy. Put the salt in a bowl. Heat the remaining water almost to boiling point and pour 3 to 4 tablespoons of it on to the salt. When the salt has dissolved, add the remaining water and the milk, pour into a saucepan and heat until lukewarm.

Make a well in the centre of the flour and pour on the yeast mixture. Cover with some of the flour, and sprinkle on the caraway and anise seeds and the orange rind. Pour on most of the milk and water, and stir vigorously with a wooden spoon, adding as much of the remaining milk and water as is required. (Different flours vary in the amount of liquid they will absorb; stop adding fluid when the dough forms itself into a sort of ball and picks up the little bits of dough in the bottom of the bowl.) Knead for 5 minutes.

Clean the bowl and grease it lightly with oil. Return the dough to the bowl and cover it with cling film (Saran wrap) or a clean cloth, and leave to stand in a warm place for 1 hour, by which time it should have roughly doubled in bulk. Take out of the bowl, knock back (punch down) and knead for a further 3 minutes. Then put back in the bowl, cover and leave to rise again for another hour.

Take out, knock back (punch down) and knead again briefly, then form into a loaf shape and put in a buttered loaf tin, 25 × 10 × 7.5cm/10 × 4 × 3in, which it fills by about half. Put it back in a warm place for 30 minutes to rise again. When the tin is nicely filled, bake for 45 minutes in a hot oven (220°C/425°F or Gas Mark 7). Tip out of the tin on to a wire rack to cool.

SAFFRON BREAD

Metric/Imperial	American
450g/1lb strong flour	1lb white bread flour
1½ teaspoons sea salt	1½ teaspoons sea salt
1 tablespoon dried yeast	1 package active dry yeast
4 tablespoons warm water	¼ cup warm water
150ml/¼ pint milk	⅔ cup milk
½ teaspoon saffron	½ teaspoon saffron
2 eggs	2 eggs

Put the flour into a large bowl and add the salt. Put the yeast in a cup with the water and leave in a warm place for 10 minutes or until frothy. Heat the milk in a small pan with the saffron; when it reaches boiling point, turn off the heat and leave to cool, stirring occasionally. Do not allow the milk to get completely cold, but keep it at blood temperature. Beat the eggs in a bowl and stir in the saffron-flavoured milk.

Make a depression in the centre of the flour with a spoon, pour in the yeast liquid and cover with flour. Pour the saffron mixture onto the flour, stirring hard with a wooden spoon. It may be necessary to add a little extra milk or water if the dough seems too dry. When it all starts to cling together nicely, turn out and knead for 5 minutes.

Wash out the bowl and dry it, rub with a little oil and put back the dough. Cover with a cloth and stand in a warm draughtproof place for about 1 hour, or until roughly doubled in volume. Knock back (punch down), turn out and knead again for a further 5 minutes then form into a loaf shape and put into a greased loaf tin, 25 × 10 × 7.5cm/10 × 4 × 3in. Cover again with a cloth and leave to rise for a further 30 to 45 minutes, until it fills the tin. Bake for 30 minutes in a moderately hot oven (190°C/375°F or Gas Mark 5), or until it sounds hollow when you tap your knuckle on the bottom of the loaf. Turn the loaf out on a rack to cool. Serve soon after cooling with fish pâtés, fish soups, vegetable soups, or vegetable hors d'oeuvre.

Burnet and cheese sandwiches; Parsley sandwiches; Rye bread; Saffron bread

BURNET AND CHEESE SANDWICH

Metric/Imperial	American
2 slices wholemeal bread	2 slices wholewheat bread
butter for spreading	butter for spreading
Cheddar, Wensleydale or cream cheese	Cheddar or cream cheese
about 16 leaves burnet	about 16 leaves burnet

Butter both slices of bread and lay a thick slice of hard cheese or spread a generous layer of cream cheese on one slice. Cover with a layer of burnet leaves and make into a sandwich. Cut into fingers or quarters. Serves 1.

PURSLANE SANDWICH

Metric/Imperial	American
3 stalks purslane	3 stalks purslane
2 slices wholemeal bread	2 slices wholewheat bread
unsalted butter for spreading	sweet butter for spreading
sea salt	sea salt

Pick the purslane leaves off the stalks, wash them, and pat them dry in a cloth. Butter both slices of bread quite thickly, lay the leaves on top, and sprinkle with sea salt. Cut into fingers or quarters. This makes a nourishing and delicious snack for 1.

PARSLEY SANDWICHES

Metric/Imperial	American
8 small slices wholemeal bread	8 small slices wholewheat bread
butter for spreading	butter for spreading
cream cheese	cream cheese
4 tablespoons chopped parsley	$\frac{1}{4}$ cup chopped parsley
black pepper	black pepper

Spread 4 of the slices of bread with butter, the other 4 with cream cheese. Strew the parsley on the cheese and sprinkle lightly with freshly ground black pepper. Cover with the buttered slices and cut into quarters.

VARIATION

Follow the recipe for *Parsley Sandwiches*, substituting for the parsley 4 tablespoons ($\frac{1}{4}$ cup) of chopped mixed herbs: chervil, dill, tarragon and chives.

Herb biscuits

HERB SCONES

Metric/Imperial	American
250ml/8fl oz water	1 cup water
65g/2½oz butter	5 tablespoons butter
175g/6oz flour	1½ cups flour
3 eggs	3 eggs
275g/10oz freshly mashed potatoes	1¼ cups freshly mashed potatoes
sea salt and black pepper	sea salt and black pepper
4 tablespoons chopped mixed herbs: chervil, dill, chives and parsley	¼ cup chopped mixed herbs: chervil, dill, chives and parsley

Boil the water and butter together in a large saucepan. When the butter has melted, remove from the heat and add the flour. Stir until it forms a thick paste. Break in the eggs, one at a time, and continue to beat until the mixture is smooth and comes away from the sides of the pan. Beat in the hot mashed potatoes and continue beating until they are amalgamated. Add salt and black pepper to taste. Stir in the chopped herbs. Leave to cool.

Heat a lightly greased griddle until very hot, then form the mixture into flat round cakes and cook them until golden brown, turning once. Serve hot, with a dish of butter on the table. Makes about 16 scones (biscuits).

HERB BISCUITS

Metric/Imperial	American
50g/2oz flour	½ cup flour
25g/1oz butter	2 tablespoons butter
pinch of sea salt	pinch of sea salt
pinch of cayenne	pinch of cayenne
50g/2oz Cheddar cheese, grated	½ cup grated Cheddar cheese
½ teaspoon caraway seeds or dried dill seed	½ teaspoon caraway seeds or dried dill seed
½ teaspoon Dijon mustard	½ teaspoon Dijon mustard
1 egg yolk	1 egg yolk
1 tablespoon iced water	1 tablespoon iced water

Sift the flour into a bowl and rub in the butter in small pieces. Add the salt and cayenne and mix in the grated cheese with the blade of a knife. (Alternatively, all this can be done in a mixer or food processor.) Stir in the caraway seeds (or dill). Stir the mustard into the lightly beaten egg yolk and stir into the mixture. Add enough of the iced water to give a soft but firm dough.

Wrap loosely in cling film (Saran wrap) and chill for 1 hour in the refrigerator. Roll out on a floured board until about 3mm/⅛in thick and cut into small rounds. Lay the biscuits (cookies) on a greased baking sheet and bake for 7 minutes in a moderately hot oven (200°C/400°F or Gas Mark 6) or until golden brown and puffed up. Serve immediately, with a clear soup. Makes approximately 20.

Drinks

There are many refreshing and nutritious drinks to be made with herbs, based on mixtures of fruit and vegetable juices, yogurt and buttermilk. These are useful for feeding invalids, convalescents and small children since they provide a valuable source of vitamins which are easily digested. Their vitamin content diminishes on standing so they should be drunk soon after making. Some of the nicest can only be made with a juice extractor, which produces juice from vegetables such as spinach, sorrel, carrots, tomatoes and cucumber, and from fruits like apples, grapes, peaches and melon. Others can be made in a blender, or simply with a whisk.

Mint is one of the most useful herbs for drinks, since it goes so well with yogurt, tea, and many blends of vegetables and fruit. Basil and chervil are both delicious with fresh tomato juice, or a mixture of carrot and tomato juice. Sorrel adds its pleasant tart flavour to bland drinks of buttermilk or yogurt, while chives are good sprinkled on glasses of cucumber or apple juice. Parsley does not yield much juice, but is excellent when finely chopped and stirred into yogurt, buttermilk or lemon juice.

APPLE JUICE WITH MINT

Metric/Imperial	American
8 juicy apples	8 juicy apples
4 tablespoons lemon juice	¼ cup lemon juice
2 tablespoons chopped mint	2 tablespoons chopped mint

Cut the unpeeled apples into quarters; do not core. Put through a juice extractor. Mix with the lemon juice and stir in the mint. Serve immediately. Makes 4 small glasses.

ROSE HIP DRINK

Metric/Imperial	American
100g/4oz rose hips	¼lb rose hips
peel of 2 large cooking apples	peel of 2 large cooking apples
900ml/1½ pints cold water	3¾ cups cold water
sugar or honey to taste	sugar or honey to taste

Chop the rose hips coarsely. Put them in a saucepan with the apple peel and cover with the water. Bring slowly to the boil and simmer for 30 minutes. Strain, add a very little sugar or honey to taste, then cool and chill. Makes 4 small glasses.

BUTTERMILK, SORREL AND CRESS

Metric/Imperial	American
600ml/1 pint buttermilk	2½ cups buttermilk
150ml/¼ pint natural yogurt	⅔ cup unflavored yogurt
2 baskets cress	2 baskets garden cress
12 young sorrel leaves	12 young sorrel leaves

Mix the buttermilk and yogurt together in a blender. Cut the heads off the cress and add them with the sorrel leaves. Blend again, and pour into glasses. Garnish with a sprig of mint, if you like. Makes 4 smallish glasses.

BUTTERMILK AND WATERCRESS

Metric/Imperial	American
600ml/1 pint buttermilk	2½ cups buttermilk
150ml/¼ pint natural yogurt	⅔ cup unflavored yogurt
1 bunch watercress	1 bunch watercress
2 tablespoons chopped chives	2 tablespoons chopped chives

Purée the buttermilk and yogurt together in a blender. Add the leaves of the watercress and blend again. Stir in the chives and pour into glasses. Makes 4 small glasses.

Buttermilk, sorrel and cress; Buttermilk and watercress

CARROT AND SORREL JUICE

Metric/Imperial	American
1kg/2lb carrots	2lb carrots
225g/8oz sorrel or sorrel and spinach mixed	½lb sorrel or sorrel and spinach mixed
1 tablespoon lemon juice	1 tablespoon lemon juice

Clean the carrots and cut into chunks. Put them through a juice extractor. Put the washed sorrel, or sorrel and spinach, through the juice extractor. Mix the two juices together, and add lemon juice. Serve immediately, or chill for 1 hour beforehand. Makes 4 small glasses.

CARROT AND TOMATO JUICE

Metric/Imperial	American
450g/1lb carrots	1lb carrots
450g/1lb tomatoes	1lb tomatoes
150ml/¼ pint natural yogurt (optional)	⅔ cup unflavored yogurt (optional)
2 tablespoons lemon juice	2 tablespoons lemon juice
1 tablespoon orange juice	1 tablespoon orange juice
1 tablespoon chopped chervil	1 tablespoon chopped chervil

Wash the carrots, cut them into chunks and put them through a juice extractor. Wash the tomatoes, cut them into quarters, and put them through a juice extractor. Mix the two juices together. Add the yogurt if you want a creamy, opaque drink, and stir in the fruit juices and the chopped herbs. Serve immediately, or chill for 1 hour. Makes 4 small glasses.

CUCUMBER JUICE WITH CHIVES

Metric/Imperial	American
1½ large cucumbers	1½ large cucumbers
250ml/8fl oz natural yogurt	1 cup unflavored yogurt
1½ tablespoons chopped chives	1½ tablespoons chopped chives

Cut the unpeeled cucumbers into chunks and put them through a juice extractor. Mix with the yogurt and stir in the chives. Serve immediately. Makes 4 small glasses.

FRUIT JUICE WITH PARSLEY

Metric/Imperial	American
450ml/¾ pint lemon juice	2 cups lemon juice
175ml/6fl oz orange juice	¾ cup orange juice
6 tablespoons chopped parsley	6 tablespoons chopped parsley

Have the fruit juices freshly squeezed. Mix them together and stir in the chopped parsley. Serve immediately. Makes 4 small glasses.

MINT FIZZ

Metric/Imperial	American
4 tablespoons chopped mint	¼ cup chopped mint
1 teaspoon sugar	1 teaspoon sugar
150ml/¼ pint boiling water	⅔ cup boiling water
juice of 1 orange	juice of 1 orange
juice of 1 lemon	juice of 1 lemon
250ml/8fl oz ginger ale or soda water	1 cup ginger ale or soda water
6 ice cubes	6 ice cubes
1 large sprig mint to decorate	1 large sprig mint to decorate

Put the chopped mint in a jug (pitcher) with the sugar and pour on the boiling water. Leave to cool, then add the freshly squeezed fruit juices. Chill for 2 to 3 hours in the refrigerator, then strain and add ginger ale or soda water, and ice cubes. Decorate with a sprig of fresh mint and serve immediately. Makes 2 to 3 large glasses.

From left to right: Carrot and sorrel juice; Yogurt and mint drink; Mint fizz; Moroccan mint tea; Cucumber juice with chives; Carrot and tomato juice; Fruit juice with parsley

MOROCCAN MINT TEA

Metric/Imperial	American
2 teaspoons China tea	2 teaspoons China tea
4 tablespoons chopped mint	¼ cup chopped mint
900ml/1½ pints boiling water	3¾ cups boiling water
sugar to taste	sugar to taste
DECORATION:	DECORATION:
4 slices lemon	4 slices lemon
4 small sprigs mint	4 small sprigs mint

Warm a teapot and put in the China tea (Lapsang Souchong for preference) and the chopped mint. Pour on the water the moment it boils and leave for 5 minutes. Pour through a strainer into glasses or tea cups, adding sugar to taste. Decorate each cup with a slice of lemon and a sprig of mint.

To make iced mint tea, add sugar to the pot and pour the tea through a strainer over cracked ice to make it cool rapidly. Serve with ice cubes, decorated in the same way.

SORREL AND BUTTERMILK

Metric/Imperial	American
225g/8oz sorrel	½lb sorrel
300ml/½ pint natural yogurt	1¼ cups unflavored yogurt
300ml/½ pint buttermilk	1¼ cups buttermilk

Put the sorrel through a juice extractor. Pour the sorrel juice into a blender and mix with the yogurt and buttermilk. Makes 4 small glasses. A delicious and healthy drink.

TOMATO JUICE WITH BASIL

Metric/Imperial	American
1kg/2lb tomatoes	2lb tomatoes
2 tablespoons chopped basil	2 tablespoons chopped basil
2 tablespoons lemon juice	2 tablespoons lemon juice

Wash the tomatoes and cut them into quarters. Put them through a juice extractor. Stir the chopped basil into the tomato juice. Add the lemon juice and chill for 2 hours before serving. Makes 4 small glasses.

YOGURT AND MINT DRINK

Metric/Imperial	American
600ml/1 pint natural yogurt	2½ cups unflavored yogurt
600ml/1 pint iced water	2½ cups iced water
pinch of sea salt	pinch of sea salt
4 sprigs mint	4 sprigs mint

Purée the yogurt in a blender with the iced water and a pinch of salt. Pour into 4 glasses. Float a sprig of fresh mint on top of each. This is a refreshing hot-weather drink from the Middle Eastern countries.

Preserves, Oils & Vinegars

The addition of herbs to pickles renders them more complex, more subtle, and at the same time milder. I only use wine or cider vinegar for making pickles, and the addition of herbs seems to make them gentler, and more interesting. Dill is one of the most successful herbs for pickling; it is best used in the form of whole stalks, complete with flowerheads and seeds. If these are not available, dill seed can be used instead. Fennel is also good, and can be used in the same way, while coriander leaves can be combined with whole dried coriander seeds in an excellent chutney. Mint is also good added to chutneys, and it can be preserved for winter use in the form of a concentrated mint sauce, or a jelly. Other good herb jellies can be made with combinations of cooking apples with lemon thyme, sage or tarragon. Rose hips make a delicious sweet jelly, as do elder flowers. These last can also be used to flavour a syrup which is then bottled and kept for adding to sweet dishes of cooked fruit throughout the winter months.

If the desired herbs are hard to get at pickling time, their flavour can be added by using a herb-flavoured vinegar (see pages 208–9) mixed with the plain vinegar in the pickling mixture. Tarragon is good in almost all pickles, especially when combined with dill. A pretty effect can be obtained by laying tiny sprigs of tarragon and dill in between the layers of cucumbers, onions, or cauliflower in a dill pickle mixture.

Both oils and vinegars will absorb the flavour of an individual herb, or of a blend of carefully chosen herbs. A shelf full of subtly flavoured oils and vinegars gives one innumerable possibilities for unusual and interesting dishes. It also provides a quick and easy way of adding herb flavours to one's diet. The fresh flavour of basil can be preserved in olive oil to add to salad dressings or to sprinkle over homemade pizzas just before baking. Both garlic and tarragon make delicious vinegars, while dill seed also gives an interesting flavour. An elder flower vinegar is delicious when added in very small amounts to cooked fruit dishes such as baked pears, stewed apples, plums, etc., while burnet vinegar adds a delicate and unusual touch to a homemade mayonnaise.

Right: Coriander chutney; Russian pickled cucumbers; Mixed dill pickles

PICKLED BEETROOT (BEET) WITH HORSE-RADISH

Metric/Imperial	American
1kg/2lb medium beetroot (raw)	2lb medium beet (raw)
1 clove garlic	1 clove garlic
4 tablespoons grated horse-radish	¼ cup grated horse-radish
600ml/1 pint white wine vinegar	2½ cups white wine vinegar
1 tablespoon sea salt	1 tablespoon sea salt
2 tablespoons sugar	2 tablespoons sugar
6 cloves	6 cloves
6 peppercorns	6 peppercorns
6 whole coriander seeds	6 whole coriander seeds

Cook the beetroot (beet) in a pressure cooker, allowing about 30 minutes. Drain and cool, reserving 450ml/¾ pint/2 cups of the water. Skin them and cut into slices. Peel the garlic and chop it finely. Pack the beetroot (beet) slices into jars, interspersed with horse-radish and garlic.

Heat the vinegar in a saucepan with the beetroot (beet) cooking water, adding the salt, sugar, cloves, peppercorns and coriander seeds. Boil for 3 minutes then pour over the beetroot (beet). Seal the jars and keep for 2 weeks in a dark place before eating. Fills four 450g/1lb jars.

MIXED DILL PICKLES

Metric/Imperial	American
1 small cauliflower	1 small cauliflower
225g/8oz carrots	½lb carrots
225g/8oz string beans	½lb snap beans
100g/4oz pickling onions	¼lb tiny onions
½ cucumber	½ cucumber
PICKLING MIXTURE:	PICKLING MIXTURE:
1.2 litres/2 pints water	5 cups water
300ml/½ pint white wine vinegar	1¼ cups white wine vinegar
2 tablespoons pickling spice	2 tablespoons pickling spice
25g/1oz sea salt	1½ tablespoons sea salt
50g/2oz sugar	¼ cup sugar
2 cloves garlic, peeled	2 cloves garlic, peeled
1 tablespoon grated horse-radish	1 tablespoon grated horse-radish
1 slice root ginger	1 slice ginger root
1 stalk dill, about 30cm/12in, with flowerhead and seeds or 1 teaspoon dill seed	1 stalk dill, about 12in, with flowerhead and seeds or 1 teaspoon dill seed
1 branch tarragon	1 branch tarragon

Put all the ingredients for the pickling mixture in a saucepan and boil for 30 minutes. Leave to cool.

Wash the cauliflower and divide it into sprigs. Clean the carrots and cut them into quarters lengthwise, then into chunks. Cut the beans into 2.5cm/1in pieces. Peel the onions and cut the unpeeled cucumber into quarters lengthwise, then into chunks. Cook the cauliflower, carrots, beans and onions separately in a saucepan of lightly salted water, using the same water for each vegetable. Drain the vegetables, discarding the cooking liquid, mix them and pack into jars.

Pour over the cooled pickling mixture through a sieve (strainer) removing the dill, tarragon, ginger and garlic. Seal the jars and keep for 2 weeks before eating. Makes about five 450g/1lb jars.

The same pickling mixture can be used to preserve gherkins (small sweet cucumbers), pickling onions, cauliflower, or carrots on their own. Allow 1kg/2lb of each vegetable.

RUSSIAN PICKLED CUCUMBERS

Metric/Imperial	American
2 cloves garlic	2 cloves garlic
1kg/2lb gherkins	2lb small pickling
8 sprigs tarragon	cucumbers
8 sprigs dill	8 sprigs tarragon
8 small black currant	8 sprigs dill
leaves	8 small black currant
PICKLING MIXTURE:	leaves
750ml/1¼ pints water	PICKLING MIXTURE:
250ml/8fl oz white wine	3 cups water
vinegar	1 cup white wine vinegar
25g/1oz sea salt	1½ tablespoons sea salt
3 bay leaves	3 bay leaves
6 black peppercorns	6 black peppercorns
6 whole coriander seeds	6 whole coriander seeds
6 whole allspice berries	6 whole allspice berries

Put all the ingredients for the pickling mixture in a pan and boil for 3 minutes. Leave to cool.

Peel and slice the garlic. Wash the gherkins (small cucumbers) and pack into glass jars with the garlic, interspersed with the sprigs of tarragon and dill and the black currant leaves. When the pickling mixture has cooled, pour it over the cucumbers and seal the jars. Keep for 2 weeks before eating.

If gherkins (small pickling cucumbers) are not available, it is possible to use large cucumbers. Cut them in quarters lengthwise, then in 5cm/2in chunks.

CORIANDER CHUTNEY

Metric/Imperial	American
1kg/2lb cooking apples	2lb cooking apples
450g/1lb onions	1lb onions
2 cloves garlic	2 cloves garlic
1 green pepper	1 green pepper
1 red pepper	1 red pepper
900ml/1½ pints red wine	3¾ cups red wine
vinegar	vinegar
450g/1lb brown sugar	2⅔ cups brown sugar
½ tablespoon whole	½ tablespoon whole
coriander	coriander
6 peppercorns	6 peppercorns
6 allspice berries	6 allspice berries
1 tablespoon sea salt	1 tablespoon sea salt
50g/2oz root ginger	2oz ginger root
2 tablespoons chopped	2 tablespoons chopped
coriander leaves	coriander leaves
2 tablespoons chopped	2 tablespoons chopped
mint	mint

Peel, core and slice the apples. Peel and chop the onions. Peel and crush the garlic. Remove the seeds and stalks from the green and red peppers and chop. Put all these ingredients in a broad heavy saucepan, add the vinegar and bring to the boil. Simmer for about 30 minutes, until soft.

Add the brown sugar, coriander, peppercorns, allspice berries, salt and the bruised ginger tied in a small piece of muslin (cheesecloth). Heat gently until the sugar has melted, then simmer until thick; this may take up to 1 hour. When done, stir in the chopped coriander and mint and spoon into hot sterilized jars. Seal. This quantity fills two 450g/1lb jars.

MINT JELLY

Metric/Imperial	American
1kg/2lb green cooking apples	2lb green cooking apples
1 bunch mint, about 15g/½oz	1 bunch mint, about ½oz
900ml/1½ pints water	3¾ cups water
approx. 450g/1lb sugar	approx. 2 cups sugar
2 tablespoons lemon juice	2 tablespoons lemon juice
2 tablespoons white wine vinegar	2 tablespoons white wine vinegar
4 tablespoons chopped mint	¼ cup chopped mint

Wash the apples and chop them, peel, cores and all. Put them in a pan with the bunch of mint and the cold water. Bring to the boil and simmer until soft and pulpy – about 30 minutes. Pour into a jelly bag and leave to drain overnight.

Next day, measure the juice and add 450g/1lb/2 cups of sugar for every 600ml/1 pint/2½ cups of fluid. Bring back to the boil in a heavy pan and boil steadily until setting point is reached – about 20 to 30 minutes. Skim off surface scum, stir in the lemon juice and vinegar, and the chopped mint. Pour into jars and seal when cool. This quantity will fill two 350g/12oz jars. It can easily be made in double or treble quantities. Serve with roast lamb.

VARIATIONS

Follow the recipe for *Mint Jelly*, substituting lemon thyme for mint. Serve with roast duck, pork and game.

Follow the recipe for *Mint Jelly*, using half as much sage as specified for mint. Serve with roast pork, duck, hare and venison.

Follow the recipe for *Mint Jelly*, substituting tarragon for mint. Serve with cold meat of all kinds.

MINT SAUCE

Metric/Imperial	American
100g/4oz mint leaves	3 cups mint leaves
350ml/12fl oz cider vinegar	1½ cups cider vinegar
100g/4oz sugar	½ cup sugar

Wash the mint leaves and pat them dry in a cloth. Chop them quite finely and pack into small jars. Boil the vinegar in a saucepan with the sugar until it has dissolved, then pour it over the mint. Mix well, then screw down the lids. Store in a dark cupboard. To use: dilute with lemon juice and water to taste.

ELDER FLOWER JELLY

Metric/Imperial	American
1.75kg/4lb cooking apples	4lb cooking apples
1.75 litres/3 pints water	7½ cups water
approx. 1kg/2lb sugar	approx. 4 cups sugar
6 large elder flowers	6 large elder flowers
4 tablespoons lemon juice	¼ cup lemon juice

Wash the apples and chop them, peel, cores and all, and put them in a pan with the water. Bring to the boil and simmer until soft and pulpy – about 30 minutes. Pour into a jelly bag and leave overnight to drain without disturbance.

Next day, measure the juice and add 450g/1lb/2 cups of sugar to every 600ml/1 pint/2½ cups of juice. Put in a pan and bring to the boil, adding the elder flowers tied in a piece of muslin (cheesecloth). Boil steadily for about 20 minutes until setting point is reached, taking out the flowers after 5 minutes, or when the jelly is sufficiently flavoured. At the last moment, skim off surface scum and stir in the lemon juice. Pour into jars and seal when cool. This quantity fills three to four 450g/1lb jars.

ELDER FLOWER SYRUP

Metric/Imperial	American
elder flowers	elder flowers
100g/4oz sugar	½ cup sugar
150ml/¼ pint boiling water	⅔ cup boiling water

Fill a wide-necked glass jar with elder flowers which have been rinsed and shaken dry. Pour over enough boiling water to fill the jar. Cool, then seal the jar and stand for 24 hours.

Make a sugar syrup by dissolving the sugar in the boiling water. Strain the water from the elder flower infusion and mix with the syrup. Pour into a clean bottle and seal tightly. Use to add to fruit dishes throughout the winter: compotes of apples and pears, fruit salad (cut fruits), etc.

ROSE HIP JELLY

Metric/Imperial	American
1kg/2lb rose hips	2lb rose hips
1.2 litres/2 pints water	5 cups water
approx. 450g/1lb sugar	approx. 2 cups sugar
3 tablespoons lemon juice, or to taste	3 tablespoons lemon juice, or to taste

Wash the rose hips and chop roughly. Put them in a pan with the water and boil for about 1 hour or until soft. Put in a jelly bag and leave to drip overnight.

Next day, measure the juice and add 450g/1lb/2 cups of sugar to every 600ml/1 pint/2½ cups of juice. Heat slowly in a pan until the sugar has dissolved, then boil steadily until setting point is reached. Skim off surface scum, add lemon juice to taste and pour the jelly into small jars. Seal when cool. Makes about 0.75kg/1½lb.

AROMATIC OIL

Metric/Imperial	American
450ml/¾ pint olive oil, preferably green olive oil	2 cups olive oil, preferably green olive oil
2 branches rosemary	2 branches rosemary
6 sprigs thyme	6 sprigs thyme
1 large clove garlic	1 large clove garlic
1 green chilli pepper	1 green chili pepper
5–6 small red chilli peppers	5–6 small red chili peppers
6 black peppercorns	6 black peppercorns
6 juniper berries	6 juniper berries

Green olive oil is the oil from the first pressing of the olives, sometimes known as virgin oil, from Provence and Tuscany. It has a marvellous strong fruity flavour, and is a fascinating translucent green in colour. It looks particularly pretty with the herbs floating in it, and its flavour also lends itself well to aromatic additions.

Pour the oil into a pretty glass bottle, stoppered with a cork for preference. Wash the herbs well and pat them dry. Peel and halve the garlic. Drop the herbs into the bottle, with the garlic, the little hot peppers, peppercorns and juniper berries. Seal tightly. Do not use for at least 2 weeks. Do not strain. If making for presents, the cork can be sealed with red sealing wax.

BASIL OIL

Metric/Imperial	American
4 tablespoons chopped basil	¼ cup chopped basil
450ml/¾ pint olive oil	2 cups olive oil

Pound the basil briefly in a mortar. Add a little of the oil and pound again. Mix with the rest of the oil and pour into a wide-mouthed bottle. Seal tightly. Keep for 2 weeks before using, shaking every 2 or 3 days. Do not strain. This is a useful way of preserving the fresh basil flavour, especially for those who do not use much vinegar. It is good in salad dressings, or for adding to pizzas just before baking.

BASIL AND GARLIC VINEGAR

Metric/Imperial	American
1 clove garlic	1 clove garlic
10 tablespoons chopped basil	10 tablespoons chopped basil
450ml/¾ pint white wine vinegar	2 cups white wine vinegar

Peel and chop the garlic and crush it in a mortar. Add the chopped basil leaves and continue to pound. Heat half the vinegar (or less if the mortar is small), and pour it while it is boiling over the garlic and basil. Pound for a minute or two, then leave to cool. Mix with the remaining vinegar and pour into a wide-necked bottle. Seal tightly, and keep for 2 weeks, shaking every few days. Pour through a strainer and rebottle.

BURNET VINEGAR

Metric/Imperial	American
10 tablespoons chopped burnet leaves	10 tablespoons chopped burnet leaves
450ml/¾ pint white wine vinegar	2 cups white wine vinegar

Pound the burnet in a mortar until well crushed. Heat the vinegar to boiling point in a saucepan and pour it over the burnet. (If the mortar is too small to hold all the vinegar, just pour on 150ml/¼ pint/⅔ cup, then mix with the rest afterwards.) Pound together for a minute or two, then leave to cool. Pour into a wide-mouthed bottle and keep for 2 weeks, shaking every few days. Strain and rebottle.

DILL VINEGAR

Metric/Imperial	American
600ml/1 pint white wine vinegar	2½ cups white wine vinegar
2 tablespoons dill seed	2 tablespoons dill seed

Pour the vinegar over the seeds in a wide-mouthed bottle. Cover tightly, and stand in a dark place for 2 to 3 weeks. Strain into a clean bottle before using. Use to flavour salads and herb sauces.

ELDER FLOWER VINEGAR

Metric/Imperial	**American**
elder flowers	*elder flowers*
white wine vinegar	*white wine vinegar*

Fill a wide-mouthed bottle with elder flowers and pour white wine vinegar over them to fill it completely. Screw on the lid tightly and stand in a dark place for 2 to 3 weeks. Strain into a regular bottle. Use in salads, or a very little to flavour cooked fruit dishes.

GARLIC VINEGAR

Metric/Imperial	**American**
3 large cloves garlic	*3 large cloves garlic*
450ml/¾ pint white wine vinegar	*2 cups white wine vinegar*

Peel the garlic and chop it quite coarsely. Pound it in a mortar until crushed. Heat half the vinegar to boiling point and pour it on to the garlic. Pound for a moment, then leave to cool. When cool, mix with the rest of the vinegar and pour into a bottle, with the garlic pieces. Leave for 2 weeks, shaking it every 2 or 3 days, then strain and rebottle. This is a quick and easy way of introducing a garlic flavour into one's salads.

VARIATION

Follow the recipe for *Garlic Vinegar*, substituting 5 shallots for the 3 cloves of garlic.

TARRAGON VINEGAR

Metric/Imperial	**American**
10 tablespoons tarragon leaves	*10 tablespoons tarragon leaves*
600ml/1 pint white wine vinegar	*2½ cups white wine vinegar*

Pull the tarragon leaves off the stalks, chop them roughly and put them in a mortar. Pound them until crushed, then heat 150ml/¼ pint/⅔ cup of the vinegar to boiling point in a saucepan and pour it over the tarragon. Pound together for a moment or two, and leave to cool. Mix with the rest of the vinegar and pour it all into a wide-mouthed bottle. Leave for 2 weeks, shaking now and then, then strain and rebottle. Delicious for making *salsa verde*.

Opposite: Aromatic oil

Below: Basil and garlic vinegar; Burnet vinegar; Tarragon vinegar; Dill vinegar; Garlic vinegar

HERBS AND THEIR USES

Herb	Culinary uses		Medicinal uses
BORAGE	Flowers Leaves	To decorate wine cups. Chopped in salads, salad dressings, egg dishes; with cucumber.	Infusion of young leaves
COMFREY	Leaves	Chopped for salads; cooked like spinach; young leaves can be dipped in batter and eaten as fritters.	Decoction of root Poultice or ointment of root or lea
HOP	Shoots	Lightly boiled and served as a vegetable.	Dried cones Dried cones, in infusion
ELDER	Flowers Berries	Flavour sorbets (sherbets), jams, jellies and vinegars. To make wine, jams and jellies.	Syrup of berries Elderflower tea
CHAMOMILE			Hot infusion of flowers
MARIGOLD	Flower petals	Add flavour and colour to soups, beef stews, salads and cheese dishes.	Flower petals, in infusion Flower petals, as ointment
SOUTHERNWOOD			Infusion of leaves
TARRAGON	Leaves	Best with chicken, fish and eggs. Chopped in sauces and as a herb butter.	
YARROW			Infusion of leaves
HORSE-RADISH	Root	Grated into sauce for hot or cold roast beef, braised beef or smoked fish.	Embrocation of root Root, in diet
WATERCRESS	Leaves and stems	Basis for hot or cold soups; in salads; garnish for steaks.	Infusion of leaves and stems
APPLE MINT	Leaves	Refreshing with fruit sorbets (sherbets).	
BASIL	Leaves	Flavour soups, egg dishes, vegetables, salads and dressings, fish, poultry, pork and veal. Pounded with garlic as a sauce.	Infusion of fresh leaves Dried powdered leaves
BERGAMOT	Leaves and flowers Leaves	Chopped in salads. In pork dishes.	Infusion of leaves and flowers
HYSSOP	Leaves	Use sparingly when roasting duck, goose or pork and in rich pâtés.	Infusion of leaves
LAVENDER			Flowers and stems, in embrocation Flowers and stems, in infusion
LEMON BALM	Leaves	Chopped in salad dressings, soups, sauces and chicken dishes.	Infusion of leaves
LEMON THYME	Leaves	Fish dishes.	Leaves and stems
MARJORAM	Leaves	Flavour game, beef and chicken dishes, sausages and tomatoes.	Leaves and stems, in infusion Leaves and stems, on hot poultice Dried and powdered leaves
PENNYROYAL			Infusion of leaves
PEPPERMINT	Leaves	Flavour fruit salads, summer drinks and sorbets (sherbets). Use for peppermint syrup.	Infusion of leaves Peppermint oil Fresh leaves
ROSEMARY	Leaves	With all meat, particularly roast lamb; in stuffings and marinades.	Infusion of leaves Fresh leaves
SAGE	Leaves	Flavour pâtés and stuffings, egg dishes, poultry and game, pork, veal and vegetables (especially onions), sauces and dressings.	Infusion of leaves
SPEARMINT	Leaves	Chopped in vegetable dishes; in mint sauce; as a sauce with garlic and yogurt; with salads.	Infusion of leaves
SUMMER SAVORY	Leaves	Chopped in stuffings and sausages; with game.	Leaves, crushed

	Cosmetic uses	
nk to reduce fevers; relieve liver and kidney ibles; as a laxative.	Fresh leaves	Face pack for dry skin
nk for coughs and bronchial ailments. plication for bruises, swellings and rheumatic ns.	Infusion of leaves Pulped leaves	Lotion for dry skin. Face pack.
ing for small pillow to aid sleep. t night-time drink for sleeplessness.		
nk for coughs and colds. ght-time drink to calm nerves.	Infusion of flowers Infusion of flowers, on compress	Softens and whitens the skin. Face pack for wrinkles, sunburn and to fade freckles.
ale the vapour to relieve a heavy cold; drink the iid for indigestion or as a tonic.	Infusion of flowers	Lotion for softening the skin; mouthwash; to bathe tired eyes; rinse for blonde hair; added to face packs for oily skin.
nk for poor circulation and varicose veins. als acne and fades old scars.	Infusion of flower petals

Infusion of flower petals, on compress | Bath for tired swollen feet; lotion for skin cleansing and softening. Soothes tired eyes. |
| nk as tonic and mild sedative. | Infusion of leaves Leaves in muslin bag | Hair rinse. Add to bath water. |
| nk as diuretic; also useful for rheumatism and ulence. | Infusion of leaves

Flower buds | Application to stimulate hair growth; lotion to cleanse skin or add to bath water. Face pack for oily skin. |
plication for chilblains and muscular stiffness. luable source of vitamin C and good for estion.		
nk to relieve indigestion, rheumatic pains or nchial catarrh.	Juice expressed from leaves and stems	Application for skin blemishes.
nk as mild laxative; good for travel- and rning-sickness. iff to clear nose cold or headache.		
othing drink for sore throat; add to hot milk as a ative.		
nk for coughs, colds, catarrh. Expectorant if en hot. Compress for muscular pains.		
es muscular pain and stiffness. ld compress applied to forehead relieves idaches and giddiness.	Infusion of flowers	Add to bath water to relax and refresh; use with other herbs in facial steam.
nic drink; relieves headaches.		
ing for cushions to relieve headache.	Infusion of leaves	Add to water for refreshing bath.
outhwash and gargle for sore throat. ieves rheumatic pain. iff for headache.		
nk to improve digestion and relieve flatulence i bronchial ailments.	Infusion of leaves	Mouthwash to sweeten breath.
nk hot as tonic and for indigestion. plication for sprains, bruises, toothache. b on forehead to ease headache.	Leaves	Facial steam to clear complexion.
nk to improve circulation, relieve nervous idaches and colds. plication for stings and bites.	Infusion of leaves Leaves in muslin bag	Rinse for dark hair. Add to water for invigorating bath.
t drink for coughs, colds and constipation; ic tea; mouthwash; eases rheumatic pain.	Leaves Infusion of leaves	Facial steam to cleanse and refine skin. Hair conditioner.
ink hot after meals to aid digestion.		
plication for swellings and bee stings.		

Herb	Culinary uses		Medicinal uses
THYME	Leaves	All savoury dishes, especially veal, chicken, game and in tomato sauce.	Infusion of leaves
BAY	Leaves	Valuable in stews, sauces, soups, pâtés, and stuffings and in fish dishes.	Infusion of leaves Oil of bay
CHIVES	Leaves	Lose flavour when cooked. Garnish for soups, eggs, fish, chicken and veal; with salads and vegetables.	Fresh leaves
GARLIC	Bulb ('cloves')	Flavour all savoury dishes, hot or cold.	Bulb ('cloves')
MARSHMALLOW	Leaves and tops	Chopped, in salads.	Decoction of root Decoction of root, in ointment Infusion of leaves
JUNIPER	Berries	Crushed into marinades; flavour stuffings for game, and pâtés.	Infusion of berries
PURSLANE	Leaves Young shoots	Chopped in salads and dressings, with egg dishes and vegetables. Lightly boiled and served as a vegetable.	Infusion of leaves
SALAD BURNET	Leaves	Delicate flavour best with creamy sauces, salads, white meats, egg dishes, tomato and cucumber.	Infusion of leaves
ROSE	Hips	Cooked with sugar for syrups, sauces, jellies.	Infusion of hips
WOODRUFF	Leaves and stems	Partially dried and added to apple juice, wine and cider cups.	Infusion of dried plant
EYEBRIGHT			Infusion of leaves
NASTURTIUM	Leaves Flowers Seeds	Add peppery taste to salads and sandwiches. Garnish for salad. Pickled; use like capers.	Leaves, in diet
ANGELICA	Stems Leaves	Crystallized (candied) for decorating cakes and desserts. Chopped, for salads or fresh fruit.	Infusion of leaves and stems
ANISE	Seeds	Tiny amounts flavour rye bread and biscuits (cookies).	Infusion of seeds
CARAWAY	Seeds	Tiny amounts flavour rye bread, cheese biscuits (crackers), and some potato dishes.	Infusion of seeds
CHERVIL	Leaves	Delicate flavour enhances chicken, fish, veal, salads, egg dishes, tomatoes. Basis of soup.	Juice expressed from leaves and st• Fresh leaves
CORIANDER	Seeds Leaves	Crushed; especially with curries and pickles. Flavouring for soups, pâtés, fish, poultry, game, lamb, pork, vegetables and sauces. Add spicy hot taste when chopped and added to curries after cooking.	
CUMIN	Seeds	Combines with coriander to flavour vegetable dishes and curries.	
DILL	Leaves Seeds and stems	Excellent with fish, chicken, rabbit, veal and salads. Goes well with mustard. Used for pickling.	Infusion of seeds
FENNEL	Leaves Seeds	Best with fish; also in soups and stuffings or with pork. Flavour stuffings for fish.	Infusion of leaves
LOVAGE	Leaves Seeds	Celery-like flavour excellent in all savoury dishes, hot or cold. Flavour stuffings, pâtés and stews.	Infusion of leaves
PARSLEY	Leaves and stalks	Flavour all savoury dishes, hot or cold; as a garnish; in sauces; basis of salad; deep-fried as a garnish.	Infusion of leaves and stalks
SWEET CICELY	Leaves	Chopped with cooked fruit. Add to water when cooking cabbage.	Seeds Seeds, in infusion
VALERIAN			Roots, in ointment Roots, decoction of
LEMON VERBENA	Leaves	Very strong lemon flavouring for fresh fruit dishes and summer drinks.	Infusion of leaves

	Cosmetic uses	
eptic rinse for cuts. Drink for headaches, hs, catarrh, asthma.	Oil of thyme	Ointment for clearing spots and pimples.
k for indigestion and headache. ication for rheumatism.		
ly laxative.		
hed in hot milk, aids digestion and relieves matism.		
k to relieve coughs and bronchial catarrh. hes skin inflammations. le for sore throat.	Root	Face pack for dry skin; in ointment for sunburn and chapped hands.
k for indigestion and bronchial complaints.	Berries	Stimulating face pack for normal skin (with other ingredients).
c if drunk regularly.		
m drink reduces fever, stimulates kidney ity.	Infusion of leaves Leaves in muslin bag	Lotion to cleanse and refine skin. Add to water for refreshing bath.
k rich in vitamin C to combat colds.	Hips, dried and crushed	In tea bag form, use moistened to soothe puffy eyes.
eshing, relaxing drink.		
k as tonic and to relieve hay fever. Lotion to e inflamed eyes.	Infusion of leaves	Lotion to soothe skin around eyes.
ce of vitamin C and iron.		
ning bedtime drink; good for colds.	Infusion of leaves or leaves in muslin bag	Add to water for relaxing bath.
k to relieve flatulence; good nightcap.		
k to aid digestion.		
lication for stings and bites. npress for bruises.	Infusion of leaves	Lotion to cleanse skin.
	Infusion of seeds	Refreshing perfumed lotion.
ching night-time drink; aids digestion.	Seeds	Chew to sweeten breath.
k to calm upset stomach; mild laxative; ves cramp if taken regularly.	Infusion of leaves	Lotion to bathe tired eyelids and as a skin tonic.
k for liver and kidney ailments; reduces fever; s flatulence.	Infusion of leaves or leaves in muslin bag	Add to water for deodorizing bath.
ic drink rich in vitamin C; eases rheumatic pain relieves piles.	Leaves	Eat raw to sweeten breath.
w for indigestion. rm drink to relieve flatulence.		
ls rashes. nk for insomnia.	Decoction of roots	Add to water for relaxing bath.
nk after heavy meal to settle digestion; at night elp sleep.	Decoction of leaves Leaves in muslin bag	Lotion to cleanse skin. Add to water for refreshing scented bath.

DIRECTORY OF PLANT NAMES

Names and species particular to the USA are given in parentheses.
*denotes a poisonous plant

Common English name	American name	Botanical name	Other popular names
AGRIMONY	Tall agrimony	Agrimonia eupatoria	Liverwort; church steeples; cockeburr; (sticklewort)
ALLSPICE	Carolina allspice	Calycanthus floridus	Jamaica pepper; (strawberry shrub); (pineapple shrub)
ANCHUSA		Pentaglottis sempervirens syn. Anchusa sempervirens	Alkanet
ANISE	Anise	Pimpinella anisum	
ANGELICA	Angelica	Angelica archangelica	
APPLE MINT	Pineapple mint (when variegated)	Mentha rotundifolia var. suaveolens	Round-leaved mint; Egyptian mint
	American elder	Sambucus canadensis	
BALM see LEMON BALM			
BANEBERRY*		Actaea spicata	Herb Christopher; toadroot; bugbane
BASIL	Sweet basil	Ocimum basilicum	
BUSH BASIL	Bush basil	O. minimum	
BASIL THYME	Basil thyme	Calamintha acinos	Calamint; mountain balm; (mother of thyme)
BAY	Sweet bay	Laurus nobilis	True laurel; Roman laurel
BERGAMOT	Oswego tea	Monarda didyma	Bee balm; scarlet monarda; (Indian plume)
BETONY	Betony	Stachys officinalis	Wood betony; bishopswort; (woundwort)
BLACK BRYONY*		Tamus communis	Blackeye root
BORAGE	Borage	Borago officinalis	Bee bread; herb of gladness; burrage; cool tankard
BURDOCK	Cockle-bur	Arctium lappa	Beggar's buttons; fox's clote; love leaves; (clot-bur)
BURNET	Burnet	Poterium sanguisorba	Salad burnet
BUTTERCUP*		Ranunculus acris	Gold knots; batchelor's buttons
CALAMINT		Calamintha spp.	
CARAWAY	Caraway	Carum carvi	
CARAWAY-SCENTED THYME		Thymus herba-barona	
CATMINT	Catnip	Nepeta cataria	Catnep
CENTAURY		Centaurium minus	Red centaury; Christ's ladder
CHAMOMILE, ROMAN	Chamomile	Anthemis nobilis	Common chamomile; maythen; manzanilla; (bowman)
CHAMOMILE, WILD		Matricaria chamomilla	Scented mayweed
CHERVIL	Chervil	Anthriscus cerefolium	
CHIVES	Chives	Allium schoenoprasum	
CINNAMON	Cinnamon	Cinnamonum zeylanicum	
CLOVES	Cloves	Eugenia aromatica	
CLOVER, RED see RED CLOVER			
COLTSFOOT	Coltsfoot	Tussilago farfara	Coughwort; horsehoof; bullsfoot
COLUMBINE*	Garden columbine	Aquilegia vulgaris	Culverwort; (European crowfoot)
COMMON BUCKTHORN*		Rhamnus catharticus	Highway thorn; hartsthorn; rams thorn
COMFREY	Common comfrey	Symphytum officinale	Knitbone; boneset; ass ear; consound; (healing herb)
CORIANDER	Coriander	Coriandrum sativum	
CORSICAN MINT see MINT			
COSTMARY	Alecost	Chrysanthemum balsamita	Balsam herb; balsamita; (mint geranium)

Common English name	American name	Botanical name	Other popular names
CUMIN	Cumin	*Cuminum cyminum*	
CURRY PLANT	Curry plant	*Helichrysum angustifolium*	
DAISY	Daisy	*Bellis perennis*	Bruisewort; (English daisy)
DANDELION	Common dandelion	*Taraxacum officinale*	Priest's crown; peasant's clock; swine's snout; (blowball)
DEADLY NIGHTSHADE*	Belladonna	*Atropa belladonna*	Devil's cherries
DILL	Dill	*Anethum graveolens*	
DOCK		*Rumex obtusifolius*	Broad-leaved dock; butter dock
DWARF ROSEMARY *see* ROSEMARY			
EAU-DE-COLOGNE MINT *see* MINT			
ELDER	(*see* American elder)	*Sambucus nigra*	Pipe tree; bore tree; sweet elder
ELECAMPANE	Elecampane	*Inula helenium*	Horseheal; scabwort; velvet dock; (yellow starwort)
ENGLISH MACE		*Achillea decolorans*	
EYEBRIGHT		*Euphrasia officinalis*	
FENNEL	Fennel	*Foeniculum vulgare*	Fenkel
FENUGREEK	Fenugreek	*Trigonella foenum-graecum*	Bird's foot; Greek hayseed
FEVERFEW	Feverfew	*Chrysanthemum parthenium*	Featherfew; featherfoil; flirtwort
FIGWORT		*Scrophularia* spp.	Throatwort; fiddlewood
FOOL'S PARSLEY*		*Aethusa cynapium*	Lesser hemlock; dog poison
FOXGLOVE*	Foxglove	*Digitalis purpurea*	Witches' gloves; dead men's bells; fairy thimbles; bloody fingers
FRENCH TARRAGON *see* TARRAGON			
GARLIC	Garlic	*Allium sativum*	Poor man's treacle
GENTIAN	Yellow gentian	*Gentiana lutea*	
GERANIUM GERANIUM, NUTMEG-SCENTED GERANIUM, PEPPERMINT-SCENTED		*Pelargonium* x *fragrans* *P. tomentosum*	
GINGER MINT *see* MINT			
GOAT'S RUE	Goat's rue	*Galega officinalis*	Italian fitch
GOLDEN BALM		*Melissa officinalis* var. *aurea*	
GOLDEN MARJORAM *see* MARJORAM			
GOLDEN SEAL		*Hydrastis canadensis*	Orange root; yellow puccoon
GOLDEN THYME *see* THYME			
GOOD KING HENRY	Good King Henry	*Chenopodium bonus-henricus*	All-good; fat hen; smearwort
GRAPE HYACINTH		*Muscari botryoides*	Starch hyacinth
GROUND IVY*	Ground ivy	*Nepeta hederacea*	Alehoof; Gill-go-over-the-ground; haymaids; Lizzy-run-up-the-hedge (field balm; creeping Charlie)
HAMBURG PARSLEY		*Petroselinum crispum fusiformis*	Turnip-rooted parsley
HAWTHORN		*Crataegus oxyacantha*	May; quick; thorn; ladies' meat; bread and cheese tree
HEMLOCK*	Poison hemlock	*Conium maculatum*	Beaver poison; poison parsley; kex; kecksies; (spotted hemlock)
HENBANE*	Henbane	*Hyoscyamus niger*	Hog's bean; cassilata; (stinking nightshade)
HONEYSUCKLE		*Lonicera periclymenum*	Woodbine; goats' leaf
HOPS		*Humulus lupulus*	
HORSE-RADISH	Horse-radish	*Cochlearia armoracia* syn. *Armoracia rusticana*	Mountain radish; red cole
HORSE-TAIL		*Equisetum* spp.	Shave grass; bottle-brush; paddock-pipes; pewterwort
HYSSOP	Hyssop	*Hyssopus officinalis*	

Common English name	American name	Botanical name	Other popular names
IVY see GROUND IVY			
JACOB'S LADDER		Polemoneum coeruleum	Charity; Greek valerian
JASMINE	Jasmine	Jasminum officinale	
JUNIPER	Juniper	Juniperus communis	(Hack matack; horse savin)
LABURNUM*		Laburnum anagyroides	Golden chain
LADY'S BEDSTRAW		Galium verum	Yellow bedstraw; Our Lady's bedstraw; cheese rennet; maid's hair
LADY'S MANTLE	Lady's mantle	Alchemilla vulgaris	Lion's foot; bear's foot; nine hooks
LARKSPUR		Delphinium ajacis	Lark's heel; knight's spur
LAVENDER FRENCH LAVENDER	English lavender French lavender	Lavandula spica L. stoechas	 Spanish lavender
LEMON BALM	Lemon balm	Melissa officinalis	Balm; sweet balm
LEMON THYME	Lemon thyme	Thymus x citriodorus	(Golden-edged thyme)
LEMON VERBENA	Lemon verbena	Lippia citriodora	Herb Louisa
LILY-OF-THE-VALLEY	Lily-of-the-valley	Convallaria majalis	May lily; Our Lady's tears; ladder to heaven
LIME (FLOWERS)	Linden	Tilia spp.	Linden flowers
LIQUORICE	Licorice	Glycyrrhiza glabra	
LOVAGE	Lovage	Levisticum officinale	Italian lovage
MACE		Myristica fragrans	
MANDRAKE		Mandragora officinarum	Devil's apples; Satan's apple
MARIGOLD	Pot marigold	Calendula officinalis	Golds; Mary gowles; marygold; ruddes
MARJORAM MARJORAM, GOLDEN MARJORAM, POT MARJORAM, SWEET MARJORAM, WILD	 Sweet marjoram 	Origanum spp. O. vulgare aureum O. onites O. majorana O. vulgare	 Knotted marjoram Oregano
MARSHMALLOW	Marshmallow	Althaea officinalis	Mallards; mauls; schloss tea; cheeses; mortification root
MEADOW SAFFRON*	Autumn crocus	Colchicum autumnale	Naked ladies
MINT MINT, APPLE see APPLE MINT MINT, CORSICAN MINT, CURLY MINT, EAU-DE-COLOGNE MINT, GINGER	 Orange mint 	Mentha spp. M. requienii M. crispa M. citrata M. gentilis	 Bergamot mint
MISTLETOE*		Viscum album	Birdlime mistletoe; lignum crucis
MOCK ORANGE		Philadelphus coronarius	
MONKSHOOD*	Aconite	Aconitum napellus	Blue rocket; friar's cap
MUGWORT	Mugwort	Artemisia vulgaris	Felon herb; St John's plant
MULLEIN	Great mullein	Verbascum thapsus	Great mullein; Aaron's rod; Hag taper; torches; Adam's flannel; Jacob's staff; shepherd's club; blanket leaf
MYRTLE	Myrtle	Myrtus communis tarentina	Tarentum myrtle
NASTURTIUM	Nasturtium	Tropaeolum majus	
NETTLE	Stinging nettle	Urtica dioica	
NUTMEG	Nutmeg	Myristica fragrans	
OPIUM POPPY	Opium poppy	Papaver somniferum	
ORRIS (ROOT)		Iris florentina	
PANSY		Viola tricolor	Heartsease; wild pansy; love-in-idleness; pink-of-my-John; love-lies-bleeding; call-me-to-you; kiss-her-in-the-buttery; kit runabout; herb constancy
PARSLEY	Parsley	Petroselinum crispum	Curly parsley; Petersylinge
PENNYROYAL	English pennyroyal	Mentha pulegium	Run-by-the-ground; lurk-in-the-ditch; pudding grass

Common English name	American name	Botanical name	Other popular names
PEPPERMINT	Peppermint	*Mentha piperita*	Brandy mint
PINEAPPLE SAGE *see* SAGE			
PINK		*Dianthus plumarius*	
PLANTAIN		*Plantago* spp.	Ripple grass; waybread; cuckoo's bread; Englishman's foot; Jackstraw; wendles
PURPLE SAGE *see* SAGE			
PURSLANE	Purslane	*Portulaca oleracea*	
RED CLOVER		*Trifolium incarnatum*	Crimson clover; trefoil

ROSE
  WILD DOG ROSE
  SWEETBRIAR
	Rose	*Rosa* spp.
		R. canina
		R. rubiginosa syn.
		R. eglanteria
			Eglantine

ROSEMARY DWARF ROSEMARY	Rosemary	*Rosmarinus officinalis* *R. lavandulaceus*	Polar plant; compass weed
RUE	Rue	*Ruta graveolens*	
SAFFRON	Saffron	*Crocus sativus*	
ST JOHN'S WORT	St John's wort	*Hypericum perforatum*	
SAGE SAGE, GOLDEN SAGE, PINEAPPLE SAGE, PURPLE SAGE, VARIEGATED	Sage	*Salvia officinalis* *S. aurea* *S. tricolor* var. *S. purpurascens* *S. tricolor*	
SALAD BURNET *see* BURNET			
SANTOLINA	Lavender cotton	*Santolina chamaecyparissus*	Cotton lavender; (grey santolina)
SAVORY *see* SUMMER SAVORY WINTER SAVORY			
SILVER QUEEN THYME *see* THYME			
SKULLCAP	Virginian scullcap	*Scutellaria galericulata* (*S. lateriflora*)	Scullcap; helmet flower; (madweed)
SLIPPERY ELM	Slippery elm	*Ulmus fulva*	Moose elm; red elm; Indian elm
SOAPWORT	Soapwort	*Saponaria officinalis*	Bouncing Bet; Fuller's herb; wild Sweet William; bruisewort
SORREL	Garden sorrel	*Rumex acetosa*	Green sauce; sour sabs; cuckoo sorrow; cuckoo's meat
SOUTHERNWOOD	Southernwood	*Artemisia abrotanum*	Old man; lad's love
SPEARMINT	Spear mint	*Mentha spicata* syn. *M. viridis*	Garden mint; mackerel mint; sage of Bethlehem; spire mint
SPINDLE TREE*		*Eonymus europaeus*	Fusoria; skewerwood; Indian arrowroot; burning bush; (wahoo)
STINKING MOTHERWORT		*Chenopodium vulvaria*	Stinking goosefoot; wild arrach
SUMMER SAVORY	Summer savory	*Satureia hortensis*	
SWEETBRIAR *see* ROSE			
SWEET CICELY	Sweet Cicely	*Myrrhis odorata*	British myrrh; anise; great chervil; smooth Cicely; shepherd's needle
SWEET MARJORAM *see* MARJORAM			
TANSY	Tansy	*Tanacetum vulgare*	Buttons

TARRAGON
  FRENCH TARRAGON
  RUSSIAN TARRAGON
	French tarragon
	Russian tarragon
		Artemisia dracunculus
		A. dracunculoides
			Little dragon
			False tarragon

THYME THYME, COMMON OR GARDEN THYME, GOLDEN THYME, LEMON THYME, SILVER	English thyme Lemon thyme	*Thymus* spp. *T. vulgaris* *T. x citriodorus* 'Aureus' *T. x citriodorus* *T. x citriodorus* 'Silver Queen'	(French thyme) (Golden-edged thyme)
TOADFLAX		*Linaria vulgaris*	Fluellin; pattens and clogs; flaxweed; churnstaff; eggs and bacon; buttered haycocks

Common English name	American name	Botanical name	Other popular names
TONKA (BEANS)		*Dipterix odorata*	Tonquin bean
VALERIAN	Garden heliotrope	*Valeriana officinalis*	Phu; phew; all-heal; setwall; cat's valerian
VANILLA	Vanilla	*Vanilla fragrans*	
VARIEGATED SAGE *see* SAGE			
VERBASCUM *see* MULLEIN			
VERVAIN	European vervain	*Verbena officinalis*	Herb of the cross; pigeon's grass; herb of grace; (simpler's joy)
VIOLET	English violet	*Viola odorata*	Sweet violet; wood violet
WATERCRESS	Watercress	*Nasturtium officinale*	
WELSH ONION	Welsh onion	*Allium fistulosum*	
WHITE BRYONY*		*Bryonia dioica*	English mandrake; wild vine; ladies' seal; tetterbury
WHITE HELLEBORE*	False Hellebore	*Veratrum viride*	
WHITE HOREHOUND	Common horehound	*Marrubium vulgare*	Hoarhound
WILLOW, BLACK AMERICAN	Pussy willow	*Salix nigra*	Pussy willow
WILLOW, WHITE		*Salix alba*	European willow
WINTERGREEN	Wintergreen	*Gaultheria procumbens*	Mountain tea; checkerberry; teaberry
WINTER SAVORY	Winter savory	*Satureia montana*	
WITCH-HAZEL	Witch-hazel	*Hamamelis virginiana*	Spotted alder; winterbloom
WOOD BETONY *see* BETONY			
WOODRUFF	Sweet woodruff	*Asperula odorata* syn. *Galium odoratum*	Wuderove; woodrova
WOOD VIOLET *see* VIOLET			
WOODY NIGHTSHADE*	Bittersweet nightshack	*Solanum dulcamara*	Bittersweet; felonwood; violet bloom
WORMWOOD	Common wormwood	*Artemisia absinthium*	Old woman; green ginger (absinthe)
YARROW	Yarrow	*Achillea millefolium*	Nosebleed; milfoil; old man's pepper; staunchweed; devil's nettle; (toothache weed)
YEW*	English yew Western yew	*Taxus baccata* *T. brevifolia*	

HERB SUPPLIERS

UNITED KINGDOM

Ashfields Herb Nursery,
Hinstock, Market Drayton,
Shropshire.
Tel. Sambrook 392
Plants and seeds

Daphne Ffiske Herb Nursery,
Rosemary Cottage, Bramerton,
Norwich, NR14 7DW.
Tel. Surlingham 8187
Plants

Dobie Seeds,
Upper Dee Mills, Llangollen,
Clwyd.
Tel. (0978) 860 119
Seeds

Heches Herbs,
St. Peter in the Wood,
Channel Islands.
Tel. 0481 63545
Plants

Hereford Herbs,
Ocle Pychard, Herefordshire.
Tel. (0432) 78 379
Plants

Hollington Nurseries Ltd.,
Woolton Hill,
Newbury, Berks.
Tel. (0635) 253908
Plants

Hullbrook House Herb Farm
Shamley Green, Guildford,
Surrey.
Tel. 0483 893 666
Plants

Manor House Herbs,
Wadeford, Chard,
Somerset.
Tel. 046 06 2213
Plants

Midsomer Herbs,
Byways, Silver Street,
Midsomer Norton, Bath.
Tel. (0761) 412168
Plants

Norfolk Lavender Ltd.
Caley Mill, Heacham,
King's Lynn, Norfolk.
Tel: (0485) 70384

Old Rectory Herb Garden,
Ightham, Nr Sevenoaks,
Kent.
Tel. Borough Green 882608
Plants

Poyntzfield Nursery Garden,
By Canon Bridge, Black Isle,
Rosshire.
No Telephone
Plants

R. V. Roger Ltd.,
The Nurseries, Pickering,
N. Yorks.
Tel. Pickering 72226
Plants

Suffolk Herbs,
Sawyers Farm, Little Cornard,
Sudbury, Suffolk.
Tel. (0787) 227247
Organically grown herbs and seeds

The Herb Farm,
Ivegill, Carlisle.
Plants

The Herb Garden,
Thunderbridge,
Nr Huddersfield,
Yorks.
Tel. Kilburton 2993
Plants

Tippell, Mrs J.
57 Ormesby Way, Kenton,
Harrow, Middlesex.
Tel. (01) 204 3663
Plants

Tresare Herb Farm,
Taman Bay, Looe,
Cornwall.
SAE with enquiries

U.S.A.

The following offer a catalog and mail order service for seeds and plants:

Borchelt Herb Gardens,
HE 474 Carriage Shop Road,
East Falmouth, Mass. 02536
Seeds only

Caprilands Herb Farm,
Silver Street,
Coventry, Conn. 06238

Carroll Gardens,
Box 310,
Westminster, Md. 21157
Plants only

Comstock, Ferre & Co.,
263 Main Street,
Wethersfield, Conn. 06109
Seeds only

Gilbertie of Westport,
7 Sylvan Lane,
Westport, Conn. 06880
Plants only

Hilltop Herb Farm,
Box 1734, Cleveland,
Texas 77327

Merry Gardens,
Camden, Maine 04843

Nichols Garden Nursery,
1190 North Pacific Highway,
Albany, Oregon 97321

Rocky Hollow Herb Farm, Inc.,
R.D.2, Box 215,
Lake Wallkill Road, Sussex,
N.J. 07461
Seeds only

Rosemary House,
120 South Market Street,
Mechanicsburg, Penn. 17055

Sunnybrook Farms Nursery,
9448 Mayfield Road,
Chesterfield, Ohio 44026
Plants only

Taylor's Garden, Inc.,
2649 Stingle Avenue,
Rosemead, Calif. 91770
Plants only

Tool Shed Herb Farm,
Turkey Hill Road,
Salem Center,
Purdy's Station,
N.Y. 10578
Plants only

Well Sweep Herb Farm,
Mt. Bethel Road,
Port Murray, N.J. 07965

CANADA

Otto Richter and Sons, Ltd.,
Locust Hill, Ontario,
Canada LO4 1JO
Seeds only

AUSTRALIA

New South Wales

Arthur Yates & Co. Pty Ltd.,
244 Horsley Road,
Milperra, N.S.W. 2214
Tel. (02) 771 2911
Seeds only

Erdman's Cottage Herbs,
59 Maiden Street,
Greenacre, N.S.W. 2190
Tel. (02) 642 4008
Plants, seeds and cuttings

Melody Farm Nursery,
616 Old Northern Road,
Dural, N.S.W. 2158
Tel. (02) 651 1176
Plants and seeds

Pennant Hills Nursery,
Yarrara Road,
Pennant Hills, N.S.W. 2120
Tel. (02) 84 2267
Plants and seeds

Somerset Cottage,
745 Old Northern Road,
Dural, N.S.W. 2158
Tel. (02) 651 1027
Plants and seeds

Victoria

Broersen Seeds & Bulbs Pty
Ltd.,
Monbulk-Silvan Road,
Silvan, Vic. 3795
Tel. (03) 737 9202
Seeds only

Lillydale Herb Farm,
61 Mangans Road,
Lilydale, Vic. 3140
Tel. (03) 735 0486
Seeds only

Nature's Store-House,
Floriston Road,
Boronia, Vic. 3155
Tel. (03) 762 4333
Plants only

Queensland

Rose-World Nursery Pty Ltd.,
Redland Bay Road,
Victoria Point, Qld. 4163
Tel. (07) 2077 350
Plants only

South Australia

Meadow Herbs,
Sims Road,
Mt. Barker, S.A. 5251
Tel. (08) 388 1611

NEW ZEALAND

Arthur Yates & Co. Ltd.,
270 Neilson Street,
Onehunga, Auckland.
Seeds only

Gardenway Nurseries Ltd.,
81 Riccarton Road,
Riccarton,
Christchurch.

Kings Herb Nursery,
17A Methuen Road,
Avondale, Auckland.
Plants and seeds

Zenith Garden Centre,
92 Epuni Street,
Lower Hutt,
Wellington.

ACKNOWLEDGMENTS

The publishers would like to thank the following individuals and organizations for their kind permission to reproduce the pictures in this book.

Special photography by Melvin Grey.

Styling for photography by Carolyn Russell

Heather Angel (Biofotos) 28; Tommy Blank 10, 58; The Bodleian Library 9 below, 63; British Library 9 above; Camera Press Limited 34, 34–35, 64; Iris Hardwick Library 23; Angelo Hornak 59, 61 above and below, 62 above and below; Bill Mason 12–13, 14, 25, 32; Allen Paterson 10; The Shaker Museum 11; Harry Smith Collection 21, 29, 65.